frank films the film and video work of robert frank

frank films
the film and video work of robert frank

Herausgegeben von / Edited by
Brigitta Burger-Utzer, Stefan Grissemann

Scalo Zurich–Berlin–New York

Filme und Videos / Films and Videos

June 2002, New York: when I finally got his telephone number from a mutual friend after several letters to him had gone unanswered, Robert Frank told me he could give me thirty minutes for a conversation. When I arrived at his building on Manhattan's Bleecker Street at 9 a.m., he sleepily took me into his tiny studio. Photographs strewn about, half-open drawers, and the wooden cot from which he had obviously just gotten up gave the impression of a monk's cell. He immediately made it clear that he wouldn't be able to come to the retrospective of his films in Graz, and refused to reconsider even after I reminded him that it wouldn't be for another sixteen months. Somewhat intimidated and at the same time touched by his natural, modest and gruff manner of greeting me, I was unable to initiate a real conversation. Frank rummaged around, looking for publications or texts about his films. In vain. He said that the Museum of Fine Arts in Houston might have some. Curator Marian Luntz would be the one to contact for videotape copies of his work. At 9:30 punctually, his wife, artist June Leaf, called to remind him that the lawyer would be right there. Their house was in danger of falling victim to real-estate speculators.

This was my first and last personal meeting with Robert Frank. He refused to give an interview for this book. He doesn't give any, anymore, I was told matter-of-factly through the Pace/MacGill Gallery in New York.

After weeks of unsuccessfully searching for material—I already had all the tapes offered by the museum in Houston and Frank's Swiss distributor was unable to provide any at all—I turned to Frank again, disheartened. He gave my number to Laura Israel, his editor and *partner in crime*, and she promised to send me video copies, a few at a time. Master tapes had to be made for a few of the films first, though this would not be possible in all cases. They would now begin to process everything. I was surprised, but suddenly understood why Frank's films, with the exception of *Pull My Daisy*, are screened so seldom. It also became clear that we were in a sense pioneers, that the book and retrospective would be the first contribution to a comprehensive assessment of his film works.

Not a single tape had arrived by November of 2002. I sent Frank the first folder announcing the retrospective, which made use of a still from *Candy Mountain* in the absence of other usable material. Frank was enraged: He doesn't like *Candy Mountain*. He also rejected the accompanying text and retracted permission to use his films, he even ordered us not to publish any of his photographs.

His modesty does not apply when essential matters are involved. The shy seismographer challenges and motivates in his own way. In December 2002, Stefan Grissemann and I went to Zurich; we wanted to finally see some of his relatively unknown films. Motivated by this experience, we then made a number of attempts to renew contact with Robert Frank, to win him over. After several weeks of

Juni 2002, New York. Eine halbe Stunde werde er für ein Gespräch zur Verfügung stehen, teilt mir Robert Frank mit, als ich nach einigen unbeantworteten Briefen an ihn über einen gemeinsamen Freund die richtige Telefonnummer bekomme. Als ich um neun Uhr morgens in seinem Haus in Manhattan, Bleecker Street, ankomme, führt mich der noch verschlafene Robert Frank in sein kleines Atelier. Herumliegende Fotos, halb offene Laden, eine Holzpritsche, auf der er offensichtlich bis gerade eben noch geschlafen hat, erwecken den Eindruck einer Mönchszelle. Er werde, das stellt er sofort fest, nicht zur Retrospektive seiner Filme nach Graz kommen können. Mein Einwand, dass diese doch erst in 16 Monaten stattfinden werde, lässt ihn von seinem Entschluss nicht abrücken. Etwas eingeschüchtert, aber auch berührt von der natürlichen, bescheidenen und gleichzeitig forschen Art, mich zu empfangen, bringe ich kaum ein Gespräch in Gang. Frank kramt, sucht Publikationen oder Texte zu seinem filmischen Werk. Vergeblich. Das Museum of Fine Arts in Houston könnte welche haben, meint er. Wenn ich Videokopien seiner Arbeiten brauche, sei die Kuratorin Marian Luntz Ansprechpartnerin. Pünktlich um 9:30 Uhr ruft Franks Frau, die Künstlerin June Leaf, in Erinnerung, dass der Anwalt gleich komme, da ihr Haus von Immobilienspekulationen bedroht sei.

      Dies ist mein erster und letzter persönlicher Kontakt mit Robert Frank. Ein Interview für dieses Buch lehnt er ab. Er gebe keine mehr, lässt er Monate später über die Pace/MacGill Gallery in New York nüchtern mitteilen. Nach Wochen vergeblicher Materialsuche – das Museum in Houston hat nur jene Tapes anzubieten, die ich ohnedies schon habe, und Franks Schweizer Verleih kann überhaupt keine Bänder schicken – wende ich mich verzagt erneut an Frank. Er gibt seiner Cutterin und *partner in crime*, Laura Israel, meine Nummer. Sie verspricht, Videokopien zu schicken. Nach und nach, wie sie sagt. Von einigen Filmen müsse nämlich *erstmals* ein Masterband angefertigt werden, in manchen Fällen sei das gar nicht möglich. Es werde jetzt begonnen, alles aufzuarbeiten. Ich bin erstaunt, verstehe aber endlich, warum, mit Ausnahme von *Pull My Daisy*, Franks Filme so selten gezeigt werden. Gleichzeitig ist klar, dass wir hier in gewisser Weise Pionierarbeit leisten, dass Buch und Retrospektive einen ersten umfassenden Beitrag zur Aufarbeitung seines filmischen Werkes darstellen.

      Im November 2002 ist noch immer kein einziges der zugesagten Bänder da. Ich schicke Frank den ersten Ankündigungsfolder, in Ermangelung brauchbaren Materials mit einem Standbild aus dem Film *Candy Mountain*. Frank ist wütend, außer sich. Er mag *Candy Mountain* nicht. Er lehnt auch den begleitenden Kurztext ab, zieht die Filme zurück, verbietet uns, auch nur ein Foto seiner Arbeit zu veröffentlichen.

      Essenzielles liegt diesseits seiner Bescheidenheit, der scheue Seismograf fordert und motiviert auf seine Art. Stefan Grissemann und ich fahren im Dezember 2002 nach Zürich, um endlich

uncertainty, through Frank's gallery we received an okay for the book and retrospective. The condition was that no images which had *ever* been published anywhere could appear in the book. And Frank insisted that video stills were the only visual material we could use. At first we were baffled why a photographer of his stature would allow publication of a book with only videostills. And after our initial communication, characterized by laborious detours and brevity, what was the source of Frank's sudden and immense trust, his willingness to put the entire visual world of his films, his visual universe, at our disposal?

The "quality" of the book and retrospective were apparently of no concern to him. He wanted additional facets to be discovered in his works, he wanted them to be subjected to new tests. His idea of creating new film and video stills, risky in an artistic sense, was his contribution to the "script," and influenced the project's character considerably. This idea wiped away his fear of repeating himself and guaranteed uniqueness. Certain of his work, he opened up new creative spaces for us. Without realizing it at first, we would be actors under Robert Frank's direction. Respected and valued actors he could constantly examine and question, in the same way he examines and questions himself and his work. Rejecting the myths surrounding his work and his person and the *icons* already published in collections of his photographs was what gave us the freedom to make selections from his visual œuvre, arrange sequences, and in fact work with him.

He was already satisfied by the first few samples that we showed him and was even concerned about the great deal of work we faced. When I told him that, despite the relatively low quality of the video images, in their mutated material form his films developed a new concentration, and at the same time a unique expressive power, he cheerfully stated, "Yes, there is still something."

While doing research for this book, and certainly as a result of our close work with individual frames, we were surprised again and again by the richness of Robert Frank's films. Karl Ulbl, who is responsible for this book's visual design, Stefan Grissemann and I, its editors, would like to thank Robert Frank for entrusting us with this invaluable treasure, enabling us to gain new insight into his works, and for allowing us to help shape the visual analyses. And we also thank him for challenging us.

Brigitta Burger-Utzer

einige seiner kaum bekannten Filme zu sehen. Motiviert von diesem Erlebnis, folgen vielfältige Versuche, die Gespräche wieder aufzunehmen, Robert Frank zu überzeugen, für uns zu gewinnen. Nach endlosen Wochen der Ungewissheit erfahren wir über Franks Galerie: OK für Buch und Retrospektive. Bedingung: Es darf kein einziges Bild im Buch erscheinen, dass schon einmal *irgendwo* erschienen sei. Und Frank bestehe darauf, dass nur Videostills als Bildmaterial verwendet werden. Dass ein Fotograf seines Ranges ein Buch zulassen will, das nur mit Video-Standbildern illustriert sein soll, ist für uns zunächst kaum begreiflich. Und: Nachdem unsere Kommunikation schon bisher von Kargheit und mühsamen Umwegen geprägt war – woher kommt plötzlich Franks immenses Vertrauen, uns die gesamte Bildwelt seiner Filme, sein visuelles Universum zur freien Gestaltung zu überlassen?

Die "Qualität" des Buches und der Retrospektive sind es offenbar nicht, was Frank reizt. Er will seiner Arbeit vielmehr neue Aspekte abgerungen wissen, will sie neuen Prüfungen ausgesetzt sehen. Mit seiner Idee der Produktion von neuen Video- und Filmstills hat er seinen – künstlerisch wagemutigen, aber das Projekt prägenden – Teil zum "Script" geliefert. Diese Idee erst hat seine tief-sitzende Angst, sich selbst zu wiederholen, in diesem Fall eliminiert und die Einzigartigkeit des Projekts garantiert. In der Gewissheit, sich auf seine Arbeiten verlassen zu können, hat er uns kreative Freiräume eröffnet. Wir wurden, ohne das gleich zu erkennen, Darsteller in einer Regie Robert Franks. Geachtete, geschätzte Darsteller, die er, wie sich selbst und seine Arbeit, permanent hinterfragt. Erst die Verweigerung des Mythos um seine Person und seine bereits in den Fotobüchern publizierten *Icons* hat uns die Freiheit gegeben, aus seiner Bildwelt auszuwählen, Sequenzen zu arrangieren, tatsächlich: mit ihm zu arbeiten.

Schon nach den ersten Mustern, die wir ihm zeigen, ist er zufrieden, sogar besorgt über die viele Arbeit, die wir da haben. Als ich ihm sage, dass seine Arbeiten trotz der vermindernden Bildqualität des Videos in der mutierten Materialität als Still ein neues Konzentrat, aber auch eine völlig eigenständige Aussagekraft entwickeln, stellt er mit heiterem Ton fest: "Yes, there is still something".

Während der Recherche an diesem Buch sind wir – gerade durch die Auseinandersetzung mit dem filmischen Einzelbild – immer wieder von dem Reichtum der (so wenig bekannten) *motion pictures* Robert Franks überrascht. Karl Ulbl, der die visuelle Gestaltung dieses Buches vorgenommen hat, Stefan Grissemann und ich danken Robert Frank, dass er uns diesen Reichtum anvertraut und uns ermöglicht hat, neue Einblicke in seine Arbeiten zu gewinnen und visuelle Analysen mitzugestalten. Danke auch dafür, dass er uns herausgefordert hat.

Brigitta Burger-Utzer

How does one approach an artist who has repeatedly avoided everyone and everything, including interpretation and critical examination? Robert Frank has always faced up to one thing only, himself. That is shown by his work, the films even more than the photographs. This book is dedicated to Frank's film and video œuvre, which grew and developed impressively in the years between 1959 and 2002, though unnoticed by most of the world. He worked in a place untouched by fashions and schools, his art literally growing out of and for itself, which is the reason it is so singular, so inimitable.

frank films, in German and English, offers an introduction to this œuvre. Published primarily to accompany a retrospective of Robert Frank's films, it also provides detailed descriptions of all his works, representing a definitive and vivid portrait. The book's structure was chosen with the intention of assembling this œuvre in a single volume, thematically and chronologically, with stylistic wrinkles and abrupt changes in direction. The introductory essay in the form of a tour of Frank's cinematic works as a whole, offers an initial overview attempting to identify his most important artistic tools and achievements. The following five essays address selected characteristics, styles and ideas which have shaped him and his work and search for recurrent themes and distinctive motifs in these divergent artworks. In the final section, each text is dedicated to one of his twenty-five films or videos.

We hope that this book will help clearly show Robert Frank as the highly original and one-of-a-kind auteur he is. What is described here from a number of different angles and points of view is the paradox of Frank's films, which are so bluntly open but in many cases also mysterious and inaccessible at the same time. What is offered here, what must be offered, is a close look at a great man who refuses to make compromises, one of the last of his kind.

Stefan Grissemann

Wie soll man, kann man einem Künstler, der sich stets allen und allem, auch Interpretationen und kritischen Annäherungen, entzogen hat, je nahekommen? Robert Frank hat sich immer nur einem gestellt: sich selbst. Davon erzählt sein Werk, das filmische mehr noch als das fotografische. Franks Film- und Videoarbeit, die zwischen 1959 und 2002, unbemerkt von der Welt, zu einem stattlichen, vielschichtigen Werk herangewachsen ist, gilt dieses Buch: einer Arbeit, die jenseits von Moden und Schulen verrichtet wurde, die buchstäblich aus sich und für sich selbst gewachsen ist und schon deswegen so singulär, so unverwechselbar anmutet.

frank films bietet, zweisprachig gehalten, einen Einstieg in diese Arbeit: Die Publikation begleitet einerseits (und idealerweise) eine Werkschau der Filme Robert Franks, andererseits soll sie – über detaillierte Beschreibungen jeder einzelnen seiner Arbeiten – auch ohne flankierende Retrospektive ein schlüssiges, möglichst plastisches Bild des Frankschen Filmschaffens vermitteln. Die Struktur des Buches ist dem Bemühen geschuldet, ein Werk, das reich ist an stilistischen Unwegsamkeiten und jähen formalen Richtungswechseln, thematisch und chronologisch zu bündeln. Der Einstiegs-Essay bietet zunächst, in Form einer Passage durch das filmische Gesamtwerk Robert Franks, einen ersten Überblick, versucht die entscheidenden künstlerischen Positionen und Mittel dieses Künstlers zu klären. Die danach folgenden fünf Essays fassen ausgewählte Eigenarten, prägende Ideen und Stile ins Auge, suchen rote Fäden, charakteristische Linien quer durch die so divergenten Arbeiten dieses Filmemachers. Der letzte Teil des Buches widmet jedem einzelnen der 25 Film- und Video-Werke Franks je eine Doppelseite.

Es steht zu hoffen, dass dieses Buch dazu beitragen wird, Robert Frank als den eigenartigen, eigensinnigen Film-*auteur* greifbar zu machen, der er zweifellos ist. Was hier im Grunde beschrieben, von vielen Seiten eingekreist wird, ist letztlich das Paradoxon der Filme Franks, die so schonungslos offen sind und doch auch, immer wieder, unzugänglich, rätselhaft bleiben. Was hier jedenfalls geboten wird, geboten werden muss, ist dies: die Nahaufnahme eines großen Kompromisslosen, eines der letzten seiner Art.

Stefan Grissemann

frank films ist durch die Kooperation und Hilfe vieler Personen zustande gekommen: Laura Israel war unsere Verbündete von Anfang an, sie hatte den besten Überblick über Franks filmisches Werk; die Pace/MacGill Gallery in New York, vor allem Lauren Panzo und Peter MacGill haben zwischen Robert Frank und uns vermittelt: danke für die permanente Unterstützung; Christa Auderlitzky hat rare Frank-Publikationen gefunden, aufwendige Recherchen betrieben und ein verlässliches, engagiertes Lektorat gemacht; die Übersetzer und Übersetzerinnen Charlotte Eckler, Barbara Pichler, Lisa Rosenblatt, Bert Rebhandl und Steve Wilder haben rasch und genau gearbeitet; Jean Perret von Visions du Réel in Nyon hat Videotapes zur Verfügung gestellt; Peter da Rin von Pro Helvetia war begeisteter Unterstützer und interessierter Beobachter unserer Arbeit; Marian Luntz hat uns mit Informationen, Material und erschwinglichen Leihgebühren unterstützt, Walter Keller vom Scalo-Verlag mit wertvollen Hinweisen. Dank auch an Alexander Horwath und Regina Schlagnitweit, die das Projekt ins Rollen gebracht haben; Herzlichen Dank besonders an die Diagonale für die Idee, Franks Arbeit im Rahmen von Graz, Kulturhauptstadt Europas 2003, mit Retrospektive und Buch zu würdigen; insbesondere an Constantin Wulff und Viktoria Salcher, die das Vertrauen in uns hatten, dass das Buch, das wir planten, trotz vieler Schwierigkeiten und Verzögerungen letztlich ohne Kompromisse zu machen sein würde.

Brigitta Burger-Utzer und Stefan Grissemann

frank films was made possible by the cooperation and help provided by numerous individuals: Laura Israel, who has the best overview of Frank's film œuvre as a whole, was our ally from the very beginning; the Pace/MacGill Gallery in New York (especially Lauren Panzo and Peter MacGill) served as an intermediary for our communication with Frank: thanks for their permanent support; Christa Auderlitzky was able to find rare publications on Frank, performed a great deal of research, and was a reliable and committed proofreader; translators Charlotte Eckler, Barbara Pichler, Lisa Rosenblatt, Bert Rebhandl, and Steve Wilder worked quickly and precisely; Jean Perret of Visions du Réel in Nyon was a source of numerous videotapes; Peter da Rin of Pro Helvetia, Switzerland's arts council, was an enthusiastic supporter and interested observer of our work; Marian Luntz helped us with information, various materials, and affordable rental fees; and Walter Keller of the Scalo-Verlag publishing house provided valuable tips. Thanks to Alexander Horwath and Regina Schlagnitweit for their inspiration for this project. Many thanks to the Diagonale for the idea of honoring Frank's work with a retrospective and a book as part of Graz's role as the 2003 European Cultural Capital, and special thanks to Constantin Wulff and Viktoria Salcher for their trust that the book we had in mind was possible despite a number of difficulties and delays, but without compromise.

Brigitta Burger-Utzer und Stefan Grissemann

Vérité Vaudeville
Passage durch Robert Franks audiovisuelles Werk

Stefan Grissemann

„Eine Entscheidung: Ich verstaue meine Leica in einem Schrank. Genug davon, auf der Lauer zu liegen, zu verfolgen, um bisweilen an die Essenz des Schwarzweiß und das Wissen um den Ort Gottes zu kommen. Ich mache Filme. Jetzt spreche ich zu den Leuten, die sich in meinem Sucher bewegen. Nicht einfach und nicht besonders erfolgreich."

So erinnert sich Robert Frank an den Schnitt, den er in seiner Arbeit Ende der fünfziger Jahre gesetzt hat: als keine große Sache, als einfach logische Folge, als mit Selbstzweifeln besetzten, aber nötigen Akt. Erfolg hat ihm die Verwandlung vom Fotografen in einen Filmemacher nicht gebracht, im Gegenteil, der Übertritt hat zum (fast vollständigen) Verschwinden dieses Künstlers aus allen öffentlichen Debatten beigetragen. Woran Frank seit 1959 arbeitet, spielt sich im (weitgehend) Verborgenen ab, sein Werk ist de facto in den Underground abgerutscht, an die äußersten Ränder der Gegenwartskunst. Als Filmemacher ist er seit mehr als vier Jahrzehnten ein gut gehütetes Geheimnis; unter denen, die Robert Frank heute noch kennen, gilt er als Fotokünstler – und vielleicht noch, da und dort, als Co-Regisseur zweier Filme, die sein Werk nicht einmal ansatzweise definieren: das filmische Beat-Poem *Pull My Daisy* (1959) und das Road-movie *Candy Mountain* (1987) – beides übrigens Arbeiten, die Frank selbst nicht zu seinen bedeutenden zählt. Bei manchen Autoren, die sich auf den Avantgardefilm spezialisieren (etwa Jonas Mekas, David E. James oder Amos Vogel), tauchen am Rande außerdem noch *Me and My Brother* (1965–68) und *The Sin of Jesus* (1961) auf. Der Rest, Franks vielteiliges Hauptwerk, ist in der Literatur ebenso wie in den Kinos so gut wie inexistent.

Nicht selten stoßen Robert Franks Filme auf heftige Ablehnung, durchaus auch auf die Ablehnung cinephiler Gemüter: Der junge Francois Truffaut, so berichtet der Filmkritiker Andrew Sarris, habe *The Sin of Jesus* einst, 1961, als den schlechtesten Film, den er je gesehen habe, bezeichnet – und US-Kritikerlegende Parker Tyler hat (in seinem Standardwerk „Underground Film") Robert Frank gewissermaßen im Vorbeigehen "inept and imitative" genannt, einen „ungeschickten und epigonalen" Filmemacher. Es gehört zu den Komplikationen im Umgang mit Franks Arbeiten, dass man solche Deklarationen offener Antipathie wenigstens zum Teil nachvollziehbar finden muss. Ein Filmemacher,

Vérité Vaudeville
Passage through Robert Frank's Audiovisual Work

Stefan Grissemann

"A decision: I put my Leica in a cupboard. Enough of lying in wait, pursuing, sometimes catching the essence of the black and white, the knowledge of where God is. I make films. Now I speak to the people who move in my viewfinder. Not simple and not especially successful."

This is how Robert Frank recalls the break that he made in his work at the end of the 1950s: as no big deal, a simple logical result, an act filled with self doubt but nonetheless necessary. The switch from photographer to filmmaker did not bring him success. On the contrary, the move contributed to the almost complete disappearance of the artist from all public discussion. The things that Frank worked on after 1959 occurred (largely) in obscurity, his work slipped *de facto* underground, to the farthest flung borders of contemporary art. As a filmmaker, he has been a well kept secret for almost four decades. Among those who still know Frank today, he is considered an art photographer—and perhaps, here and there, as the co-director of two films, which are in no way definitional for his work: the filmic Beat poem *Pull My Daisy* (1959) and the road movie *Candy Mountain* (1987)—both, by the way, works that Frank himself does not consider among his most important. For some authors who specialize in avant-garde film (such as Jonas Mekas, David E. James, or Amos Vogel), appearing peripherally are also *Me and My Brother* (1965–68) and *The Sin of Jesus* (1961). The remainder, Frank's complex œuvre, is virtually non-existent in the relevant literature and in the cinemas.

Frank's works often meet with strong rejection, and even disapproval among cinephiles. As the film critic Andrew Sarris reports, the young Francois Truffaut once described *The Sin of Jesus*, 1961, as the worst film he had ever seen—and the legendary U.S. critic Parker Tyler in his classic work *Underground Film*, called Frank—as an aside, so to speak—"inept and imitative," an "untalented and unoriginal" filmmaker. One of the complications in dealing with Frank's works is being able to find such declarations of open antipathy at least somewhat understandable. A filmmaker like this, who is so demonstratively *not* interested in mediation, but instead only in his own ideas of living up to odd visions, will constantly encounter a great deal of misunderstanding along with the respect that he deserves.

der sich so demonstrativ wie dieser *nicht* um Vermittlung bemüht, sondern einzig darum, eigenen Ideen, verqueren Visionen zu entsprechen, wird stets neben dem Respekt, den er verdient, auch einer Menge Unverständnis begegnen.

Wenn es einen Begriff gibt, der Robert Franks Arbeit ästhetisch umreißt, so ist das die Flüchtigkeit. Robert Franks dokumentarischen Arbeiten, aber durchaus auch seinem fiktionalen Werk ist eine unbändige Liebe zum Gegenwärtigen zu eigen, eine Hingabe an die Flüchtigkeit des Augenblicks. Frank ist ein Künstler des radikalen Understatement, der Verweigerung. Sein Stil, seine Sprache, seine Zeit ist die Gegenwart – als wollte er das Wesen seines Mediums durchkreuzen, das die Zeit einfriert und als Erinnerung, für immer reproduzierbar, wieder ausspuckt. Franks Filme und Videos enthalten, wenigstens scheinbar, kaum große Bilder und keine „bedeutenden" Momente, sie verweigern, was man „Kino" nennt – und auf der Höhe irgendeiner „Kunst" zu sein, daran hat Frank sowieso kein Interesse. Diese Filme wollen, in zweierlei Hinsicht, grundsätzlich nur für den Moment da sein – den Moment, den sie wiedergeben, ebenso wie für den Moment, in dem sie betrachtet werden –, um sich unmittelbar danach aus dem Bewusstsein wieder „zurückzuziehen", als wären sie nie da gewesen: wie Träume, die man nach dem Wachwerden nicht mehr recht rekonstruieren kann. Diese Filme legen es nicht darauf an, Erinnerungsspuren zu hinterlassen, sie bleiben blass, ungreifbar, sind „atmosphärisch" eher als „bildlich". (Blickt man ein wenig tiefer, ändert sich dieser Eindruck allerdings: Betrachtet man etwa Standfotos aus Franks Filmen, so fällt an ihnen sofort eine eigenartige kompositorische Schönheit auf, eine visuelle Genauigkeit, die an den Filmen selbst zu bemerken schwer fällt. Es gehört zur anhaltenden Faszination dieses Werks, dass es seine eigene Schönheit so sehr unterspielt, zu leugnen scheint.)

Als Künstler ist Frank, 1924 in Zürich geboren, Ende der fünfziger Jahre im Begriff, berühmt zu werden (sein umstrittener Fotoband "The Americans" wird im November 1958 publiziert); ohne zu zögern, als langweilte ihn die jähe Aufmerksamkeit, die man ihm entgegenzubringen beginnt, schon wieder, tritt er in sein neues Fach über: ins Kino. Der Einstieg ist Legende: Mit den schönen Worten "Early morning in the universe" leitet die melodische Stimme Jack Kerouacs *Pull My Daisy* ein, Franks bekanntesten Film, in Co-Regie realisiert mit dem Künstler Alfred Leslie. Basierend auf einer poetischen Tour de force Kerouacs, der hier – in einer veritablen *verbal jazz performance* – aus dem Off spricht, singt, heult, vollzieht sich *Pull My Daisy* als Innenansicht des New Yorker Bohemien-Lebensstils und des Selbstverständnisses der Beatniks, Ende der fünfziger Jahre in der Lower East Side, Manhattan. Franks und Leslies *Pull My Daisy* – finanziert übrigens von zwei Wall-Street-Investoren – führt ein

Pull My Daisy – Gregory Corso

Pull My Daisy – Allen Ginsberg

If there were a term that could aesthetically outline Frank's work, it would be "fleeting." Frank's documentary works, but also his fictional works, possess an unbridled love of the present, a devotion to the transience of the moment. Frank is a master of the radical understatement, the refusal. His style, his language, and his time is the present—as though he wanted to cross through the being of his medium, to freeze time, and having it eternally reproducible to spit it out as a memory. Frank's films and videos contain—at least seemingly—hardly any great pictures and no "meaningful" moments. His films refuse what one calls "cinema." Anyway, Frank is not interested in being at the height of any type of "art." These films aim to be present for only a moment in two respects—the moment that they are played, just as much as the moment that they are observed—to then immediately "retreat" from consciousness once again, as though they had never been there, like dreams that you can't really piece together when you wake up. These films are not interested in leaving behind tracks, they remain pale, ungraspable, are more "atmospheric" than "pictorial." (If one looks a bit deeper, however, this impression changes: when viewing still photos from Frank's films, for example, a unique compositional beauty is immediately noticeable, a visual precision that is difficult to recognize in the films themselves. A constant fascination with this work lies in that it seems to play down its own beauty to such an extent, to deny it.)

Frank, born in 1924 in Zurich, was on the verge of artistic fame at the end of the 1950s (his controversial photo book "The Americans" was published in November 1958). Without hesitation, as though the sudden attention which he was beginning to be given bored him, he once again stepped into a new field: cinema. The entry is legendary: with the beautiful words "Early morning in the universe," Jack Kerouac's melodic voice introduces *Pull My Daisy*, Frank's best known film, co-produced together with the artist Alfred Leslie. Based on Kerouac's poetic *tour de force*, which he speaks, sings, and howls from off-camera in a veritable verbal jazz performance, *Pull My Daisy* takes place in Manhattan's Lower East Side as an inside view of the New York Bohemian lifestyle and the Beatniks' self perception at the end of the 1950s. Frank and Leslie's *Pull My Daisy*—financed, by the way, by two Wall Street investors—very demonstratively presents a remarkable artistic credo: what is cinema there for if not for the everyday, the banal? The filmmakers and their artist friends (including: Allen Ginsberg, Gregory Corso, and Peter Orlovsky) show themselves, present their own world, and put on no greater airs than is necessary when people decide to film their own lifestyle.

A room, an environment monopolized by art: the camera pans across an apartment, a loft downtown in New York, past bare walls and a few paintings. Disorder reigns, precious, valuable chaos, but only inside—the world outside is hazy, desolate, or at least it looks that way: the windows do not

markantes künstlerisches Credo vor, sehr demonstrativ: Wozu soll das Kino da sein, wenn nicht für das Alltägliche, das Banale? Die Filmemacher und ihre Künstlerfreunde (mit dabei: Allen Ginsberg, Gregory Corso, Peter Orlovsky) zeigen sich also selbst, führen die eigene Welt vor, und sie nehmen sich dabei nicht wichtiger, als es sein muss, wenn man beschließt, seinen Lebensstil zu verfilmen.

Ein Raum, Lebensraum, von der Kunst vereinnahmt: Die Kamera schwenkt durch eine Wohnung, ein Loft in downtown New York, an kahlen Wänden und ein paar Gemälden vorbei. Es herrscht Unordnung, kostbares, lebenswertes Chaos, aber nur innen – die Welt draußen ist dunstig, verödet, wenigstens sieht es so aus: Die Fenster geben nicht viel preis, das Tageslicht, das durch sie in die Zimmer dringt, ist milchig, undurchdringlich, als gäbe es hinter diesen Fenstern keinen Himmel, keine Straßen, keine Menschen. Die Protagonisten des Films, die Dichter, Dichterfamilien und Dichter-freunde, halten sich im Inneren auf, verschanzt im Privaten, halb verschluckt vom Rauch ihrer Zigaretten, im Dunstkreis von Bier und Poesie: Beatniks (das kann man hier lernen) sind Innenraummenschen, *living room people*, Pendler zwischen Clubs und Schlafzimmern und Bars und Stiegenhäusern. *Pull My Daisy* – ein *home movie* in jedem, auch im besten Sinn des Wortes – hält sich daher programmatisch im Inneren auf: im Inneren seiner Figuren, für die und von denen der Film spricht; und im Inneren der Räume, die diese Figuren beleben. Kerouac, der Demiurg der Erzählung, synchronisiert und rhythmi-siert mit „spontaner Prosa" das Treiben der Menschen, allwissend und motivierend, liebevoll distanziert. Die sprunghafte Voice-Over übernimmt fremde Stimmen, spielt Dialoge nach, um sich Sekunden später davon auch wieder zu distanzieren, zurück in den Kommentar, in eine Erzählung zu flüchten, die vage auf dem dritten Akt eines nie gespielten Theaterstücks Jack Kerouacs beruht.

Was andere für Kino halten, wirft *Pull My Daisy* leichtherzig über Bord: Der Film liefert keine „Geschichte", kaum Bewegung, keinen Glamour und keine großen Schauwerte. Statt dessen: einen filmischen Bewusstseinsstrom, einen Akt der angewandten Poesie. Alles hat mit allem zu tun, wenn man es nur gut genug dreht und wendet, genau wie die Worte, die Kerouac sich selbst (oder man einander) im Mund umdreht: Baseball und Religion, Amerika und Küchenschaben, die Selbstverlieb-heit und die Selbstvergessenheit. Der Maler Alfred Leslie und der Fotograf Robert Frank inszenieren Dokumentarisches, Zufälliges, Improvisiertes, zugleich dokumentieren sie die Inszenierung, die sie vornehmen: Der Tonfall des Komischen stellt sich über die Selbstreflexivität, über die Offenheit her, mit der sich *Pull My Daisy* bereitwillig infiziert. Die Grenzen zwischen Fiktion und Dokumentarismus verwischen sich: eine Konstante auch im späteren Werk Robert Franks. *Pull My Daisy*, keine halbe Stunde lang, jongliert mit genuin filmischen Widersprüchen, mit Paradoxien, die nur das Kino zustande bringt: „Dialoge" werden als Monologe repräsentiert, eine „Story" als Delirium, als Fantasie, als reiner Klang, zunehmend losgelöst von „Sinn" und Ambition – das Kino musikalisiert sich, wird lyrisch, gestisch, expressiv.

Pull My Daisy ist eine Art Avantgardefilm – und auch wieder *nicht* in seinen sehr konkreten sozialen, halbdokumentarischen Lebensbildern, die nicht unbedingt die Nähe zu den sich formierenden Pionieren des New American Cinema suchen; jedenfalls aber ist Franks Debüt ein tausendprozentig *unabhängiger* Film, der durch seine bewusst „amateurhafte" Form auch als piece de resistance gegen den hochpolierten Stil des US-Erzählkinos jener Zeit zu lesen ist. Gemeinsam mit *Shadows*, dem zeitgleich entstehenden, ebenfalls betont jazzig angelegten Regiedebüt John Cassavetes', wird *Pull My Daisy* im November 1959 im New Yorker Cinema 16 uraufgeführt: ein double feature als Blick in die Zukunft der Filmkunst.

reveal much, the daylight that penetrates through them into the room is milky, impenetrable, as though there were no sky behind these windows, no streets, no people. The film's protagonists—the poets, the poets' families and friends—stay indoors, take refuge in the private space, half swallowed by the smoke of their cigarettes, in the orbit of beer and poetry: Beatniks (we learn here) are inside people, *living room people,* commuters between clubs and bedrooms and bars and apartment buildings. *Pull My Daisy*—a *home movie* in every and also the best sense of the word—thus remains programmatically in the inner space: inside of its characters, for whom and of which the film speaks; and inside of the rooms that these characters inhabit. Kerouac, the demiurge of the narrative, synchronizes and rhymes the goings on of the people in a "spontaneous prose" that is omniscient and motivating, affectionately distant. The erratic voice-over takes on a foreign voice, repeats dialogues to then distance from them a second later, to move back to the commentary, to escape into a narration based vaguely on the third act of a never produced play by Jack Kerouac.

Pull My Daisy lightheartedly throws overboard what others think of cinema: the film delivers almost no "story," movement, glamour, or great viewing value but instead, a cinematic stream of consciousness, an act of related poetry. Everything has to do with everything else if we only twist and turn it well enough, just like the words that Kerouac to himself, and we to each other, turn around in our mouths: baseball and religion, America and cockroaches, self love and oblivion. The painter Alfred Leslie and the photographer Frank stage the documentary, coincidental, and improvised elements, and simultaneously document the staging that they undertake. A comical tone is generated over the self reflection, the openness, and *Pull My Daisy* is willingly infected. The borders between fiction and documentary blur into one another. This also remains a constant in Frank's later works. *Pull My Daisy*, not even half an hour long, juggles with genuine cinematic contradictions, with paradoxes that only the cinema can create: "Dialogues" are represented as monologues, a "story" as delirium, as fantasy, as pure sound increasingly released from "sense" and ambition—cinema becomes musical, lyrical, expressive, gesture.

Pull My Daisy is a type of avant-garde film—but then again, it's *not* in its very concrete social, semi-documentary pictures of life, which do not necessarily seek affiliation with the forming pioneers of the New American Cinema. But, in any case, Frank's debut is a truly, 1,000 percent *independent* film, which through its conscious "amateur-like" form can be read as a *piece de resistance* directed at the highly polished style of the U.S. narrative cinema of the times. Together with *Shadows,* the contemporaneous, likewise decidedly jazzy directing debut from John Cassavetes, *Pull My Daisy* had its premiere in November 1959 in New York's Cinema 16: a double feature as a glance into the future of film art.

Pull My Daisy permanently damaged the relationship between Alfred Leslie and Frank. As soon as the film was complete, each began accusing the other of illegally and falsely stylizing himself as the actual creator, the director of the work. Until the present day it is not clear which of the two is right. Actually, one of the stories that reports on this argument sounds like a cruel fable. Leslie, three years younger than Frank, reports on the genesis of the film (in a detailed interview in the book, "The Naked Lens," 1997) as follows: he, Leslie, had to first convince the "totally disinterested" Frank to participate in *Pull My Daisy* as a cameraman. When they then finished the film, Frank suddenly became interested in being named as co-director. Because Leslie at the time considered Frank to be his best friend, he agreed to share everything. He would give him the co-director credit if Frank in return allowed him to be

Pull My Daisy

Pull My Daisy beschädigt die Freundschaft zwischen Alfred Leslie und Robert Frank nachhaltig. Seit Fertigstellung des Films bezichtigt einer den anderen, sich widerrechtlich und fälschlich zum eigentlichen Schöpfer, zum Regisseur der Arbeit stilisiert zu haben. Es ist bis heute nicht zu klären, wer von beiden recht hat. Tatsächlich nimmt sich eine der Geschichten, die von diesem Streit erzählen, wie eine böse Fabel aus. Leslie, drei Jahre jünger als Frank, berichtet (in einem detaillierten Interview in dem Buch "The Naked Lens", 1997) von der Genese des Films folgendes: Er, Leslie, habe den „total desinteressierten" Frank erst überreden müssen, als Kameramann an *Pull My Daisy* mitzuwirken. Als sie den Film fertiggestellt hatten, sei plötzlich Franks Interesse daran erwacht, als Co-Regisseur genannt zu werden. Weil Leslie aber nun Frank für seinen besten Freund gehalten habe, habe er zugestimmt, alles zu teilen: Er wolle ihm den Co-Regie-Credit überlassen, wenn ihm Frank im Gegenzug die Nennung als Co-Kameramann gestatte. Leslie habe nur eine Bedingung gestellt: Nach zehn Jahren müssten die wahren Verhältnisse wiederhergestellt werden – und Leslie als alleiniger Regisseur im Vorspann verzeichnet stehen. Und von dieser Minute an, erzählt Alfred Leslie, habe Robert Frank alles getan, um als treibende Kraft hinter *Pull My Daisy* wahrgenommen zu werden. Er habe in Interviews gelogen, habe jede Möglichkeit genutzt, um Leslies Zutun herunterzuspielen. – Es versteht sich fast von selbst, dass Franks Version dieser Geschichte in die entgegengesetzte Richtung zielt.

1966 brennt Alfred Leslies Atelier nieder. Zwölf Feuerwehrleute kommen dabei ums Leben. Unzählige Werke Leslies – Gemälde, Schriften, Filme – werden in den Flammen vernichtet, darunter auch eine Menge unverwendetes Filmmaterial aus *Pull My Daisy*. Man sagt, dass die Beat-Poeten darin in Cowboy-Kostümen zu sehen gewesen seien.

Die sarkastische Debatte um die *holiness*, die Kerouac an einer (berühmten) Stelle in *Pull My Daisy* führt, das Nachdenken über die Heiligkeit in allem, in allen Dingen und Bildern und Lebewesen, sie setzt sich in Franks zweitem Film fort: *The Sin of Jesus* (1961) wagt sich an ein spirituelles Thema, das der Filmemacher indes sehr dezidiert im Irdischen verankert. Franks Adaption der gleich-

The Sin of Jesus

named co-cameraman. Leslie placed only one condition on this: after ten years the truth had to be reestablished—and Leslie was to be recorded as the sole director in the credits. From this moment on, Leslie recounts, Frank did everything possible to be recognized as the driving force behind *Pull My Daisy*. He lied in interviews, used every possibility to play down Leslie's participation. It seems almost natural that Frank's version of this story leads in the opposite direction.

In 1966, Leslie's studio burned to the ground. Twelve firefighters died in the blaze. Innumerable works from Leslie—paintings, writings, films—were destroyed in the flames, including a great deal of unused film material from *Pull My Daisy*. It was said that one could see the Beat poets in cowboy costumes in this material.

The sarcastic debate about *holiness*, which Kerouac introduces in a (famous) spot in *Pull My Daisy*, the contemplation of the holiness in everything, in all things and pictures and living beings, continues in Frank's second film. *The Sin of Jesus* (1961) risks approaching a spiritual theme, which the filmmaker anchors quite decisively in the worldly realm. Frank's adaptation of the like-named tale by Isaac Babel (Leslie also claimed the idea to film this material) begins with the picture of a field with a view of the gray earth. At first *The Sin of Jesus* is a film about work, about the earth and the housework of a young woman who reports from off-camera and complains about the monotony of her existence ("day after day, winter, summer, winter"), while her marriage falls apart under the pressure of routine. The heroine's husband, played by a young Telly Savalas (according to the credits: "Telli Savales"), decides to leave "for a while," as it's called, but one suspects that he will most likely be gone for good.

For the time being, Frank maintains the jazz in his work, and the impression of the introvert is thus reinforced. The music of Morton Feldman very softly accompanies this chronic of a Fall of Mankind by Jesus. A soft tone penetrates the film, which depicts what it has to show in a way that, although not beautiful, is strangely gentle: the animals, the landscape, the people. Even though Isaac Babel's short story is categorized as magical realism, Frank holds less to the magical than he does to the

namigen Erzählung Isaac Babels (auch die Idee der Verfilmung dieses Stoffes übrigens reklamiert Leslie für sich) beginnt mit dem Bild eines Ackers, mit einem Blick auf graue Erde. *The Sin of Jesus* ist zunächst ein Film über Arbeit, über die Land- und Hausarbeit einer jungen Frau, die aus dem Off von sich berichtet, die Monotonie ihrer Existenz beklagt ("Day after day, winter, summer, winter"), während sich ihre Ehe, unter dem Druck der Routine, schon erledigt hat. Der Gefährte der Heldin, gespielt vom jungen Telly Savalas (laut Vorspann: „Telli Savales"), beschließt wegzugehen, "for a while", wie es heißt, aber man ahnt, dass es wohl eher für immer sein wird.

Der Jazz bleibt Robert Franks Arbeit vorerst erhalten, und dabei verfestigt sich der Eindruck des Introvertierten: Die Musik Morton Feldmans begleitet, sehr leise, diese Chronik eines Sündenfalls Jesu. Ein sanfter Ton durchdringt den Film, der, was er zu zeigen hat, nicht schön, aber eigenartig weich abbildet: die Tiere, die Landschaft, die Menschen. Auch wenn Isaac Babels Kurzgeschichte der Kategorie magischer Realismus zugeordnet worden ist, so hält sich Frank doch weniger ans Magische als an den Realismus. Er forciert den hohen dokumentarischen Anteil seiner Inszenierung einer Geschichte, die an sich, wie man sehen wird, schon bizarr genug ist. Zunächst scheint diese auf ein Drama hinauszulaufen: Die Frau ist schwanger, sie versucht, ihren Mann zum Bleiben zu überreden, scheitert daran aber; sie provoziert ihn nur zu einem Ausbruch, roh weist er ihre Liebe, ihren Hilferuf zurück: Er habe sie satt, herrscht er sie an, ebenso wie er diesen Ort satt habe. Und man kann sehen, was er meint: die Hütte, in der sie in Armut leben, und die grauen Felder vor der Tür. Hilfe bringt erst der Rückzug in die Transzendenz: Die Verlassene (mit Stummfilmgesicht: Julie Bovasso) meint in ihrem Stall Jesus zu begegnen. Frank führt ihn und die seinen als frühe Hippies vor, hier kippt der Film in die (seltsam stille) Groteske: Ein hagerer Jesus spricht der Frau, um deren Not zu lindern, einen Engel zu, einen *unhappy angel* namens Alfred, den sie ab sofort für vier Jahre haben könne, nur so, zum Spaß. So findet eine Hochzeit statt, gleich an Ort und Stelle, im Stall: Ein Hippie-*happening* ergibt sich, eine Liebesparty unter Bohemiens. Das Glück des neuen Paares wird jäh gekappt: Der Sex, den die Frau, allen Warnungen zum Trotz, von ihrem neuen Gemahl einfordert, führt zum Tod des Engels.

Gott zürnt fortan der Frau, anstatt ihre menschliche Fehlbarkeit zu verzeihen, macht sich mithin der Sünde der nicht stattfindenden Vergebung schuldig. Die Heldin verzweifelt darüber, wird depressiv, vereinsamt. Sie brauche keinen Engel, ruft sie Jesus zu, gefangen in immer extremeren psychischen Zuständen. Im offenen Feld, wieder ganz in Grau, endet der Film, mit einer letzten Konfrontation zwischen dem reumütigen Heiland und der stolzen einsamen Frau: Jesus sinkt vor ihr auf die Knie, bittet sie, ihm zu vergeben ("forgive your sinful God"). Sie lässt ihn hinter sich, verstößt ihn. Die Rollen haben sich verkehrt.

Während der frühen sechziger Jahre befindet sich der Filmemacher Robert Frank noch in einer Phase des Suchens. Er befasst sich auch mit Themen und (spiel-)filmischen Formen, die ihm wenig später schon abhanden kommen, die sein folgendes Werk nicht weiter prägen werden: *OK End Here* gerät, nach der spröden Jesus-Parabel, zu einer fast schon über-eleganten, an Antonioni gemahnenden urbanen Alltagsgeschichte – zu einer weiteren gut halbstündigen Beziehungsstudie, deren reibungslose Erzählung ein Fremdkörper im Schaffen dieses Künstlers bleiben wird. Eine Art Suchmanöver leitet den Film ein, eine tastende Bewegung vorwärts, zum Kern der Erzählung, zum Privaten hin: Nach einer schnellen Fahrt an einem New Yorker Wohnblock vorbei bewegt sich Franks Kamera durch die Gänge eines weitläufigen Apartments dem Schlafzimmer seiner Protagonisten entgegen, findet ein Paar vor, noch im Bett, gerade erst erwacht.

realism. He imposes a great deal of documentary elements in his staging of a story, which, as we will see, is already bizarre enough in and of itself. At first it seems to lead into a drama: the woman is pregnant, she attempts to talk her husband into staying, but fails to do so. Instead, she only provokes him to an outburst. He crudely rejects her love and her call for help. He has had enough of her and this place, he barks at her. And we can see what he means: the hut, in which they live in poverty and the fields of gray before the door. Help is first attained by a retreat into transcendence. The abandoned Julie Bovasso (with an expression like in a silent movie) says that she met Jesus in her stall. Frank presents him and his companions as early hippies. Here the film slips into a (strangely silent) grotesque tale: a gaunt Jesus promises the woman an angel to ease her desperation, an *unhappy angel* named Alfred, whom she can have immediately for four years, just for fun. Thus a marriage takes place, right then and there. A hippie *happening* results, a love fest among Bohemians. The new couple's happiness is abruptly cut short: sex, which the woman demands of her new husband despite all warnings, leads to the angel's death.

Rather than forgiving her for her human fallibility, God scorns the woman from then on and therefore becomes guilty of the sin of not forgiving. The heroine despairs over this, becomes depressed, lonely. She does not need an angel, she calls out to Jesus, imprisoned in ever more extreme mental states. The film ends in the open field, which is once again entirely gray, with a final confrontation between the remorseful Savior and the proud, lonely woman: Jesus sinks to his knees in front of her, pleads with her to forgive him ("forgive your sinful God"). She leaves him, walks away behind his back, disowns him. The roles have been reversed.

During the early 1960s, the filmmaker Robert Frank was still in a searching phase. He was also occupied with themes and (feature) film forms, which he would shortly drop, which would not influence his later work. After the unwieldy Jesus parable, *OK End Here* turned out as an almost overly elegant urban story of everyday life reminiscent of Antonioni—a further half-hour long examination of a relationship, whose smooth narration would remain out of place among the artist's works. A type of search maneuver introduces the film, a tentative movement forward, to the core of the story, to the private: after a fast drive past a New York residential block, Frank's camera moves through the hallways of a spacious apartment toward its protagonists' bedroom, finds a couple still in bed, just waking up at that moment.

The young woman speaks more to herself, formulates the question of what a "deus ex machina" actually is. The man next to her talks about something else, namely that it is time to get up. The day that they are beginning is no special day; it has nothing to offer them. They are waiting for something that they just can't name, they live here, alongside one another. They don't have anything to do, and obviously don't know what to do with each other (or themselves). There is calm between them, in a good and also bad sense. Images of the city outside reflect in their windows. The conversations that they strive for have more characteristics of a monologue than a dialogue. The television has more of a tonal life of its own than they do. It temporarily drives away the silence between them; blaring, dramatic, enervating.

It seems as though a love has come to an end, which is what the film tells of: the young couple, apparently leading successful lives, are ossified in the ennui, they paralyze each other. The early scenes in the couple's bedroom, the soft jazzy rhythm in the narration and the soundtrack once again recall Cassavetes' *Shadows*, the scenes show intimate moments, also those of doing nothing, of waiting, moments nonetheless, which are unheard of in American cinema at the time. The title of the film,

Die junge Frau spricht, mehr zu sich selbst, formuliert die Frage, was ein "Deus ex machina" eigentlich sei. Der Mann neben ihr spricht von etwas anderem, nämlich davon, dass es an der Zeit sei aufzustehen. Der Tag, den sie beginnen, ist kein besonderer, er hat ihnen nichts zu bieten. Sie warten auf etwas, das sie nicht benennen können, leben nebeneinander her. Sie haben nichts zu tun, fangen offensichtlich miteinander (und sich selbst) nichts an. Zwischen ihnen ist Ruhe, im Guten wie im Schlechten. Bilder der Stadt draußen spiegeln sich in ihren Fenstern. Die Gespräche, die sie anstreben, tragen eher monologische als dialogische Züge. Das Fernsehen hat mehr klangliches Eigenleben als sie, vertreibt zeitweilig die Stille zwischen ihnen, lärmend, dramatisch, enervierend.

Eine Liebe scheint an ihr Ende gekommen zu sein, davon erzählt der Film: Das junge, im Leben offenbar erfolgreiche Paar ist im Ennui erstarrt, einer lähmt den andern. Die frühen Szenen im Schlafzimmer des Paares, der sanft jazzige Rhythmus in der Erzählung und der Tonspur, erinnern erneut an Cassavetes' *Shadows*, zeigen intime Momente, auch solche des Nichtstuns, des Abwartens, Augenblicke jedenfalls, die im amerikanischen Kino jener Zeit unerhört sind. Der Titel des Films, der auf das Scheitern der Beziehung zwischen den Protagonisten gemünzt sein dürfte, verweist nebenbei auch auf das Handwerk des Inszenierens, spielt mit dem Klang einer Regieanweisung. Nur insofern ist *OK End Here* ein typischer Frank-Film: In der Weigerung, zwischen Abbildung und Sein, zwischen Kunst und Leben einen Unterschied zu sehen, gewinnt er auch hier an Energie und Sogwirkung; die filmischen Mittel, derer sich Frank dabei bedient, führen einen Regisseur vor, der bereits erstaunlich sicher, *stilsicher* arbeitet: Gegen die Langeweile seiner Helden setzt Frank, mit Lust an der Paradoxie, eine nervöse Montage und eine überaus bewegliche Kamera. Zu den autobiografischen Resten dieses Films zählt wohl die Beschäftigung mit der Fotografie: Der Mann hantiert nebenbei mit Bildern, die er unter anderem auf einem Lichttisch betrachtet; später wird die Frau öffentlich erklären, dass Fotografien „wenigstens alles aufhalten", dass sie „das Vergehen der Zeit beenden". Genau davon wird in den Jahren und Jahrzehnten danach Robert Franks Arbeit handeln.

Man muss dem Filmemacher zugute halten, dass er die Beziehung, von der sein Film handelt, nicht nur aus *einer* Perspektive zeigt, dass er diese nicht polemisch, sondern analytisch sieht. *OK End Here* betrachtet die Liebe als ambivalentes Phänomen, als fragile Angelegenheit. Zwischen seinen beiden Hauptfiguren ist so etwas wie Innigkeit durchaus spürbar, zugleich beginnt man aber auch

OK End Here

 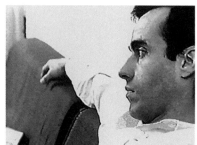

which seems to be coined for the failure of the relationship between the protagonists, also refers to the craft of staging by playing with the sound of a director's orders. It is only in this regard that *OK End Here* is a typical Frank film. In the refusal to see a difference between reproduction and reality, between art and life, it also gains energy and a drawing-in effect. With the cinematic means used for this, Frank presents himself as a director who is already working with amazing certainty, *stylistic certainty*. Enjoying paradox, Frank counters his heroes' boredom with a nervous montage and an extremely mobile camera. Certainly numbering among the autobiographical remnants of this film is the occupation with photography: the man is busy, on the side, with pictures that he observes, among other ways, on a light table; later the woman will publicly explain that photographs "at least hold everything," that they "stop the passing of time." In the following years and decades, Frank's works will deal precisely with this point.

One must consider that the filmmaker does not show the relationship around which his film revolves from only *one* perspective, that he does not see it polemically, but rather, analytically. *OK End Here* observes love as an ambivalent phenomenon, as a fragile affair. Something like an intimacy is definitely traceable between his two main characters, yet at the same time one begins to feel the tight borders of this intimacy. The most minor interpersonal discrepancy can ruin everything; one word is enough to end a life together. Love exists on the blade of a knife, on silk threads. It doesn't take much to reach the edge. The man uses the lazy day to openly terminate communication: what should one talk about? he asks cynically, about politics? Films? Proust? "Just talk to me," she counters with resignation, and the honesty of this request shatters his cynicism. *OK End Here* is a bourgeois tragedy: without arriving at reconciliation, the two receive guests and chat with them because the situation demands it. Almost the entire film takes place inside an apartment, just like in *Pull My Daisy*, and basically, like Frank's first film, it is essentially about presenting a specific lifestyle, revealing the actions and reactions of certain people under certain conditions: a laboratory experiment—art as an arranged experiment. For the last few minutes of the film the people leave their inside space, go out into a gray day. The couple walks through the fog, near the water, and reasons about the dreariness of their existence: they are childless; perhaps the relationship grew cold for this reason. In a small restaurant where they eat, a woman is crying; she reads a letter out loud. No one pays attention to her, not even those at her table react to her. Everyone lives for themselves, everyone keeps to themselves. On the way home at night she tells him that he will also become old. She had seen that in the morning. It is hard to decide if she sounds horrified or merely resigned. *OK End Here* concentrates on things that one cannot speak about: a type of psychodrama, only without tragic peaks.

Frank is in no hurry with cinema. After three short films, in the mid-1960s he dares to make a feature-length film. Frank risks a great deal with *Me and My Brother*, a film that arose between 1965 und 1968, and, as should be noted, his main aim was not to achieve success. He shocks all of those who until then had come to know his "directness" rather than his "realism" (Jonas Mekas, for example, in his "Movie Journal" in the "Village Voice" even reacted to *Me and My Brother* with outrage)—and thereby flung himself into one of his most complicated projects: truly experimental, erratic, formally manneristic cinema about a handicapped, catatonic, young man (Julius Orlovsky, the brother of the poet Peter Orlovsky, Frank's friend), who accompanied the beat poets on their tour and in their hippie life. Frank spent almost four years creating this film: it is without a doubt one of his major works, an opus magnum, far superior to both of his other longer works (*Cocksucker Blues* and *Candy Mountain*) in terms of ambition and substance. Here, for the first time, Frank also filmed some sequences in color.

die engen Grenzen dieser Innigkeit zu fühlen. Die kleinste zwischenmenschliche Unstimmigkeit kann alles ruinieren, ein Wort genügt, um ein Zusammenleben zu beenden. Die Liebe existiert: auf Messers Schneide, am seidenen Faden. Es braucht nicht viel, um an die Grenzen zu gehen. Der Mann nützt den faulen Tag zu einer offenen Aufkündigung der Kommunikation: Worüber soll man reden, fragt er zynisch – über Politik? Filme? Proust? "Just talk to me", entgegnet sie resignativ, und die Ehrlichkeit dieses Ansinnens zerreißt seinen Zynismus in der Luft. *OK End Here* ist ein bürgerliches Trauerspiel: Unversöhnt empfängt das Paar Gäste, macht Small-Talk, weil die Situation dies verlangt. Fast zur Gänze spielt der Film im Inneren einer Wohnung, genau wie *Pull My Daisy*, und im Grunde gilt er, wie Franks Erstling, der Vorführung eines spezifischen Lebensstils, der Erkundung von Aktion und Reaktion bestimmter Menschen unter bestimmten Bedingungen: ein Labor-Experiment – die Kunst als Versuchsanordnung. Für die letzten paar Minuten des Films verlassen die Menschen ihren Innenraum, begeben sich hinaus in einen grauen Tag. Das Paar spaziert im Nebel, am Wasser, räsoniert über die Tristesse seines Daseins: Es ist kinderlos, vielleicht ist die Beziehung auch daran erkaltet. In einem kleinen Restaurant, das sie aufsuchen, weint eine Frau; sie liest aus einem Brief vor. Niemand kümmert sich um sie, nicht einmal an ihrem Tisch reagiert man auf sie. Jeder lebt für sich, jeder bleibt nur sich selbst. Er werde auch alt, sagt sie noch zu ihm, nachts, am Weg nach Hause. Das habe sie am Morgen gesehen. Es ist nicht zu entscheiden, ob dies grausam klingt oder bloß resignativ. *OK End Here* stellt Dinge in sein Zentrum, von denen man nicht sprechen kann: eine Art Psychodrama, nur ohne tragische Spitzen.

Robert Frank hat es nicht eilig mit dem Kino. Nach drei kurzen Filmen wagt er sich nun, Mitte der sechziger Jahre, an einen abendfüllenden. Nicht primär um „Erfolg" zu haben, wohlgemerkt: Mit *Me and My Brother*, einem Film, der zwischen 1965 und 1968 entsteht, riskiert Frank viel; er stößt all jene vor den Kopf, die bis dahin stets seinen Realismus, seine „Unmittelbarkeit" zu schätzen wussten (Jonas Mekas etwa reagiert in seinem "Movie Journal" in der Village Voice sogar empört auf *Me and My Brother*) – und er stürzt sich damit in eines seiner kompliziertesten Projekte: in tatsächlich experimentelles, sprunghaftes, formal manieristisches Kino über einen behinderten, einen katatonischen jungen Mann (Julius Orlovsky, Bruder des Poeten und Frank-Freundes Peter Orlovsky), der die Beat-Dichter hier auf Tourneen und in deren Hippieleben begleitet. Fast vier Jahre bringt Frank damit zu, diesen Film herzustellen: Er ist zweifellos eines seiner Hauptwerke, ein Opus magnum, das den beiden

Me and My Brother

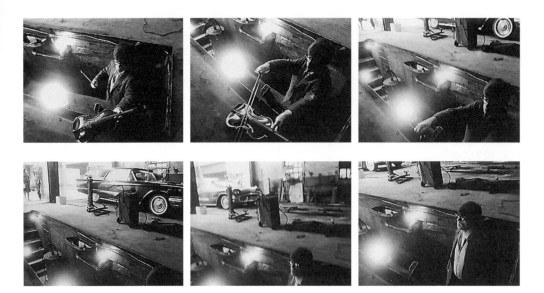

Me and My Brother

Afterwards, he still felt a greater affinity to the black and white of his earlier films. It was only after the switch in 1985 from film to video material that Frank would stick to color when filming.

What *Me and My Brother* carries out for an exhausting ninety-one minutes, is self-reflection: studies about the conflict between the real and the imaginary—as well as about the cinema's more or less automatic process of exchange between reality and "reality." Frank's first opus magnum intensifies to an artificially blazing, and in that sense, paradoxically only slightly "fictional" film, that persistently deals with cinema itself: staging, projecting, acting. It is also a film, however, that questions and doubts its "documentational power." If everything that is filmed (every idea, every body, every room) is inevitably fiction anyway, Frank seems to say, then one can instantly dismiss realism as a concept—and begin to consider a new, completely different cinema: for example, a cinema of the—only apparently formless—cinematic assemblage, which would become Frank's new form with *Me and My Brother*.

Subsequent to this film, which also marks an endpoint, only a return to simplicity can result: *Conversations in Vermont* (1969) is actually the antithesis to *Me and My Brother*—one of the sleekest types of documentary film structure, an examination of oneself, of the private, with no major formalistic intervention; seemingly pure nature, set in the simplest words and images. Frank uses the cinema to ask his two children, Pablo and Andrea, how they feel about the life that they now lead in the countryside (and to document it). Was this normal for them, after they had been in New York City for so long; but what is "normal" anyway? *Conversations in Vermont* also once again emphasizes the cinematic, the artificiality of cinematic representation, no matter how "authentic" it may look. At the beginning of the film, the filmmaker is cleaning his camera lens in the picture, up close and out of focus. "Let's see," he says again and that sounds appropriate. Afterwards, he presents photos, goes through moments of his life, or at least the few that he has captured. Frank "films" personal moments that he had

anderen langen Arbeiten dieses Regisseurs (*Cocksucker Blues* und *Candy Mountain*) an Ambition und Substanz weit überlegen ist. Dabei dreht Frank erstmals, in manchen Sequenzen, auch in Farbe. Dem Schwarzweiß seiner frühen Filme fühlt er sich dennoch auch danach näher. Erst ab 1985, mit dem Übertritt vom Film– zum Videomaterial, wird Robert Frank beim Drehen in Farbe bleiben.

Was *Me and My Brother*, anstrengende einundneunzig Minuten lang, betreibt, ist Selbstreflexion: Studien über den Widerstreit zwischen Realem und Imaginärem – sowie über den im Kino quasi mechanisch einsetzenden Austauschprozess zwischen Wirklichkeit und „Wirklichkeit". Franks erstes Hauptwerk verdichtet sich zu einem künstlich gleißenden, dabei paradoxerweise kaum „erfundenen" Film, der unentwegt vom Kino selbst handelt, vom Inszenieren, Projizieren, Schauspielen; ein Film aber auch, der sich in seiner „Dokumentationsmacht" befragt und bezweifelt. Wenn alles Verfilmte (jede Idee, jeder Körper, jeder Raum) unausweichlich ohnehin Fiktion wird, scheint Frank zu sagen, so kann man Realismus als Konzept sofort verwerfen – und über ein neues, ganz anderes Kino nachzudenken beginnen: etwa jenes der – nur scheinbar formlosen – filmischen Assemblage, das mit *Me and My Brother* zu Franks neuer Form wird.

Von diesem Film aus, der auch einen Endpunkt markiert, kann dennoch nur die Rückkehr in die Simplizität erfolgen: *Conversations in Vermont* (1969) ist tatsächlich die Antithese zu *Me and My Brother* – ein Dokumentarfilm der schlichtesten Bauart, eine Untersuchung des Eigenen, des Privaten, ohne große formalistische Intervention, scheinbar bloße Natur, in einfachste Worte und Bilder gesetzt. Robert Frank benutzt das Kino, um seine beiden Kinder, Pablo und Andrea, über ihre Haltung zum Leben am Land, das sie nun führen, zu befragen (und zu dokumentieren). Ob das normal für sie sei, nachdem sie so lange in New York City gewesen sind. Aber was ist das schon: „normal"? *Conversations in Vermont* betont nebenbei auch wieder das Filmische, die Künstlichkeit filmischer Repräsentation, mag sie auch noch so „authentisch" aussehen. Zu Beginn des Films reinigt der Filmemacher, ganz nah und unscharf im Bild, das Objektiv seiner Kamera. "Let's see", sagt er noch, und das klingt passend. Danach

Me and My Brother – Julius Orlovsky

once captured in still images, gives them back a measure of time, makes them "alive" once again. This film, says Frank, deals with the past. But not only: it also tells of the present—of a present that he preserves with cinematic means, thereby directly making it a thing of the past once again. Frank gropes back through his own history, gazes meditatively at events that occurred nearly two decades prior, reports on his first marriage (with the artist Mary Lockspeiser), on the birth of his children. He shows all of this in pictures, in a consciously casually staged photo/film home movie.

Pablo and Andrea are at the center of the *conversations* carried out here. Frank approaches them cautiously, patiently, like someone who has something to clear up with them. Pablo reacts appropriately in the conversations that his father wants to have with him: he seems to have retreated into himself, remains for the most part reserved. That which is not stated in these conversations seems significantly stronger, more painful than everything that is actually formulated. Even though the distance between Pablo and his father (their "growing apart," that would become Frank's lifelong trauma) is directly addressed and articulated at least once, Frank's self-referentiality can't be overlooked—by appearing in front of the camera he makes himself the theme although the film should actually be about his children. He has to do this, he has no choice: the author is too strong. "Maybe this film is about growing older," Frank says; a short phase of silence follows.

The filmmaker does not glorify life in and with nature somewhere in far-off Vermont; he views it as though it were something self evident, in no way lends it romantic traits. They work in a dark stall, eat in an untidy room, and live in the circle of an extended family. Frank stages the occurrences before his lens; he gives instructions not only to his children, but by force of habit, also to everyone else; and one gets the impression that what is meant to be shown and proven here is not so

Conversations in Vermont

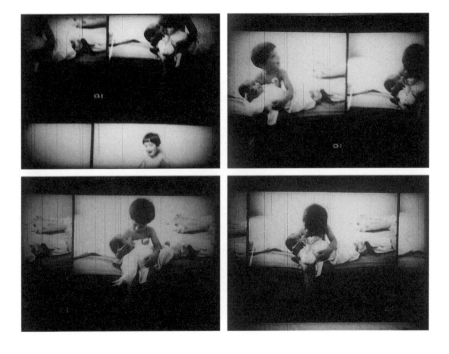

Conversations in Vermont – Robert & Pablo Frank

führt er Fotos vor, geht Momente seines Lebens durch, wenigstens die paar, die er festgehalten hat. Frank „verfilmt" persönliche Augenblicke, die er einst in Standbildern fixiert hat, gibt ihnen ein Zeitmaß zurück, macht sie wieder „lebendig". Dieser Film, sagt Frank, handle von der Vergangenheit. Aber nicht nur: Er erzähle auch von der Gegenwart – von einer Gegenwart, die er mit den Mitteln des Kinos bewahrt und gerade damit wieder zu Vergangenheit macht. Robert Frank tastet sich in seine eigene Geschichte zurück, blickt versunken auf Ereignisse, die fast zwei Jahrzehnte zurück liegen, berichtet von seiner ersten Ehe (mit der Künstlerin Mary Lockspeiser), von der Geburt seiner Kinder. Er zeigt all das in Bildern, in einem bewusst beiläufig inszenierten Foto/Film-Home-movie.

Pablo und Andrea bilden das Zentrum der *conversations*, die hier geführt werden. Frank nähert sich ihnen behutsam, geduldig, wie einer, der an ihnen etwas wieder gut zu machen hat. Pablo reagiert in den Gesprächen, die sein Vater mit ihm sucht, dementsprechend: Er wirkt in sich zurückgezogen, bleibt meist reserviert. Das Unausgesprochene dieser Konversationen scheint bedeutender, stärker, schmerzhafter als alles tatsächlich Formulierte. Auch wenn die Distanz zwischen Pablo und seinem Vater (ihr "growing apart", das Franks lebenslanges Trauma sein wird), wenigstens einmal direkt an- und ausgesprochen wird: Franks Selbstbezogenheit ist unübersehbar – er macht vor allem sich, indem er selbst vor die Kamera tritt, zum Thema, wo es eigentlich um seine Kinder gehen soll. Er muss das tun, er hat keine Wahl; der Autor ist zu stark. "Maybe this film is about growing older", meint Frank; eine kurze Phase der Stille folgt.

Das Leben mit und in der Natur, irgendwo im weiten Vermont, glorifiziert der Filmemacher nicht; er blickt es wie etwas Selbstverständliches an, verleiht ihm keineswegs romantische Züge. In einem dunklen Stall wird gearbeitet, in unaufgeräumten Zimmern wird gegessen; im Kreise der erweiterten Familie wird gelebt. Frank inszeniert, was ihm vors Objektiv gerät, er gibt Anweisungen, nicht nur seinen Kindern, sondern gewohnheitsmäßig auch allen anderen; und man gewinnt den Eindruck, dass dies hier nicht so sehr die Autorität des Filmemachers zeigen und bezeugen soll, sondern vor allem: ein kleines Stück Wahrheit. Ein Schwieriger wirft, noch einmal, einen kritischen Blick auf sich selbst. *Conversations in Vermont* benötigt für die vielen Themen, die Frank darin anschlägt, keine halbe Stunde: Die große Gestaltungssouveränität des Filmemachers, dem es offensichtlich nicht darum zu tun ist, dokumentarfilmischen oder erzählerischen Konventionen zu genügen, stellt das kleine Wunder dieses

About Me: A Musical

much the authority of the filmmaker, but rather: a small slice of truth. Once again a difficult person casts a critical gaze upon himself. *Conversations in Vermont* requires less than half an hour for the many themes that Frank strikes up. The filmmaker's great gestalt sovereignty, which is obviously not to satisfy documentary or narrative film conventions, assures the small wonder of this unbelievably tightly woven, yet totally relaxed film. These conversations carry a belief in spontaneity, in the potential of the moment. The film ends with music, a choir, and from the off the trailer credits spoken by the director. Finally, in the end he says, "I call this film *Conversations in Vermont*," then the pictures come to an end.

The years 1968 to 1970 present a productive time in the life of the filmmaker Frank. Two further works arose: in addition to *Liferaft Earth*, the cinematic documentation of a public hunger strike, an improvised *starve-in* in a parking lot in Hayward, California. With *About Me: A Musical* Frank mainly achieves a new, ironic study of his own inner life, a self portrait that hides much more than it reveals. The slightly absurd sounding film title refers both to the contract that Frank took on, as well as the rejection of this contract: beginning with the idea of making a film about music in America, Frank discards this right from the start, quite explicitly, to then return to that which he knows best: himself. He decides to produce a self portrait, naturally one that again immediately seeks Dadaist rupture: Frank introduces a young actress who is meant to play him. His enjoyment of his audience's and producer's perplexity can't be overlooked. *About Me* demonstrates the filmmaker's pleasure in the fragmentary, the idiosyncratic. His films are personal (and also this one in particular) simply because Frank does not take his consumers into consideration at all, because requests for explanation are not enough and as a rule he offers no help in understanding.

About Me: A Musical deals (also/again) with its own creation. Rather than the authenticity, which the first part of the film title seems to promise, Frank places acting at the center, allowing moments of his psychologically unstable private life to be played by actors. The fiction, the artificiality of this venture, contributes to elevating the lies that are likewise buried in every self portrait. Again, music is at the center, and again it leads to the end of that which Frank's tales never want to bring to an end: hippies make music ecstatically, in cacophony, and recite poetry. Later, the black inmates of a prison, dressed in white prison garb, sing a gospel in the corridor of the building. Music overtakes the film, turns Frank's supposed self portrait into a mini-musical (which, likewise, also permits social reflection,

ungeheuer dicht gewobenen, dabei völlig entspannten Films sicher. Ein Glaube an die Spontaneität, an das Potential des Moments trägt diese Conversations. Der Film endet mit Musik, einem Chor und einem aus dem Off vom Regisseur selbst eingesprochenen Nachspann. "I call this film *Conversations in Vermont*", sagt er schließlich, dann reißen die Bilder ab.

Die Jahre 1968–70 sind eine produktive Zeit im Leben des Filmemachers Robert Frank. Zwei weitere Arbeiten entstehen: Neben *Liferaft Earth*, der filmischen Dokumentation eines öffentlichen Hungerstreiks, eines improvisierten *starve-in* auf einem Parkplatz im kalifornischen Hayward, gelingt Frank vor allem mit *About Me: A Musical* eine neue ironische Studie des eigenen Innenlebens, ein Selbstporträt, das mehr verbirgt als es enthüllt. Der ein wenig absurd klingende Filmtitel verweist sowohl auf den Auftrag, den Frank angenommen hat, als auch auf die Verweigerung dieses Auftrags: Ausgehend von der Idee, einen Film über Musik in Amerika zu drehen, verwirft Frank diese gleich zu Beginn, ganz explizit, um zu dem zurückzukehren, was er besser kennt: sich selbst. Er beschließt, ein Selbstporträt herzustellen, freilich eines, das sofort wieder den dadaistischen Bruch sucht: Frank führt eine junge Schauspielerin ein, die ihn darstellen soll. Franks Freude angesichts der Ratlosigkeit seines Publikums und seiner Produzenten ist unübersehbar. *About Me* demonstriert die Lust dieses Filmemachers am Fragmentarischen, an der Idiosynkrasie. Persönlich sind seine Filme (und ganz besonders auch dieser) schon deswegen, weil Frank kaum Rücksicht nimmt auf seine Konsumenten, weil er Erklärungsanforderungen nicht genügt und in der Regel keine Verständnishilfe leistet.

About Me: A Musical handelt (auch/wieder) von seiner eigenen Entstehung. Frank stellt, statt der Authentizität, die der erste Teil des Filmtitels zu versprechen scheint, Gespieltes in den Mittelpunkt, lässt Augenblicke seines psychisch instabilen Privatlebens von Akteuren nachspielen. Die Fiktion, die Künstlichkeit dieses Unterfangens tragen dazu bei, die Lüge hervorzuheben, die jedes Selbstporträt auch birgt. Wieder steht Musik im Mittelpunkt, wieder führt sie zu Ende, was Franks Erzählungen nicht zu Ende bringen wollen: Hippies musizieren ekstatisch, kakophonisch, und Poesie wird rezitiert, später intonieren die schwarzen Insassen eines Gefängnisses in weißer Anstaltskleidung einen Gospel im Korridor des Hauses. Die Musik übernimmt den Film, verdreht das vermeintliche Selbstporträt Franks doch noch in ein kleines Musical (das sich aber wiederum nebenbei auch soziale Reflexionen, knappe Außenseiterstudien erlaubt): Die Musik regiert am Ende alles hier, die Straßen, die Gefängnisse und die

About Me: A Musical

concise outsider studies): in the end, the music directs everything here; the streets, the prisons, and the artists' bars. "Life dances on," someone says here, thereby announcing the title of a film that Frank would shoot ten years later; but it occurs as it seems to occur in all of Frank's films: life dances on, incessantly, inexorably while we are seldom able to take notice, so persistently involved with ourselves.

A more explicitly political project than *About Me*, a film that is naturally only seemingly directed at the personal, *Liferaft Earth* is the documentation of an action in the battle against over-population and under-nutrition in the Third World. *Liferaft Earth* is not a documentary report, but rather, a subjective film: Frank doesn't remove himself from his film, he joins the hippies' hunger strike and he doesn't take it easy on himself. But at first his political activism is not strong enough, he fails in his own good intentions. Frank subjects himself to his own camera (once again as though to repent), tells how deeply he has understood and felt the issues of the *hunger circus*—and how bad he felt when he had to prematurely leave his colleagues because of heavy rain. "I didn't have the guts," he admits, standing alone in the picture. Penitently, Frank once again joins the hard core of the group, which has meanwhile moved its hunger show to the woods near San Francisco. He records hippie rituals: trance exercises, group humming, howling, and shouting. "Are you alive?" becomes the filmmaker's standard ironic question after days of fasting as he gropes his way from person to person in the big house that they all live in together. The film's style is impressionistic, the autumn sun pours into the house and onto the images. Frank continually finds ways to briefly break the apathy that has fallen upon those participating in the action. Some consider the fasting as a game, as they say, others as a serious political duty; one admits on record that he got "pretty high" from it. At the end there are fifty-two, proud strike "survivors." Frank makes the extent to which we should also consider *Liferaft Earth* as agitprop explicit: after a mention of Richard Nixon, he polemically cuts to a grunting pig.

Liferaft Earth

Künstlerstuben. "Life dances on", sagt jemand hier und nennt damit den Titel eines Films, den Frank elf Jahre später drehen wird; aber es passt, wie es auf eigentlich alle Filme Robert Franks zu passen scheint: Das Leben tanzt weiter, unaufhörlich, unaufhaltsam, während man selbst davon selten Notiz nehmen kann, weil man unentwegt nur mit sich zu tun hat.

Ein explizites politisches Projekt als – der freilich nur scheinbar ins Private zielende – Film *About Me* ist *Liferaft Earth*, das Dokument einer Aktion im Kampf gegen die Überbevölkerung und die Unterernährung der Dritten Welt. *Liferaft Earth* ist keine Reportage, sondern ein parteiischer Film: Frank nimmt sich selbst aus seinem Kino nicht aus, er schließt sich dem Hungerstreik der Hippies an, und er beschönigt sich dabei nicht. Sein Politaktivismus ist aber zunächst nicht stark genug, er scheitert am guten Vorsatz. Frank setzt sich (wieder: wie um zu büßen) seiner eigenen Kamera aus, erzählt, wie tief er das Anliegen des *hunger circus* verstanden und mitgefühlt habe – und wie schlecht er sich gefühlt habe, als er seine Kollegen wegen starken Regens vorzeitig verließ. "I didn't have the guts", gesteht er, allein im Bild. Frank schließt sich dem harten Kern der Gruppe, die ihre Hunger-Show inzwischen in die Wälder bei San Francisco verlegt hat, reumütig wieder an. Er zeichnet Hippierituale auf: Tranceübungen, gemeinsames Summen, Heulen und Schreien. "Are you alive?" wird zur ironischen Standardfrage des Filmemachers, als er sich nach Tagen des Fastens von Mensch zu Mensch im großen Haus, das sie alle gemeinsam bewohnen, tastet. Der Stil des Films ist impressionistisch, die Herbstsonne dringt ins Haus und in die Bilder. Frank findet Wege, die Apathie, die die Aktionsteilnehmer befallen hat, immer wieder kurzfristig zu unterbrechen. Manche betrachten das Fasten als Spiel, wie sie erzählen, andere als ernste politische Pflicht; einer gibt zu Protokoll, dass er davon "pretty high" geworden sei. Am Ende verzeichnet man 52 stolze „Überlebende" des Streiks. Wie sehr *Liferaft Earth* auch als Agit-prop zu verstehen sein soll, verhehlt Frank nicht: Nach einer Erwähnung Richard Nixons schneidet Frank polemisch auf ein grunzendes Schwein.

Es scheint, als sei Robert Frank nach 1970 ausgelaugt, vorerst am Ende mit dem Kino. Auch privat setzt er in dieser Zeit Schlussstriche und Neuanfänge. Er trennt sich 1969 von Mary, um wenig später mit der Künstlerin June Leaf ein neues Leben, anderswo zu beginnen. Sie ziehen nach Neuschottland, ins kanadische Nova Scotia, „an das Ende einer Straße", wie er später sagen wird. June und Robert bauen sich ein Haus mit Blick aufs Meer. „Ich sehe aus dem Fenster. Oft. Für lange Zeit. Die Kameras bleiben im Schrank. Ich warte."

Nicht mehr als zwei Kinoarbeiten, insgesamt kaum mehr als zwei Stunden Film, stellt Robert Frank nach *About Me* in den siebziger Jahren her. Das Tournee-Dokument *Cocksucker Blues*, Franks zweite abendfüllende Arbeit, wächst sich für den Filmemacher 1972 zum Desaster aus. Die Rolling Stones, die er mit der Kamera begleitet, zeigen sich mit seinem Blick nicht einverstanden. Mick Jagger, auf dessen Initiative hin der Film während der Nordamerika-Tour der Band gedreht wird, zieht die Arbeit nach Fertigstellung zurück, verbietet seine öffentliche Auswertung. Bis heute darf der Film laut gerichtlicher Verfügung nur einmal im Jahr und nur im Beisein Robert Franks gezeigt werden. Das hat ihn zu einem Werk des Underground gemacht: Er kursiert weltweit nur noch als Video-Raubkopie, ein verblichener, verschrammter Schatten seiner selbst. Über die Gründe der Ablehnung Jaggers kann nur spekuliert werden: Natürlich ist der Pessimismus nicht zu übersehen, mit der Robert Frank die Maschine Rock'n'Roll betrachtet, andererseits hat die Band gerade ihn wohl auch nicht verpflichtet, um sich besonderen Glamour zu verschaffen. Es ist unklar, was genau dazu geführt hat, dass ausgerechnet die wilden Rolling Stones Einspruch gegen einen Film erheben, der kompromisslos, ungeschönt zeigt,

After 1970 it seems as though Frank is exhausted, for the time being finished with film. At this time he also finishes with some things and makes new beginnings in his personal life. He separates from Mary in 1969 to then shortly thereafter begin a new life elsewhere with the artist June Leaf. They move to Nova Scotia, Canada, "at the end of a road," as he would later say. June and Robert build a house with an ocean view. "I look out of the window. Often. For a long time. The cameras stay in the cupboard. I wait."

In the 1970s, Frank produced no more than two cinematic works after *About Me*, barely more than two hours of film. The documentation of the tour, *Cocksucker Blues*, Frank's second feature-length work, developed into a disaster for the filmmaker in 1972. The Rolling Stones, whom he accompanied with his camera, didn't seem to agree with his way of looking at things. Mick Jagger, who provided the initiative for the film to be shot during the band's North American tour, withdrew the work after it was completed, prohibited its public scrutiny. According to a court order, even today the film can only be shown once a year and Frank must be present at the screening. This turned it into an underground work: the film circulated the world as only a pirated video copy, a deceased, scratched shadow of itself. We can only speculate on Jagger's reasons for rejecting it: naturally, it is not possible to ignore the pessimism with which Frank views the rock'n'roll machine. On the other hand, the band never really obliged him, specifically, to create a special glamour around them. It is unclear what exactly led to the wild Rolling Stones' objection to a film that shows without compromise, without touching up, the less earth-shaking things that happen around a world renown rock band on concert tour. All that is clear is what Frank concentrates on: loneliness. Happiness is elsewhere. They take drugs, have quick sex in the airplane, but everyone mainly just waits desperately for the next step: for the arrival in some new city, for the check-in at a reception desk, which once again looks like all of the others, for the concert to begin, for the night to end.

However, except for the "musical numbers," everything that happens in *Cocksucker Blues* is fictitious; at least it says so right at the beginning—"No representation of actual persons and events is intended." But it seems obvious that we should consider these words as an imposition from the producers; none of Frank's other films work in such a bluntly documentary style as this one; fictional interventions in the apparently "authentic," which are not rare in this author's creations, are reduced to a minimum in *Cocksucker Blues*. Frank refuses all orientational guidelines; he introduces neither persons nor places, neither well-known nor unknown faces, he works without inserts or narrative swerves, without the trap door of pre-formed, user friendly "documentary" film. That which can be seen and heard in *Cocksucker Blues* is often incomprehensible—acoustically and in terms of content. No one speaks to the public here; everyone keeps to themselves, within themselves, withdrawn, in the end: a riddle. Frank's extremely raw visual surfaces, his cold images, contribute considerably to the impression of a certain lack of form: a consciously vague, radically contemporary film.

In terms of content, *Cocksucker Blues* delivers something that we thoroughly expect: Frank shows people at work, at work on music, at practices and concerts, he looks without prejudice at faces, bodies, and spaces. "Exile on Main Street"—the cover of which Frank designed—is incidentally the album that the Rolling Stones were currently promoting on the tour being filmed. Almost none of that can be traced in *Cocksucker Blues*. Frank is not at all interested in doubling the promotion effects, he is not even interested, for example, in making his clients look good. Frank does not consider the Stones to be stars; as a filmmaker he doesn't even give preference to them over their entourage, they are part of

was im Umfeld einer weltberühmten Band auf Konzertreise an wenig weltbewegenden Dingen eben passiert; klar ist nur, worauf sich Frank konzentriert: die Einsamkeit. Das Glück ist anderswo. Man nimmt Drogen zu sich, hat schnellen Sex im Flugzeug, vor allem aber wartet jeder hier nur verzweifelt auf den jeweils nächsten Schritt: auf ein Ankommen in irgendeiner neuen Stadt, auf das Einchecken an einer Rezeption, die wieder aussieht wie alle anderen, auf den Beginn des Konzerts, auf das Ende der Nacht.

Allerdings: Alles, was in *Cocksucker Blues* passiere, abgesehen nur von den "musical numbers", sei fiktiv, heißt es gleich am Anfang – und: "No representation of actual persons and events is intended". Es liegt nahe, diese Worte als von den Produzenten aufgezwungen zu betrachten, denn kein zweiter Film Franks arbeitet so unverblümt dokumentarisch wie dieser hier; fiktionale Eingriffe im scheinbar „Authentischen", die zwar nicht selten sind im Schaffen dieses Künstlers, sind in *Cocksucker Blues* auf ein Minimum reduziert. Frank verweigert jede Orientierungshilfe; er stellt weder Orte noch Menschen vor, weder die bekannten noch die unbekannten Gesichter, er arbeitet ohne Inserts und narrative Bögen, ohne den doppelten Boden des vorgeformten, bedienerfreundlichen „dokumentarischen" Films. Was in *Cocksucker Blues* zu sehen und zu hören ist, ist oft – akustisch wie inhaltlich – unverständlich; niemand hier spricht zum Publikum, jeder bleibt bei sich, in sich, zurückgezogen, letztlich: ein Rätsel. Die extrem rauen visuellen Oberflächen, die abweisenden Bilder Franks tragen zu dem Eindruck einer gewissen Ungeformtheit maßgeblich bei: ein bewusst vage gehaltener, radikal gegenwärtiger Film.

Inhaltlich liefert *Cocksucker Blues* durchaus Erwartbares: Frank zeigt Menschen bei der Arbeit, der Arbeit an der Musik, bei Proben und Konzerten, er blickt vorurteilsfrei auf Gesichter, Körper und Räume. "Exile on Main Street", dessen Cover übrigens ebenfalls Robert Frank gestaltet hat, ist die Platte, die die Rolling Stones auf der Tournee, der der Film gilt, aktuell bewerben. Davon ist praktisch nichts zu spüren in *CS Blues*: Frank liegt nichts daran, Werbeeffekte zu verdoppeln, es liegt ihm nicht einmal daran etwas, seine Auftraggeber selbst gut aussehen zu lassen. Die Stones nimmt Frank nicht als Stars, er zieht sie als Filmemacher nicht einmal ihrer Entourage vor, sie sind Teil der Welt dieser Rock-Tour, nicht mehr. So gibt es über die Band selbst hier nicht sehr viel Wissenswertes zu erfahren (oder auch nur zu sehen): Keith Richards kippt, offenbar unter Einfluss, einmal bewusstlos weg – und eine sehr inszenierte Sequenz, die entfernt an Nicolas Roegs und Donald Cammells *Performance* (1970)

Cocksucker Blues

the world of this rock tour, no more. Thus we do not really learn (or even see) much of value here about the band itself: at one point, Keith Richards falls over unconscious, obviously under the influence—and a very staged sequence, which vaguely recalls Nicolas Roeg and Donald Cammell's *Performance* (1970), shows Jagger in bed, how he touches himself and films it in a mirror. Despite everything, reputation obliges: Richards throws a hotel television out of the window for Frank's camera. A girl, who is taking a shot of heroine, asks Frank in another scene why he is filming everything anyway. He doesn't reply.

The shaky camera encircles or peers at the musicians, the technicians, the stage workers and the groupies, but constantly remains "outside," foreign to that which it shows. In contrast to *Liferaft Earth*, Frank does not get mixed up with involvement or participation; no fraternization between those filming and those filmed takes place here. With *Cocksucker Blues* Frank bids a final adieu to the utopia of the Beat generation: the free spaces, which the casual dealings with sex and drugs had once promised, have been transformed here into a series of dreary hotel rooms in which there is nothing left to do and nothing left to gain. Boredom reigns, they play cards, talk, are silent or numbing themselves (often in precisely this order). *Cocksucker Blues* is a depression piece, populated by the living dead who no longer even spread fear: a zombie film without peaks of stimulation and no refuge in artistic dramaturgies or explanatory side paths. Frank's path is direct cinema, in every sense of the word: cinema can't be any more direct than it is in this film. Frank's friend and technician, Daniel Seymour, who shortly thereafter disappeared without a trace on one of his long journeys (and, whom the filmmaker would recall with nostalgia in *Life Dances On...* eight years after this collaboration), was named co-director in *Cocksucker Blues*. In the credits, Frank and Seymour make every effort despite everything (or, maybe, under pressure) to once again cloud the borders between fact and fiction: they assign roles, as is done for actors, to all of those who have made an appearance. It is impossible to miss the sarcasm in this: Keith Richards, for example, is named as "1st TV Repairman."

In 1974 Frank's daughter Andrea, only twenty years old, died in an airplane crash in Tikal, Guatemala. Frank began to travel, to teach, he tried to generate new energy from his marriage with June and their life together on the ice-cold sea, to desperately prove himself. He is not sure how to proceed with his filmmaking. Nonetheless, he tries. For the time being, he sticks decidedly to the "primitive": In an initial collaboration in 1975 with the screenwriter Rudy Wurlitzer, he begins to shoot a small, basic feature film, outside, in the wind and in the sun, on the water, under the sky: they call it *Keep Busy*.

Cocksucker Blues

erinnert, zeigt Jagger im Bett, wie er sich betastet und in einem Spiegel dabei selbst filmt. Aber der Ruf verpflichtet, trotz allem: Richards wirft, Franks Kamera zuliebe, in einer Szene einen Hotelfernseher aus dem Fenster. Ein Mädchen, das sich einen Schuss Heroin verpasst, fragt Frank in einer anderen Szene, warum er das alles eigentlich filme. Er erwidert darauf nichts.

Die wackelige Kamera umkreist oder beäugt die Musiker, die Techniker, die Bühnenarbeiter und die Groupies, bleibt dabei aber stets „außen", bleibt denen, die sie zeigt, fremd. Frank lässt sich, ganz anders als etwa in *Liferaft Earth*, nicht ein auf Teilnahme oder Anteilnahme; Verbrüderungen zwischen Filmenden und Gefilmten finden hier nicht statt. Mit *Cocksucker Blues* nimmt Frank endgültig Abschied von den Utopien der Beat-Generation: Die Freiräume, die der lockere Umgang mit Sex und Drogen einst versprochen hat, haben sich in eine Reihe trostloser Hotelzimmer verwandelt, in denen nichts mehr zu tun und zu holen ist. Die Langeweile regiert, man spielt Karten, man redet, schweigt oder betäubt sich (oft auch in genau dieser Reihenfolge). *CS Blues* ist ein Depressionsstück, bevölkert von lebenden Toten, die nicht einmal mehr Schrecken zu verbreiten haben: ein Zombiefilm ohne Erregungshöhepunkte und ohne Zuflucht in kunstvolle Dramaturgien oder erklärende Nebenwege. Robert Franks Weg ist das Direct Cinema, ganz im Sinne des Begriffs: Direkter, unvermittelter als in diesem Film kann Kino nicht sein. Franks Freund und technischer Begleiter Daniel Seymour, der wenig später auf seinen Fernreisen spurlos verschwinden wird (und an den sich der Filmemacher acht Jahre nach dieser Zusammenarbeit in *Life Dances On...* wehmütig erinnern wird), wird in *Cocksucker Blues* als Co-Regisseur genannt. Im Nachspann bemühen sich Frank und Seymour trotz allem (oder eben auf Druck) wieder um Vernebelung der Grenzen zwischen Fakt und Fiktion: Sie ordnen allen Auftretenden, wie Schauspielern, Rollen zu – der Sarkasmus ist dabei nicht zu verkennen: Keith Richards etwa ist als "1st TV Repairman" genannt.

1974 kommt Robert Franks Tochter Andrea, sie ist erst 20, bei einem Flugzeugabsturz in Tikal, Guatemala ums Leben. Frank selbst beginnt zu reisen, zu lehren, er versucht, aus seiner Ehe mit June und ihrem gemeinsamen Leben am eiskalten Meer neue Kraft zu schöpfen, sich krampfhaft seiner selbst zu vergewissern. Wie es mit dem Filmemachen weitergehen soll, ist ihm selbst nicht klar. Er gibt sich dennoch Mühe. Das „primitive" Kino bleibt vorerst bestimmend: Er beginnt, in einer ersten Zusammenarbeit mit dem Drehbuchautor Rudy Wurlitzer, 1975 einen kleinen, elementaren Spielfilm zu drehen, im Freien, im Wind und in der Sonne, am Wasser, unter dem Himmel: Sie nennen ihn *Keep Busy*. Wovon der Film genau erzählt, ist nicht leicht zu sagen; nur soviel: Ein paar Leute kommen auf einer kleinen Insel mit Leuchtturm zusammen, zwischen Holzabfällen und industriellem Müll, um dort miteinander absurdes Theater zu spielen, ein Stück vor Franks Kamera zu improvisieren, in eigenwilligen Ritualen und insistierenden, betont künstlichen Texten: Eine schief stehende, desolate Holzhütte soll – offenbar – gerade gestellt, später zerlegt werden. Die Holzhütte ist immerhin ein wiederkehrendes Motiv in Franks Filmen, von *The Sin of Jesus* bis zu der location, in der Patti Smith und ihre Band, inszeniert von Robert Frank, den Song von den *Summer Cannibals* zum Besten geben. Die schmucklose Hütte fasst alles, wovon Frank in seiner Arbeit träumt: ein einfaches Leben, eine arme Kunst.

In *Keep Busy* bleiben die Menschen wahrlich *busy*, geschäftig; man spricht ununterbrochen über Wind und Wetter, turnt, tollt und plappert unaufhörlich, assoziiert frei, redet Nonsens, Nichtsinn. Während die Schauspieler sich wie die Kinder geben, stellt auch Frank spielerisch Bilder auf den Kopf; was die Akteure hier tun, grenzt an Performances, erstmals rückt Frank der bildenden Kunst nahe. Unter den Mimen: der Künstler Richard Serra. Der Stil der Inszenierung ist fahrig, der Film dazu fast uner-

Keep Busy

Exactly what the film is about is hard to say. Several people converge on a small island with a lighthouse, to play absurd theater with one another between wood trash and industrial waste, to improvise a piece before Frank's camera in obstinate rituals and insistent, emphatically artificial texts. Apparently, a crooked, desolate wooden hut should be erected and, later, taken down. The wooden hut is, after all, a repetitive motif in Frank's films, from *The Sin of Jesus* to the location where Patti Smith and her band give their best to the song about *Summer Cannibals* as staged by Frank. The undecorated hut surmises everything that Frank dreams of in his work: a simple life, Arte Povera.

In *Keep Busy* the people truly do remain *busy*, occupied; they talk nonstop about wind and weather, they clamber, romp about, and chat incessantly, make free associations, talk nonsense, make no sense. While the actors are acting like children, Frank also playfully turns around pictures; what the actors are doing here borders on performance art, for the first time Frank nudges towards the fine arts. The artist Richard Serra is among the actors. The style of the staging is agitated; what is more, the film is almost unbearable, nihilistic. Because there is nothing to bring to an end, it breaks off with a few bars of pop music and a radio report about the weather, which has delivered the film's mysterious running gag.

Frank's cinema also ended along with it; for a few years at least. At the beginning of the 1970s he rediscovered photography, the doors of the cupboard at home were wide open. In retrospect, Frank would say: "Since 1972, in the time left over between films or film projects, I have been taking photographs. In black and white or in colour. Sometimes I put several images together to make one. I tell of my hopes, my little hope, my joy. When I can, I put in a bit of humour. I destroy the descriptive elements in the photos so I can show how I am, myself. Before the negatives are fixed, I scratch words on: soup, strength, blind confidence... I try to be honest. Sometimes it's too sad."

Only five years after *Keep Busy* that Frank resumed his cinematic work. With *Life Dances On...*, his tenth film, he began again in 1980 and it seems as though this introduced a phase of consolidation, a new concentration on the essential. Frank has worked (relatively) steadily since 1980. He has completed new films or videos every one or two years since 1985. The commemorative works led him back to film: "In memory of my daughter Andrea," can be read in *Life Dances On...*—along with the

träglich, nihilistisch. Er reißt ab, weil es nichts zu Ende zu bringen gibt, mit einem Radiobericht übers Wetter, das den mysteriösen running gag des Films abgegeben hat, und ein paar Takten Popmusik.

Damit endet auch Franks Kino, für ein paar Jahre wenigstens. Anfang der siebziger Jahre hat er die Fotografie wiederentdeckt, die Türen des Schranks daheim stehen weit offen. Im Rückblick wird Robert Frank das so formulieren: "Since 1972, in the time left over between films or film projects, I have been taking photographs. In black and white or in colour. Sometimes I put several images together to make one. I tell of my hopes, my little hope, my joy. When I can, I put in a bit of humour. I destroy the descriptive elements in the photos so I can show how I am, myself. Before the negatives are fixed, I scratch words on: soup, strength, blind confidence... I try to be honest. Sometimes it's too sad."

Erst fünf Jahre nach *Keep Busy* setzt Frank seine filmische Arbeit fort. Mit *Life Dances On...*, seinem zehnten Film, steigt er 1980 wieder ein, und es scheint, als leitete dieser eine Phase der Konsolidierung ein, eine neue Konzentration auf das Wesentliche. Seit 1980 arbeitet Frank (relativ) kontinuierlich, seit 1985 stellt er alle, zwei Jahre neue Film- und Videoarbeiten fertig. Die Erinnerungsarbeit führt ihn zurück ins Kino: "In memory of my daughter Andrea", steht in *Life Dances On...* zu lesen – und ihre knappe Lebenszeit: 1954-1974. Die Erinnerung an Andrea (und nebenbei auch an Danny Seymour) steht über dem Film, aber Frank sucht zunächst doch wieder das Gegenwärtige: eine Konversation mit seinem Sohn Pablo. Warum er das Leben nicht genießen könne, fragt ihn sein Vater. Pablo antwortet, indirekt, mit einem Wunsch. Er wolle den Mars erkunden, denn er schätze die Schwerkraft der Erde nicht.

Life Dances On... verweist zurück auf *Conversations in Vermont*. Wieder sind die beiden Kinder Franks das Ziel des Films, nur ist nun eines der beiden bereits abwesend – und auch der (noch) Anwesende entzieht sich bereits, es steht zu vermuten: lange schon. Pablo pfeift gelassen vor sich hin, weicht den Fragen und dem Blick seines Vaters aus. *Life Dances On...* zeichnet eine Tragödie auf, die Tragödie eines Vaters: den Verlust beider Kinder. Der zweite Teil des Films bewegt sich immer wieder auch weg von diesen familiären Szenen, hin zu Anekdoten, Episoden, die scheinbar nichts oder kaum mit den Einstellungen davor zu tun haben. Der Film handle von Menschen "walking on the edge", wird Frank später sagen: Ein beleibter Mann leert seine Taschen in einem heruntergekommenen Raum, der auch ein Gefängnis sein könnte. Ein Junge in den Straßen konfrontiert aggressiv einen Mann, der die Kamera auf ihn gerichtet hat, eröffnet eine Debatte, die eher einer Reihe von Beleidigungen gleicht.

Life Dances On...

dates of her brief life: 1954-1974. The remembrance of Andrea (and, along with her, also Danny Seymour) hovers over the film, but at first Frank seeks the opposite: a conversation with his son Pablo. Why can't he enjoy life? his father asks him. Pablo answers indirectly with a wish. He wants to explore Mars, because he doesn't appreciate the earth's gravity.

Life Dances On... refers back to *Conversations in Vermont.* The film once again centers on Frank's two children, with one of the two now absent. The one who is (still) present is withdrawn, and, it seems, has been for a long time. Pablo calmly whistles, avoids his father's questions and his gaze. *Life Dances On...* sketches out a tragedy, a father's tragedy: the loss of both children. The second part of the film also constantly moves away from these familiar scenes to anecdotes, episodes that apparently have nothing or hardly anything to do with the prior shots. The film deals with people "walking on the edge," as Frank will claim later: A corpulent man empties his pockets in a rundown room that could also be a prison. A boy in the street aggressively confronts a man who has directed a camera at him, opening up a debate that seems more like a series of insults. On another street, Frank and his little team stop a few people and half jokingly ask them to name five famous photographers. None mention the name Robert Frank. Only after the film team introduces the name, is there someone who has once heard of Frank, vaguely. This art of fragmentation is one of the characteristics that make Frank's work so difficult to comprehend and assess. But it is always at that point, when one thinks that his films are falling to ruins, that Frank finds his way back to what is essential, to the personal. In the case of *Life Dances On...*, he finds his way back to Pablo and Andrea, to the mourning, to pictures in pictures, to films within the film, to this very special inscrutable mixture of found and staged material.

Nothing comes about without energy: no life, no art. Frank's next film after *Life Dances On...* reports on energy and how one can gain it, or at least this is the title's blunt promise: *Energy and How to Get It* (1981) turns out to be one of the director's most unique projects, perhaps his most per-plexing exercise in terms of veiling the border between *fact* and *fiction.* It is about science and the desire to invent ("it's science-fiction," it says here, and that captures the point of the film), about the connection between talent and terrorism, the mechanisms of the (very artificial) detective film and life in (very real) isolation. *Energy and How to Get It* tells the story of a brilliant inventor and constructor of an energy-

Energy and How to Get It

In einer anderen Straße hält Frank mit seinem kleinen Team ein paar Menschen auf, bittet sie – halb scherzhaft – darum, ihm doch fünf berühmte Fotografen zu nennen. Auf den Namen Robert Frank kommt niemand; erst als das Filmteam diesen ins Spiel bringt, findet sich jemand, der schon mal entfernt von Frank gehört hat. Das Fragmentarische gehört zu jenen Eigenschaften, die Robert Franks Werk so schwer zu begreifen und einzuschätzen machen. Aber immer dann, wenn man meint, seine Filme zerfallen zu sehen, findet Frank doch wieder zurück zum Eigentlichen, zum Privaten: im Fall von *Life Dances On...* zu Pablo und Andrea, zur Trauerarbeit, zu Bildern-in-Bildern und zu Filmen-im-Film, zu dieser ganz speziellen unergründlichen Mischung aus Gefundenem und Inszeniertem.

Ohne Energie entsteht nichts: kein Leben, keine Kunst. Von der Energie und wie man sie gewinnt, berichtet Franks nächster Film, wenigstens verspricht dies sein unverblümter Titel: *Energy and How to Get It* gerät 1981 zu einem der eigenartigsten Projekte des Regisseurs, zu seiner vielleicht verblüffendsten Übung, was die Verschleierung der Grenzen zwischen *fact* und *fiction* betrifft. Es geht um Wissenschaft und Erfindungslust ("it's science-fiction", heißt es hier einmal, und das bringt diesen Film schon auf den Punkt), um den Zusammenhang zwischen Talent und Terrorismus, um die Wirkungsweisen des (sehr künstlichen) Kriminalfilms und das Leben in der (sehr realen) Einöde. *Energy and How to Get It* erzählt die Geschichte eines brillanten Erfinders und Energiemaschinen-Konstrukteurs, dem – in einem Hangar an der Arbeit – einerseits der Ausverkauf droht und andererseits die psychische Zerrüttung durch stetige behördliche und industrielle Behinderungen. Wieder wirkt Franks alter Freund William S. Burroughs, der bereits 1966 gemeinsam mit dem jungen Kameramann Robert Frank an Conrad Rooks' Psychedelia-Studie *Chappaqua* gearbeitet hat, als charismatischer (Selbst-)Darsteller mit: als King of Cool, mit schnarrender Stimme und, natürlich, mit Revolver. Außerdem treten der Musiker Dr. John (ein paar Jahre danach auch in Franks *Candy Mountain*) sowie ein junger kanadischer Schauspieler und Filmemacher namens Allan Moyle auf (er wird mit *Pump Up the Volume* ein knappes Jahrzehnt später zu einer Regie-Hoffnung des Independentkinos aufsteigen). Und erneut ist der Film auf eine halbe Stunde hin angelegt, womit er genau jenem Zeitmaß entspricht, das Robert Frank seit jeher als das für seine Zwecke passendste betrachtet. (Nicht weniger als 14 seiner bisher 25 audiovisuellen Arbeiten sind zwischen 23 und 40 Minuten lang. Zieht man die beiden Musikvideos und seine drei langen Filme als strukturelle und dramaturgische Ausnahmeerscheinungen in dieser Werkliste ab, so bleiben nicht mehr als sechs Produktionen, die andere Laufzeiten als um die 90 oder um die 30 Minuten aufweisen.)

Robert Franks Umstieg von Film- auf Videomaterial findet zu Beginn der achtziger Jahre statt. *Home Improvements*, zwischen 1983 und 1985 entstanden, ist seine erste große Videoarbeit, zugleich eines seiner bedeutendsten Werke. Zwar tritt Frank damit nicht rückhaltlos zum neuen Medium über, zwar kehrt er zwischendurch, für einzelne Projekte oder Szenen, zur klassischen Filmfotografie zurück; aber der Weg ist vorgezeichnet: Ab 1990 ist Robert Franks zentrales Medium die Videoaufzeichnung: Von *C'est vrai! (One Hour)* (1990) bis zu *Paper Route* (2002) schießt er alle wichtigen Filme mit der kleinen Videokamera. Ehe er seine sehr privaten *Home Improvements* in Angriff nimmt, stellt Frank 1983 einen anderen, weniger ambitionierten Film fertig: *This Song for Jack*, ein Nebenwerk von tatsächlich nicht viel mehr als dokumentarischem Wert: Eine Gruppe von Leuten findet sich, in memoriam Jack Kerouac, in einem einsamen Haus irgendwo in Boulder, Colorado ein, um zu plaudern, einander wiederzusehen, sich zu erinnern: eine *beat congregation,* die 1982, aus Anlass des 25jährigen Jubiläums der Publikation von Kerouacs "On the Road", über das poetische Erbe ihrer Bewegung nach-

Energy and How to Get It

machine, who—in a hangar at work—is threatened by selling out on the one hand and mental ruin through constant bureaucratic and industrial hurdles on the other. Frank's old friend William S. Burroughs—who had already worked together with the young cameraman Robert Frank on Conrad Rooks' 1966 psychedelic study *Chappaqua*—again joins in as the charismatic star (playing himself): as King of Cool, with a raspy voice and, naturally, a revolver. In addition, the musician Dr. John makes an appearance (as he would a few years later in Frank's *Candy Mountain*) as does a young Canadian actor and filmmaker named Allan Moyle (who with *Pump Up the Volume* would become one of independent cinema's directing hopefuls just one brief decade later). And once again, the film is laid out for half an hour, thus corresponding precisely with that amount of time that Frank always considered the most suitable for his purposes. (Fourteen of his hitherto twenty-five audio-visual works are between twenty-three and forty minutes long. If one subtracts from this work list two music videos and three long films as structural and dramaturgical exceptions, only six productions remain with a running time of other than either approximately ninety or thirty minutes.)

Frank's transition from film to video material took place at the beginning of the 1980s. *Home Improvements*, which arose between 1983 and 1985, is his first major video work, and at the same time one of his most important works. Admittedly, Frank did not completely dive into a new medium; he returned to classical film photography for single projects or scenes. But his route was laid out. From 1990, Frank's central medium would be video: from *C'est vrai! (One Hour)* (1990) through to *Paper Route* (2002) he shot all important films with the little video camera. Before he tackled his very personal *Home Improvements* in 1983, Frank completed a different, less ambitious film. *This Song For Jack* is a secondary work that actually has no more than documentary value: a group of people gather in memory of Jack Kerouac in a lonely house somewhere in Boulder, Colorado, to chat, see each other again, and reminisce. A *beat congregation,* which reflected on the poetic legacy of their movement, was created in 1982 on the occasion of the twenty-fifth anniversary of Kerouac's "On the Road." From a distance, the (emphatically unglamorously arranged) black-and-white images naturally recall bored, hanging out poets and friends of poets and later hippies from the Bohemian studies in *Pull My Daisy,* but nowhere does it even remotely gain the energy which, twenty-three years earlier, Kerouac's recitation alone had radiated.

Frank's distinctive melancholy, the basis for his artistic work, however, penetrates *Home Improvements*. Conceived as a type of diary film, *Home Improvements* is fascinating with its consciously sketchy, open form, but also perplexing through its desire to condense, its wealth of detail. Frank once

denkt. Natürlich erinnern die (betont unglamourös arrangierten) Schwarzweißbilder gelangweilt herumsitzender Dichter und Dichterfreunde und später Hippies von fern an die Boheme-Studien in *Pull My Daisy*, aber nirgendwo gewinnt dieser Film auch nur entfernt jene Kraft, die 23 Jahre davor allein Kerouacs Rezitativ ausstrahlte.

Robert Franks ausgeprägte Melancholie, die Basis seiner künstlerischen Arbeit, durchdringt dagegen *Home Improvements*. Als eine Art Tagebuchfilm konzipiert, fasziniert *Home Improvements* durch eine bewusst skizzenhafte, offene Form, verblüfft aber auch durch seine Verdichtungslust, seinen Detailreichtum. Frank verhandelt hier erneut das eigene Leben, weit weg von der großstädtischen Zivilisation, spricht über Alter, Krankheit und über die Qual des angekündigten Todes seines Sohns Pablo. Die Ruhe in Franks Filmen ist mit Beschaulichkeit nicht zu verwechseln. Sie malen ganz grundsätzlich keine Idyllen, versuchen vielmehr, die bemerkenswerte Bandbreite der Einsamkeit (von unwirtlichem Frieden bis zum Terror der Depression) zu erfassen. Frank beginnt seine Ballade von der eigenen Existenz an einem Tag, der wie jeder andere ist: Der 9. November 1983 ist nebenbei auch Robert Franks 59. Geburtstag, aber das spielt keine große Rolle. Franks Frau ist krank, möglicherweise ernstlich. *Home Improvements* ist auch, ganz am Rande nur, ein Liebesfilm, vor allem aber eine viel weiterreichende Konstruktion aus filmischen Notizen und Splittern, ein Film, der unentwegt an scheinbar Irrelevantem hängen bleibt: an einer Fliege am Fenster, an Graffitis in der U-Bahn, an einem Stück Papier, das im Wind auf der Straße tanzt. "I like to look at the most banal things", hat Frank einmal gesagt. "Things which move." Franks Sohn ist in sichtlich schlechtem psychischen und physischen Zustand, verliert sich in seiner Krebskrankheit und der Metaphysik. Frank ist von Pablos Qual erschüttert, sein Film bildet diese Erschütterung ab. "Let's be more happy, Pablo", sagt er, und es klingt wie eine Bitte, verzweifelt, insistierend.

Home Improvements ist ein (ungewöhnlicher) Film über Gewohntes – über den Winter in Nova Scotia, über das Morgengrauen in Rot und Blau, über den Müll, der zur Straße hinunter gebracht werden muss, über das Warten und das Leben: ein Film, gemischt aus Bewegungs- und Standbildern, aus alten Schlagern und Fernsehabfallbildern. Denken, Sprechen und Filmen werden da in eins gesetzt, finden gewissermaßen zugleich statt, ohne eins vors andere zu setzen; es wird gefilmt und aufgezeichnet, was gerade gedacht und gesprochen wird, was sich ereignet, das Momentane gewinnt ungeahnten Raum in dieser sehr unmittelbaren Arbeit. Robert Franks Farben, auch das sieht man hier, sind bleich, „alltäglich", dem Grau und dem Weiß eher zugeneigt als allen anderen Farbtönen. Frank legt keinen Wert auf *eyecatcher*, seine großen Augenblicke sind die kleinen Tagesereignisse, das Unscheinbare. "It's a big moment", sagt Frank, mehr zu sich selbst als zu seinem Zuschauer, ironisch *und* ernst, als der Wagen des Müllmanns frühmorgens an der einsamen, vereisten Landstraße endlich auftaucht.

This Song for Jack

again deals with his own life here, far away from the civilization of the big city; he speaks about age, sickness, and the torture of his son Pablo's impending death. The calm in Frank's films is not to be confused with tranquility. Quite fundamentally, they paint no idyllic scenes but instead attempt to encompass the remarkable range of loneliness (from inhospitable peace through to the terror of depression). Frank begins the ballad of his own existence on a day that is just like any other: 9 November 1983. Incidentally it is also Frank's fifty-ninth birthday, but that does not play a major role. Frank's wife is sick, possibly seriously. *Home Improvements* is also, quite peripherally, a love film, but mainly a much further-reaching construction of film notes and fragments, a film that persistently remains stuck on what is apparently irrelevant: a fly on the window, graffiti in the underground, a piece of paper that dances in the wind on the street. "I like to look at the most banal things," Frank once said, "things which move." Frank's son is in a visibly poor physical and mental state, he is becoming lost in cancer and in metaphysics. Frank is shaken by Pablo's suffering, his film depicts this distress. "Let's be more happy, Pablo," he says and it sounds as though a plea, despairing, insistent.

    Home Improvements is an (uncommon) film about the common—about the winter in Nova Scotia, about daybreak's red and blue, about the trash that has to be brought down to the street, about waiting and about life: a film mixed from moving and still images, from old pop hits and trash television images. Thinking, speaking, and filming are united as one here, take place simultaneously so to speak, without placing the one before the other; that which is spoken and thought at the moment is filmed and recorded, that which happens, the momentary, gains undreamed-of space in this intensely direct work. Frank's colors, which one also sees here, are pale, "everyday," leaning more toward gray and white than all other shades. Frank places no value in *eyecatchers*, his great moments are the little daily occurrences, the nondescript. "It's a big moment," Frank says, more to himself than to his viewers, ironic *and* serious, as the garbage truck finally emerges in the early morning on the lonely iced-over country road.

    That which most of the others find great gives Frank difficulties. It is first in 1986 that he once again risks a feature-length film; for the first (and last) time in Frank's creative career, this undertaking is meant to be a "real" feature film, a work that takes the customs of the genre into consideration

Candy Mountain

Home Improvements

Was die meisten anderen als groß empfinden, macht Robert Frank Schwierigkeiten. Erst 1986 wagt er sich erneut an einen abendfüllenden Film; erstmals (und letztmals) in Franks Schaffen soll dieses Unternehmen ein „echter" Spielfilm werden, ein Werk, das die Gepflogenheiten der Gattung soweit berücksichtigt, das so (verhältnismäßig) bruchlos arrangiert ist, dass man von Mehrheitsfähigkeit sprechen kann. Der alte Pessimismus ist dennoch weiterhin präsent: "There Ain't No Candy Mountain" lautet noch der Arbeitstitel des Films, den Frank gemeinsam mit Drehbuchautor Rudy Wurlitzer inszeniert. Später wird man den Film einfach nur *Candy Mountain* nennen, vielleicht auch, weil das den ursprünglichen Titel ins Gegenteil verdreht, ins Positive wendet. Die geradlinige Erzählung ist Franks Sache nicht, das ist *Candy Mountain* – obwohl ansehnlich fotografiert von Pio Corradi – anzumerken. Immerhin setzt er sich mit dem jungen Helden des Films, gespielt von Kevin J. O'Connor, wieder in Bewegung – *on the road again*: Von New York City aus reist der junge Mann nordwärts, bis nach Kanada, nach Nova Scotia, um einen legendären, leider verschollenen Gitarrenkonstrukteur zu finden, der ihm viel Geld einbringen könnte. Frank und Wurlitzer nehmen den dünnen Handlungsfaden zum Anlass, eine Reihe mehr oder weniger motivierter Gastauftritte zu inszenieren: O'Connor trifft unterwegs auf Musiker wie Arto Lindsay, Tom Waits, Joe Strummer und Dr. John, auf Leute, die das Interesse der Filmemacher am Marginalen, an der Subkultur dokumentieren. Frank schätzt *Candy Mountain* heute nicht mehr, betrachtet den Film wenn nicht als Niederlage, so mindestens als faulen Kompromiss; "heavy machinery" nennt er schon unmittelbar nach dem Dreh abfällig die technische Basis des Films, an dem er ganz grundsätzlich Spontaneität vermisst. Es sei, sagt er, einfach nicht nötig, "25 Leute um mich zu haben, wenn ich einen Film drehe". Auch die Zusammenarbeit mit Rudy Wurlitzer endet hier, jäh, mit dem dritten Film, den die beiden miteinander drehen.

Und wieder schlittert Frank in eine Phase der künstlerischen Desorientierung. Sein 37minütiger Fernsehfilm *Hunter*, im Herbst 1989 für den WDR gedreht, zeugt von der inneren Unsicherheit, in der sich Robert Frank in diesen Jahren befindet: verloren zwischen präzisem Dokumentarismus und bemühter Spielhandlung, zwischen Autorenfilm und Sozialreportage. Deutschland im

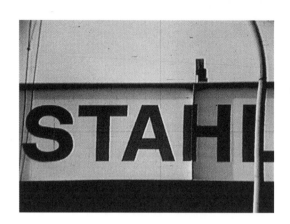

Hunter

so seriously that it is arranged (relatively) without breaks and it is possible to speak of it as suitable for mass viewing. Nonetheless, the old pessimism is still evident. The working title of the film, which Frank made together with screenwriter Rudy Wurlitzer, was: "There Ain't No Candy Mountain." Later, one would simply call the film *Candy Mountain*, perhaps because that turns the original title into its opposite, to the positive. Linear tales are not Frank's forte and despite Pio Corradi's handsome photography, this is noticeable. Nonetheless, he goes out on the road again with the young hero of the film played by Kevin J. O'Connor—from New York City, the young man travels north to Canada, to Nova Scotia, to find a legendary but unfortunately absent luthier who could possibly bring him a great deal of money. Frank and Wurlitzer take the thin threads of plot as an occasion to stage a series of more or less motivated guest appearances: on the road, O'Connor meets musicians such as Arto Lindsay, Tom Waits, Joe Strummer, and Dr. John; people who document the filmmaker's interest in the marginal, in the subculture. Today, Frank no longer appreciates *Candy Mountain*, views the film as a defeat, or at least as a lazy compromise; he will call the technical basis of this feature piece of fiction unfavourably "heavy machinery," missing spontaneity quite fundamentally. It is, he says, simply "not necessary to have twenty-five people around me when I make a film." Also his collaboration with Rudy Wurlitzer ends here, abruptly, with the third film that the two shoot together.

And again, Frank slides into a phase of artistic disorientation. His thirty-seven minute TV film *Hunter*, shot in autumn 1989 for the German television station WDR, provides evidence of the inner uncertainty that envelopes Frank in these years: literally lost between precise documentary work and forced feature film plot, between author film and social report. Germany in the autumn, at a time of unrest, somewhere in the Ruhrgebiet: *Hunter* is again the product of a tight creative collaboration. Together with the screenwriter (and main actor) Stefan Balint, Frank realizes a not very accessible little road movie about Germany shortly before reunification, a film that touches upon themes such as fascism, music history, prostitution, and xenophobia in clever associative leaps. The monotonous acting is countered by the vitality of several of the passers-by whom Frank questions, a vitality that the staging can only dream of.

Once again the filmmaker changes course: at sixty-five, Frank staged the first of his two music videos, although as the cover designer and documentarist of the Stones he was no newcomer to the pop industry. In 1989 he designed a clip for the song "Run" from the British band New Order. He fulfilled the contract as though he despised it, like someone who desperately seeks a way to insert

Herbst, in einer Zeit des Umbruchs, irgendwo im Ruhrgebiet: *Hunter* ist wieder das Produkt einer engen kreativen Kooperation: Gemeinsam mit Drehbuchautor (und Hauptdarsteller) Stephan Balint realisiert Frank mit *Hunter* ein wenig zugängliches kleines Road-movie über Deutschland kurz vor der Wende, einen Film, der in kühnen assoziativen Sprüngen Themen wie Faschismus, Musikgeschichte, Prostitution und Xenophobie streift. Dem monotonen Schauspiel Balints halten viele der Passanten, die Frank befragt, immerhin eine Lebensenergie entgegen, von der die Inszenierung selbst nur träumen kann.

Wieder wechselt der Filmemacher überraschend die Spur: 65jährig inszeniert Robert Frank, allerdings (als Covergestalter und Stones-Dokumentarist) kein Neuling in der Popindustrie, das erste seiner bislang zwei Musikvideos: Für die britische Band New Order gestaltet er 1989 einen Clip zu dem Song "Run" – und er führt den Auftrag aus, als hasste er ihn, wie einer, der verzweifelt einen Weg sucht, Bilder und Montagen einzusetzen, die im Feld der Videoclips nicht tauglich sind. Das ist keine einfache Aufgabe, denn gerade in dem Genre ist bekanntlich fast alles möglich. Frank findet dennoch eine Lösung: Das einzige, was die Popbranche kategorisch verbietet, ist das Unmodische. Genau dies aber scheint Frank hier zu suchen: Er konfrontiert eine bewusst nachlässig inszenierte Straßenszene, in der ein grüblerischer älterer Mann höhnisch zu lachen beginnt (vermutlich über sich selbst), mit wenig charismatischen Stand- und Live-Bildern der Band sowie Aufnahmen einer Gruppe anonymer Menschen. So wird *Run* zu einem dreieinhalbminütigen Anti-Clip, schwerfällig, unansehnlich, gemischt aus nicht nachvollziehbaren Assoziationen. Es ist kaum vorstellbar, dass Franks Auftraggeber mit dem Resultat zufrieden waren. Ungleich besser (und wohl auch fernsehtauglicher) gelingt sieben Jahre später *Summer Cannibals*, Franks Adaption des gleichnamigen Songs von Patti Smith; vielleicht ist diese Arbeit auch deshalb fruchtbarer, weil die Sängerin und Songschreiberin als amerikanische Slam-Poetin der siebziger Jahre Frank näher steht als der britische Elektronikpop von New Order. Zwar dient sich der Regisseur auch in diesem Fall keineswegs dem MTV-Mainstream an, zwar bemüht er sich auch hier sehr entschieden *nicht* um zeitgemäße Bilder, sondern ganz im Gegenteil: um größtmögliche Zeitlosigkeit. In der Wahl des Schauplatzes greift er auf ein altes, bei Frank seit *The Sin of Jesus* spirituell besetztes Lieblingsmotiv zurück: die heruntergekommene Behausung seiner Figuren. In Ställen, Holzhütten, ärmlichen Wohnungen sind viele der Menschen daheim, von denen Frank erzählt. Patti Smith und ihre Band sind in diesem Sinn Geschwister der (stets halbrealen, ungreifbaren) Figuren, die in *Conversations in Vermont*, in *Keep Busy* oder auch *Energy and How to Get It* zu sehen sind.

Run

Summer Cannibals

unsuitable images and montages into the field of video clips. This is no simple task as precisely in this genre, as is well known, almost everything is possible. Nonetheless, Frank finds a solution: The only thing that is categorically forbidden in the pop branch is to be unfashionable. But this is precisely what Frank seems to be looking for here: he juxtaposes a consciously carelessly staged street scene, in which a brooding older man begins to laugh scornfully (presumably about himself), with not very charismatic still and live images of the band as well as shots of a group of anonymous people. *Run* thus becomes a three-and-a-half minute anti-clip, ponderous, plain, a blend of incomprehensible associations. It is difficult to imagine that Frank's client was pleased with the result. Seven years later, Frank's adaptation of Patti Smith's like-named song *Summer Cannibals* fares oddly better; perhaps this work was much more fruitful because the singer and songwriter, as an American slam poet of the 1970s, was more familiar to Frank than New Order's British electronic pop. Admittedly, in this case as well, the director in no way offered anything to the MTV mainstream, and for sure he did *not* make great efforts to produce contemporary images, but on the contrary, the greatest timelessness possible. For the choice of settings, he returned to an old, spiritually occupied motif, one of Frank's favorites since *The Sin of Jesus*: the falling down dwelling of his characters. Many of the people whose stories Frank tells are at home in stalls, wooden huts, and run down apartments. Patti Smith and her band, in this sense, are siblings of the (constantly semi-real, untouchable) characters who can be seen in *Conversations in Vermont, Keep Busy,* and also *Energy and How to Get It.*

If we were to name a time, an era, around which Frank's work constantly orbits, it would be 1930s, North America. It appears symbolically in the photos, as well as in many of the films, as a vague association, like a signal. It is as though Frank, as a *visual artist*, would always belong to the Depression era. *Summer Cannibals* is no exception to this—and as a music video, it is much more clearly associated with the rest of Frank's work than *Run*. The great aesthetic clarity of the staging—photographed in richly contrasting black and white—preserves the riddle of the recitation and the text. The gutturally expressed "eat, eat," that Patti Smith so distinctly repeats in the refrain of her song, seems also to once again recall the hunger show in *Liferaft Earth*, a distant echo from 1969.

Truth can't be fixed in art, and not at all by a well-versed, fact-fiction twister like Frank. A film that is called *C'est vrai!* therefore deserves the mistrust that one tends to show it. All that is "true" with any certainty in this film is its time: set up as an experiment with cinematic *real time, C'est vrai!* (logical additional or alternative title: *One Hour*) records exactly one hour and an (almost) uncut journey

Wenn doch eine Zeit, eine Ära zu nennen wäre, um die Franks Arbeit immer wieder kreist, so wären dies Amerikas dreißiger Jahre: Sie scheinen in den Fotos ebenso wie in vielen Filmen zeichenhaft auf, als vage Assoziation nur, wie ein Signal. Es ist, als ob Robert Frank, als *visual artist*, für immer einer Zeit der Depression angehören würde. *Summer Cannibals* ist darin keine Ausnahme – und als Musikvideo viel deutlicher mit Franks restlichem Werk verbunden als *Run*. Gerade die große ästhetische Klarheit der – in kontrastreichem Schwarzweiß fotografierten – Inszenierung bewahrt die Rätsel des Vortrags und des Textes. Das guttural vorgebrachte "Eat, eat", das Patti Smith im Refrain ihres Songs so markant wiederholt, scheint außerdem noch einmal an die Hunger-Show in *Liferaft Earth* zu erinnern, ein fernes Echo des Jahres 1969 zu sein.

Die Wahrheit ist in der Kunst nicht festzumachen, schon gar nicht bei einem routinierten Fakt-Fiktions-Verdreher wie Robert Frank. Ein Film, der *C'est vrai!* heißt, verdient daher das Misstrauen, das man ihm entgegenbringen mag. Das einzige, was mit einiger Sicherheit an diesem Film „wahr" ist, ist seine Zeit: Als Experiment mit filmischer *real time* angelegt, zeichnet *C'est vrai!* (logischer Zusatz- oder Alternativtitel: One Hour) eine genau einstündige und (fast) ungeschnittene Reise durch Lower Manhattan auf, die der Filmemacher als strukturalistisches Road-movie mit vielen Stationen, überraschenden Wendungen und scheinbar dokumentarischen Obertönen durchspielt. Mit der Videokamera gedreht, entfaltet sich der Film als Bewegung durch die Stadt, an einem Tag im Juli des Jahres 1990 zwischen 15.45 Uhr und 16.45 Uhr. Die Reise, die in *C'est vrai!* unternommen wird, führt in Kilometern nicht sonderlich weit; man kommt an nicht mehr als ein paar Blocks in den Straßen New Yorks vorbei, zu Fuß und im Auto – aber diese Reise verläuft nicht geradlinig, sondern labyrinthisch: von innen nach außen und von dort aus wieder in Innenräume zurück (in ein Diner, in den Minivan, mit dem das Filmteam sich fortbewegt) – und letztlich auch von oben nach unten, von der Straße in eine U-Bahn-Station.

Das Faszinierende an dem Unternehmen *C'est vrai!*, gedreht für ein (von dem Künstler Philippe Grandrieux für die TV-Station La Sept initiiertes) mehrteiliges Fernsehprojekt namens "Live", ist seine Mischung aus Präpariertem und Zufälligem: Nach wenigen Minuten auf der Straße trifft man hier etwa einen Mann an, der an einem öffentlichen Münztelefon offenbar gelernten Text zitiert, also als Schauspieler handelt, ebenso wie – das wird schrittweise klar – unzählige andere Figuren dieses Films; daneben scheinen aber immer wieder auch tatsächlich Passanten, Unvorbereitete vor Franks Kamera zu geraten. *C'est vrai!* spielt Robert Franks altes Vorhaben, die Grenzen zwischen Sein und Schein in der filmischen Repräsentation konsequent zu verwischen, noch einmal durch, allerdings auf durchaus neue, überraschende Weise. So wird *C'est vrai!* zu einer Kette von Mini-Dramen und Story-Fragmenten; den roten Faden gibt die gestresst durch die Straßen hetzende Crew vor: Kevin O'Connor spielt dabei wieder eine Hauptrolle, als übelgelaunte, im hinteren Teil des Teamwagens lümmelnde Figur, der die Funktion des Narren, wie er etwa bei Shakespeare auftaucht, zukommt – er verweist, als einzig reflexive, distanzierte Gestalt auf die Künstlichkeit und Theatralizität des Unterfangens. Er zitiert hier nicht nur unentwegt Filme und zischt Sarkastisches, Respektloses in Richtung Regie ("I didn't mean to interrupt your 60 minutes"), sondern belebt und hysterisiert Franks Realzeit-Groteske zusehends, assistiert auch von dem später zusteigenden Peter Orlovsky, der – ununterbrochen redend und drohend – den klassischen New Yorker Maniac gibt.

Von etwa Michael Snows avantgardefilmischen Vermessungen des Begriffs Zeit unterscheidet sich *C'est vrai!* jedenfalls deutlich, schon durch die „Unreinheit" der Inszenierung. Franks

C'est vrai! (One Hour)

through Lower Manhattan, which the filmmaker plays through as a structuralist road movie with several stations, surprise twists, and seemingly documentary overtones. Shot with a video camera, the film unfolds as a trip through the city on a day in July in 1990 between 3:45 and 4:45 p.m. The journey that is embarked upon in *C'est vrai!* does not lead especially far in kilometers; one doesn't get much further than a few blocks on New York's streets, both walking and riding in a car—yet this journey does not take place in a linear fashion, instead, it is labyrinthic: from the inside to the outside and from there again back inside (in a diner, in the minivan that the film team uses for transportation)—and finally also from above to below, from the street to a subway station.

The fascinating thing about the venture *C'est vrai!*, shot for a multipart television project called "Live," (initiated by the artist Philippe Grandrieux for the TV station La Sept) is its mixture of prepared material and coincidence: after just a few minutes, one encounters a man on the street reciting texts, which he has obviously memorized, into a payphone. He is *acting*, just like countless other characters in this film—which becomes clear step by step. Alongside, however, other actual passers-by seem to land unprepared in front of Frank's camera. *C'est vrai!* once again plays out Frank's old project of

Versuchsanordnungen sind weiter gefasst, lassen mehr zu, sind kaum je überblickbar. In der Mitte des Films setzt plötzlich das Bild aus, nur der Ton läuft weiter, bis eine zweite Kamera aufblendet. So formuliert Frank seine Abneigung gegen vorgefertigte Konzeptkunst und filmische „Artistik": Wenn er schon einen Film in einer Einstellung dreht, muss erst recht ein ironisch gesetzter Schnitt, ein Einschnitt her, der das eigene, viel zu „schlüssige" Konzept leichterhand entsorgt. Franks *C'est vrai! (One Hour)* will offensichtlich weniger als technisch virtuose Leistung brillieren, die man darin durchaus sehen könnte, denn als absurde philosophische Komödie zwischen Improvisation und präziser Planung. Dass diese zweifellos zu den Hauptwerken dieses Regisseurs zu zählen ist, liegt auch an der Bedeutung, die sie für sein weiteres Schaffen gewinnt. Mit *C'est vrai!* vollzieht Frank den entscheidenden Schritt weg vom klassischen Kino (das er ohnehin kaum je korrekt zu bedienen wusste) hin zur bildenden Kunst, zum Video-Kunstbetrieb. Eine letzte Arbeit an der Schnittstelle zwischen Spiel- und Dokumentarfilm, noch einmal mit – für Robert Franks Verhältnisse – großem logistischen Aufwand verbunden, entsteht 1991. *Last Supper* kreist erneut um eine Antiklimax. In einem Hinterhof in Harlem findet eine Party statt, aber der Schriftsteller, dem sie gilt, taucht dort nicht auf. Die verarmte schwarze Bevölkerung der Gegend nimmt das weltferne Treiben der weißen Festgesellschaft gleichgültig zur Kenntnis. In *Last Supper* hält Frank seiner sehr speziellen Spielart des sozialrealistisch getönten Independentfilms verwackelte Videobilder und stark theatralische Einschübe entgegen. Das Motiv des letzten Abendmahls wird übrigens, in ebenfalls leicht beunruhigenden Zusammenhängen, vier Jahre später auch in *Summer Cannibals* auftauchen.

Robert Franks Spätwerk, das sich bis heute mit bemerkenswerter Konstanz entwickelt, beginnt somit 1990: Über Jahre hinweg sammelt Frank Material, das er, wenn ihm der Augenblick richtig erscheint, zu knappen Filmen verdichtet und veröffentlicht. Zwei hochkomplexe Videoarbeiten, radikal in ihrer Offenheit (*offen* sind sie im doppelten Sinn des Begriffs: uneingegrenzt *und* selbstentblößend), stellt er Mitte der neunziger Jahre fertig. *Moving Pictures*, gedreht zwischen 1990 und 1994, nimmt Franks alte Themen wieder auf: Erinnerung und Fotografie. *The Present*, 1994 begonnen, 1996 abgeschlossen, versteht sich eher als Tagebuchfilm im Stil der *Home Improvements*, zeigt sich aber, verglichen mit dem älteren Film, (noch) sprunghafter, elliptischer.

Last Supper

consistently blurring the borders between image and reality in cinematic representation, however he does it in a completely new, surprising way. *C'est vrai!* thus becomes a chain of mini dramas and fragments of stories; the stressed out film crew rushing through the streets provides the red line: Kevin O'Connor once again plays a starring role, as an ill-tempered character sitting flopped in the back of the team's wagon, who befits the function of the fool, such as he appears in Shakespeare—he refers, as the only reflective, distanced figure, to the artificiality and theatricality of the undertaking. He not only incessantly recites films and hisses sarcastically, disrespectfully towards the directors ("I didn't mean to interrupt your sixty minutes"), but also visibly enlivens Frank's real-time grotesque tale and adds hysteria, assisted by Peter Orlovsky who joins later, playing the classic New York maniac, with his nonstop talking and threats.

However, *C'est vrai!* differs clearly from Michael Snow's measurement of the concept of time, for example, simply through the "impurity" of the staging. The set up for Frank's experiment is more extensive, allows more, can almost never be assessed. In the middle of the film, suddenly the picture is cut; only the sound continues until they switch over to a new camera. This is how Frank formulates his dislike of pre-arranged concept art and the cinematic "artistic": If he is going to shoot a film in one shot, then it will be an ironically placed cut, an incision, that easily disposes of his own much too "logical" concept. Frank's *C'est vrai! (One Hour)* obviously wants to shine less as a virtuoso technical achievement, which one can definitely see in it, than as an absurd philosophical comedy situated between improvisation and precise planning. The fact that this can be considered without a doubt among the main works of this director is also due to the importance it would have for his future creative work. With *C'est vrai!,* Frank made the decisive step away from classical cinema (that he hardly knew how to operate properly, anyway) towards fine art, towards the video-art industry. A final work at the interface between feature and documentary film, once again tied up with major—for Frank— logistical extravagance, was created in 1991. *Last Supper* once again revolves around an anticlimax. In a backyard in Harlem, a party takes place but the writer for whom the party is being thrown doesn't show up. The impoverished Black population in the area is indifferent to the unrealistic activities of the White party society. In *Last Supper*, Frank contrasts his very special variety of socio-realist tinged independent film with blurred and shaky video images and strongly theatrical insertions. The motif of the Last Supper would also appear, by the way, in a likewise slightly worrying context four years later in *Summer Cannibals.*

Frank's later works, which have developed until the present day with a remarkable con-sistency, thus begin in 1990: For years Frank collected material which, when the moment seemed right, he condensed to concise films and then made public. In the mid-1990s he completed two highly complex video works, radical in their openness (they are *open* in both senses of the term: limitless and self-revealing). *Moving Pictures*, shot between 1990 and 1994, picks up on Frank's old themes: memory and photography. *The Present*, begun in 1994 and completed in 1996, is more of a diary film in the style of *Home Improvements*, but compared with the older film, reveals itself as (even) more erratic, more elliptic.

The formal brittleness of the sixteen minute work, *Moving Pictures*, carries it away from the field that its title actually names: it is more of an art-exhibition piece than a movie (although, naturally, taken strictly, it is both). It seems more at home in the museum space than in the cinema. The video is silent, operates only with text inserts, as though created for a video monitor in the framework of an installation. In terms of content, Frank remains personal and with the past. He presents himself at his

Moving Pictures

Die formale Sprödheit der 16minütigen Arbeit *Moving Pictures* entrückt diese dem Feld, den ihr Titel eigentlich benennt: Sie ist eher Kunst-Ausstellungsstück als Film (obwohl sie natürlich, streng genommen, beides ist), scheint eher im musealen Raum als im Kino am Platz zu sein. Das Videoband ist stumm, operiert nur mit Text-Inserts, wie geschaffen für einen Videomonitor im Rahmen einer Rauminstallation. Inhaltlich bleibt Frank persönlich und beim Alten. Er führt sich selbst vor, am Grab seiner Eltern in Zürich, und er macht das Erinnerte wieder zum Thema, zeigt Fotos und Fotocollagen, die bereits auf Basis assoziativer Verbindungen entstanden sind und nun ihrerseits eine Serie von Assoziationen (über Amerika, Jean-Luc Godard, die Natur, June Leafs Kunstarbeit, Gesicht und Präsenz) auslösen, eine Art Bewusstseinsstrom, den Frank hier eben *Moving Pictures* nennt: eine Meditation über das Wesen des Bildlichen und die Denk- und Blickrichtungen, die es vorgibt; die Arbeit eines verschlossenen, in der Kunst dennoch mitteilsamen alten Mannes, der sich die Freiheit nimmt, einfach auch, wenn es (ihm) passt, alte Freunde zu zeigen – den Dichter Allen Ginsberg, den Bildhauer Raoul Hague, den Filmemacher Harry Smith.

The Present gibt sich elementarer, macht sich selbst, als intime Erzählung, zum Thema: Was (und wie) soll man filmen? Was aufzeichnen? Was soll man, *muss* man behalten, erinnern? Robert Frank stellt sich, während er schon dreht, entscheidende Fragen, vor allem die Frage nach dem Sinn dessen, was er da überhaupt tut. Es gehe darum, sagt er, eine Story zu finden. Aber genau darum geht es nicht; sein Werk beweist das Gegenteil. Und er erkennt, dass alles, was er benötigt, schon da ist in seinem eigenen unaufgeräumten Zimmer, dass da eine ganze Welt vor seinen Augen liegt: ein zerwühltes Bett, eine Fliege am Fenster, ein Filmemacher im Zweifel. In *The Present* bespiegelt sich, auch ganz buchstäblich, ein Künstler selbst, der es gewohnt ist, schonungslos gegen sich selbst vorzugehen. Dabei stößt Frank an die Grenzen des Selbstreflexiven: Er denkt über die Erinnerungsarbeit nach, um an ihr zu arbeiten, zwanghaft fast, um – wie in einem Akt der Buße – auch die Vergessensmühe zu durchleiden, die ihm manche Erinnerung abverlangt. Er denkt zurück an seine Kinder, die nicht mehr bei ihm sind, denkt an Andrea, die an einem der Tage, an dem er seinen Film dreht, vierzig geworden wäre; er denkt aber auch an die kleinen Wunder der Welt, die sich ihm bieten, wenn er nur genau genug hinschaut. *The Present* zeigt, in weniger als einer halben Stunde, Robert Franks brüchige, flüchtige Kunst: eine autobiografische Erzählung aus tausend Einzelteilen, Ansichten und Gedankenblitzen. Gegen Ende hin lässt Frank den Schriftzug "Memory" mühselig von einer Glasplatte kratzen, als wollte er ein Zeichen setzen, um die Erinnerung zu überwinden. Was am Ende (stehen) bleibt, ist nur man selbst: "Me".

The Present

parents' grave in Zurich, and as a theme, he takes that which he remembers; he shows photos and photo collages, which have already been created on the basis of associative connections and now, for their part, set off a series of associations (about America, Jean-Luc Godard, nature, June Leaf's artwork, face and presence), a type of stream of consciousness that Frank calls here *Moving Pictures*: a meditation about the essence of the pictorial and the lines of thought and sight that it sets; the work of a taciturn old man who is nonetheless communicative through art, who takes the liberty of also showing old friends when he wants—the poet Allen Ginsberg, the sculptor Raoul Hague, and the filmmaker Harry Smith.

    The Present is even more basic, makes itself—as an intimate tale—the main theme: What (and how) should one film? What should be recorded? What should, *must* one keep? remember? While already involved with the shooting, Frank asks himself decisive questions, primarily the question of the sense of what he is doing. It is about finding a story he says. But that isn't exactly what it is about; his work proves the opposite. And he knows that everything that he needs is already there in his own untidy room, that a whole world is lying there in front of his eyes: a disheveled bed, a fly on the window, a filmmaker in doubt. In *The Present,* an artist who is used to proceeding ruthlessly against himself, mirrors himself, also quite literally. In doing so, Frank stumbles upon the borders of self-reflection. He thinks about commemorative work in order to work on it, almost compulsively, in order—as though in an act of repentance—to also endure the effort of forgetting, which some of his memories demand. He thinks back to his children, who are no longer with him, thinks about Andrea, who would have been forty on the day that he is shooting his film; but he also thinks of the small wonders of the world which are offered to him if he only looks carefully enough. *The Present* shows Frank's fragmentary, fleeting art in less than half an hour: an autobiographical story made from a thousand individual parts, views, and flashes of thought. Towards the end, Frank has the lettering "Memory" arduously scratched away from a plate of glass, as though he wants to set an example in order to overcome memory. That which remains at the end is only one's self: "Me."

    In the aesthetic minimalism that Frank worked on in these years there is also a trace of progressive revocation of the autarchic I in favor of poetic condensation. As usual, Frank carries out this revocation radically, seems to approach his own self-dissolution in art. What now becomes obvious throughout the course of his work is the effort to reduce to what is absolutely essential: with two video pieces produced in Canada, *Flamingo* and *What I Remember from My Visit (with Stieglitz)*, which he presented in 1997/98, Frank pushes the principle of fleetingness to the extreme. He produces these

In der ästhetischen Verknappung, an der Robert Frank in diesen Jahren arbeitet, ist auch eine fortschreitende Zurücknahme des auktorialen Ich zugunsten poetischer Verdichtung zu spüren. Frank betreibt diese Zurücknahme gewohnt radikal, scheint einer Selbstauflösung in der Kunst entgegenzugehen. Das Bemühen um Reduktion auf das äußerst Notwendige wird nun auch in den Laufzeiten seiner Werke offensichtlich: Mit zwei in Kanada produzierten Videoarbeiten, genannt *Flamingo* und *What I Remember from My Visit (with Stieglitz)*, die er 1997/98 vorlegt, treibt Frank das Prinzip der Flüchtigkeit auf die Spitze. Er stellt diese Arbeiten, nur noch jeweils wenige Minuten lang, fast im Alleingang her, begleitet lediglich von seiner Cutterin Laura Israel (im einen Fall) und einem jungen Kameramann (im anderen Fall); beide Werke präsentieren sich wie filmische Haikus, knappe Gedichte, die keine Spur von modischer Verfremdung mehr in sich tragen, völlig jenseits der Zeit zu existieren scheinen.

In Schwarz und Weiß, in rasanter Montage vollzieht sich *Flamingo*: Frank fusioniert, wie gewohnt, wieder die Fotografie mit dem Filmischen, zeigt eine kleine Dia-Projektionswand, geht Fotos von Landschaften, Tieren, Dingen durch – Reste einer Erinnerung, durch die Kunst unterstützt und wachgerufen. Man nimmt Franks Foto-Inschriften wahr: Er zeichnet einer Gruppe von Bildern Himmelsrichtungen ein, gibt seinen Fotos Begriffe wie "blind", "love" und "faith" mit auf ihren Weg. Miranda Dali liest im Off einen lyrischen, das Visuelle nur streifenden Text vor, der der einzige Ton dieser Produktion bleiben wird. Wenn die Erzählerin schweigt, sind die Bilder auf sich allein gestellt; man sieht: den Wind, der in die Blätter eines dunklen Baumes fährt; Arbeiter, die den Bau eines Hauses in der offenen Natur vorantreiben; ein Auto, auf dessen verschneiter Windschutzscheibe ein Datum zu lesen ist; June, wie sie ums Haus geht; June, wie sie in die Kamera blickt. "OK, we're done", heißt es am Ende. Und: "Paint it black". Ein Mann beginnt, das Haus schwarz anzustreichen. Am Ende steht es dunkel da, in offenem, weitem Land. *Flamingo* ist einem der amerikanischen Avantgarde-Road-movies des großen österreichischen Filmemachers Kurt Kren nahe, *Breakfast im Grauen*. An eine Begegnung mit dem 1946 verstorbenen amerikanischen Fotografen Alfred Stieglitz erinnert sich Robert Frank in der anderen der beiden kurzen Arbeiten. Im kalten Mabou, im Oktober 1998, rekonstruieren Robert und June als „Schauspieler", gemeinsam mit dem die Kamera führenden Jerome Sother, einige der alltäglichen Ereignisse, die während eines lange zurückliegenden Treffens mit Stieglitz und dessen Frau Georgia O'Keeffe stattgefunden haben. *What I Remember* ist wieder ein Film über die Natur, über das

Flamingo

What I Remember from My Visit (with Stieglitz)

works, each only a few minutes long, almost alone—accompanied only by his cutter Laura Israel (in the case of one) and a young camera man (in the case of the other); both works appear as though cinematic haikus, terse poems that no longer carry any traces of fashionable alienation in them; they seem to exist completely outside of time.

Flamingo is realized in black and white, in a rapid montage: As usual, Frank once again fuses the photographic with the cinematic, shows a small slide projection wall, goes through photos of landscapes, animals, things—the remains of a memory, supported and awoken by art. One believes Frank's photo inscriptions: he draws arrows to the sky on a group of pictures, gives his photos terms such as "blind," "love," and "faith" to take with them on their way. Miranda Dali reads a lyrical text from off-camera, which only touches upon the visual. This remains the only sound in this production. When the narrator is silent, the pictures are left to themselves; one sees the wind moving through the leaves of a dark tree; workers who persevere in building a house out in the open nature; a car, on whose snowed in windshield it is possible to read a date; June, as she walks around the house; June, as she gazes into the camera. "OK, we're done," is stated at the end. And: "paint it black." A man begins to paint the house black. At the end it stands there, dark, in the wide open land. Flamingo is somewhat similar to Breakfast im Grauen, one of the American avant-garde road movies by the great Austrian filmmaker Kurt Kren. In the other short work, Frank recalls an encounter with the American photographer Alfred Stieglitz, who died in 1946. In cold Mabou, in October 1998, Robert and June, together with Jerome Sother, who takes over the camera, reconstruct one of the everyday events that took place during a long-past meeting with Stieglitz and his wife, Georgia O'Keeffe. What I Remember is again a film about nature, about the engaging, harsh land that has become Frank's home. And again the brief film collects found objects, which flash briefly in the picture to then disappear again immediately. That is the fate of things and people. A photo album being flipped through here is empty.

Both of Frank's most recent works seem to move away again from this extreme point of cinematic solipsism, back to simpler, more accessible documentary forms. San Yu (2000) once again picks up the red line of commemoration of dead friends and relatives that runs through Frank's creative output. The Chinese painter San Yu, whom Frank met in New York during an apartment exchange in the early 1950s, thus stands in a line with Pablo and Andrea Frank, Danny Seymour, Jack Kerouac, and Alfred Stieglitz. (San Yu's premature death in 1966, which towards the end of the film can be read on a gravestone, is falsely indicated as 1964 at the beginning of the film. One might ask whether this error

anziehende, abweisende Land, das Frank zur Heimat geworden ist. Und wieder versammelt der kleine Film gefundene Objekte, die im Bild kurz aufblitzen, um gleich wieder zu verschwinden: Das ist das Schicksal der Dinge und der Menschen. Ein Fotoalbum, das hier aufgeblättert wird, ist leer.

Die beiden jüngsten Werke Franks scheinen sich von diesem äußersten Punkt des filmischen Solipsismus wieder weg zu bewegen, zurück zu simpleren, zugänglicheren dokumentarischen Formen. *San Yu* (2000) nimmt den durch Franks Schaffen verlaufenden roten Faden der Erinnerung an verstorbene Freunde und Verwandte wieder auf. Der chinesische Maler San Yu, den Frank in den frühen fünfziger Jahren in New York im Zuge eines Wohnungsaustauschs kennengelernt hat, steht somit in einer Linie mit Pablo und Andrea Frank, mit Danny Seymour, Jack Kerouac und Alfred Stieglitz. (San Yus frühes Todesjahr, 1966, das gegen Ende des Films auf einem Grabstein abzulesen ist, wird übrigens zu Beginn dieses Films mit 1964 falsch angegeben. Man mag sich fragen, ob dieser Fehler einer Nachlässigkeit des Filmemachers entspringt – oder ob auch dies letztlich der Idee der sanften Fiktionalisierung und „Verfälschung" realer Figuren geschuldet ist.)

"Is this a requiem?" fragt ein Insert in *San Yu* – und tatsächlich ist das nicht so klar: Frank kehrt an den Ort zurück, an dem sein Freund San Yu den Hauptteil seines Werks geschaffen hat, reist nach Paris, um ein Künstlerleben zu rekonstruieren; aber er tut dies weniger im Stil eines Requiems als in Form vieler kleiner Geschichten, die ihn, Robert Frank, ebenso sehr betreffen wie San Yu. Der Film präsentiert eine Reihe von Briefen, die zu Franks Parisreise geführt haben, er zeigt die wunderbar schlichte Kunst San Yus, aber auch den physischen Umgang mit seiner Arbeit bei Ausstellungen und einer Auktion seiner Gemälde. Der Filmemacher versucht, den Blick des Malers nachzuvollziehen: Wie hat San Yu die Tiere, sein Lieblingsthema, angeschaut? Ist das Geheimnis dieses Blicks zu entschlüsseln? In einer Reihe inszenierter pseudo-dokumentarischer Filmaufnahmen tritt ein Schauspieler in Schwarz-weiß an San Yus Stelle. "All my work is a declaration of simplicity", lässt Frank ihn sagen. In knappem, fragmentarischem Stil tastet *San Yu*, der Film, das Leben und die Kunst eines Fremden ab – und die zaghaften, letztlich zum Scheitern verurteilten Versuche, sich diesem zu nähern. Frank selbst stellt hier jedenfalls en passant noch einmal fest, worum sein Werk sich primär dreht: "It's all about memory". Der Erzähler, heißt das, kann stets nicht mehr als das Eigene, nur die persönliche Erinnerung an etwas wiedergeben, niemals aber das Leben oder den Blick anderer.

San Yu

stems from the filmmaker's carelessness—or if it can be attributed to the idea of a gentle fictionalization and "falsification" of real characters.)

An insert in *San Yu* asks, "Is this a requiem?"—and, actually, it is not so clear: Frank returns to the location where his friend San Yu created the majority of his works, travels to Paris to reconstruct the artist's life; but rather than doing this in the style of a requiem, he uses a number of little stories that are just as pertinent to him, Frank, as San Yu. The film presents a series of letters that led to Frank's trip to Paris, it shows San Yu's wonderfully simple art, but also the physical dealing with his work at exhibitions and at an auction of his paintings. The filmmaker attempts to reconstruct the painter's gaze: how did San Yu look at animals, his favorite theme? Is the secret to decode this gaze? In a series of staged pseudo-documentary film recordings in black and white, an actor appears in place of San Yu. Frank has him say, "All my work is a declaration of simplicity." In concise, fragmentary style, *San Yu* makes its way through the life and art of someone else—and hesitantly attempts to approach this person, and in the end is doomed to fail. Frank once again establishes, in passing, the prime concern of his work: "It's all about memory." What this says is that a narrator can only recite the personal, only his personal memory of something, and never the life or the way of seeing of another.

It is only consistent that Frank's own view is once again present at the beginning of *Paper Route* (2002), (even if this is broken by the off-narration of a women's voice with Asian-style English): Frank films a series of his photos and derives history and stories from them—and he films himself, solitary, waiting for the first light of day. This provides the prologue to *Paper Route*. Afterward, the actual protagonist comes into the picture, the newspaper deliverer Bobby McMillan, whom Frank accompanies on his rounds, on the "paper route" through the lonesome area in and around Mabou, on 5 March 2002. A night worker at the wheel: McMillan delivers 158 editions of the Herald Tribune every night. While doing so, he talks pleasantly with Frank and the other sleepless people in the area who are already waiting for their morning paper. Frank's gaze encounters the morning through the broken windshield of the old car that Bobby drives through the vast wintry nature. He eats his breakfast on the road, also he, one of the lucky ones, on the journey through a snowy land, in the day's first sun. The final shot belongs to Bobby, this time after work, alone in his living room, at home, in a chair, a vacuum cleaner at his feet. How does it feel to be filmed, Frank asks him. He simply says, "good."

As simple as it appears, this little road movie is a surprise in the filmmaker's work: an unblemished documentary film, the portrait of a job, a life, a landscape. "Making the circle, that's what we all do," remarks Frank, feeling philosophical in the car behind Bobby McMillan: living in a circle. *Paper Route* is not the sum and not the end of an uncompromising life work, but rather, like everything of Robert Frank's, a new path: the result of the attempt to always take a new route each time.

When Frank was asked in the mid-1980s to come up with a list of the essential stations of his life and comment on them, he recalled the journey through America which he began in 1955 for his famous photo book with the words: "I work all the time. I don't speak much. I try not to be seen."

Es ist also nur konsequent, wenn am Anfang von *Paper Route* (2002), wieder der eigene Blick steht (wenn dieser auch durch die Off-Erzählung einer Frauenstimme mit asiatisch gefärbtem Englisch gebrochen wird): Frank filmt eine Serie seiner Fotos ab, aus denen er Geschichte und Geschichten ableitet – und er filmt sich selbst, einsam, auf das Morgengrauen wartend. Das ist der Prolog von *Paper Route*, erst dann kommt der eigentliche Protagonist ins Bild, der Zeitungslieferant Bobby McMillan, den Robert Frank auf seinem Weg, der „Zeitungsroute", durch die einsame Gegend in und um Mabou begleitet, am 5. März 2002. Ein Nachtarbeiter, am Steuer: 158 Exemplare der Herald Tribune liefert McMillan allnächtlich aus, plaudert dabei freundlich mit Frank und den Schlaflosen der Gegend, die schon auf die Morgenzeitung warten. Der Blick Franks fällt durch die gesprungene Scheibe des alten Autos, mit dem Bobby durch die weite winterliche Natur fährt, dem Morgen entgegen. Sein Frühstück nimmt er unterwegs ein, *on the road* auch er, ein Glücklicher, auf der Reise durch ein Land im Schnee, in der frühen Sonne des Tages. Die letzte Einstellung gehört Bobby, diesmal nach der Arbeit, allein in seinem Lebensraum, daheim, im Sessel, einen Staubsauger zu seinen Füßen. Wie es sich anfühle, gefilmt zu werden, fragt ihn Frank noch. Gut, meint er nur.

Im Werk des Filmemachers ist dieses kleine Road-movie, so simpel es aussieht, eine Überraschung: ein makelloser Dokumentarfilm, das Porträt einer Arbeit, eines Lebens, einer Landschaft. "Making the circle, that's what we all do", bemerkt Frank, philosophisch gestimmt, im Auto hinter Bobby McMillan: Leben im Kreis. *Paper Route* ist nicht die Summe und nicht das Ende eines kompromisslosen Lebenswerks, sondern, wie alles bei Robert Frank, ein neuer Weg: das Ergebnis des Versuchs, jedes Mal wieder eine neue Route zu nehmen.

Als Robert Frank Mitte der achtziger Jahre aufgefordert wird, eine Liste wesentlicher Stationen seines Lebens zu erstellen und zu kommentieren, erinnert er sich mit folgenden Worten an die Amerikareise, die er 1955 für sein berühmtes Fotobuch begonnen hatte: „Ich arbeite immer. Ich spreche nicht viel. Ich versuche, nicht gesehen zu werden."

Paper Route

Philip Brookman im Gespräch mit Allen Ginsberg

Philip Brookman

Philip Brookman interviewte Allen Ginsberg am 13. Oktober 1985 in New York über Robert Frank, während der Produktion der Fernsehdokumentation *Fire in the East: A Portrait of Robert Frank*. Dies ist ein Auszug aus ihrem Gespräch. *Fire in the East* wurde von Anne Wilkes Tucker und Paul Yeager produziert, Regie führten Philip Brookman und Amy Brookman für das Museum of Fine Arts Houston und KUHT Public Television Houston. Eine Sammlung von Interviews und Videos aus diesem Projekt befindet sich in den Archiven des Museum of Fine Arts Houston.

WIE PASSTE ROBERT FRANK IN IHRE WELT UND DIE IHRER FREUNDE?

Einmal machte Robert ein Foto von mir. Er lebte auf der 3rd Avenue in der Bowery und wir gingen hinunter in den Hinterhof, der ein Haufen von altem Gerümpel und Müll vor einer alten Ziegelmauer in der Bowery war. Und ich stieg da hinunter in eine Art Grube aus altem Gerümpel und rostigem Eisen, Schluchten und Teilen eines Boilers und stand darauf und er machte vor dieser Mauer ein Foto von mir. Das ist immer noch eines seiner besten Fotos. Ich lernte Robert erst 1958 kennen und über ihn als Fotografen wusste ich eigentlich nichts. Ich hatte gehört, er sei ein großer Fotograf aber das hat mir nicht viel bedeutet. Ich war nicht der Ansicht, dass Fotografen so wichtig wie Dichter oder Schriftsteller wären. Ich war ein bisschen geschmeichelt, dass dieser Fotograf denkt, wir wären wichtig genug, um Fotos von uns zu machen. Aber wir mussten nicht posieren, weil er einen Film machte.

Wir machten einen Film mit dem Titel *Pull My Daisy*, der auf einem Skript von Jack Kerouac basierte. Ich hatte es nie zuvor gesehen, ich wusste nicht, dass Kerouac es geschrieben hatte. Und es ist eine sehr einfache und gewöhnliche Geschichte über das Familienleben, beobachtet in Neil Cassidys Haus in Los Gatos, Kalifornien, mit seiner blonden Frau und vermutlich einigen seiner Kinder, drei Kleinkinder. In einer realen Szene, bei der ich tatsächlich anwesend war, traf gerade ein Priester, irgendein kalifornischer Priester von irgendeiner Psychosensekte, mit seiner Mutter ein. Der Priester besuchte Neils Mutter und ich glaube, ich war mit Peter Orlovsky da.

A conversation with Allen Ginsberg

Philip Brookman

Philip Brookman interviewed Allan Ginsberg about Robert Frank on 13 October, 1985 in New York City, during production of the television documentary *Fire in the East: A Portrait of Robert Frank*. This is an excerpt from their conversation. *Fire in the East* was produced by Anne Wilkes Tucker and Paul Yeager, and directed by Philip Brookman and Amy Brookman for The Museum of Fine Arts, Houston and KUHT Public Television, Houston. A collection of interviews and videos from this project is housed in the Archives of The Museum of Fine Arts, Houston.

HOW DID ROBERT FRANK FIT INTO YOUR WORLD AND THE WORLD OF YOUR FRIENDS?

So once Robert took my picture. He was living on 3rd Avenue on the Bowery and we went downstairs to the backyard, which was a pile of old lumber and garbage, against an old Bowery brick wall. And I went down there in sort of like a pit of old lumber and rusty iron, canyons, and pieces of boiler, and stood on it, and he took my picture against the wall. That's still one of the best pictures he took. I didn't meet Robert until 1958, and I actually didn't know anything about him at all as a photographer. I heard he was supposed to be a big photographer, but that didn't mean that much to me. I didn't think photographers were as important as poets or prose writers. I was a little flattered seeing that this photographer thinks we're important enough to take pictures of. But he didn't require us to pose because he was making a movie.

We were making a movie that was called *Pull My Daisy*, which was built on a script of Jack Kerouac. I'd never seen it before. I didn't know Kerouac had written it. And it's a very simple and down-home story of family life, seen in Neil Cassidy's Los Gatos, California household, with his blond wife and I guess a couple of his kids, 3 young babies, and a scene that I was actually present at in real life, when a visiting priest, some kind of a California priest from some kind of psychosis sect, arrived with his mother. This priest came visiting Neil's mother, and I think I was there with Peter Orlovsky.

Ja. Ja. Aber die tatsächliche Szene wurde in meiner Erinnerung durch den Film ersetzt. Der Film ist jetzt in Hinblick auf die Bilder lebendiger. Robert und Al Leslie, der Maler, lebten beide in der Bowery und es ist immer erstaunlich, wenn man in der Bowery Lofts bekommen kann. Während dieser Zeit war eine Gemeinschaft von Künstlern wie Willem De Kooning und Franz Kline mit Robert befreundet. Anscheinend hatte er einen ganzen Freundeskreis, der sich entwickelte, nachdem wir uns zum ersten Mal getroffen hatten – gewissermaßen eine Art von Familienleben. Ich lebte mit Peter ungefähr fünf Blocks weiter auf der 2nd Street. Also gingen wir einige Wochen lang jeden Tag oder jeden zweiten Tag in Al Leslies Loft. Robert brachte Gregory Corso dazu, sich selbst zu spielen oder es zu versuchen, und er hatte den Maler Larry Rivers, der Neil Cassidy spielte. Er strahlte eine gewisse Energie aus, aber er war nicht so süß wie Cassidy. Und Delphine Seyrig, die später eine berühmte Schauspielerin wurde, spielte Neil Cassidys Frau. Die Frau war wütend, weil alle diese Bohemiens ihren hart arbeitenden Mann, einen Eisenbahner, besuchten, der auch ein wilder Partybesucher und Party-Veranstalter war. Sie waren alle ein bisschen spirituell und sprachen über Heiligkeit, ach, aber sie benahmen sich ein wenig albern. Wir mussten also etwas erfinden und dem Skript auf sehr allgemeine Weise folgen, wir mussten uns nicht an den tatsächlichen Dialog halten oder den tatsächlichen Szenen folgen. Und darin war Robert gut. Weder ließ er uns das Skript auswendig lernen, noch mussten wir im Grunde genommen schauspielern.

Sogar sehr – Kerouac hatte nur gegen eine Kleinigkeit einen Einwand, einen Anflug von Gewalt. Ich weiß nicht, wer das einbrachte, Robert oder Al Leslie, als jemand im Film sich auf den Schlips getreten fühlte und eine imaginäre Fingerpistole auf seinen Kopf richtete, auf den Kopf des anderen Mannes, und „Peng" machte. Vielleicht tat es Larry Rivers bei Gregory. Und auch eine Szene, in der jemand geohrfeigt wurde, obwohl Kerouac das in seinem Soundtrack sehr gut überdeckte, indem er sagte: „Außer bei Frank Sinatra ist unerwiderte Liebe langweilig."

Im Rückblick weiß ich das nicht mehr, aber damals schien sie mehr Roberts Angelegenheit zu sein. Es war sein Mitgefühl oder seine Sympathie, seine Aufmerksamkeit, die ich am reizvollsten fand – eine gewisse Qualität der verdrießlichen Zustimmung, der verdrießlichen Aufmerksamkeit. Während all dieser frühen Jahre dachte ich an ihn als den verdrießlichen Schweizer. Ach, und ich entwickelte eine Art väterliche Zuneigung zu ihm. Er erschien mir wie eine Vaterfigur, er hatte eine Familie und einige Kinder. Zumindest sein Sohn Pablo war da.

Ja, im Laufe der Jahre haben wir immer wieder gemeinsam etwas gemacht. Ich weiß nicht, anfangs war es ein wenig dürftig. Ich glaube, er mochte Kerouac, weil sie beide so spontan waren, sie berücksichtigten zufällige Ereignisse, und sie berücksichtigten zufällige Ereignisse im Geiste oder zufällige Ereignisse im Raum, als einen Teil des Realen. Sie konnten anderen Menschen in geschriebener Form oder in Bildern zeigen, was sie interessierte. Das mag ich an Roberts Arbeit vielleicht am liebsten,

YOU WERE ACTUALLY THERE WHEN THE PRIEST CAME?

Yeah. Yeah. But the actual scene has been replaced by the movie in my memory. The movie is now more vivid, pictorially. Robert and Al Leslie, the painter, both of them lived on the Bowery, and it's always amazing when you can get lofts on the Bowery. During this time it was a community of artists like Willem De Kooning and Franz Kline, who were friends of Robert's. Apparently he had a whole circle of friends that developed after we first met—kind of a home life in a way. I lived on 2nd Street about five blocks away with Peter. So we went to Al Leslie's loft, oh every day or every other day for a couple weeks. Robert made Gregory Corso play himself, or try to, and he had the painter Larry Rivers play Neil Cassidy. He had a certain amount of energy but he wasn't as cute as Cassidy. And Delphine Seyrig, who later got to be a famous actress, played Neil Cassidy's wife. It was the wife pissed off because all these Bohemian guys were coming to visit her hard-working railroad husband, who was also a kind of a wild party-goer, party-giver, all of them a little spiritual, talking about holiness. Ah, but acting a little silly. So what we had to do was invent, following the script in a very general way, not keeping to the actual dialogue and not keeping to the actual scenes. And that's where Robert was good. He didn't make us memorize the script and we didn't have to act, basically.

DO YOU THINK THAT *PULL MY DAISY* WAS A REFLECTION OF WHAT WAS HAPPENING AT THE TIME?

Very much so—Kerouac objected to only one thing that was there, a little tiny note of violence. I don't know who put that in, Robert or Al Leslie, when someone in the film got miffed and put an imaginary finger pistol to his head, to the other guy's head and went, pow! Maybe Larry Rivers to Gregory. And also a slapping scene, although Kerouac covered that nicely in his soundtrack by saying, "Out of Frank Sinatra, unrequited love is a bore."

HOW MUCH OF THE FILM DIRECTION DO YOU THINK WAS ROBERT'S AND HOW MUCH WAS FROM ALFRED LESLIE?

I don't know in hindsight, but it seemed to relate more to Robert at the time. It was his compassion or sympathy, his attention that I've found most attractive—some quality of glum approval, glum attentiveness. I kept thinking of him as the glum Swiss man all those early years. Ah, and I began to develop a kind of paternal liking for him. He seemed like a father figure, he had a family and a couple of kids. His son Pablo, at any rate, was there.

IS THIS A RELATIONSHIP THAT YOU HAVE EXTENDED FROM THAT TIME?

Yes, over the years we've kept doing some things together. I don't know how, at first it was a little tenuous. I think he liked Kerouac, because they both had this spontaneity, an allowance of accidents, and an allowance of accident in mind or accident of space, as part of what was real. They could show other people what interested them in writing or in pictures. That may be the thing that I liked most in Robert's work, his helplessness for the actual fact of chance, and his acceptance of that, and his willingness to include that.

HE USED IT TO HIS ADVANTAGE, TOO. HE SAW THAT HE WAS ABLE TO USE CHANCE IN HIS WORK.

Yes. Two years ago Robert had bought a JVC video camera, a new toy, and he came over to my house. I hadn't seen him in a while, and we had a long relationship over my *Kaddish* project.[1] I was

seine Hilflosigkeit gegenüber der Tatsache des Zufalls und seine Akzeptanz und seine Bereitwilligkeit, das mit einzuschließen.

ER NUTZTE DAS AUCH ZU SEINEM VORTEIL. ER ERKANNTE, DASS ER DEN ZUFALL IN SEINER ARBEIT VERWENDEN KONNTE.

Ja. Vor zwei Jahren hatte Robert eine JVC Videokamera gekauft, ein neues Spielzeug, und er kam zu mir. Ich hatte ihn eine Zeit lang nicht gesehen, und wir hatten eine lange Beziehung in Zusammenhang mit meinem *Kaddish*-Projekt.[1] Ich brannte darauf, ihm dieses neue Gedicht vorzulesen. Es war 25 Jahre später, ein Epilog zu *Kaddish*. Die Vision und der Traum, den ich von meiner Mutter hatte, in einem weißen Totenhemd. Ich saß also in dem Stuhl und begann ihm vorzulesen, und er hatte seine Kamera und filmte mich dabei, wie ich ihm dieses Gedicht zum ersten Mal vorlas, samt meinem ganzen Interesse daran, es vorzulesen. Und nachher sagte er, dass er die Videokamera deshalb mag, weil sie genauso wie Standfotos sei. Zufälle passieren. Man kann das Kratzen des Stuhls hören, das hupende Taxi von draußen, Menschen, die sich räuspern. Sie schloss die Realität mit ein. Sie konnte die Realität flexibler mit einschließen, ebenso wie das zufällige Ereignis des Standfotos.

GLAUBEN SIE, DASS DAS VIDEO VIELLEICHT EINE ERWEITERUNG VON *ME AND MY BROTHER* WAR?

Nun, das ist eine andere Geschichte. Natürlich war er deshalb daran interessiert. Er mochte *Kaddish*, oder irgendwie sprach *Kaddish* ihn an. Es war kurz zuvor geschrieben worden. Ich war verschwunden, hatte es, veröffentlicht von City Lights, zurückgelassen, ich war in Indien, reiste um die Welt, kam zurück nach New York. Ich war ziemlich pleite, hatte nicht viel Geld und schließlich eine billige Wohnung auf der Lower East Side. Keine Arbeit, ich wusste nicht, was ich tat, lebte eigentlich von Tag zu Tag. Und er hatte die Idee, aus *Kaddish* einen Film zu machen. Und *Pull My Daisy* hatte so großen historischen Erfolg.

Pull My Daisy – Allen Ginsberg, Gregory Corso

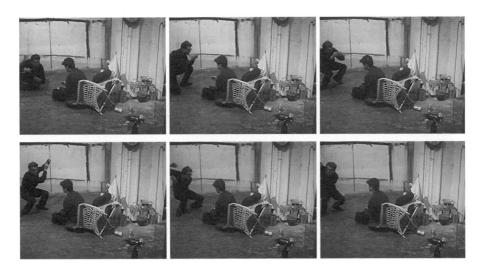

really eager to read him this new poem. It was twenty-five years later, an epilogue to *Kaddish*. The vision and the dream I had about my mother, white shroud. So I sat in the chair and started reading it to him, and he had his JVC and he filmed me reading this poem to him for the first time, with all the interest I had in reading it. And afterwards he said the reason he likes the JVC, the video, was that it's like stills. Accidents happen. You can hear the scraping of the chair, the taxi honk outside, people clearing their throat. It included reality. It was more flexible to include reality, like the accident of the still photo.

DO YOU THINK MAYBE THAT VIDEO WAS AN EXTENSION OF *ME AND MY BROTHER*?

Well that's another story. Sure, that's why he was interested. He liked *Kaddish*, or somehow *Kaddish* appealed to him. It was recently written. I had gone, left it behind, published by City Lights, I was in India, went around the world, got back to New York. I was relatively broke, didn't have much money, had a cheap apartment on the Lower East Side finally. No work, I didn't know what I was doing, was living day-to-day, actually. And he had the idea of making the film of *Kaddish*. And *Pull My Daisy* had such great historical success.

I know I didn't say much about that, but *Pull My Daisy* was one of the first totally improvised films, and in a way it completely changed Hollywood. It affected the entire film world. That and a few other films, like John Cassavetes' *Shadows*, films from the underground, really did have a catalytic effect, altering people's awareness of what you could do: improvise and be open and sexual if necessary. So I was glad Robert was interested in *Kaddish*. We had to make a script and I didn't know anything about film scripts. We went out and I came to Robert's house every day or every other day, a couple of times a week, and we'd sit down at his typewriter, at his office, at his desk, and write a scene. I took the poem and cut it into pieces and arranged it exactly chronologically and made an arrangement of all the images in it that were pictorial and photographic. And then he paid me something like ten dollars a day, something like five or six dollars an hour, or eight an hour, depending on how long it took me to do it. And I lived on that money for about two months. I felt amazed that anybody would take me that seriously.

FOR ME, LOOKING BACK AT THAT TIME, IT WAS ALMOST A VISIONARY THING TO LOOK AT A POEM LIKE "KADDISH" AND TRY TO DO A FILM OF IT.

Later I thought about it. I followed my story chronologically but Robert wanted to flash forward, also to my present day life, and depart from the enclosed historical narrative up to the present. I resisted it quite a bit because I felt that the integrity of the film was in danger. But I was willing to try to figure out what he was trying to do, and try to work with that. I didn't have much choice. It was his movie, anyway. I argued about it a little, I read about fifteen scenes. Then we had to raise money, or he had to raise money. I was too shy about it, sort of standoffish. I thought he couldn't raise enough money to do it, actually. So the film never got made.

So finally after about a year, in 1964, '65, he began filming around the house, filming Julius Orlovsky, who is also from a mental hospital like my mother had been, and Peter, and their relationship. So what began as *Kaddish*, a study of mental family tragedy and mental illness, finally became *Me and My Brother*. Peter had two brothers, Lafcadio and Julius. Julius was the one. And the only role I had was one as a waiter. Once in a while, Robert would set up a scene that we would have to act out. In my house, Julius and Peter were eating, and I was coming on as a sort of funny Hungarian waiter, serving them food. So that was funny, improvising scenes. So it took maybe two years of just solitary labor on

Me and My Brother

Ich weiß, ich habe nicht viel darüber gesagt, aber *Pull My Daisy* war einer der ersten völlig improvisierten Filme und in gewisser Weise hat er Hollywood völlig verändert. Er hat die gesamte Filmwelt beeinflusst. Er und einige andere Filme wie John Cassavetes' *Shadows*, Filme aus dem Untergrund, hatten wirklich einen katalytischen Effekt, sie veränderten das Bewusstsein der Menschen darüber, was möglich war: improvisiere und sei offen und sexuell, wenn nötig. Also war ich froh, dass sich Robert für *Kaddish* interessierte. Wir mussten ein Skript schreiben, und ich wusste nichts über Filmskripts. Wir gingen aus und ich kam jeden Tag oder jeden zweiten Tag zu Robert nach Hause, einige Male pro Woche, und wir setzten uns an seine Schreibmaschine, in seinem Büro, an seinem Tisch und schrieben eine Szene. Ich nahm das Gedicht und zerstückelte es und arrangierte es genau chronologisch und machte ein Arrangement all jener Bilder, die malerisch oder fotografisch waren. Und dann bezahlte er mir ungefähr zehn Dollar pro Tag, ungefähr fünf oder sechs Dollar die Stunde oder acht Dollar die Stunde, abhängig davon, wie lange ich dafür brauchte. Und ich lebte ungefähr zwei Monate von diesem Geld. Ich war erstaunt, dass mich irgendjemand so ernst nahm.

FÜR MICH WAR ES, IM RÜCKBLICK AUF DIESE ZEIT DAMALS, BEINAHE ETWAS VISIONÄRES,
SICH EIN GEDICHT WIE "KADDISH" ANZUSEHEN UND EINEN FILM DARAUS ZU MACHEN.

Ich habe später darüber nachgedacht. Ich folgte meiner Geschichte chronologisch, aber Robert wollte nach vorne springen, auch in mein gegenwärtiges Leben, und von der geschlossenen historischen Erzählung weg bis in die Gegenwart gehen. Ich leistete ziemlichen Widerstand, weil ich dachte, die Integrität des Films sei gefährdet. Aber ich war gewillt, es zu versuchen und herauszufinden, was er vorhatte und zu versuchen, damit zu arbeiten. Ich hatte keine große Wahl. Es war immerhin sein Film. Ich diskutierte ein wenig darüber, ich las ungefähr 15 Szenen. Dann mussten wir das Geld aufbringen, oder er musste das Geld aufbringen. Ich war dafür zu scheu, irgendwie reserviert. Ich dachte, er könnte nie genug Geld aufbringen, um ihn tatsächlich zu machen. Also wurde der Film nie gemacht.

Also begann er schließlich nach ungefähr einem Jahr, 1964 oder 1965, in der Umgebung des Hauses zu filmen, Julius Orlovsky aufzunehmen, der ebenso wie meine Mutter aus einer Nervenheilanstalt kam, und Peter und ihre Beziehung. Was als *Kaddish* begann, eine Studie einer geistigen Familientragödie und Geisteskrankheit, wurde schließlich zu *Me and My Brother*. Peter hatte zwei Brüder,

his part, like a still-photographer going out, you know, certain scenes, he went out with maybe one photographer, had only one guy as his crew, maybe two at most, friends or amateurs. Then at one point, Peter's brother Julius wandered off and got lost in the mental hospital. So the main character was gone. So I think Robert got Joseph Chaiken, the actor, and he used him as a stand-in for Julius for some scenes. Then at the very end, toward the last scene in the film, Robert turns to Julius and asks him what he thinks about making a movie. Julius has been almost silent all through the film. Then Julius comes up with some astoundingly conscious answer. Later he became almost like one of Julius' best friends. Julius still asks after Robert Frank, and Robert goes and sees him whenever Julius is around, there is generally a meeting.

There's a funny compassion in Robert. Maybe not for himself but for other people, for not exactly clochards, but for people whose condition on earth is not what it looks like in the White House, not what it looks like in a middle class home, not what it looks like in a good Swiss Berger family, but for the outcasts, and the outcasts that are exactly real, somebody really stuck in the world, brought out of his control, maybe.

HE CAME FROM AN UPPER-MIDDLE CLASS SWISS FAMILY, YOU KNOW.

I knew very little about that although by now he was already a very mature fifty-eight or fifty-nine years old man. I never managed to ask him about it, or overcome my shyness and impose upon him, and start asking him about his family.

HOW DO YOU THINK HE WAS TRANSFORMED FROM THE MIDDLE CLASS SWISS KID TO ROBERT FRANK, THE ARTIST? WAS IT COMING TO AMERICA?

No, I don't think it was that, because in his pictures in Europe, first pictures in Europe, he seemed to be the same, solitary guy. So he worked, he got out of his family and worked. And he was technically qualified by all the apprentice work he did there in the Old World European photography outfit. So I guess he just got out on his own, and I don't know if he was transformed. There's still some element of some of the European Bohemian about him—tolerance, I guess. Years later, Robert had a lot of tragedies in his life, with his daughter in a plane crash and his son was very ill, his marriage broke up, a long period of solitude and withdrawal from the world after all the tragedy. And his own work got out of his hands for a while, his own photography, some other people owned it.

Pull My Daisy

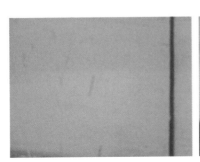

Lafcadio und Julius. Es war Julius, um den es ging. Und meine einzige Rolle war die eines Kellners. Manchmal richtete Robert eine Szene ein, die wir dann spielen mussten. Julius und Peter aßen in meiner Wohnung, und ich trat als eine Art lustiger ungarischer Kellner auf, der ihnen das Essen servierte. Es hat Spaß gemacht, Szenen zu improvisieren. Er musste ungefähr zwei Jahre einsam vor sich hin arbeiten, wie ein Standfotograf, der hinaus geht, wissen Sie, gewisse Szenen, er ging vielleicht mit einem Kameramann, er hatte nur einen Kerl als Crew, höchstens zwei vielleicht, Freunde oder Amateure. An einem bestimmten Punkt verlor sich dann Peters Bruder Julius und verschwand in einer Nervenheilanstalt. Die Hauptperson war fort. Ich glaube, Robert holte Joseph Chaiken, den Schauspieler, und setzte ihn in manchen Szenen als Double für Julius ein. Ganz am Ende, beinahe in der letzten Szene des Films, wendet sich Robert dann Julius zu und fragt ihn, was er davon hält, einen Film zu machen. Julius war den ganzen Film über beinahe stumm. Dann liefert er eine erstaunlich bewusste Antwort. Später wurde er fast einer von Julius' besten Freunden. Julius fragt noch immer nach Robert Frank, und Robert besucht ihn, wann immer Julius in der Nähe ist, dann gibt es gewöhnlich ein Treffen.

Robert hat ein seltsames Mitgefühl. Vielleicht nicht für sich selbst, aber für andere Menschen, nicht unbedingt Landstreicher, aber für Menschen, deren Lebensbedingungen auf dieser Welt nicht dem entsprechen, wie es im Weißen Haus aussieht, nicht wie es in einem weißen Mittelklassehaushalt aussieht, nicht wie es in einer guten Schweizer Familie Berger aussieht, sondern für die Ausgestoßenen, und die Ausgestoßenen, die eben gerade real sind, jemand, der wirklich in der Welt feststeckt, die vielleicht seiner Kontrolle entglitten ist.

ER STAMMTE AUS EINER SCHWEIZER FAMILIE DER OBEREN MITTELKLASSE.

Ich wusste sehr wenig darüber, obwohl er nun schon im reifen 58., 59. Jahr ist. Ich konnte ihn nie darüber befragen oder meine Schüchternheit überwinden oder mich ihm aufdrängen und anfangen, ihn über seine Familie auszufragen.

WIE HAT ER SICH VON DEM SCHWEIZER JUNGEN AUS DER MITTELKLASSE IN ROBERT FRANK, DEN KÜNSTLER, VERWANDELT? HAT ES DAMIT ZU TUN, DASS ER NACH AMERIKA KAM?

Nein, ich glaube nicht, dass es daran lag, denn in seinen Bildern in Europa, den ersten Bildern in Europa, schien er derselbe, einzelgängerische Typ zu sein. Er arbeitete, er machte sich von seiner Familie frei und arbeitete. Und durch seine Lehrjahre in der Schule der Fotografie des alten Europa war er technisch qualifiziert. Ich glaube, er hat sich alleine freigemacht und ich weiß nicht, ob er sich verwandelt hat. Er hat immer noch etwas vom Flair des europäischen Bohemiens – wahrscheinlich ist es Toleranz. Jahre später erlebte Robert eine ganze Reihe Tragödien, seine Tochter stürzte mit einem Flugzeug ab und sein Sohn war sehr krank, seine Ehe zerbrach, eine lange Periode der Einsamkeit und des Rückzugs von der Welt, nach all den tragischen Ereignissen. Und eine Zeit lang verlor er die Kontrolle über seine Arbeit, andere Menschen besaßen die Rechte für seine Fotografien.

DANN ZOG ER INMITTEN ALL DIESER EREIGNISSE NACH KANADA?

Ja, es war interessant, auf der Höhe seines Ruhmes zog er weg und zog sich von der Welt zurück. Er zog sich lediglich von der Welt zurück, nachdem ihm persönliche Tragödien zugestoßen waren, die jeden umwerfen würden. Wahrscheinlich hat es ihn eine Zeit lang umgeworfen.

THEN HE MOVED TO CANADA IN THE MIDDLE OF ALL THIS.

Yeah, he moved out and retired from the world, it was interesting, at the height of his celebrity. He merely retired from the world, having encountered personal tragedy that would have knocked anybody over. It knocked him over for a while, I guess.

WHAT DID HE RESPECT IN PEOPLE?

I think integrity. I think dumbness, in the sense of genius dumbness. There's some kind of wise, well, first of all, workmanship. He understands that. And say with Sid Kaplan, the photographer, several times when he's talked to me about Sid, he said you know, the thing about Sid, he's real slow. He's immovable, like sort of slow and immovable, but he knows what he's doing. I think Robert liked that, the fact that Sid is totally himself, like a rock. Robert has this ability to work with people who you would think would be the opposite of his glamour. Not that he's so glamorous, but there is some glamour about him in the sense that he's this extraordinary photographer.

DO YOU HAVE A SENSE THAT YOUR OWN WORK, AS WELL AS ROBERT'S, AS WELL AS THAT OF OTHER PEOPLE WHO WERE WITH YOU IN THE 1960s, WAS AUTOBIOGRAPHICAL? CAN YOU EXPLAIN IT THAT WAY?

I never thought of Robert's work as autobiographical, but now in hindsight I realize it was autobiographical and had become increasingly open. In seeing himself objectively as part of the scene, it's an odd thing that he does with it. Years later in Boulder, Colorado, in 1982, we had the twenty-fifth anniversary of Kerouac's publication of "On the Road" and Robert went out, somewhat unwillingly, he wasn't sure he wanted that, but I was very eager to come out and do some little film 'cause it was like *Pull My Daisy* twenty-five years later, except with more characters. Like Burroughs was going to be there, Gregory Corso was going to be there as himself, Peter and myself, and Jack Micheline, the poet that Jack Kerouac liked, and John Clellon Holmes, and Carolyn Cassidy, who was played by somebody else in *Pull My Daisy*, she was Kerouac's first wife who was a really photogenic, amazing person, but most of all, Herbert Huncke, who was an extremely intelligent talker and very charming and ingenious as a personage. I wanted Robert to come out and we managed that he was able to get funding for another film, which he did mostly on his own. Robert simply sat on the porch, stations himself on the porch where we were all living, it was up in the one old dark, multi-roomed dormitory place where most of the writers were staying. And every morning, everybody would get up and chew the fat, and have coffee together, and figure out what they were supposed to do for the day, and where the symposium, poetry reading, was, and meet old friends that were coming up, people who haven't seen each other for twenty-five years like ah, I think John Holmes and Carl Solomon and Herbert Huncke and John Holmes hadn't seen each other for decades and decades and decades. So they were all part of the same mythology, the Beat Generation or *Pull My Daisy* or whatever it was, San Francisco renaissance, poetry, 1950s art. So Robert stationed himself on the front porch with a cup of coffee, soundman, and a silent camera— silent in the sense that it didn't make noise, but he could—it recorded everything. He just recorded everybody's morning chewing the fat and conversation and meetings and ordinary, everyday, no big deal, the fellows among themselves and the girls with each other, just talking. Burroughs coming up to visit and talking about trying to get more out of his Bowery loft and Robert asking him a question, "is it worth money, what are you trying to sell," and Burroughs saying, "I've got to sell it, I've got a key and an eviction notice," and odd people just talking to each other, David Amram singing, skipping around

WELCHE EIGENSCHAFTEN RESPEKTIERTE ER BEI MENSCHEN?

Ich glaube Integrität. Ich glaube, Sprachlosigkeit, im Sinne einer Sprachlosigkeit des Genies. Es gibt eine Art weise, nun ja, in erster Linie Kunstfertigkeit. Er versteht das. Beispielsweise bei Sid Kaplan, dem Fotografen, mehrmals als er mit mir über Sid sprach, sagte er, „Weißt du, was Sid angeht, er ist wirklich langsam. Er ist unbeweglich, irgendwie langsam und unbeweglich, aber er weiß, was er tut." Ich glaube, Robert mochte das, die Tatsache, dass Sid ganz er selbst war, wie ein Felsen. Robert hat diese Fähigkeit mit Menschen zu arbeiten, von denen man annehmen würde, dass sie das Gegenteil von seinem Glamour sind. Nicht dass er so glamourös ist, aber es umgibt ihn ein gewisser Glamour in dem Sinn, dass er ein außergewöhnlicher Fotograf ist.

HABEN SIE DAS GEFÜHL, DASS IHRE EIGENE ARBEIT, WIE AUCH DIE VON ROBERT ODER DIE ANDERER PERSONEN, DIE IN DEN SECHZIGER JAHREN MIT IHNEN ZUSAMMEN WAREN, AUTOBIOGRAFISCH WAR? KÖNNEN SIE SIE AUF DIESE WEISE ERKLÄREN?

Ich dachte an Roberts Arbeit nie als autobiografisch, aber wenn ich jetzt darauf zurückblicke verstehe ich, dass sie autobiografisch war und immer offener wurde. Indem er sich selbst objektiv als Teil der Szene sah, es ist seltsam, was er damit anstellt. Jahre später in Boulder, Colorado im Jahr 1982, begingen wir den 25. Jahrestag der Veröffentlichung von Kerouacs "On the Road" und Robert kam hin, etwas unwillig, er war sich nicht sicher, ob er das wollte, aber ich wollte sehr gerne dorthin und einen kleinen Film machen, weil es wie *Pull My Daisy* war, nur 25 Jahre später und mit mehr Figuren. Burroughs würde dort sein, Gregory Corso würde als er selbst dort sein, Peter und ich, und Jack Micheline, der Dichter, den Jack Kerouac mochte, und John Clellon Holmes und Carolyn Cassidy, die in *Pull My Daisy* von jemandem anderen gespielt wurde, sie war Kerouacs erste Frau, eine wirklich fotogene, erstaunliche Person, aber vor allem Herbert Huncke, ein äußerst interessanter Redner und eine sehr charmante und geistreiche Persönlichkeit. Ich wollte, dass Robert kommt, und wir konnten es einrichten, dass er einen weiteren Film finanziert bekam, den er beinahe alleine machte. Robert saß einfach auf der Veranda, positionierte sich selbst auf der Veranda wo wir alle lebten, es war oben in dem einen alten, dunklen Haus mit den vielen Schlafsälen, in dem die meisten Schriftsteller wohnten. Und jeden Morgen standen alle auf und plauderten gemütlich und tranken gemeinsam Kaffee und fanden heraus, was sie heute tun sollten und wo das Symposion und die Gedichtlesung stattfinden würden und trafen alte Freunde, die hinaufkamen, Menschen, die sich seit 25 Jahren nicht gesehen hatten, ich glaube John Holmes und Carl Solomon und Herbert Huncke hatten sich seit Jahrzehnten nicht gesehen. Sie waren alle Teil derselben Mythologie, der Beat Generation oder *Pull My Daisy* oder was immer es auch war, San Francisco Renaissance, Dichtung, die Kunst der 50er Jahre. Also hat sich Robert mit einer Tasse Kaffee, einem Tonmann und einer stummen Kamera auf der Veranda positioniert – stumm in dem Sinn, dass sie keine Geräusche machte, während er es konnte – sie hat alles aufgezeichnet. Den morgendlichen Tratsch und die Konversation und die Treffen und das Normale, Alltägliche, nichts Besonderes, die Jungs unter sich und die Mädchen, die sich miteinander unterhalten, er nahm einfach alles auf. Burroughs, der auf Besuch kommt und darüber spricht, dass er versuche, mehr aus seinem Loft in der Bowery herauszuholen und Robert, der ihn fragt, „Ist das, was du verkaufen willst, Geld wert?", und Burroughs, der sagt, „Ich muss es verkaufen, ich habe einen Schlüssel und einen Räumungsbefehl", und einzelne Menschen, die sich einfach miteinander unterhalten, den singenden David Amram, der herumspringt und alte Lieder aus den 1920ern singt. Es war alles ganz heimelig, und es bekam den Titel

and singing some old 1920s song. So it was all completely home-like, and it was called *This Song for Jack*. And in one of the opening scenes Robert had this really funny group of boozers, sort of Hells Angels boozers down on the mall in Boulder, he'd gone out in the rain and found a couple of bum-like ancient Beatniks and stopped them and asked them what they thought of Kerouac. This is the documentary aspect, a crazy documentary. He was talking to aging Beatniks and said, "what do you think of Kerouac?"

WHEN DID YOU FIRST SEE "THE AMERICANS"?

I don't remember. It must have been some time after 1959 when Grove Press put it out.

DID IT HAVE AN IMPACT ON YOU?

No, it took quite a while before—I just took it for granted. Kerouac really liked Robert, and Kerouac's mother did. Robert was one of the very few people that Kerouac's mother would accept, because he was Swiss and spoke French, and he had a European background and wasn't queer, had a family. He had a thing of his own that he was doing but he also had a car. And so Robert, I think, one time moved Kerouac's entire family from wherever it was, Long Island, down to Florida. And Kerouac constantly had to move his mother around. She would be dissatisfied living in Ozone Park or Northport, and so Jack moved her down to Florida and he had to move her back once, he moved his mother about five times. Burroughs she rejected, me she rejected, a queer Jew, and Lucien Carr, an old friend of Jack's, she disapproved of. And I think Jack's father, on his deathbed, made his mother swear to protect Jack from all his friends. But Robert was a later friend, after Jack's father died, and was one of the rare people who were sort of anonymous to Mrs. Kerouac—just a friendly presence, not an aggressive presence. I guess he took it easy with her, Robert probably knew that kind of peasant.

WHAT DO YOU THINK OF ROBERT AS A WRITER? YOU WERE TALKING A BIT ABOUT THAT.

Ah, there is some kind of basic sincerity about him. You know, he doesn't say much. The main subject matter very often is how to avoid the consequences of fame. How do you avoid the hyper-consciousness of being an artist, how do you stay with life as it is with an ordinary eye? That's one reason why he gave up the still photographs; he got tired of looking through the camera, through like a frame.

Me and My Brother

This Song for Jack. Und in einer der Eröffnungsszenen hatte Robert diese wirklich lustige Gruppe von Säufern, so etwas wie Säufer von den Hells Angels im Einkaufszentrum in Boulder, er war im Regen unterwegs gewesen und hatte einige herumgammelnde, uralte Beatniks gefunden und sie aufgehalten und sie gefragt, was sie von Jack Kerouac hielten. Das ist der dokumentarische Aspekt, eine verrückte Dokumentation. Er sprach mit alternden Beatniks und sagte: „Was halten sie von Kerouac?"

WANN HABEN SIE "THE AMERICANS" ZUM ERSTEN MAL GESEHEN?

Ich kann mich nicht erinnern. Es muss einige Zeit nach 1959 gewesen sein, als es bei Grove Press herauskam.

HAT ES SIE BEEINFLUSST?

Nein, das hat eine ganze Weile gedauert – ich nahm es als selbstverständlich. Kerouac mochte Robert wirklich und Kerouacs Mutter auch. Robert war einer der wenigen Menschen, die Kerouacs Mutter akzeptierte, weil er Schweizer war und Französisch sprach, und er hatte einen europäischen Hintergrund und war nicht schwul, hatte eine Familie. Er zog sein eigenes Ding durch, aber er hatte auch ein Auto. Also hat Robert einmal Kerouacs gesamte Familie von wo auch immer, Long Island, hinunter nach Florida übersiedelt. Und Kerouac musste seine Mutter ständig übersiedeln. Sie war nicht mehr damit zufrieden in Ozone Park oder Northport zu leben, also übersiedelte Jack sie nach Florida, und er musste sie einmal zurück übersiedeln, er übersiedelte seine Mutter ungefähr fünf Mal. Burroughs hat sie abgelehnt, mich hat sie abgelehnt, einen schwulen Juden, und sie hat Lucien Carr, einen alten Freund von Jack, nicht gutgeheißen. Und ich glaube, Jacks Vater hat auf seinem Totenbett seine Mutter schwören lassen, Jack vor all seinen Freunden zu beschützen. Aber Robert war ein späterer Freund, nachdem Jacks Vater gestorben war, und er gehörte zu den wenigen Menschen, die für Mrs. Kerouac anonym waren – nur eine freundliche Präsenz, keine aggressive Präsenz. Ich denke, er ist entspannt mit ihr umgegangen, Robert kannte wahrscheinlich diese Art von Banausen.

WAS HALTEN SIE VON ROBERT ALS AUTOR? SIE HABEN EIN WENIG DARÜBER GESPROCHEN.

Ach, er hat so eine Art grundlegende Ehrlichkeit an sich. Wissen sie, er sagt nicht viel. Das Hauptthema ist sehr oft, wie man den Konsequenzen des Ruhmes entgehen kann. Wie vermeidet man das Überbewusstsein, ein Künstler zu sein, wie bleibt man dem Leben, wie es ist, mit einem alltäglichen Auge verhaftet? Das ist einer der Gründe, warum er die Fotografie aufgab; er war es Leid, durch die Kamera zu blicken, wie durch einen Rahmen. Er wollte etwas Größeres. Er wollte in der Welt sein. Und ich glaube, darum sind sowohl seine Schriften als auch seine Kommentare zu seinen Fotos so bunt zusammengewürfelt und beziehen seine Familie, seine Freunde mit ein. Das Thema seiner Schriften scheint zu sein: Wie steigen wir aus, wie führen wir den Kampf fort, wie bleiben wir in Bewegung?

Robert sagte, „Nun, sobald man alle seine Fotografien katalogisiert und einzeln aufgeführt hat, sie mit Nummern versehen geordnet hat, dann ist die Arbeit getan, es gibt nicht so viel Arbeit." Also sagte ich, „Nun, ich habe Probleme am Laufenden zu bleiben, ich muss eine Sekretärin einstellen, um den Überblick über die Nummern zu behalten und sie abzulegen. Wie machst du das?", fragte ich. „Oh, ich mache nur zehn Fotos pro Jahr." „Zehn Fotos", sagte ich, „wie machst du das?" Nun, er arbeitete mit dieser gigantischen Polaroidkamera in Cambridge, die die Firma Polaroid eine Zeit lang am MIT hatte, glaube ich. Und er arbeitet mit Video, und wenn er die Bilder im Video mochte, fotogra-

He wanted something larger. He wanted to be in the world. And that's I guess why both his writing and comments on his photographs were so scratchy and include his family, his friends. The subject of his writings seems to be: how do we get off, how do we continue the struggle, how do we keep moving?

Robert said, "well, once you've got all your photographs catalogued and itemized, put in place with the numbers on them, then the work is done, there's not so much work." So, I said, "well, I'm having trouble keeping up with it, I have to hire a secretary to keep the numbers together and file them. How do you do it?" I asked. "Oh, I, I only take ten pictures a year." "Ten pictures," I said, "how do you do that?" Well, what he was doing was working with this giant big Polaroid camera in Cambridge that the Polaroid company had for a while at MIT, I think. And he was working with video, and then when he liked the images on the video he photographed them with this giant 20 x 24-inch Polaroid, and then lined them up as a triptych, quadruptych, or whatever. I saw that. I didn't realize how he did it. He was just taking life-size or even larger than life-size photographs of the video screen. I said, "Well, that's an interesting thing." He said, "Well, if you're a photographer you've got to keep moving on. In this business, you've got to keep moving on. Otherwise you fall asleep or otherwise you settle in to some kind of repetition."

WHY DO YOU THINK THAT ROBERT CHOSE KEROUAC TO WRITE AN INTRODUCTION TO "THE AMERICANS"? ORIGINALLY WALKER EVANS WROTE THAT TEXT AND ROBERT REJECTED IT AND CHOSE KEROAUC INSTEAD. DO YOU THINK THAT WAS A TRANSITIONAL MOMENT FOR HIM?

Robert told me about that the other day. He said Walker Evans was very aristocratic, although he took popular American scenes. His nature was aristocratic. And in fact, when he came to visit the set of *Pull My Daisy*, apparently Evans was wondering why was Robert hanging around with these American ruffian Bohemians. Then, I suppose, Walker meant security and respectability as a preference writer in historicity, but Kerouac meant creation. If I had been Robert, I would have been so scared to move away from Walker Evans and jump into something new. That's amazing, an amazing human choice that he would jump into unknown Kerouac instead of classic Walker Evans as his patron, or introducer.

DO YOU THINK THAT ROBERT WAS AN INTREGRAL PART OF THE BEAT GENERATION?

Well he was apparently working independently on the same principles, which were spontaneous mind. He was looking for some supreme reality, actually, depending on his own Whitman, from the lineage of Whitman, depending on his own nature rather than on a received aesthetic, or a received moral, or a received sociology, but reflecting his own helplessness, hopelessness, his own failure, his own inability, his own inability to live up to whatever super ideal standard he was supposed to live up to, but depending on his own senses, like Jack…. Jack's was a more romantic, national ambition. Robert was more world-weary and unillusioned. But on the other hand they both had an eye for wild detail, eccentric detail, crazy people, crazy Americana…. In that sense certainly, they created things together that were remarkable.

[1] Kaddish = A Jewish prayer recited by mourners during the year of the death and on its anniversary.

fierte er sie mit dieser gigantischen 20x24-Inch Polaroidkamera und ordnete sie als Triptychon, als Quadruptychon oder was auch immer an. Ich habe das gesehen. Ich wusste nicht, wie er es macht. Er machte einfach lebensgroße oder sogar überlebensgroße Fotografien des Videomonitors. Ich sagte, „Nun, das ist eine interessante Sache." Er sagte, „Nun, als Fotograf musst du dich weiterentwickeln. In diesem Geschäft musst du dich weiterentwickeln. Sonst schläfst du ein oder du verfällst in irgendeine Form der Wiederholung."

WARUM HAT ROBERT IHRER MEINUNG NACH JACK KEROUAC AUSGEWÄHLT, UM EINE EINLEITUNG ZU "THE AMERICANS" ZU SCHREIBEN? URSPRÜNGLICH HAT WALKER EVANS DEN TEXT GESCHRIEBEN, UND ROBERT HAT IHN ABGELEHNT UND STATTDESSEN KEROUAC GEWÄHLT. GLAUBEN SIE, DAS WAR FÜR IHN EIN ÜBERGANGSMOMENT?

Robert hat mir vor kurzem davon erzählt. Er sagte Walker Evans sei sehr aristokratisch, obwohl er populäre amerikanische Szenen fotografierte. Er hatte eine aristokratische Natur. Und tatsächlich fragte sich Evans anscheinend bei seinem Besuch am Set von *Pull My Daisy*, warum sich Robert mit diesen amerikanischen rüpelhaften Bohemiens abgab. Außerdem nehme ich an, dass Walker als bevorzugter Autor für den historisierenden Kanon Sicherheit und Ansehen bedeutete, aber Kerouac bedeutete Neuschöpfung. Ich an Roberts Stelle hätte entsetzliche Angst davor gehabt, mich von Walker Evans abzuwenden und mich auf etwas Neues einzulassen. Das ist erstaunlich, eine erstaunliche menschliche Wahl, dass er sich auf den unbekannten Kerouac einließ anstelle des klassischen Walker Evans als seinen Förderer oder Vorstellenden.

GLAUBEN SIE, ROBERT WAR EIN INTEGRALER TEIL DER BEAT GENERATION?

Nun er hat scheinbar unabhängig nach denselben Prinzipien gearbeitet, nämlich einem spontanen Geist folgend. Tatsächlich suchte er, wie Jack, nach einer allerhöchsten Realität, die auf seinem eigenen Whitman beruhte, von Whitman ausging, die eher auf seiner eigenen Natur beruhte, als auf einer allgemein anerkannten Ästhetik, oder einer allgemein anerkannten Moral, oder einer allgemein anerkannten Soziologie, die stattdessen seine eigene Hilflosigkeit und Hoffnungslosigkeit reflektierte, sein eigenes Scheitern, seine eigene Unfähigkeit, seine eigene Unfähigkeit welchen auch immer überidealen Standards gerecht zu werden, denen er gerecht werden sollte und die stattdessen auf seinen eigenen Sinnen beruhte... Jacks Ambition war romantischer, nationaler. Robert war eher der Welt müde und ohne Illusionen. Aber andererseits hatten sie beide ein Auge für das wilde Detail, das exzentrische Detail, verrückte Menschen, verrückte Americana ... In diesem Sinn haben sie sicherlich gemeinsam bemerkenswerte Dinge geschaffen.

---

[1] Kaddisch (engl. Kaddish): das jüdische Gebet der Trauernden im Trauerjahr und jährlich am Todestag.

Im Kreis
Anfänge, Weiterführungen, Erneuerungen: Robert Franks
persönliches New American Cinema

Amy Taubin

> „Wir machen die Runde. Verstehst du, Robert?"
> „Die Runde? Das ist alles, was wir machen."
>
> (Aus einem Gespräch zwischen Bobby McMillan und Robert Frank
> in dem Video Paper Route, 2002)

„1. Oktober 1960: Robert Frank kam morgens. Wir gaben ihm 4000 Fuß altes Filmmaterial. Er war müde, zornig, mitgenommen von der Arbeit, von Geldmangel, Geschäftsleuten und Verträgen. ‚Ich werde nie wieder so einen Film machen', sagte er. Unrasiert, schwarz, müde, sprach er beinahe zu sich selbst." (Aus den Tagebüchern von Jonas Mekas, die in limitierter Auflage von Anthology Film Archives herausgegeben wurden)

Robert Frank dachte schon wie ein Filmemacher, bevor er noch seinen ersten Film *Pull My Daisy* (1959) gemacht hatte. Sein Buch "The Americans" (1958) enthält 83 Fotografien, die er auf verschiedenen Reisen auf und ab, quer durch und rundherum in den USA zwischen 1955 und 1957 gemacht hat. Sie ergeben, neben vielem anderen, vor allem ein Road Movie. Beim Fotografieren gehorchte Frank dem Imperativ des „entscheidenden Moments" (dem er später widersprach). Aber "The Americans" ist nicht einfach eine Sammlung solcher Momente. Das Buch ist mehr als nur eine Reihe von Aufnahmen unter einem Titel – so eindrücklich, schön, und, ja, ikonisch eine jede von ihnen auch ist. "The Americans" ist ein narratives Werk. Es erzählt die Geschichte einer Reise, die Robert Frank – ein schweizerisch-jüdischer Immigrant, der kurz nach dem 2. Weltkrieg in New York, einer Stadt von Immigranten, ankam – unternahm, auf der Suche nach den richtigen Amerikanern. Wie allgemein bekannt ist, leben die richtigen Amerikaner nicht in New York, denn New York ist nicht wirklich ein Teil von Amerika. Überraschenderweise fand Frank, als er New York verließ, Leute, die auch nicht mehr daheim waren als er selbst. Die Gesichter in "The Americans" zeigen „Fremde in einem fremden Land" – irritiert, einsam, verzweifelt, zornig noch in einer Umarmung. Alt und jung, reich und arm, Schwarze und Weiße sind bei Frank in ihrer Isolation vereint.

Circling
Beginnings, Continuations, Renewals: Robert Frank's personal New American Cinema

Amy Taubin

"So we make the circle. You understand now, Robert."
"Make the circle? That's what we all do."

(From a conversation between Bobby McMillan and Robert Frank
in Frank's 2002 videotape *Paper Route*)

"October 1, 1960: Robert Frank came, in the morning. We gave him 4000 feet of outdated
film for leader. He was tired, angry, beaten down by work, lack of money, businessmen, and contracts.
'I'll never make a film like this again,' he said. Unshaven, black, tired, he was almost talking to himself."
(From the diaries of Jonas Mekas, published in limited edition through Anthology Film Archives, NY)

Even before Robert Frank made his first movie, *Pull My Daisy* (1959), he was already
thinking like a filmmaker. Frank's "The Americans" (1958), a book of 83 photographs shot during
various trips up and down, across and all around the United States between 1955 and 1957, is, above all
else, a road movie. In making the images, Frank was guided by the photographic imperative of "the decisive moment," (an imperative he later renounced); but "The Americans" is not simply a collection of
such moments. The book is more than the sum of the photographs within its covers—resonant, beautiful,
and, yes, iconic as each of them is. "The Americans" is a narrative work. It tells the story of a journey
that Robert Frank—a Swiss-Jewish immigrant who arrived in New York, a city of immigrants, just after
World War II—took, in search of real Americans. As everybody knows, real Americans do not reside in
New York because New York is not really part of America. What Frank found, perhaps to his surprise,
when he left New York, were people who were no more at home than he was. The faces in "The Americans" are those of "strangers in a strange land"—bewildered, lonely, despairing, angry, isolated even when
caught in an embrace. What unites the young and the old, the rich and the poor, the Black people and
the White people in Frank's photographs is their isolation.

"The Americans" is a deliberate, devastating attack on the air-brushed, happy-face image
of America in the Eisenhower era. The book is not a side-show—it is an encompassing vision. (The
title is not "The Other Americans" but "The Americans" plain and simple.) Derided by the cultural

"The Americans" ist eine bewusste, vernichtende Attacke auf das retuschierte Image des gutgelaunten Amerika der Eisenhower-Zeit. Das Buch spielt keineswegs an einem Nebenschauplatz, sondern enthält eine umfassende Vision. (Deswegen heißt es klar und deutlich "The Americans", und nicht The Other Americans.) Als es erschien, machte sich das kulturelle Establishment darüber lustig, aber es wurde eines der einflussreichsten Werke der Kunst des 20. Jahrhunderts, das Spuren hinterließ nicht nur in der Fotografie, sondern auch im Film. Das Auge von Robert Frank hat so unterschiedliche Filmemacher wie Jim Jarmusch, Wim Wenders, Gus Van Sant und Curtis Hanson geprägt.

Frank war nicht der erste Fotograf, der aus der Schnappschuss-Ästhetik (ausgefallene Kompositionen, Körnigkeit, gedämpfte graue Farbtöne) eine poetische, persönliche Vision entwickelte, aber er tat dies mit einer bis dahin unbekannten Wut. Der Zorn in "The Americans" richtet sich im großen und ganzen nicht gegen die Menschen in den Bildern, sondern gegen die Heuchelei, mit der sowohl die kommerzielle wie die künstlerische Fotografie sich weigerten, das Scheitern des amerikanischen Traums einzugestehen und sichtbar zu machen. Frank kannte diese Heuchelei aus erster Hand. Er verdiente sein Geld in der Modefotografie, und einige der wichtigsten Repräsentanten dieser Hochglanzwelt unterstützten seinen Antrag bei der Guggenheim Foundation um Förderung für "The Americans". Jeder von ihnen hätte zweifellos auch ein Vorwort zu "The Americans" beigesteuert; doch Frank fragte Jack Kerouac, dessen Roman "On the Road" die Beat-Ästhetik kulturell etablierte. Kerouacs kurzer Essay machte Geschichten aus den Fotografien, die durch Franks Auge verbunden waren. Der Blick des Fotografen wurde zum Äquivalent der Erzählstimme des Autors.

Nach der Vollendung von "The Americans" unternahm Frank zwei „proto-kinematische" Projekte. Er schuf eine Reihe von Fotografien von New York aus den Fenstern fahrender Busse – auf diese Weise setzte er sich über das Konzept der Stand-Fotografie hinweg. Und er arbeitete an einer Werbekampagne für die New York Times, bei der Bildsequenzen – manche davon aus einer 16-mm-Kamera – in einen gemeinsamen Bildrahmen collagiert wurden. Die Filmkamera war, wenn auch noch nicht so allgegegenwärtig wie zur Mitte der sechziger Jahre, bereits ein verführerisches Werkzeug geworden, nicht nur für Leute, die sich als Filmemacher verstanden. In den frühen fünfziger Jahren versuchten sich einige Fotografen mit Film: *In The Street* (1951) von Janet Loeb, James Agee und Helen Levitt sowie *Little Fugitive* (1953) von Morris Engel, Ruth Orkin und Ray Ashley sind Meilensteine der New Yorker Filmgeschichte. Auch Franks erster Film *Pull My Daisy* war eine Teamarbeit. In den Schlusscredits heisst es "adapted, photographed und directed by Robert Frank and Alfred Leslie, written by Jack Kerouac".

"The Americans" beruht auf der gebräuchlichen Form des Schnappschusses, und *Pull My Daisy* ist das Home Movie der Untergrundkunstszene. Der Originaltitel des Films (der einzige, der tatsächlich zu sehen ist) lautet "The Beat Generation". Aber schon bei der ersten Vorführung lief er unter dem sexuell beziehungsreichen Titel *Pull My Daisy*. Er basiert lose auf einem Stück von Kerouac. Ort der Handlung während der 28 Minuten des Films ist eine unordentliche, schmuddelige Loft in Downtown im Verlauf eines Tages. Hier wohnen der Eisenbahnarbeiter und Saxophonist Milo (gespielt von dem Maler Larry Rivers), seine Frau, eine Malerin (gespielt von Delphine Seyrig, der einzigen professionellen Schauspielerin in dem Film; sie war zu dieser Zeit mit dem amerikanischen Maler Jack Youngerman verheiratet), und ihr kleiner Sohn (gespielt von Pablo Frank, dem Sohn von Robert Frank und seiner ersten Frau, der Künstlerin Mary Frank). Sehr zum Ärger der Frau tauchen Milos Freunde in der Wohnung auf – drei Dichter (Allen Ginsberg, Peter Orlovsky, und Gregory Corso, die alle sich selbst spielen) und ein Musiker (gespielt von David Amram, der die Musik zum Film schrieb). Die Dichter

establishment when it first appeared, it became one of the most influential works of twentieth[th] century American art, affecting not only photography but film as well. Filmmakers as various as Jim Jarmusch, Wim Wenders, Gus Van Sant, and Curtis Hanson are indebted to the eye of Robert Frank.

Frank was not the first photographer to marry the snapshot aesthetic (off-kilter compositions, graininess, muted gray scale) with a poetic, personal vision, but he did so with a ferocity that had not been seen before. The anger in "The Americans" is directed, by and large, not at the people in the photographs, but at the hypocrisy of both commercial and art photography in refusing to expose the failure of the American dream. It was a hypocrisy Frank knew first-hand; he earned his living in the glossy fashion photography world, and some of its most celebrated figures sponsored his application to the Guggenheim Foundation for funding for "The Americans." Frank could have requested almost any one of them to write an introduction to the U.S. edition of the book. Instead, he asked Jack Kerouac, whose novel "On the Road" (1957) put the Beat aesthetic on the cultural map. Kerouac's short essay turned the photographs into stories, linked to one another by Frank's eye. The photographer's vision became the equivalent of the writer's narrating voice.

After completing "The Americans" Frank took on two "proto-cinematic" projects. He produced a series of images of New York, shot through the windows of moving buses—thus defying the concept of the still photograph. And he worked on an advertising campaign for the New York Times, which involved sequences of images—some of them shot with a 16mm film camera—collaged within a single frame. While not as ubiquitous as it would become by the mid-1960s, the movie camera was already a seductive tool, and not just for people who defined themselves as filmmakers. In the early 1950s, several still photographers made forays into film: Janet Loeb, James Agee, and Helen Levitt's *In the Street* (1951) and Morris Engel, Ruth Orkin and Ray Ashley's *Little Fugitive* (1953) are groundbreaking works in the history of New York movie-making. Frank's first film, *Pull My Daisy* (1959) was also a collaboration. The end credits on the film read "adapted, photographed, and directed by Robert Frank and Alfred Leslie, written by Jack Kerouac."

If "The Americans" is based in the vernacular form of the travel snapshot, *Pull My Daisy* is the underground art world's home movie. The film's original title (the only title that actually appears in the film) was "The Beat Generation", but by the time of its first public screening, it was going by the slyly sexual handle of *Pull My Daisy*. Loosely based on a play by Kerouac, the twenty-eight minute film is set in a cluttered, grubby downtown loft and takes place within a single, ordinary day. The loft is home to railroad worker and saxophonist Milo (played by painter Larry Rivers), his painter wife (played by Delphine Seyrig, the only professional actor in the film who was, at that time, married to American painter Jack Youngerman), and their young son (played by Pablo Frank, the son of Robert Frank and his first wife, the artist Mary Frank.). Much to the annoyance of the wife, the loft is invaded by Milo's friends—a trio of poets (Allen Ginsberg, Peter Orlovsky, and Gregory Corso, playing themselves) and a musician (played by David Amram, who wrote the score for film.) The poets poke fun at the wife's guests, "the Bishop" (a Bowery preacher, played by art dealer Richard Bellamy), his wife, and sister. The wife berates Milo for mistreating the Bishop. Milo shrugs her off and departs with his friends.

Although he never appears on the screen, the star of *Pull My Daisy* is Kerouac, who improvised the descriptive voice-over while watching a fine-cut of the picture. Since the film was shot without sound, it was left to Kerouac not only to explain what's happening but also to give voice to the words the actors are saying. His verbal riffs combined with Amram's jazzy score and the antics of

Pull My Daisy

machen sich über die Gäste der Ehefrau lustig – den „Bischof" (einen Prediger von der Bowery, gespielt von dem Kunsthändler Richard Bellamy), seine Frau und seine Schwester. Milo bekommt den Ärger seiner Ehefrau zu spüren, weil er den Bischof schlecht behandelt. Er kümmert sich nicht weiter darum und verlässt mit seinen Freunden das Haus.

Obwohl er selbst nie im Bild zu sehen ist, ist Jack Kerouac der eigentliche Star von *Pull My Daisy*. Er improvisierte die beschreibende Off-Erzählung, als er eine weitgehend fertiggestellte Schnittfassung sah. Da der Film ohne Ton gedreht worden war, musste Kerouac nicht nur die Geschehnisse erläutern, sondern auch den Schauspielern eine Stimme verleihen. Seine Wortkaskaden tragen, zusammen mit Amrams jazziger Musik und den Späßen von Ginsberg, Orlovsky und Corso, viel zu der übermütigen Spontaneität von *Pull My Daisy* bei. (Ginsberg berichtet, dass Frank sie in ihrem Geblödel ausdrücklich bestärkte.) Der abrupte, synkopierte Rhythmus der Montage trägt auch viel zu dem Eindruck bei, der Film wäre wie von selbst entstanden. Um ein Jahr nur nahm dieser Stil die Cinéma-Verité-Ästhetik von den Maysles-Brüdern, Ricky Leacock und D. A. Pennebaker vorweg. Tatsächlich aber drehte Frank mehrere Aufnahmen von jeder Einstellung (was bei einem Spielfilm ganz normal ist, aber strikt gegen die Regeln von Cinéma Verité) und hatte am Ende angeblich 30 Stunden Material. (Wie in seiner ganzen späteren Karriere arbeitet Frank mit einem professionellen Cutter zusammen – in diesem Fall Leon Prochnik.) Durch das schwarzweiße 35mm-Material hat *Pull My Daisy* eine körnige, dabei aber scharf konturierende Qualität, die den Fotografien in "The Americans" ähnelt. Mit der Ausnahme eines einzigen, unterbrochenen 360-Grad-Kreisschwenks über die Wohnung blieb Frank bei statischen Einstellungen und kurzen Kamerabewegungen. Auch wenn die Bilder wie „aus der Hüfte geschossen" wirken, blieb die Kamera doch durchgehend auf dem Stativ.

Pull My Daisy hatte 1959 Premiere in einer Vorstellung zusammen mit *Shadows*, dem ersten Spielfilm von John Cassavetes. Schauplatz war das Cinema 16, das in einer wöchentlichen Reihe alles zeigte, was nicht Mainstream war: osteuropäisches Kunstkino, medizinische Kurzfilme, Avantgardefilme von Leuten wie Stan Brakhage und Maya Deren. Die Zusammenstellung der beiden Filme provozierte eine polemische Auseinandersetzung auf den Seiten des Magazins Film Culture, das Jonas Mekas mitherausgab, in seiner vielgelesenen Kolumne in der Village Voice. Mekas feierte *Pull My Daisy*, er sah darin „einen Wendepunkt für das Kino, wie es "The Connection" für das Theater war". Jack Gelbers Stück "The Connection" war ein Jahr zuvor vom Living Theater produziert worden, und wurde 1961 von Shirley Clarke verfilmt. Es ging darin um ein paar Junkies, die in einer heruntergekommenen Wohnung herumhingen und auf ihren Dealer mit der täglichen Heroin-Ration warteten. *Pull My Daisy*

Ginsberg, Orlovsky, and Corso give *Pull My Daisy* its sense of spontaneity and high spirits. (Ginsberg reported that Frank encouraged them to horse-around.) The abrupt, syncopated rhythms of the editing also add to the sense that the film was caught on the fly—the editing style pre-figured, but only by a year, the cinema-verite editing approach of the Maysles brothers, Ricky Leacock, and D. A. Pennebaker. But, in fact, Frank shot multiple takes of each scene (a customary practice in fiction filmmaking but definitely against the rules of cinema verite) and is said to have accumulated as much as thirty hours of footage. (As he would continue to do throughout his career, Frank collaborated with a professional editor—here Leon Prochnik) Shot in 35mm black and white, *Pull My Daisy* has a grainy but etched look that resembles the photographs in "The Americans." Except for one slow, 360-degree broken pan around the loft, Frank employed a combination of static shots, small pans and tilts. And while the image gives the impression of having been "shot from the hip", the camera remained on its tripod throughout.

    Pull My Daisy premiered in 1959 on a double bill with John Cassavetes' first feature *Shadows*. The venue was Cinema 16, the weekly series that showcased all manner of non-mainstream film from Eastern European art flicks to medical shorts to avant-garde work from the likes of Stan Brakhage and Maya Deren. The juxtaposition of the two films generated a flurry of polemics in the pages of "Film Culture Magazine" which Jonas Mekas co-edited and in Mekas's influential column in the Village Voice. Mekas championed *Pull My Daisy*, deeming it "as much a signpost in cinema as 'The Connection' was in theater." Jack Gelber's play "The Connection," which had been produced by "The Living Theater" just a year before *Pull My Daisy* was shot and which would be made into a film by Shirley Clarke in 1961, involved a group of junkies hanging out in a crummy apartment waiting for their dealer to bring them their daily heroin supply. Similar in their anti-dramatic structure, their circumscription within a single space, and their drug-warped sense of time passing, *Pull My Daisy* and "The Connection" influenced a strain of American avant-garde filmmaking that includes most notably Jack Smith's *Flaming Creatures*, the early 1960s films of Ken Jacobs, and many Warhol films from the silent *Haircut* (1963) to *The Chelsea Girls* (1966).

    In 1960, Jonas Mekas and producer Lewis Allen invited two dozen filmmakers to the first meeting of the New American Cinema Group. Among the invitees were Frank, Leslie, Peter Bogdanovich, Emile De Antonio, Shirley Clarke, and Gregory Markopoulos. The group was not limited to filmmakers. It included a distributor, two actors, a lawyer, several producers—all of them passionately devoted to making films outside the commercial system. There were as yet no clear divisions between avant-garde, narrative, and documentary filmmakers. The heterogeneity of the group was reflected in the films they made during the early 1960s. And indeed, that heterogeneity has sparked Frank's moves from fictional narrative to documentary to home movie and around and around again for more than forty years. Often, he see-saws between genres within a single film. This restlessness distinguishes Frank from almost all his early film colleagues. (Clarke is another exception.) Even Jonas Mekas, whose work and life have striking parallels with Frank's, had, by 1965, settled into the diary form that would define all his future films.

    But in the early 1960s, the European art film still exerted a powerful hold on the imagi-nations of the emerging New American Cinema. Mekas's first film *Guns of the Trees* (1961), like *Shadows*, was a feature length slice-of-New-York-life that owes more to early Visconti than to *Pull My Daisy*. A fascinating failure, the film evidences both the near impossibility of making convincing narrative features with the meager financial resources American independents had at their disposal, and also

und "The Connection" haben eine antidramatische Struktur gemeinsam, die Beschränkung auf einen Ort der Handlung, und eine durch Drogenkonsum verzerrte Zeitwahrnehmung. Eine Reihe wichtiger amerikanischer Avantgardefilme entstand bald darauf unter diesem Eindruck, vor allem *Flaming Creatures* von Jack Smith, die Filme der frühen sechziger Jahre von Ken Jacobs, und viele Warhol-Filme von dem stummen *Haircut* (1963) bis *zu The Chelsea Girls* (1966).

1960 luden Jonas Mekas und der Produzent Lewis Allen zwei Dutzend Filmschaffende zum ersten Treffen der New American Cinema Group ein. Unter den Eingeladenen waren Frank, Leslie, Peter Bogdanovich, Emile De Antonio, Shirley Clarke und Gregory Markopoulos. Die Gruppe bestand nicht ausschließlich aus Filmemachern. Ein Verleiher, zwei Schauspieler, ein Anwalt und einige Produzenten waren dabei – allen ging es vor allem darum, Filme außerhalb des kommerziellen Systems zu machen. Es gab noch keine klaren Unterscheidungen zwischen Avantgarde-, Erzähl- und Dokumentarfilmemachern. Die Heterogenität der Gruppe spiegelt sich in den Filmen wider, die während der frühen sechziger Jahre entstanden. Frank ließ sich vierzig Jahre lang, in all seinen Übergängen vom fiktionalen Erzählfilm zum Dokumentarischen zum Home Movie und immer wieder rundherum, von dieser Heterogenität anstecken. Manchmal springt er in einem einzigen Film zwischen den Formen hin und her. Diese Rastlosigkeit unterscheidet Frank von allen seinen Kollegen aus dieser frühen Zeit. (Mit Ausnahme von Clarke.) Selbst Jonas Mekas, dessen Arbeit und Leben auffällige Parallelen zu Frank aufweist, hatte 1965 die Tagebuchform gefunden, die alle seine weiteren Filme bestimmen sollte.

In den frühen sechziger Jahren hatte der europäische Kunstfilm noch großen Einfluss auf das entstehende New American Cinema. *Guns of the Trees* (1961), der erste Film von Jonas Mekas, wie *Shadows* ein abendfüllender Ausschnitt aus dem Leben in New York, verdankt dem frühen Visconti mehr als *Pull My Daisy*. Der Film ist auf faszinierende Weise gescheitert, er zeigt sehr deutlich sowohl die finanziellen Probleme, vor denen die unabhängigen Filmemacher in ihrem Bemühen um überzeugende Erzählformen standen, als auch Mekas' nachlassendes Interesse an der Form des Spielfilms selbst. Sein zweiter Film *The Brig* (1964) ist die Aufzeichnung einer Produktion des Living Theater von Kenneth Browns Stück über den Alltag in einem Militärgefängnis. Mekas drehte mit einer 16mm-Handkamera mitten auf der Bühne, so als bewegte er sich durch eine alltägliche Situation. Der Film unterlief die Unterscheidung zwischen Dokument und Fiktion so gründlich, dass beim Festival in Venedig, wo er den Großen Dokumentarpreis gewann, viele Zuschauer das Militärgefängnis für echt hielten.

Praktisch vom Moment seiner Ankunft in New York im Jahr 1949 an hatte Mekas ein 16mm-Tagebuch geführt. Aber erst Mitte der sechziger Jahre begann er, diese kontinuierlichen Auf-

Pull My Daisy

Mekas's flagging commitment to the feature narrative form itself. Mekas's second film *The Brig* (1964) is a film recording of the Living Theater's production of Kenneth Brown's play about the daily experience of prisoners in an army stockade. Mekas shot the production with a hand held 16mm camera, moving amid the on-stage action as if he were responding to a real-life situation. The film confounded categories of fiction and documentary so thoroughly that many in the audience at the Venice Film Festival, where it won the documentary grand prize, believed that they were watching a film of an actual army prison.

Almost from the moment of his arrival in New York in 1949, Mekas had been keeping a 16mm diary. It was not until the mid-Sixties, however, that he began editing this on-going record of his life and the life of the fragile and fractious cultural community, in which he was a galvanizing force, into a series of films that includes at least two of the greatest works of the New American Cinema: *Walden: Diaries, Notebooks and Sketches* (1964-1969) and *Lost Lost Lost* (1975). Mekas's hand-held shooting style and his rapid-fire montage was clearly influenced by Stan Brakhage, but unlike Brakhage himself and the diaristic filmmakers also indebted to him (Bruce Baillie, Warren Sonbert, Andrew Noren), Mekas gave equal weight to both picture and sound. If *Pull My Daisy* was a "signpost" for Mekas's own filmmaking, it was because he learned at least two things from it. One was the necessity of recording—from an insider's position—an incredibly rich and passionate moment in cultural history. The other was that voice-over narration could do something more than provide information. It could be an expressive element, shaping the rhythm and emotional tone of a film. When Frank's films became more directly diaristic, beginning with *Conversations in Vermont* (1969), he also came to rely on his own voice as an expressive instrument. There is something plaintive in the voices of both filmmakers, suggesting feelings of loss too deep to be assuaged by the images on the screen. And although Mekas and Frank have both lived in New York for over a half century, their speech remains heavily accented with the sounds of their first languages (Mekas's was Lithuanian, Frank's was German.) The accents mark them as permanent outsiders to the culture they've memorialized in their art.

Frank followed *Pull My Daisy* with two short fiction films. *The Sin of Jesus* (1961) is a bleak, heavy-handed allegory somewhat influenced by Bergman and only slightly redeemed by its stark black-and-white cinematography. In *OK End Here* (1963), a photographer and his girlfriend realize that their relationship is quietly falling apart. Filled with Antonioni-like silences, the film suffers from the inability of the actors who play the couple to convince us that they've known each other for more than five minutes. The failure lies as much with Frank's direction as with the actors themselves.

The associative, fragmented, multi-layered *Me and My Brother* (1968) reunites Frank with beat poets Allen Ginsberg and Peter Orlovsky. The film is a portrait of Peter's catatonic-schizophrenic brother Julius, and it's also a film about the problem of "portraying" Julius, who is the ultimate non-actor, in a film. "He has to be told each thing to do, otherwise he just stands there and looks at his mattress," says Peter, at one point. And that's on a good day. Frank tries various strategies. Indeed, he seems to have made up the film as he went along, using whatever stock—black-and-white or color—he could get his hands on and developing scenes—some improvised, some scripted in advance—in response to the stubborn object that was Julius.

Me and My Brother was four years in the making. Frank films Julius at home with Allen and Peter. We learn from a psychiatrist's report that Julius had his first psychotic break while working for the Sanitation Department, so Frank takes Julius to a garbage depot, and films him shoveling refuse. Allen and Peter go on a poetry reading tour. They take Julius on the road with them and Frank tags along

zeichnungen aus seinem Leben und dem des fragilen und streitlustigen kulturellen Milieus, in dem er eine bestimmende Kraft war, zu Filmen zu montieren, von denen zwei unbestritten zu den größten Werken des New American Cinema gehören: *Walden: Diaries, Notebooks and Sketches* (1964) und *Lost Lost Lost* (1975). Der Gebrauch der Handkamera und die frenetische Montage waren deutlich von Stan Brakhage beeinflusst, aber anders als Brakhage und die ebenfalls von ihm beeinflussten Filmchronisten (Bruce Baillie, Warren Sonbert, Andrew Noren) achtete Mekas auf ein Gleichgewicht zwischen Bild und Ton. *Pull My Daisy* war ein „Wendepunkt" für Mekas' eigenes Filmemachen, weil er zwei Dinge daraus lernte: Erstens war es unumgänglich, einen (aus der Perspektive des Insiders) unerhört reichen und intensiven Augenblick der kulturellen Geschichte zu überliefern. Zweitens aber begriff er, daß eine Off-Stimme mehr als nur Information geben kann. Sie konnte selbst ein Ausdrucksmittel sein, bestimmend für den Rhythmus und die Emotionalität eines Films. Als Franks Filme tagebuchartiger wurden, mit *Conversations in Vermont* (1969), begriff auch er seine Stimme als expressives Instrument. Es klingt eine Trauer in den Stimmen beider Filmemacher an, eine Ahnung von Verlustgefühlen, die durch kein Bild auf der Leinwand gelindert werden können. Und obwohl sowohl Mekas wie Frank mehr als ein halbes Jahrhundert in New York gelebt haben, trägt ihre Rede immer noch deutlich den Akzent ihrer ersten Sprache (Litauisch bei Mekas, Deutsch bei Frank). Sie sind dadurch als Aussenseiter ausgewiesen in einer Kultur, zu deren Gedächtnis sie so viel beitragen.

Frank ließ auf *Pull My Daisy* zwei kurze Spielfilme folgen. *The Sin of Jesus* (1961) ist eine düstere, schwerfällige Allegorie, die auf Einflüsse durch Ingmar Bergman schließen läßt und höchstens durch die kühle Schwarzweiß-Fotografie ein wenig gewinnt. In *OK End Here* (1963) begreifen ein Fotograf und seine Freundin, dass ihre Beziehung zu Ende geht. Es wird viel geschwiegen wie bei Antonioni, aber die beiden Schauspieler vermögen niemals den Eindruck zu erwecken, daß sie einander länger als fünf Minuten kannten. Das Problem des Films ist ebenso eines der Regie von Frank wie eines der Schauspieler.

Bei dem assoziativen, zersplitterten, vielschichtigen *Me and My Brother* (1968) arbeitete Frank wieder mit den Beat-Poeten Allen Ginsberg und Peter Orlovsky. Der Film ist das Porträt von Peters katatonisch-schizophrenem Bruder Julius, zugleich geht es um die Problematik der Darstellung des ultimativen Nicht-Schauspielers Julius in einem Film. „Man muss ihm jede Kleinigkeit ansagen, sonst steht er nur herum und starrt auf seine Matratze", sagt Peter an einer Stelle. Und das ist noch ein guter Tag. Frank probiert verschiedene Strategien aus. Es sieht aus, als hätte er den Film während des Drehens entworfen, unter Verwendung verschiedensten Materials (schwarzweiß und farbig), dessen er habhaft wurde, in immer neuen szenischen Anläufen, improvisierten und vorab geschriebenen, auf das widerspenstige Objekt Julius.

Es dauerte vier Jahre, *Me and My Brother* fertigzustellen. Frank filmt Julius daheim mit Allen und Peter. Aus dem Bericht eines Psychiaters erfahren wir, dass Julius seinen ersten psychotischen Schub hatte, als er für das Gesundheitsamt arbeitete. Also bringt Frank Julius zu einer Müllabladestätte und filmt ihn dabei, wie er Abfälle schaufelt. Allen und Peter gehen auf eine Lesetournee. Sie nehmen Julius mit, und Frank läuft mit seiner Kamera hinterher. Auf dieser Tour geht Julius für viele Wochen verloren, weswegen Frank einen Schauspieler an seiner Stelle anheuert. (Wie so viele Anekdoten im Zusammenhang mit dem Film ist auch diese, wenn nicht wahr, so zumindest gut erfunden.) Der Schauspieler ist Joe Chaikin, zu diesem Zeitpunkt der Leiter des Open Theater, einer experimentellen Truppe. Frank wandte sich auch an den Dramatiker Sam Shephard, der häufig mit Chaikin arbeitete, und bat

with his camera. It's on this tour that that Julius goes missing for many weeks, forcing Frank to bring in a professional actor to take his place. (Like everything in the film, this anecdote may be fact or fiction or one superimposed on the other.) The actor is Joe Chaikin, then the leader of the Open Theater, an experimental theater troupe. Frank also turned to playwright Sam Shephard, who often worked with Chaikin, to script some scenes for the film. In the end, the actors, many of them Open Theater members, outnumbered the non-actors (people who were playing themselves, rather than characters). Frank also recruited two young Broadway actors, Christopher Walken and Roscoe Lee Browne, to alternate in the role of the director. Often when we see them speaking, it's Frank's voice that we hear.

Frank doesn't ask Chaikin to create the illusion that he is Julius. Rather, he films the actor's process of engaging with Julius as a character. *Me and My Brother* is a film about performance—not only the performance of an actor for the camera, but also the performance of the filmmaker shooting a movie. More broadly, it's about life as a performative act. All of Frank's work grapples with the connection between inside and outside—between feeling, thought, and perception (interiority), and expression. How do they come together in taking a photograph, putting paint on canvas, making a film. In an open letter published in 1969 in "Creative Camera", Frank wrote: "In 1958, right after finishing 'The Americans' I made my first film. I knew film was first choice. Nothing comes easy, but I love difficulties and difficulties love me. Since being a filmmaker I have become more of a person. I am confident that I can synchronize my thoughts to the image and that the image will talk back to me. It's like being among friends."

But for Julius, interior and exterior do not come together. The connection between emotion and expression, thought and action, is blocked or severed. We don't know what, or even if, Julius thinks, feels, perceives, because most of the time he's silent and immobile. Amazingly, however, when Julius returns to the film at the end, he can speak. (It seems that when he wandered away, he ended up in a psychiatric institution where he was given shock treatment.) Julius delivers a rather devastating critique of the film, which suggests he knew all along what Frank was up to with his camera. "The camera seems like a reflection of disapproval or disgust or disappointment or unhelpfulness, inexplainability to disclose any real truth that might possibly exist," says Julius, nailing the two-way relationship of projection and introjection and of filmmaker and subject.

A more pleasurable, rewarding, and generous depiction of performing artists at work and play, *Cocksucker Blues* (1972) is a documentary of the Rolling Stones on tour in North America. Mick Jagger refused to allow the film to be released because of the possible legal repercussions from the depiction of behind-the-scenes sex and drug-taking, but he has allowed limited museum and benefit screenings. (It's hard to believe that Frank and Jagger didn't know what they were getting into from the start—that Frank would be incapable of censoring his own eye and that Jagger would never allow what Frank recorded to be available for public consumption.) In the U.S., the film is available on VHS bootlegs, where the degraded image and sound quality have little effect on its power as a road movie (among the more extraordinary scenes is one where Jagger and Richards wander into a Black juke joint somewhere. in the Deep South and the locals gradually realize who they are) and as a performance documentary. Other Rolling Stones documentaries have on-stage sequences as exhilarating as those in *Cocksucker Blues*. What Frank captures that no one else has is the moment in the underground passageway that leads to the stage, when, in response to the distant roar of the crowd, Jagger's energy shifts and he transforms himself from the disciplined professional musician we've seen in his dressing room into a superhuman.

Me and My Brother

ihn um ein paar Szenen für den Film. Am Ende waren zahlreiche Schauspieler beteiligt, viele aus dem Open Theater, und die Laien (Leute, die sich selbst und keine Figuren spielten) gerieten in die Minderheit. Frank bezog auch zwei junge Broadway-Schauspieler ein, Christopher Walken und Roscoe Lee Browne, die einander in der Rolle des Regisseurs abwechselten. Häufig ist es Franks Stimme, die wir hören, wenn wir sie sprechen sehen.

Frank verlangte von Chaikin nicht den Anschein, er wäre Julius. Er filmt den Prozess des Schauspielers in der Aneignung dieser Figur. *Me and My Brother* ist ein Film über Rollen – nicht nur die Darstellung des Schauspielers vor der Kamera, sondern auch die Rolle des Filmemachers während der Dreharbeiten. Allgemeiner gesagt, geht es um das Leben als einen darstellerischen Akt. Die ganze Arbeit von Frank dreht sich um die Verbindung zwischen Innen und Außen – zwischen Gefühl, Gedanke, Wahrnehmung (Innerlichkeit) und Ausdruck. Wie verbinden sie sich während des Fotografierens, des Malens auf einer Leinwand, des Filmemachens? In einem offenen Brief, den er 1969 in Creative Camera veröffentlichte, schrieb Frank: „1958, gleich nach der Fertigstellung von "The Americans", machte ich meinen ersten Film. Das war ganz selbstverständlich. Nichts kommt von selbst, aber ich liebe Schwierigkeiten, und die Schwierigkeiten lieben mich. Seit ich Filmemacher bin, bin ich eine stärkere Persönlichkeit. Ich habe das Vertrauen, dass meine Gedanken synchron zum Bild sind, und dass das Bild zu mir zurückspricht. Es ist, als wäre man unter Freunden."

Für Julius aber kommen Innen und Außen nicht zusammen. Die Verbindung zwischen Gefühl und Ausdruck, Gedanke und Tat ist blockiert oder gestört. Wir wissen nicht, was (und ob überhaupt) Julius denkt, fühlt, wahrnimmt, denn die meisten Zeit ist er still und bewegungslos. Als er jedoch am Ende in den Film zurückkehrt, kann er überraschenderweise sprechen. (Anscheinend war er während seiner Abwesenheit in einer psychiatrischen Institution, wo er eine Schockbehandlung erfuhr.) Julius gibt eine ziemlich vernichtende Kritik des Films, die vermuten lässt, daß er Franks Absichten die ganze Zeit durchschaut hatte. „In der Kamera spiegelt sich Missbilligung oder Abscheu oder unterlassene Hilfe, die ganze Unerklärlichkeit in der Enthüllung einer wirklichen Wahrheit, die vielleicht existiert", sagt Julius, mit Blick auf die zweifache Relation zwischen Projektion und Introspektion, zwischen Filmemacher und Subjekt.

Cocksucker Blues (1972) ist ein vergnüglicheres, lohnenderes und großzügigeres Porträt von Künstlern bei der Arbeit und beim Spiel. Er dokumentiert eine Tour der Rolling Stones durch Nordamerika. Mick Jagger untersagte die Veröffentlichung des Films, weil er juristische Probleme aufgrund von Szenen mit Sex und Drogenkonsum hinter den Kulissen fürchtete. Gelegentliche Vorführungen in

Conversations in Vermont

Conversations in Vermont (1969) was Frank's first openly autobiographical film, a form that has subsequently dominated his work for over thirty years. Its subject is his relationship with his then teenage children, Pablo and Andrea. Andrea died in a plane crash in 1974 at age 20. After many years of mental and physical illnesses, Pablo committed suicide in 1995. It's impossible not to attribute the change in Frank's work during the 1970s to the tragedy of Andrea's death and Pablo's deterioration. In addition to making films, he returned to the more immediate medium of photography. Rather than single image photographs, however, he produced multiple-panel pieces and collages that combined images and words. During the 1970s, the photographic object became the sign of postmodernism, all but displacing painting and sculpture. Unlike most of this work, which was basically conceptualist, Frank's pieces were flagrantly emotional—a direct translation of personal anguish into object. They were even more raw than the writing of the Beats, mediated as it was by the ethos of "cool." One has the sense, looking at these pieces, not merely that feeling has taken precedence over form, but that it would have been some kind of obscene cover-up to bring form into the picture at all.

And perhaps, the photographic pieces are also an attack on the so-called "structuralists" who dominated avant-garde film from the mid-1960s to the late 1970s, specifically on the work of Michael Snow and Hollis Frampton. Like Frank, Frampton was a photographer before he turned to film while Snow has become as celebrated for his photographic pieces as for his films. In this context, "Mute/Blind" (1989) can be read as an angry response to Snow's piece "Venetian Blind" or to a number of other pieces where Snow arranges photographs as a grid and employs the loaded word "blind" as part of a punning title. "Venetian Blind" is made up of a series of black-and-white poloroids that Snow took of his own face with the cityscape of Venice in the background. The images were taken blind, in the sense that Snow held the camera at arms-length in front of him and clicked the shutter without looking through the viewfinder. Their arrangement in vertical and horizontal columns suggests the slats of that shutter-like household object—the venetian blind. Frank's "Mute/Blind", on the other hand, is a grid-like arrangement of photographs of a small blind dog surrounding photographs of the statue of a male deer. The photographs of the deer statue have been treated with dye so that the deer's eyes look as if they're gouged out and streaming blood. The photos are messily tacked to a piece of creased, crimson fabric. They effect is as if Frank were muttering between clenched teeth, "You want blind? I'll give you blind."

In the 1990s, Frank replaced the cumbersome 16mm film camera with a lighter, more flexible video camera. With it, he has produced pieces that have a grace and spontaneity absent from his moving picture works since *Pull My Daisy*. *The Present* (1996) and *Paper Route* (2002) are among

Kinematheken oder zu wohltätigen Zwecken sind allerdings gestattet. (Es ist schwer vorstellbar, dass Frank und Jagger nicht wussten, worauf sie sich mit diesem Filmprojekt einließen – dass Frank unmöglich sein eigenes Auge zensieren konnte, und dass Jagger diese Aufnahmen niemals an die Öffentlichkeit gelangen lassen würde.) In den USA ist *Cocksucker Blues* als VHS-Bootleg erhältlich, mit schlechtem Bild und Ton, die weder seine Qualitäten als Road-movie trüben (zu den besten Szenen gehört eine, in der Jagger und Richards in eine schwarze Kaschemme irgendwo im tiefen Süden eintreten, und die Leute allmählich mitbekommen, um wen es sich da handelt) noch die der Konzertszenen. Es gibt andere Rolling-Stones-Filme, die ähnlich aufregende Eindrücke von den Bühnenshows geben. Frank aber erfasst als Einziger den Moment auf dem Weg zur Bühne, in dem Jagger die noch unsichtbare Menge zum ersten Mal hört, sein Energiezustand sich verändert und er sich aus dem disziplinierten, professionellen Musiker, den wir eben noch in der Garderobe gesehen haben, in einen Übermenschen verwandelt.

Conversations in Vermont (1969) war Franks erster offen autobiografischer Film. In den vergangenen dreißig Jahren hat diese Form sein Werk dominiert. Es geht um die Beziehung zu seinen Kindern Pablo und Andrea. Andrea starb 1974 im Alter von 20 Jahren bei einem Flugzeugunglück. Pablo beging 1995, nach vielen Jahren mit psychischen und körperlichen Krankheiten, Selbstmord. Es ist unmöglich, die Veränderungen in Franks Arbeit während der siebziger Jahre nicht mit Andreas Tod und Pablos Verfall in Zusammenhang zu bringen. Neben dem Filmemachen kehrte er zu der größeren Unmittelbarkeit des Mediums Fotografie zurück. Anstatt einzelner Bilder produzierte er jedoch Tafeln und Collagen, in denen Bilder und Worte kombiniert waren. Während der siebziger Jahre wurde das fotografische Objekt die Signatur der Postmoderne, in Ablösung von Malerei und Skulptur. Im Unterschied zu vielen, hauptsächlich konzeptuellen Arbeiten dieser Zeit waren Franks Werke immer ungeniert emotional – eine direkte Übersetzung der persönlichen Wut in Objekte. Sie waren noch roher als die Dichtung der Beats, die immerhin durch das Ethos von „cool" bestimmt war. Man hat beim Anblick dieser Werke den Eindruck, dass Gefühl vollständig über die Form gesiegt hat, ja mehr noch, dass es eine obszöne Ablenkung wäre, das Bild mit Form zu belasten.

Und vielleicht sind diese fotografischen Arbeiten ja auch eine Attacke gegen die sogenannten „Strukturalisten", die den avantgardistischen Film von Mitte der sechziger bis in die späten siebziger Jahre dominierten, insbesondere gegen Michael Snow und Hollis Frampton. Wie Frank war Frampton auch Fotograf, bevor er sich dem Film zuwandte, während Snow sowohl für seine fotografischen wie für seine filmischen Arbeiten gefeiert wird. In diesem Zusammenhang kann "Mute/Blind" (1989) als ungehaltene Reaktion auf Snows Arbeit "Venetian Blind" oder eine Reihe weiterer Werke, in denen Snow Fotografien nach einem Muster ordnet und das bedeutungsschwere Wort „blind" im Titel verwendet. "Venetian Blind" besteht aus einer Reihe von Polaroids, die Snow von sich selbst gemacht hat. Im Hintergrund ist immer die Stadt Venedig zu sehen. Die Bilder entstanden „blind", insofern Snow die Kamera im Arm hielt, sie auf sich selbst richtete und den Verschluss öffnete, ohne durch den Sucher zu blicken. In vertikalen und horizontalen Reihen angeordnet, ergeben diese Bilder eine Analogie zu den Leisten in dem Fensterladen-Verschluss auf so vielen venezianischen Gebäuden. Franks "Mute/Blind" hingegen arrangiert Fotos von einem blinden Hund rund um Fotos von der Statue eines Hirschs. Diese Aufnahmen sind mit Farbe nachbehandelt, sodaß der Hirsch aussieht, als hätte man ihm die Augen ausgestochen, und Blut rinne aus den Augen. Die Fotografien sind nachlässig zu einer rissigen, rötlichen Struktur zusammengeheftet. Es ist, als würde Frank zwischen zusammengepressten Zähnen hervorstoßen: „Ich werde euch zeigen, was blind heisst."

the most beautiful and elegantly shaped works Frank has made in any medium. Both are diaristic pieces that begin with Frank wondering what story he's going to tell. The search for a story becomes a kind of running gag throughout the twenty-three minutes of *The Present*. The piece is extremely fragmented. Hop-scotching between his New York loft, his house in Mabou, Nova Scotia, and various European cities, Frank encounters old friends and neighbors, contemplates his messy workspaces, and talks to himself, the birds, the deer, his wife, June Leaf, and whomever else crosses in front of the lens. Movie-making becomes a conversational act. The artist is part of the world he records. The effect is very different from Mekas's voice-overs, which are responses to recorded images (memories) rather than to real life. Which may be why the video is titled *The Present*.

   Paper Route is similarly conversational, but its subject is a single person, performing a single activity within a circumscribed space. Frank rides with a middle-aged man, Bobby McMillan, as he delivers the morning newspaper to subscribers in and around Mabou. As they drive through the wild, bleak, North Atlantic landscape, night slowly changes to day, and Mr. McMillan offers thumbnail sketches of the people on his route (some of whom we glimpse as they come to out to fetch their papers). The piece is filled with aleatory moments that John Cage might envy. Even before Mr. McMillan describes how he "makes the circle" in getting from one house to another, we might realize that the phrase *Paper Route* could be a metaphor for Frank's life and the trail of photographs and movies and writing he has left behind him and which also leads him into the future.

   The circle, as metaphor and image, reoccurs throughout Frank's work. When Mr. MacMillan talks about "making the circle" his reference is geographic. When Frank responds, "Make the circle? That's what we all do," he has something more metaphysical in mind. For a moment, the shadow of death falls across this seemingly casual and good-humored little piece. But the reference can also be read purely in terms of Frank's films, circling us back to *Pull My Daisy* which opens with an incomplete pan around the empty loft then cuts to an overhead shot of the round table in the middle of the floor. And although *Pull My Daisy* does its best to dispense with narrative, its climactic sequence is a 360-degree pan, which reveals, as if by accident, a violent quarrel erupting between the husband and the wife—the domestic drama the film has tried to suppress. After Milo shrugs off his angry wife, and he and his friends go out the door into the night, the camera lingers for a second or two on the circular ornament on the stairway balustrade. It's the last image before the final fade to black.

Paper Route

In den neunziger Jahren ersetzte Frank die beschwerliche 16mm-Kamera durch eine leichtere, flexiblere Videokamera. Er hat damit Arbeiten produziert, deren Anmut und Spontaneität er seit *Pull My Daisy* nicht mehr erreicht hatte. *The Present* (1996) und *Paper Route* (2002) gehören zu den schönsten und elegantesten Werken, die Frank überhaupt geschaffen hat, in allen Medien. Beide sind in Tagebuchform gehalten und beginnen damit, dass Frank sich Gedanken über eine mögliche Geschichte macht. Die Suche danach ist eine Art Running Gag während der 23 Minuten von *The Present*, das sehr stark fragmentiert ist. Wie ein verspieltes Kind springt er zwischen seinem Loft in New York, dem Haus in Mabou, Nova Scotia, und verschiedenen europäischen Städten hin und her. Frank begegnet alten Freunden und Nachbarn, betrachtet seine unaufgeräumten Arbeitsstätten, und spricht mit sich selbst, den Vögeln, dem Wild, seiner Frau June Leaf, und wer ihm sonst noch vor das Objektiv kommt. Der Unterschied zu der Erzählerstimme von Jonas Mekas, der auf die Bilder als Aufzeichnungen (Erinnerungen) antwortet, ist deutlich. Deswegen vielleicht trägt das Video auch den Titel *The Present*.

Paper Route ist ähnlich kommunikativ, aber es geht um eine einzelne Person, um eine einzelne Aktivität in einem fest umrissenen Raum. Frank begleitet einen Mann in mittleren Jahren, Bobby McMillan, der in und um Mabou die Morgenzeitung zustellt. Während der Fahrt durch die wilde, kalte nordatlantische Landschaft wird es allmählich hell, und Mr. McMillan gibt kurze Charakterisierungen der Menschen auf seiner Route (manche sind auch einen Moment zu sehen, wenn sie aus dem Haus kommen, um die Zeitung an sich zu nehmen). Das Video hat zahlreiche aleatorische Momente, wie John Cage sie geliebt hätte. Auch wenn Mr. McMillan beschreibt, wie er „die Runde macht" von einem Haus zum nächsten, liegt es nahe, den Titel *Paper Route* als eine Metapher für Franks Leben zu begreifen, für diese Spur aus Fotografien und Filmen und schriftlichen Äußerungen, die er gezogen hat und von der er sich nun in die Zukunft leiten lässt.

Der Kreis, als Metapher und als Bild, erscheint in Franks Werk immer wieder. Mr. McMillan versteht den Kreis geografisch als „die Runde". Wenn Frank antwortet: „Die Runde machen? Genau das machen wir alle", dann klingt das deutlich metaphysischer. Der Schatten des Todes fällt für einen Moment auf diese entspannte und heitere Arbeit. Der Kreis kann sich aber auch im engeren Sinn auf Franks Filme beziehen. Er lässt sich schließen mit Blick auf *Pull My Daisy*, den Frank mit einem unvollständigen Schwenk durch die Loft eröffnete, und dann auf ein Bild des runden Tisches in der Mitte schnitt. Obwohl *Pull My Daisy* die Narration so weit wie möglich suspendiert, gibt es einen Höhepunkt in Form eines 360-Grad-Schwenks, der wie zufällig einen wütenden Streit zwischen dem Mann und der Frau preisgibt – das private Drama, das der Film verdrängen wollte. Nachdem Milo seiner Frau die kalte Schulter zeigt, und mit seinen Freunden in die kalte Nacht hinausgeht, hält die Kamera kurz vor einem Rundornament auf dem Stiegengeländer inne. Es ist das letzte Bild, bevor der Film im Schwarz endet.

Geisterbeschwörungen
Das Drama der Stimme in den Filmen von Robert Frank

Bert Rebhandl

"Deus ex machina", sind die ersten Worte der Frau in Robert Franks Kurzfilm *OK End Here.* "What does that mean?" Es ist eine Äußerung, die noch dem Assoziationsmaterial des Traums zugehört. Sie bedarf der Übersetzung aus einer Fremdsprache. Es ist aber auch ein analytischer Begriff aus einem bestimmten Kontext – dem des Theaters –, der durch die Umstände dieser Morgenszene vielfache, sexuelle und andere Bedeutungsmöglichkeiten annimmt. Neben der Frau liegt ihr Freund, der Film handelt von dem Tagesbeginn eines Liebespaars, das die Nacht miteinander verbracht hat. Die Gespräche des Vormittags werden dem Schweigen abgerungen. Der Mann widmet sich den alltäglichen Dingen, das Gerede aus dem Fernsehgerät scheint ihn zu entlasten. Die Frau hängt noch immer ihrem Traum nach: "At home my dreams are different."

Reden wäre ein Beweis der Liebe, den der Mann nicht erbringen kann. "Do I bore you?", fragt die Frau. Erst das Eintreten eines befreundeten Paars beendet diese schwierige Situation. Der Besuch in einem Restaurant führt in die Polyphonie der Außenwelt, der die entropische Schweigsamkeit in dem New Yorker Appartement entgegengesetzt ist. Eine ältere Frau liest inmitten des Stimmengewirrs des Lokals einen Brief vor, verzweifelt aber am Desinteresse der Nachbarn. "I told you, she's a bore", äußert jemand über sie, als sie schon gegangen ist. Das Urteil wird aus demselben Off gesprochen, in das die Frau flüchtet. Ist das nicht genau die Funktion eines "Deus ex machina" – aus dem Off eine Szene entscheidend zu verändern?

Robert Frank war zuerst Fotograf, dann wurde er Filmemacher. Standbilder sind stumm und unveränderlich, Filme aber können über Ton und Zeitlichkeit verfügen. Jack Kerouac schrieb im Vorwort zu dem Fotoband "The Americans", Frank habe darin „mit der seltsamen Verschwiegenheit eines Verfolgers" gearbeitet. Auch die Ansicht der Fotografien stiftet einen Schweigepakt, der erst in der Begegnung mit Literatur und Film, vor allem aber: mit Sprache gelöst wird. Der Referent im Foto, also dessen Gegenstand, sei ein Gespenst, schreibt Roland Barthes in „Die helle Kammer". Die Fotografie sei „ohne Zukunft (darin liegt ihr Pathos, ihre Melancholie); sie besitzt nicht den geringsten Drang nach vorn, indes der Film weiterstrebt und somit nichts Melancholisches hat (was aber ist er letztendlich? – Nun, er ist ganz einfach ‚normal', wie das Leben auch.)"[1]

Exorcisms
The Drama of the Voice in Robert Frank's Films

Bert Rebhandl

In Robert Frank's short film *OK End Here* the woman's first words are: "Deus ex machina. What does that mean?" The comment still belongs to the associations from a dream. It requires translation from a foreign language. But it is also an analytical term from a specific context—the theater—which takes on multiple, sexual, and other possible meanings through the circumstances of this morning scene. The woman's boyfriend is lying next to her; the film deals with the start of the day for two lovers who have spent the night together. Their morning conversation is wrested from silence. The man devotes himself to everyday things; the chatter from the television set seems to offer him some relief. The woman still dwells on her dreams: "At home my dreams are different."

Talking would be proof of love, which the man is not able to produce. "Do I bore you?" asks the woman. It is the arrival of a befriended couple that first ends this difficult situation. The visit to a restaurant leads into the outer world's polyphony, which opposes the entropic silence of the New York apartment. In the midst of the maze of voices in the bar an older woman reads a letter out loud, but despairs at the disinterest of her neighbors. "I told you, she's a bore," someone says about her after she has already left. The verdict is spoken from the same off to which the woman escapes. Is that not precisely the function of a "deus ex machina"—to decisively influence a scene from off stage?

Robert Frank was first a photographer and then later became a filmmaker. Still images are silent and unchanging; films, however, can have sound and chronology. In the foreword to the photo volume "The Americans" Jack Kerouac wrote that in it, Frank works "with the strange silence of someone who is following something." Also the photographs' perspective establishes a pact of silence that is first resolved in the encounter with literature and film, and above all with language. In "Camera Lucida" Roland Barthes wrote that the reference point in the photo, its object, is a ghost. Photography is "without future (and its pathos, its melancholy can be found in that); it does not contain the slightest urge for continuation, whereas film pushes onward and thus has nothing melancholic (but in the end, what is it?—Well, it is quite simply 'normal,' like life itself)."[1]

Through photography, Barthes misunderstood cinema, because he preferred to remain a visionary. But Robert Frank first really understood his photography through cinema, because he could

Barthes missverstand das Kino durch die Fotografie, weil er lieber ein Geisterseher bleiben wollte. Robert Frank aber begriff seine Fotografie erst durch das Kino richtig, weil er sie darin zu einem Teil eines größeren Diskurses machen konnte. Er konnte die Fotografien im Film besprechen. Er konnte die Einsamkeit des Betrachters überwinden. Dazu bedurfte es aber eines Umwegs über den Stummfilm. In *Pull My Daisy* passt das „Weiterstreben" des Lebens mit der Melancholie der Bilder nicht recht zusammen, weil es nur durch die Sprache vermittelt ist. Die Stimme von Jack Kerouac in *Pull My Daisy* entspricht einem "Deus ex machina", der es sich nicht verkneifen kann, mit einem kleinen Schöpfungsakt zu beginnen: "Early morning in the universe", lautet der erste Satz. Michel Chion spricht vom „akusmatischen Wesen", das der Tonfilm nicht erfunden hat, „denn der große ursprüngliche AKUSMATIKER ist Jehova". All das kommt mit Kerouacs Stimme ins Spiel. Er agiert wie ein Stumm-filmerzähler, dem die langsamen Schwenks durch das Loft in der New Yorker Bowery ein wenig zu geduldig sind. Er provoziert durch die Kaskaden seiner Worte den Slapstickmoment über den Dichter Apollinaire, der am Grab Balzacs hinfällt; er beschwört durch die insistierende Frage "Is everything holy?" eine Qualität des visuellen Materials, die weit über den Zufall (die Kontingenz, schreibt Barthes) des Moments hinaus will. Der Text ist primär, das Sichtbare wird durch ihn definiert. In einem langen Sprachspiel über das Wort "cockroach" bringt Kerouac buchstäblich das Unsichtbare zum Vorschein, weil Frank nicht viel mehr tun kann, als über die Wände und Möbel zu schwenken, hinter denen sich die Kakerlaken verbergen. Die Stimme bekommt hier eine geisterbeschwörende Funktion, die Bilder aber werden Objekte der Melancholie, je weiter sich der historische Moment entfernt und die Personen der Handlung selbst zu Phantomen werden. (Schon hier tritt Pablo auf, der Sohn von Robert Frank, um dessen An- und Abwesenheit es später immer wieder gehen wird.)

Das filmische Werk von Robert Frank enthält in Summe tatsächlich so etwas wie ein akusmatisches Drama: Am Beginn von *Pull My Daisy* steht ein starkes Wort über den Bildern, in den späten Videos ist die Stimme zwar immer noch allgegenwärtig, aber nur noch Teil einer melancho-lischen Registratur, nahe an der brüchigen "ecstasy" von Jonas Mekas. Dem Ausdrucksoptimismus der Beat-Bewegung, ihr Verständnis des Körpers als eines Schallraums, der Literatur mehr oder minder natürlich freigibt ("bursting with poetry", sagt Kerouac), setzt Frank eine wesentlich komplexere Auseinandersetzung mit den Zusammenhängen von Leib und Sprache, Subjektivität und Kommuni-kation entgegen. Die Szene von einer berühmten Lesung der Beats Allen Ginsberg und Peter Orlovsky in *Me and My Brother* ist unvergesslich. Im Bühnenhintergrund sitzt Julius Orlovsky, und starrt vor sich

Pull My Daisy

integrate photography into a larger discourse within it. He was able to discuss photography in film. He could overcome the loneliness of the viewer. But to do that he needed a detour through silent movies. In *Pull My Daisy* the "forward momentum" of life, because it is only represented through language, does not quite fit right with the melancholy of the images. Jack Kerouac's voice in *Pull My Daisy* corresponds with a "deus ex machina," which cannot manage to refrain from beginning with a little act of creation. The opening line begins: "Early morning in the universe." Michel Chion speaks of "acousmatic beings," that were not invented by sound films, "since Jehova is the great original ACOUSMATIC." All of this comes into play with Kerouac's voice. He acts like a silent film narrator for whom the slow pan through the loft in the New York Bowery moves a little too patiently. Through his cascade of words he provokes the slapstick moment about the poet Apollinaire, who falls at Balzac's grave. Through the insistent question "Is everything holy?" he invokes that quality in the visual material that strives to go far beyond the chance (or, as Barthes writes, the contingency) of the moment. The text is primary; through it, the visible is defined. In a long play on words about the word "cockroach," Kerouac literally makes the invisible appear because Frank cannot do much more than pan over the walls and the furniture behind which the cockroaches hide. The voice is given an exorcizing function, but the further away the historic moment is, the more the images become objects of melancholy, and the persons involved become phantoms. (Pablo, Robert Frank's son, already makes an appearance here. Later, everything will revolve around his presence and absence.)

In sum, Robert Frank's cinematic work actually contains something similar to an acousmatic drama: at the beginning of *Pull My Daisy* the words over the images are strong. In the later videos the voice is still omnipresent, but only as part of melancholic registration, approaching Jonas Mekas's fragile "ecstasy." Frank opposes the expressive optimism of the Beat movement—its understanding of the body as a sound space that more or less naturally releases literature ("bursting with poetry," says Kerouac)—with an essentially more complex confrontation with the relationship between body and language, subjectivity, and communication. There is an unforgettable scene of a famous reading by the Beat poets Allen Ginsberg and Peter Orlovsky in *Me and My Brother*. At the back of the stage, Julius Orlovsky sits and stares. The poets attempt to integrate him into their performance and besiege him with their microphones: "Say something!" Julius remains silent but the entire film takes on the task of transporting outward the "voices" from within the mentally ill man and even assigning them with pictures, which are surely no more than invention.

This achieved construction is so meaningful because in it, a media historical statement is made. The film—and not the poetry, like for the Beats, or the photography, like in Frank's "The Americans"—is the "common denominator," for the mediation between subject and object, between inner and outer worlds. However, for Frank, film is not the medium of an enthusiastic subjectivity, as it is for Stan Brakhage, for example, but instead, already with *Me and My Brother* is very much influenced by a revaluation of the relationship of image (which follows) and language (which is prior). The presence of the photographic moment is broken by the absent subject of Julius Orlovsky. From the first take onward, linguistic signs shower down on Orlovsky, a neon sign in the image's darkness with a warning voice: "Watch out for the cars, Julius!" This indifferent witness, however, cannot even be lured out of his reserve by two homosexuals' "sex experiment" carried out in front of the camera—because he is at a different place: "Where he is seems like a meeting place."

Similar to the Beats' meeting point in *Pull My Daisy*, this place is composed linguistically. The pictures, first discovered on the path of visual digression, are compiled entirely by association and can

Me and My Brother

hin. Die Poeten versuchen, ihn in ihre Performance zu integrieren, und bedrängen ihn mit ihren Mikrophonen: "Say something!" Julius schweigt, der ganze Film aber unternimmt es, die „Stimmen" aus dem Inneren des psychisch kranken Mannes nach außen zu tragen und ihnen sogar Bilder zuzuordnen, die nichts anderes sein können als Erfindungen.

Diese Konstruktionsleistung ist so bedeutend, weil darin auch eine medienhistorische Aussage getroffen wird: Der Film – und nicht die Poesie, wie bei den Beats, oder die Fotografie, wie in Franks "The Americans" – ist der "common denominator", der gemeinsame Nenner für die Vermittlung zwischen Subjekt und Objekt, zwischen Innenwelt und Außenwelt. Film ist bei Frank aber nicht das Medium einer enthusiastischen Subjektivität, wie etwa bei Stan Brakhage, sondern steht schon mit *Me and My Brother* im Zeichen einer Umwertung des Verhältnisses von Bild (das nachträglich wird) und Sprache (die vorrangig wird). Die Gegenwärtigkeit des fotografischen Augenblicks zerbricht an dem abwesenden Subjekt Julius Orlovsky, auf den von der ersten Einstellung an sprachliche Zeichen einprasseln, eine Leuchtschrift in der Dunkelheit des Bildes, dazu eine warnende Stimme: "Watch out for the cars, Julius!" Der teilnahmslose Zeuge an einem "sex experiment" zweier Homosexueller vor der Kamera lässt sich nicht aus der Reserve locken, weil er an einem anderen Ort ist: "Where he is seems like a meeting place".

Dieser Ort ist, wie schon der Treffpunkt der Beats in *Pull My Daisy,* sprachlich verfasst. Die Bilder werden dazu erst gefunden, auf dem Weg von visuellen Abschweifungen, die ganz assoziativ verfasst sind und nur über die Tonspur integriert werden. Das „sensitive mike" – und eben nicht die Kamera – ist das Gerät, das den Zugang zur rätselhaften Subjektivität von Julius Orlovsky ermöglicht. Das Stimmengewirr, mit dem er mutmaßlich lebt, hat eine äußere Entsprechung in der Vielfalt der Diagnosen und Annahmen über seinen Zustand. Der Einwand einer Frau (aus dem Off) ist romantisch: "Julius isn't replaceable. Why use an actor?" Der Film aber ist modern, weil er sich nicht mit dem Bild des (geisterhaft) schweigenden Julius zufriedengibt, sondern ihn sprachlich einzuholen versucht. Der Schauspieler tritt an die Stelle von Julius, gerade weil dessen Ort unerreichbar ist. Es geht nicht darum, ihn zu ersetzen *(replace),* sondern ihn zu *deplazieren,* ihn an einen Ort zu holen, an dem die Stimmen akusmatisch werden, also hörbar sind. Es gibt markante Einstellungen, die Julius in Spiegelungen zeigen, ihn in gerahmte Bilder überblenden oder ihn in einem Film-im-Film zeigen, aber keine dieser Metaphern für seinen „anderen Ort" kommt an die Worte heran, die „über" ihn gesprochen werden.

Julius ist das „Satori"-Ereignis in einer künstlerischen Bewegung, die glaubte, sich den Buddhismus aneignen zu können; aber er ist Leere nicht auf transzendente, sondern auf psychotische

Conversations in Vermont

only be integrated through the soundtrack. The "sensitive mike"—and not the camera—is the instrument that enables access to Julius Orlovsky's enigmatic subjectivity. The maze of voices, with which he presumably lives, has an outer correspondent in the multiplicity of diagnoses and assumptions about his state. The objection of a woman (from off-camera) is romantic: "Julius isn't replaceable. Why use an actor?" The film, however, is modern because it is not satisfied with the picture of the silent (ghostly) Julius, but instead attempts to catch up with him linguistically. The actor enters in Julius's place, precisely because this place is unreachable. It is not about *replacing* him, but *displacing* him, to catch up with him at a location where the voices become acousmatic, and are thus audible. There are striking takes that show Julius mirrored, that dissolve him in framed pictures and show him in a film-in-film, but none of these metaphors for his "other place" can come close to the words that are spoken "about" him.

Julius is the "Satori" event in an artistic movement that believes it can appropriate Buddhism; yet it is not an emptiness through transcendent, but rather, psychotic means, and only a particularly elaborate montage of picture and sound can even come close to this experience. Freud, in his conception of language, differentiated between the idea of the word and the idea of the thing, and he understood the relationship between these two kinds of ideas as a memory: the sound of a word results in an idea of the word, which invokes a picture—the idea of a thing. In psychotic persons, this communication is disturbed. They can read headlines from the newspaper without any problem, but these words do not produce any images in their imagination. Julius would therefore not be moved to say anything because he cannot recall pictures belonging to the sound of a word. He lives in a hell of ideas of words; he has become an object of the voices.

In 1969 Frank began a film by turning on a record player: "Something's the matter with the record player." (Music is his ideal path for leading beyond the melancholy of photography, although that is another theme.) Voice is also dominant here: "This film is about the past and the present. The present comes back in actual film footage." The formulation is traitorously ambivalent: the past comes back. At the end Frank speaks from off-camera, his "deus ex machina" formula: "I call this film *Conversations in Vermont*." This is followed by the word "cut," which is already there at the end of *Me and My Brother*. For the conversations in Vermont, Frank visits his children Pablo and Andrea, who live in the countryside, go to school, and are part of a group that manages a farm and sings together, "Jubilate deo." The father speaks with remorse of his behavior during Pablo and Andrea's early child-hood, at the same time he presents them with photographs dating back to this time and challenges them to recognize themselves in the pictures.

Weise, und nur eine besonders elaborierte Montage aus Bild und Ton kommt auch nur in die Nähe dieser Erfahrung. Freud unterschied in seiner Auffassung von Sprache zwischen der Wortvorstellung und der Sachvorstellung, und er begriff die Beziehung zwischen diesen beiden Vorstellungen als eine Erinnerung: Der Klang eines Wortes ergibt eine Wortvorstellung, die ein Bild – eine Sachvorstellung – heraufbeschwört. Beim Psychotiker ist diese Kommunikation gestört, er liest zwar Schlagzeilen aus der Zeitung problemlos, sie produzieren in seiner Vorstellung aber kein Bild. Julius wäre also deswegen nicht dazu zu bewegen, etwas zu sagen, weil er sich nicht an Bilder erinnern kann, die zum Klang eines Wortes gehören. Er lebt in einer Hölle der Wortvorstellungen, er ist zum Objekt der Stimme geworden.

1969 beginnt Frank einen Film, indem er einen Plattenspieler einschaltet: "Somethings's the matter with the record player." (Die Musik ist sein Königsweg, der über die Melancholie der Fotografie hinausführt, aber das ist ein anderes Thema.) Auch hier ist die Stimme dominant: "This film is about the past and the present. The present comes back in actual film footage." Die Formulierung ist verräterisch ambivalent: Die Gegenwart kommt zurück. Am Ende spricht Frank aus dem Off seine "Deus ex machina"-Formel: "I call this film *Conversations in Vermont*." Dann folgt noch das Wort "Cut", mit dem schon *Me and My Brother* endete. Für die Gespräche in Vermont sucht Frank seine Kinder Pablo und Andrea auf, die auf dem Land leben und zur Schule gehen, in der Gruppe einen Hof bewirtschaften und gemeinsam "Jubilate deo" singen. Der Vater äußert sich schuldbewusst über sein Verhalten während der frühen Kindheit von Pablo und Andrea, zugleich präsentiert er ihnen Fotografien aus dieser Zeit und fordert sie auf, sich darin wiederzuerkennen.

"I don't remember any of those pictures", sagt Pablo, und gibt damit zum Ausdruck, dass er nicht daran interessiert ist, diese Bilder zum Sprechen zu bringen. Auch er spricht ambivalent, denn die Bilder sind ja gegenwärtig (der Vater hat sie mitgebracht), er findet nur keine Entsprechung in seinen Kindheitserinnerungen. Das Familienalbum bleibt stumm, weil es nur mit der Stimme des Vaters spricht. Frank selbst erzählt von den Jahren in New York und Europa, die Kinder finden diese Zeit gar nicht so außergewöhnlich: "We've all come from normal to this": New York war normal, Vermont ist die Gegenwart. Pablo und Andrea verweigern sich der Linearität von Schuldgefühl und Schuldzuweisung. Wie in einer psychoanalytischen Sitzung geht es darum, den verborgenen Sinn ihrer Aussagen zu enthüllen.

Die Fotografien aus der Kindheit haben in diesem Film einen ganz anderen Status als den, den Barthes als „das Unveränderliche" beschrieb („Es-ist-so-gewesen") – sie sind Material in einem Streit darüber, wie es gewesen ist. Diese Auseinandersetzung verliert nur dort an Bedeutung, wo Frank einen alten Film dazwischen montiert, eine mythologische Spielerei, ein stummes Holiday-movie mit Musik, mit dem die Bilder insgesamt in die Freiheit entlassen werden. Sie stehen nicht länger unter dem Bann einer Aussagepflicht, über die Kerouac noch mit der ganzen Chuzpe der Beat-Generation verfügt hatte, und die Franks autoritative Vaterstimme zu Beginn und am Ende ebenfalls für sich reklamiert. Er ist mit seinem Vorhaben gescheitert, die Bilder zum Medium einer gemeinsamen, versöhnenden Deutung der Kindheit von Pablo und Andrea zu machen. Die Kinder stellen sich dumm, sie verweigern die Aussage. Die Fotografien (das Medium, das Frank zu diesem Zeitpunkt „aufgegeben" hatte) fallen wieder unter den Schweigepakt. Nur das "film footage" ist "actual".

„Nichts Proustisches ist in einem Foto", schreibt Barthes. „Die Wirkung, die sie (die Fotografie) auf mich ausübt, besteht nicht in der Wiederherstellung des (durch Zeit, durch Entfernung) Aufgehobenen, sondern in der Beglaubigung, dass das, was ich sehe, tatsächlich da gewesen ist." Die *Conversations in Vermont* scheinen dies zu bestätigen, die ursprüngliche Familie lässt sich durch deren

"I don't remember any of those pictures," Pablo says and thus expresses that he is not interested in making these pictures talk. He also speaks ambivalently, because the pictures are in the present (his father brought them), only he doesn't find any correspondence with his childhood memories. The family album remains silent because it only speaks with the father's voice. Frank tells of the years in New York and Europe; the children do not find this time at all unusual: "We've all come from normal to this": New York was normal, Vermont is the present. Pablo and Andrea refuse the linearity of sentiments of guilt and assignments of guilt. Similar to a psychoanalytical session, it is about uncovering the hidden sense of their statements.

In this film the childhood photographs have a completely different status than those that Barthes describes as "the unchangeable" ("It was like this ...")—they are material in a fight over how it was. This confrontation loses significance only at the point where Frank inserts an old film, a mythological game, a silent holiday movie with music that frees the pictures as a whole. They are no longer under the spell of having to make a statement, which Kerouac still had at his disposal with the entire chutzpah of the Beat generation, and which Frank's authoritative fatherly voice claimed for itself at the beginning and also at the end. He has failed in his plans to make the pictures a medium for a common, reconciling interpretation of Pablo and Andrea's childhood. The children act dumb, they refuse to make the statement. The photographs (the medium that Frank had "given up" by this point in time) again fall within the pact of silence. Only the "film footage" is "actual."

Barthes wrote, "there is nothing Proustian in a photo." "The effect, that it (the photograph) has on me does not comprise the re-establishment of that which has been removed (through time, through distance), but rather the confirmation of that which I see, which is actually there." *Conversations in Vermont* seems to confirm this; the original family cannot be re-established through its album. Frank then continually comes back to the line of questioning of how memory and the present relate to each other in the topicality of the film (later the video) and in the presence of the developed picture.

The short video *What I Remember from My Visit (with Stieglitz)* from 1997 also contains a whole series of suppositions that do not attribute much value to the material picture, whereas memory is once again present through language. "What I remember from my visit with Stieglitz"; a voice with a French accent repeats the title insert, and a light bulb lights up (one of the many light associations: "Little light, lit up!", from *The Present*). The speaker is Jerome Sother. With Frank in the main role, they re-stage a visit with Alfred Stieglitz in 1943. All that is left of the actual event is an empty photo album, and a series of details that Sother enumerates: there were cookies, there was a hospitable atmosphere, chicken was served at lunch, Stieglitz could not mow the lawn as it was too damp from the rain. Particularly conspicuous were the "steel toes," that Stieglitz put on before going out to cut wood. In *What I Remember*, there is a video picture from 1996 for each moment within this memory protocol. These pictures, however, work only as illustrations while the commentary from off-camera seems to be the genuine act of memory, although it is being spoken by the wrong man. Frank plays the role of Stieglitz without any trace of irony; there is no evidence of a "visit with Stieglitz," and the portrait that has been shot with the old camera shows Jerome Sother.

What I Remember is a play with voices. Remembering becomes polyphonous. The outer occasion for a visit from Sother to Frank becomes the motif to reflect on another visit—that of a young photographer to an old master, which possibly never even took place. In any case, the film leaves both possibilities open. There is no more "it was like this ..." accompanying the video images, remaining is the

Flamingo

Album nicht wiederherstellen, und Frank kommt danach immer wieder auf diese Fragestellung zurück: wie sich Erinnerung und Gegenwart in der Aktualität des Films (später des Videos) und in der Präsenz des entwickelten Bildes zueinander verhalten.

Das kurze Video *What I Remember from My Visit (with Stieglitz)* aus dem Jahr 1997 enthält dazu eine ganze Reihe von Vermutungen, die dem materiellen Bild wenig Wert beimessen, während das Erinnern wieder über die Sprache verläuft. "What I remember from my visit with Stieglitz", wiederholt eine Stimme mit französischem Akzent das Titel-Insert, dazu wird eine Glühbirne zum Leuchten gebracht (eine weitere der vielen Schöpfungsassoziationen: "Little light, lit up!", heißt es in *The Present*). Der Sprecher heißt Jerome Sother, er reinszeniert mit Frank in der Hauptrolle dessen Besuch bei dem Fotografen Alfred Stieglitz im Jahr 1943. Von dem tatsächlichen Ereignis ist nur ein leeres Fotoalbum übriggeblieben, und eine Reihe von Details, die Sother aufzählt: Es gab Kekse, die Atmosphäre war gastfreundlich, zum Lunch wurde ein Huhn serviert, die Wiese war vom Regen zu feucht, als dass Stieglitz sie hätte mähen können. Besonders auffällig sind die "steel toes", die Stieglitz überzieht, bevor er zum Holzhacken nach draußen geht. Zu jedem Moment dieses Gedächtnisprotokolls gibt es in *What I Remember* ein Videobild aus dem Jahr 1996, das aber immer nur wie eine Illustration wirkt, während der Kommentar aus dem Off wie die genuine Erinnerungsleistung erscheint, obwohl er von dem falschen Mann gesprochen wird. Die Rolle des Stieglitz spielt Frank selbst, ohne jeden Anflug von Ironie, dabei gibt es keinen Beweis für einen "visit with Stieglitz", und das Porträt, das mit der alten Kamera geschossen wird, zeigt Jerome Sother.

What I Remember ist ein Spiel mit Stimmen. Das Erinnern wird selbst polyphon. Der äußere Anlass, ein Besuch von Sother bei Frank, wird zum Motiv, eines anderen Besuchs – den eines jungen Fotografen bei einem alten Meister – zu gedenken, der möglicherweise nie stattgefunden hat, jedenfalls hält der Film selbst beide Möglichkeiten offen. Mit den Videobildern geht kein „So-ist-es-gewesen" mehr einher, was bleibt, ist die Überzeugungskraft einer Stimme, die einfach beginnt, aufzuzählen. "This is the time to say a few words", äußert eine andere Stimme in *Flamingo*. Sie gehört Miranda Dali, obwohl Robert Frank diesen Text ebensogut sprechen könnte, denn er handelt von seiner Arbeit: "projecting slides" und "building a house". Die Aufnahmen vom Bau seines Hauses im kanadischen Nova Scotia haben wieder die Qualität eines Stummfilms, es ist nur konsequent, dass der Kommentar lange Pausen enthält und am Ende den Film selbst skeptisch relativiert: "Okay, we're done. Paint it black." Gemeint ist das Haus, das aber von Beginn an selbst nur ein Bild ist, ein Schemen in dunkler

power of persuasion of a voice, which simply begins to enumerate. "This is the time to say a few words," says another voice in *Flamingo*. It belongs to Miranda Dali, although Frank could have said the text just as well since it is about his work: *projecting slides* and *building a house*. The photographs of building his house in the Canadian province of Nova Scotia once again have the quality of a silent film. It is logical that the commentary contains long pauses and at the end skeptically makes the film itself relative: "Okay, we're done. Paint it black." What is meant is the house, which from the beginning on is only a picture, a scheme in a dark landscape. In these late videos, the language itself is afflicted with melancholy, which grows still stronger with aging and with life's experiences (the early death of both children).

The video *The Present* leads Robert Frank to a point at which he can no longer expect anything from language: "I'm glad I found my camera. Now I can film. But I don't know what." He finds himself surrounded by objects of melancholy, most of which are connected with his son Pablo who died after experiencing drug problems and mental illness. "The suffering, the silence of Pablo" is on a folder, the cover of which Frank films but does not open. The view from the window opens a dimension of objectivity, which could approach the Satori of Buddhism. Frank shoots a "crow film," and he films a dog who stares out the window, dissociated. "What does he see?" This question is asked from the same position where Frank stood years earlier facing Julius Orlovsky. In the meantime, all answers are forbidden; all that is still possible is an image in which also language is, quite literally, dissolved. MEMORY is written as lettering on a wall, a friend is called to eradicate this word. "It's actually impossible," after he has honestly tormented himself two letters remain: ME.

"Me and My Memory" has become the theme of Robert Frank's life, the filmmaker who found his way out beyond the presence of his pictures. "The evil (perhaps also the bliss) of language lies there: in that it cannot vouch for itself," wrote Barthes. "According to its essence, language is invention: if one wants to enable it to render actuality, this requires an enormous effort, we make an effort at the logic, or if that is missing, at the oath." The invoking voice of Jack Kerouac, the "ex machina" that could create an entire world, the fatherly voice of Robert Frank, which wanted to tell a story together with Pablo and Andrea, are silenced. The acousmatic drama is not preserved in any holy story; it can only be differentiated from a variety of voices, which—as a choir or as a murmuring—stand entirely on the side of the natural. They are all united in a gaze at the silent being (the psychotic, the animal, the dead), whose subjectivity can no longer be uttered or reproduced: "What does he see?"

1) Roland Barthes, "Camera Lucida: Reflections on Photography". Translated by Richard Miller. Hill and Wang: New York.

Landschaft. In diesen späten Videos ist die Sprache selbst von einer Schwermut befallen, die wiederum mit den Erfahrungen des Lebens (der frühe Tod beider Kinder) und des Alters wächst.

Das Video *The Present* führt Robert Frank an einen Punkt, an dem er von der Sprache nichts mehr zu erhoffen hat: "I'm glad I found my camera. Now I can film. But I don't know what." Er findet sich umgeben von Objekten der Melancholie, von denen die meisten mit dem Leben seines Sohnes Pablo zusammenhängen, der nach Drogenproblemen und psychischer Krankheit starb. "The suffering, the silence of Pablo" steht auf einem Ordner, dessen Umschlag Frank filmt, den er aber nicht aufschlägt. Der Blick aus dem Fenster öffnet eine Dimension der Objektivität, die dem Satori des Buddhismus nahekommen könnte. Frank dreht einen „Krähenfilm", und er filmt einen Hund, der unverwandt aus dem Fenster starrt. "What does he see?" Diese Frage ist aus der gleichen Position gestellt, mit der Frank viele Jahre zuvor Julius Orlovsky gegenüberstand. Inzwischen verbieten sich alle Antworten, möglich ist nur noch ein Bild, in dem auch die Sprache noch ganz buchstäblich ausgelöscht wird. MEMORY steht als Schriftzug an einer Wand, ein Freund wird gerufen, um dieses Wort zu beseitigen ("erase"). "It's actually impossible", nachdem er sich rechtschaffen geplagt hat, bleiben zwei Buchstaben übrig: ME.

„Me and My Memory" ist zum Lebensthema des Filmemachers Robert Frank geworden, der damit über die Präsenz seiner Bilder hinausfand. „Darin liegt das Übel (vielleicht aber auch die Wonne) der Sprache: dass sie für sich selbst nicht bürgen kann", schreibt Barthes. „Die Sprache ist ihrem Wesen nach Erfindung; will man sie zur Wiedergabe von Tatsächlichkeit befähigen, so bedarf es eines enormen Aufwands, wir bemühen die Logik oder, wenn es daran mangelt, den Schwur." Die beschwörende Stimme von Jack Kerouac, die "ex machina" eine ganze Welt entstehen lassen konnte, die väterliche Stimme von Robert Frank, die mit Pablo und Andrea eine gemeinsame Geschichte erzählen wollte, sind verstummt. Das akusmatische Drama ist in keine Heilsgeschichte aufzuheben, es ist nur zu differenzieren in eine Vielfalt von Stimmen, die – als Chor oder als Gemurmel – ganz auf der Seite des Kreatürlichen stehen. Sie sind alle vereint im Blick auf das stumme Wesen (den Psychotiker, das Tier, die Toten), dessen Subjektivität nicht aussagbar und nicht abbildbar ist: "What does he see?"

1) Roland Barthes: "Die helle Kammer. Bemerkung zur Fotografie". Übersetzt von Dietrich Leube. Suhrkamp: Frankfurt/Main 1985 (Taschenbuch 1989)

The Present

Vom Feuer verzehrt
Über Musik und existentielle Rhythmen in einigen Filmen von Robert Frank

Thomas Mießgang

Julius Booke ist ein Verlierer. Im Windschatten der Wall-Street-Hysterie im New York der achtziger Jahre sucht er den Notausgang zu einer Karriere als Songwriter oder Rockstar. Seinen Job hat er hingeschmissen, seine Gitarre verborgt, und als Aushilfsmusiker in einem Ballroom macht er keine besonders gute Figur. Die große Chance sieht Julius, als eine Gruppe von Veteranen des Musikgeschäfts den legendären Gitarrenbauer Elmore Silk erwähnt: Der habe die besten Instrumente gebaut, jedes davon mittlerweile gut 20.000 Dollar wert: "I would buy every guitar that Elmore ever built". Leider hat der Instrumenten-Designer die Stadt verlassen und alle Kontakte zu seiner früheren Welt abgebrochen. Julius macht sich erbötig, das enigmatische Genie auszuforschen und ihm einen Deal für den Verkauf seiner Gitarren vorzuschlagen.

So beginnt *Candy Mountain*, ein Film, den Robert Frank mit Rudy Wurlitzer im Jahr 1987 gedreht hat. Ein klassisches Road-movie, das seinen Protagonisten aus den Schluchten von New York in den Norden der USA, dann nach Kanada und Nova Scotia transportiert. Das bescheidene Spesenkonto ist bald ausgeschöpft, die Reise kann nur durch den Tausch von Julius' gutem Auto gegen immer schlechtere Fahrzeuge fortgesetzt werden. Schließlich steht er mit dem Daumen im Wind am Straßenrand. "How can you do the road with no car?" fragt ein zahnloser Fahrer, der ihn ein Stück weit mitnimmt.

Die Odyssee von Julius Booke ist eine *quest* im klassischen Sinne, zugleich eine Parodie auf die Sinnsuche. Der Fährtensucher folgt einer Spur der emotionalen Verwüstung: Verlassene Familienmitglieder und gepeinigte Frauen in unterschiedlichen Graden der Verbitterung begegnen ihm. Niemand will wissen, wo Elmore, der längst weitergezogen ist, sich gerade herumtreibt, niemand will ihn je wiedersehen. Den dürftigen Hinweisen folgend stöbert Julius den Gitarrenbauer schließlich in der Mitte des Nichts auf: Einen Mann in mittleren Jahren, vom unsteten Leben und vom Alkohol leicht angenagt, aber immer noch attraktiv. Einen Drifter, der seinen Welthass in Stoizismus transformiert hat und ganz offensichtlich an Geschäften völlig desinteressiert ist. Noch glaubt Julius an seinen Deal, doch bald muss er erkennen, dass Elmore ganz andere Dinge im Sinn hat: "You`re not even at the bottom end of my dance card."

Consumed by Fire:
On Music and Existential Rhythms in a Number of Films by Robert Frank

Thomas Mießgang

Julius Booke is a loser. In the wake of the 1980s Wall Street hysteria in New York he searches for an emergency exit to a career as a songwriter and rock star. He throws away his job, lends out his guitar, and doesn't really cut much of a figure as a hired musician in a ballroom. Julius sees his big chance when a group of veterans from the music business mention the legendary guitar maker Elmore Silk. Silk built the best instruments, each of which is meanwhile worth 20,000 dollars: "I would buy every guitar that Elmore ever built." Unfortunately, the luthier has left the city and broken off all contacts to his prior life. Julius offers to hunt down the enigmatic genius and propose a deal for the sale of his guitars.

Thus begins *Candy Mountain*, a film that Robert Frank shot with Rudy Wurlitzer in 1987. It is a classic road movie that transports its protagonist from the depths of New York to the north of the U.S., and then over into Canada and Nova Scotia. His modest expense account is soon exhausted and Julius can only continue the journey by constantly exchanging his car for a more run-down vehicle. In the end he stands there with his thumb in the wind at the side of the road. "How can you do the road with no car?" asks a toothless driver who takes him a bit further.

Julius Booke's odyssey is a *quest* in the classical sense, and simultaneously a parody of the search for meaning. The path seeker follows a track of emotional devastation: he encounters abandoned family members and tormented women in various states of embitterment. No one wants to know where Elmore is at the moment. Elmore has long moved on; no one ever wants to see him again. Following meager clues, Julius finally tracks down the guitar maker in the middle of nowhere: A middle-aged man, restless and somewhat worn away by alcohol but nonetheless still attractive: A drifter who has transformed his hatred of the world into stoicism and is quite obviously completely uninterested in doing business. Julius still believes in his deal, but he must soon recognize that Elmore has completely different things in mind: "You're not even at the bottom end of my dance card."

After several days of holding out, Silk signs a contract with a devious Japanese woman. He must produce twelve guitars for her, burn all the rest, and then never produce anymore. A Faustian pact, which provides Elmore with the necessary small change to keep on going, but extinguishes his

Nach einigen Tagen des Hinhaltens unterzeichnet Silk den Kontrakt einer undurchsichtigen Japanerin, der ihn verpflichtet, ihr 12 Gitarren auszuhändigen, alle anderen zu verbrennen und keine weiteren mehr herzustellen. Ein faustischer Pakt, der Elmore zwar das nötige Kleingeld beschert, um sich weitertreiben zu lassen, seinen kreativen Funken aber endgültig zum Erlöschen bringt. So endet seine *quest* in einer großen Gitarrenverbrennung. Julius sieht fassungslos zu, wie Elmore seine Instrumente auf einem Scheiterhaufen in Flammen aufgehen lässt und damit gleichzeitig seine eigenen Träume verheizt. Der Mythos des archetypischen *Noisemaker*-Instruments, das Chaos in die Ordnung der gesellschaftlichen Regulative bringt und mit der Zungenrede seiner Oberton- und Feedback-Symphonien vom Leben auf der anderen Seite, dem existenziellen Szenario der *angelheaded hipsters* erzählt, wird zur glühenden Asche. Der Akt der Gitarrenverbrennung, bei Jimi Hendrix in Monterey noch eine Geste der optimistisch gestimmten Subversion, ist nun eine Chiffre der Resignation: Sag' mir, wo die Blumen sind, wo sind sie geblieben? „In girum imus nocte et consumimur igni"[1] heißt es bei Guy Debord: Im Kreise gehen wir in der Nacht und werden vom Feuer verzehrt.

Hello Darkness, my old friend

Candy Mountain ist ein Film, der über die Metapher der Musik von der Gegenkultur erzählt. Und so, wie in den meisten Arbeiten von Robert Frank treten prononcierte Vertreter populärkultureller und literarischer Gegenströme in Cameos auf: Arto Lindsay, Tom Waits, Leon Redbone, Joe Strummer. Die Straße ist das Skelett des Narrativs, das den Film zusammenhält. An jedem Stop werden dem Protagonisten Julius Booke interessante Typen zugeführt, die je eine dramatische Szene oder einen pointierten Sketch aufführen dürfen, um dann für immer aus dem Bildrand zu kippen. Das graue Asphalt-Band wird zur einzigen Beglaubigung eines immer brüchiger werdenden Vertrauens in den *pursuit of happiness*.

Dumpf und stoisch begleitet ein basslastiger Rhythm-and-Blues-Takt den irrationalen Trip auf der Road to Nowhere: Das Versprechen einer Transsubstantiation durch die Beschleunigung des Körpers im unbegrenzten Raum – seit Kerouacs "On the Road" und Woody Guthries Liedern aus der Dust Bowl ein klassisches Motiv des gegenkulturellen Selbstverständnisses – wird zur Wiederkehr des Immergleichen. "Freedom doesn`t have much to do with the road one way or another", sagt Elmore Silk im Film einmal. Obwohl Musik in *Candy Mountain* neben dem zerzausten Protagonisten Julius die eigentliche „Heldin" ist, wird sie nur sporadisch zum Klingen gebracht: etwa wenn Arto Lindsay mit Joe Strummer in einem New Yorker Loft eine Grobversion seiner D.N.A.-Krachästhetik hinlegt oder ein zittriges Lo-Fi-Lied erklingt, das eine kranke Frau in den Schlaf geleiten soll. Während der Klimax des Films greift sich Julius ein Instrument aus dem brennenden Gitarrenhaufen: Unter hysterischem Gelächter schlägt er auf die Saiten ein; Neonlichter am Korpus leuchten auf, doch kein einziger Ton ist zu hören. Katatonische Starre des geräuschtoten Raumes: "Hello darkness, my old friend, I've come to talk with you again."

Candy Mountain mag eine eher ungewöhnliche Einstiegsluke in das filmische Werk von Robert Frank sein. „Wir hatten zu viel Geld, und wir mussten zu viele Bedürfnisse des Geldes befriedigen", sagt der Regisseur selbst. „Die Regeln waren zu strikt, man konnte nicht spontan sein." Andererseits bietet gerade der Filter eines relativ konventionellen Road-movie die Möglichkeit, gewissermaßen ex negativo einiges über die Verwendung von Musik in den Filmen von Frank zu erfahren.

creative sparks once and for all. Thus his *quest* ends in a huge guitar burning. Julius watches stunned as Elmore allows his instruments to burn at the stake, simultaneously burning his own dreams. The myth of the archetypical *noisemaker* instruments, which bring chaos into the order of social regulation and by talking in the tongues of their overtones and feedback symphonies tell of life on the other side, of the existential scenario of *angel headed hipsters*, now become glowing embers. The act of guitar-burning—for Jimi Hendrix in Monterey still an act of optimistic subversion—is now a symbol of resignation: where have all the flowers gone? Where are they? "In girum imus nocte et consumimur igni"[1] says Guy Debord: We go in circles at night and are consumed by fire.

Hello Darkness, my Old Friend

Candy Mountain is a film that tells of the metaphor of music from the counterculture. Therefore, like in most of Robert Frank's works, appearing in cameo roles are staunch representatives of popular culture and literary countercurrents: Arto Lindsay, Tom Waits, Leon Redbone, Joe Strummer. The road is the skeleton of the narrative that holds the film together. At every stop the protagonist, Julius Booke, is introduced to interesting characters who are each allowed to present a dramatic scene or a meaningful sketch to then fall away forever off the edge of the picture. The gray stretch of asphalt becomes the only confirmation of an ever more brittle trust in the *pursuit of happiness*.

Muffled and stoic, a heavy bass rhythm and blues beat accompanies the irrational trip on the road to nowhere: the promise of transubstantiation through acceleration of the body in indefinite space—a classical motif of the way counterculture has seen itself ever since Kerouac's "On the Road" and Woody Guthrie's songs from the Dust Bowl—turns into a constant recurrence of the same. "Freedom doesn't have much to do with the road one way or another," says Elmore Silk in the film. Although music is the real hero in *Candy Mountain*, alongside the disheveled protagonist Julius, it is only sporadically played: for example, when Arto Lindsay puts on a rough version of his D.N.A. noise aesthetic together with Joe Strummer in a New York loft, or a shaky lo-fi song rings out that is meant to lull a sick woman to sleep. At the climax of the film, Julius pulls an instrument out of the burning heap of guitars: laughing hysterically, he strikes the guitar's strings; neon lights glow from the body yet no single tone can be heard. Catatonic rigidity of a sound-dead space: "Hello darkness, my old friend, I've come to talk with you again."

Candy Mountain is perhaps an unusual porthole into Robert Frank's cinematic work. "We had too much money, and we had to satisfy too many needs of the money," the director conceded. "The rules were too strict; it wasn't possible to be spontaneous." On the other hand, the filter of a relatively conventional road movie offers, to a certain extent, the possibility to experience a bit about the use of music in Frank's films via a counter example. In hardly any of his other works is music introduced simply to set the emotion as occurs in the street scenes in *Candy Mountain*. The diagnosis, entirely in keeping with the disillusioned spirit of the times, is that desire for the impossible does not necessarily produce livable alternatives to the despised conventions of the "American way." This leads to a deconstruction of aesthetic strategies that bring the closed narrative to explosion, and in the intuitive unfolding of the materials attempt "the consolidation of a spiritual void."[2] Strategies, whose variation and perfection Robert Frank had been working on since *Pull My Daisy*. On no account should one overrate *Candy Mountain* within the director's œuvre: for one, it is not possible to definitively confirm the extent

Candy Mountain

So gibt es von ihm kaum eine andere Arbeit, in der Klänge lediglich zur simplen Emotionalisierung eingesetzt werden, wie das in den Straßenszenen von *Candy Mountain* geschieht. Die durchaus im Einklang mit dem desillusionierten Zeitgeist gestellte Diagnose, dass das Verlangen nach dem Unmöglichen nicht unbedingt lebbare Alternativen zu den verhassten Konventionen des "American Way" produziert, führte zu einem Rückbau jener ästhetischen Strategie, die die geschlossene Narrative zur Explosion bringen und in der intuitiven Entfaltung der Materialien „die Befestigung eines geistigen Nichts"[2] betreiben wollte. Strategien, an deren Variation und Vervollkommnung Robert Frank seit *Pull My Daisy* gearbeitet hatte. Man darf *Candy Mountain* im Gesamtwerk des Regisseurs keinesfalls überbewerten: Zum einen lässt sich nicht zweifelsfrei bestimmen, in welchem Ausmaß Regie-Co-Pilot Rudy Wurlitzer das Endprodukt beeinflusste, zum anderen konnte Frank nur selten unter vergleichsweise komfortablen finanziellen Bedingungen arbeiten. Trotzdem ist diese Arbeit nicht bloß ein Auftragswerk, sondern ein markantes Interpunktionszeichen; eine beklemmende Manifestation negativer Energie, die zu diesem Zeitpunkt wohl notwendig war, um als dialektisches Korrelat den Befreiungsimpulsen einen Realitätsdamm entgegenzustellen.

Speaking in Tongues

Viel ist geschrieben worden über den spontanen, intuitiven, improvisatorischen Gestus bei der Kreation von *Pull My Daisy*, jenem heute kanonischen Debüt von Robert Frank, das er gemeinsam mit Alfred Leslie erarbeitet hat. Beim Lesen der zeitgenössischen Rezensionen gewinnt man den Eindruck, dass dieser Film gedreht wurde wie eine Zigarette: schnell, sorglos, rauschhaft. Eine Ausstülpung schöpferischer Energien, die sich quasi selbst zum Werk formten. Eine Selbstdarstellung der noch jungen Beat-Generation im Einklang mit ihrem kategorischen Imperativ einer Elevation des Daseins durch Jazz, Drogen, Religion und radikale Politik. Jonas Mekas bezeichnete *Pull My Daisy* als

to which co-director Rudy Wurlitzer determined the final product, and for another, Frank only rarely had the opportunity to work under comparably comfortable financial conditions. Nonetheless, the film is not simply contracted work, but rather, a striking punctuation mark; an oppressive manifestation of negative energy that was certainly necessary at this time in order to place, as a dialectical correlate, a reality dam resisting the impulses for liberation.

Speaking in Tongues

Much has been written about the spontaneous, intuitive, improvisational gestures in the creation of *Pull My Daisy*, Robert Frank's currently canonic debut made together with Alfred Leslie. Reading the contemporary reviews, one gets the impression that this film was made in the same way that one rolls a cigarette: fast, carefree, and ecstatic. Rolled-up creative energies that formed themselves, as it were, into a work: A self presentation of the still young Beat generation in harmony with their categorical imperative of elevating existence through jazz, drugs, religion, and radical politics. Jonas Mekas described *Pull My Daisy* as "free improvisation" and its creators as "the true independents, the conscious rebels who reject every type of compromise."[3] Later analyses have bathed the magical primeval scene in another light. Above all, the claim that Jack Kerouac improvised the text track for the final cut of the film in a tenor saxophonist style, proved untenable: "His wonderfully skewed narration had already been written out word for word," wrote William Anthony Nericcio:[4] "He spoke the text four times altogether, and the final version was mixed from three different takes."

Although perhaps the myth can be deconstructed in this way, not the aura, which the film still radiates today: *Pull My Daisy* is a thoroughly musical "adventure in sound." The combination of Jack Kerouac's finely modulated narrative voice, that lends the silent actors acoustic contours, with fragments of a driving bebop rhythm, an oboe solo, the sounds of a heavily panting harmonium and occasional blend-ins of chamber music epigrams, created an arrhythmic kinetic energy that keeps the

Pull My Daisy

„freie Improvisation" und seine Schöpfer als „die wahren Unabhängigen, die bewussten Rebellen, die jede Art von Kompromiss ablehnen."[3] Spätere Analysen haben die magische Urszene in ein anderes Licht getaucht. Vor allem die Behauptung, Jack Kerouac habe im Stile eines Tenorsaxophonisten zu dem fertig geschnittenen Film eine Textspur improvisiert, erwies sich als unhaltbar: „Seine wundervoll schräge Erzählung war vorher Wort für Wort aufgeschrieben worden", schreibt William Anthony Nericcio[4]. „Er sprach den Text insgesamt viermal, und die endgültige Fassung wurde aus drei verschiedenen Takes zusammengemischt."

Der Mythos mag sich auf diese Weise dekonstruieren lassen, nicht jedoch die Aura, die der Film auch heute noch abstrahlt: *Pull My Daisy* ist ein durch und durch musikalisiertes "Adventure in Sound". Das Zusammenwirken von Jack Kerouacs fein modulierter Erzählerstimme, die den stummen Darstellern akustische Konturen verleiht, mit Fragmenten eines treibenden BeBop-Rhythmus, einem Oboensolo, den Geräuschen eines schwer schnaufenden Harmoniums und gelegentlich eingeblendeten kammermusikalischen Epigrammen schafft eine arhythmische Bewegungsenergie, die den Film am Laufen hält, ohne jene Absorptionskraft zu entfalten, die im konventionellen Hollywood-Kino den Zuschauer das Gemachte vergessen lassen will. In *Pull My Daisy* ist man sich stets der Bausteine bewusst, deren Amalgamierung zur Ekstase führen soll. Der Zaubertrick dabei ist, dass sie trotzdem eintritt. Und zwar nicht durch eine emotionale Ganzkörpermassage, sondern durch kleine Rhythmusverschiebungen, diskret erhöhte Intensitätsgrade und asynchrone Schichtungen von Klang- und Sprachpartikeln. Wenn Kerouac in der berühmten "Holy"-Sequenz den Sinngehalt seines Raps zum Tanzen und Taumeln bringt – "is everything holy, is alligators holy, Bishop? Is the world holy? Is the organ of man holy?" – dann beginnt der „innere Puls" (Isidor Isou) des Films zu schlagen, die isolierten Elemente fallen wie selbstverständlich ineinander, und die propulsive Motorik erzeugt eine Druckwelle, die, im Sinne Rimbauds, jenes *dérangement* der Sinne bewirkt, in dem „alle Formen der Liebe, des Leidens, des Wahnsinns"[5] sich zur Apotheose der existenziellen Entgrenzung verdichten.

Erstaunlich ist, dass *Pull My Daisy* auch heute noch diese transgressive Wirkung entfalten kann, obwohl die Klangmodule, die das akustische Chiaroscuro seines Soundtracks konstituieren, unter der verlorenen Zeit und den Kontextverschiebungen im populärkulturellen Paralleluniversum gelitten haben.

Der Score von David Amram mag zu seiner Zeit eine Ahnung jener spirituellen Qualitäten vermittelt haben, die die Beats in den Jazz hineinphantasierten. Von jener Odyssee eines Tenorsaxophonisten, die der Autor John Clellon Holmes beschreibt: „Alles, was er weiß, ist, dass etwas in ihm spricht und die Mechanismen der Prophezeiung ihm gehorchen. Der Tenorspieler swingt weiter hinein in ein Vakuum, er ist völlig selbstverloren, und doch ist es möglich, dass er in jedem Augenblick uns andere alle errettet mit seiner ernsthaften Anstrengung, Gnade zu erlangen."[6]

Heute klingen die betulichen Harmonien und milden Dissonanzen des Soundtracks von *Pull My Daisy* wie Opas Jazz; mehltaubestäubte Klänge aus der Bar jeder Vernunft nach Mitternacht, wenn die Zigarettenasche achtlos unter den Nierentisch fällt. Wie konnte es gelingen, die Vorstellung von einem Versprechen, das nur in der Unendlichkeit eingelöst wird, durch einen Zeitkorridor von 45 Jahren zu transportieren, ohne dass der Glanz der Verheißung matt geworden wäre? Es hat mit dem „der Leere nächsten Zustand" zu tun, von dem die Lettristen, eine französische Avantgarde-Bewegung der fünfziger Jahre, gesprochen haben; mit der Idee des *détournement* – der Zweckentfremdung eines Stoffes von seinen nützlichen Zwecken für unbegründete ästhetische Arrangements.

film going without displaying that power of absorption that in conventional Hollywood cinema seeks to have the viewers forget the fact that it is a made thing. In *Pull My Daisy* one is constantly aware of the building blocks whose amalgamation is meant to lead to ecstasy. The magic trick is that this ecstasy still appears. Not through an emotional full-body massage, but rather, through little rhythmic shifts, discretely elevated degrees of intensity and asynchronous layers of sound and speech particles. When Kerouac brings the emotional content of his rap into a dance and frenzy—"is everything holy, is alligators holy, Bishop? Is the world holy? Is the organ of man holy?"—then the "inner pulse" (Isidor Isou) of the film begins to beat, the isolated elements fall seemingly naturally into one another and the propulsive motor function creates a shockwave, which, in the sense of Rimbaud, causes that *dérangement* of the senses in which "all forms of love, of suffering, of madness"[5] concentrate to the apotheosis of existential delimitation.

What is amazing is that *Pull My Daisy* can still lead to this transgressive effect today although the sound modules, which constitute the acoustic chiaroscuro of its soundtrack, have suffered from the lost time and the shift in context in the parallel universe of popular culture.

The score by David Amram, in its day quite possibly mediated some idea of those spiritual qualities that the Beats fantasized about in Jazz: Knowledge of that odyssey of a tenor saxophonist, as described by the author John Clellon Holmes: "All that he knows is that something in him speaks and the mechanisms of prophesizing listen to it. The tenor player swings further into a vacuum, he is completely lost in himself, and yet it is possible that at every moment he saves the rest of us with his earnest efforts to obtain mercy." [6]

Today, the unhurried harmonies and mild dissonances of the soundtrack to *Pull My Daisy* sound like the jazz of our grandfathers; mildew-flecked sounds from after midnight, when cigarette ashes fall unnoticed under kidney-shaped tables. How might it be possible, to transport through a forty-five year time corridor the idea of a promise that can only be kept through eternity without letting the gloss of promise fade? It has something to do with the "state closest to emptiness," which the Lettristes, a French avant-garde movement of the 1950s, spoke of; with the idea of *détournement*—the estrangement of a material from its useful purposes to ungrounded aesthetic arrangements.

Despite an exuberant abundance of reality and an initial sense-oriented dynamics, in *Pull My Daisy*, major existential exhaustion occurs: Neo-dadaist choreography of movement and ecstatic un-leashing of language sketch out a paradigm beyond pure reason and the practical appropriation of reality. The musical fragments continue to decompose on the soundtrack. They are robbed of their social functionality and circle solipsistically around the masks of an existence that seems self-referentially obliged only to the here and now: a materialized emptiness in the universe of blind mirrors. Cold ecstasy. It is this sense of a concentrated eradication of sense under the sign of convulsion that has remained modern, even if some of the strategic means employed have long become dated. The film knew more than its authors and actors, who dreamed of making "…the complete step across chronological time into timeless shadows."[7]

Shock Corridor

Pull My Daisy and *Candy Mountain*, two works committed to music and its connotations, oppose each other asymmetrically. Through a plot perforated straight through, the debut formulated "the story of that seductive power that tears the hero, as though magically, from the monotonous existence of

Trotz einer überbordenden Wirklichkeitsfülle und einer anfänglich sinnorientierten Handlungsdynamik findet in *Pull My Daisy* eine große existenzielle Auszehrung statt: Neo-dadaistische Bewegungschoreographien und extatische Sprachentfesselung skizzieren ein Paradigma jenseits von Ratio und lebenspraktischer Realitätsaneignung. Die musikalischen Fragmente, die auf der Tonspur die Zersetzungsarbeit fortführen, werden ihrer gesellschaftlichen Funktionalitäten beraubt und kreisen solipsistisch um die Masken eines Seins, das selbstreferenziell nur noch dem schieren Hic et Nunc verpflichtet zu sein scheint: materialisierte Leere in einem Universum der blinden Spiegel. Kalte Ekstase.

Es ist diese Idee einer konzentrierten Sinnvernichtung im Zeichen der Konvulsion, die modern geblieben ist, auch wenn manche der strategischen Mittel, die zum Einsatz kommen, längst von einer Patina überdeckt sind. Der Film wusste mehr als seine Autoren und Darsteller, die davon träumten, „den totalen Schritt über die chronologische Zeit hinweg hinein ins zeitlose Schattenreich"[7] zu tun.

Shock Corridor

Pull My Daisy und *Candy Mountain* sind zwei der Musik und ihren Konnotationen verpflichtete Arbeiten, die einander asymmetrisch gegenüberstehen: Das Debüt formuliert durch einen perforierten Plot hindurch noch „die Geschichte jener verführerischen Macht, die den Helden wie mit Zauber aus der einförmigen Existenz seines Alltags reißt" (Kerouac)[8] und denkt in der absurden Überspitzung der nihilistischen Gestik den Widerspruch gleich mit (auf der Ebene der Literatur hat derweil Burroughs längst die Metaphysik des "On the Road" dekonstruiert). *Candy Mountain* ist, fast 30 Jahre später, die Rückführung des unsagbaren Anderen in ein Gehege der Erzählkonventionen und der kleinen Fluchten. Robert Frank hat immer zwischen diesen antipodischen Haltungen navigiert und einer Ästhetik vertraut, die der Poet Allen Ginsberg folgendermaßen beschrieb: „Geschwinder Fokus ‚unsichtbar' ... Schuss aus der Hüfte – das Auge zur Seite gedreht, dann abdrücken, mit der Chance eines ‚Fensters auf eine andere Zeit', auf einen anderen Ort."[9]

Diesseits der Metaphysik konnte jener andere Ort auch einfach ein fremdes Milieu sein, in dem Robert Frank, der Reisende durch die Subkulturen eines illegitimen Amerika, mit stets schussbereiter Kamera die Mysterien des Organismus hinter den Fassaden des gesellschaftlichen Funktionierens erkundete.

Als er 1972 den Auftrag bekam, die Amerika-Tour der Rolling Stones zu dokumentieren, hatte die Befreiungstheologie der Beats längst abgewirtschaftet. Sie war durch Transformationen gegangen: durch die Flower-Power-Ideologie der Hippies, die Acid Tests von Ken Kesey, die Schlammfeste von Woodstock. Und sie hatte in Altamont von jenem "Spirit of Evil" gekostet, der der euphorischen Energie der Entgrenzung „das heilige Nichts der unerschaffenen Leere" (Kerouac)[10] entgegenstellte.

Die Rolling Stones, die in Altamont zusehen mussten, wie ein Mann vor der Bühne erstochen wurde, waren die doppelköpfigen Priester von Ekstase und Vernichtung, sie kreisten in ihrer eigenen Umlaufbahn: „Ich kam mir vor wie in einem Raumschiff", sagte Robert Frank einmal. „Ich dachte, die Stones seien normale Leute. Doch ich fand schnell heraus, dass sie nicht dieselbe Luft atmen wie wir anderen. Sie reisen in dünner Luft und sie ziehen dich in ihrem Sog mit."

Cocksucker Blues, der Film, der die Tour dokumentiert, ist berühmt und berüchtigt geworden: Er zeigt Partyrausch und sexuelle Freizügigkeit, vor allem in der Entourage der Band, er kontrastiert zenbuddhistisches Geschwafel mit der Heroinnadel, die Hysterie der Fans mit dem Ennui im

his everyday life."[8] and in the absurd exaggeration of nihilistic gestures, at the same time includes its contradiction (in literature, Burroughs had meanwhile long deconstructed the metaphysics of "On the Road"). *Candy Mountain* is the return, almost thirty years later, of the indescribable other in a preserve of narrative conventions and little places of refuge. Robert Frank always navigated between these antipodean positions and trusted an aesthetic that the poet Allen Ginsberg described as "'focus swiftly,' 'invisible' … shoot from the hip—turn the eye aside, then click chance in the 'window on another time, on another place.'"[9]

From this world of metaphysics, everywhere else could also simply present a foreign milieu in which Robert Frank—the traveler through the subcultures of an illegitimate America, with an ever-ready camera—discovers the mysteries of the organism behind the façade of social functioning.

When he got the contract to document the Rolling Stones tour in 1972, the liberation theology of the Beats was long over. It had gone through transformations: through the flower power ideology of the hippies, Ken Kesey's acid tests, the mud fests of Woodstock. And it tasted that "spirit of evil" in Altamont, that opposed the euphoric energy of limitlessness, "the holy void of uncreated emptiness."[10]

The Rolling Stones, who had to watch as a man was stabbed in front of the stage in Altamont, were the double-headed priests of ecstasy and extermination; they revolved in their own orbit: "I felt as though I were in a space ship," Robert Frank once said. "I thought that the Stones were normal people. But I quickly found out that they don't breathe the same air as other people. They travel in thin air and they draw you along in their wake."

Cocksucker Blues, the film that documented the tour, became both famous and infamous: it shows a party frenzy and sexual permissiveness, but mainly, within the entourage of the band, it contrasts the waffles of Zen Buddhists with heroin needles, the hysteria of the fans with the ennui in the backstage area. The Rolling Stones' lawyers prohibited public screenings of *Cocksucker Blues* because it cast the group in a bad light. Thus, through the withdrawal of the images, an over-dimensional myth was created that the actual work couldn't live up to. Robert Frank constantly played down the scandal value of his work by saying that he "…didn't see one single orgy during the entire tour. Unless you describe a girl getting laid by two guys as an orgy."

It is not the chronic of alleged excess that is remarkable, but much more so how little this film, which in terms of content and chronology marks the midpoint between *Pull My Daisy* and *Candy Mountain*, deviates from Frank's other works in its inner design: one finds the nomadic camera that constantly loses its protagonists and entirely abandons itself to the intuition of a *dérive* without any specific purpose such as in *About Me: A Musical* or in the music videos for Patti Smith's *Summer Cannibals*. One becomes lost in an acoustic labyrinth of a sound score built according to complex switchboards that condense the tangle of voices, snatches of conversations, noise of departing aircraft, and brutally chopped elements of Stones songs into a type of brooding.

The most penetrating image in *Cocksucker Blues* shows the gladiators striding down an endless corridor that leads to the stage. It is a motif that also surfaces in the film *About Me: A Musical* created one year earlier. Here, however, it is a chain gang that treads a long hallway in a prison, behind bars, past the sullen, gazing guards.

The corridor and the light bulb, which casts a naked unprotected light on events, are two visual symbols that continually surface in different constellations and serial arrangements in Robert

Summer Cannibals

Backstagebereich. Die Anwälte der Rolling Stones verboten die öffentliche Aufführung von *Cocksucker Blues*, weil er die Gruppe in einem zu schlechten Licht zeige. So wurde durch den Entzug der Bilder ein überdimensionaler Mythos geschaffen, dem das Werk selbst nicht standhalten kann. Robert Frank hat den Skandalwert seiner Doku immer heruntergespielt: „Ich habe während der ganzen Tour keine einzige Orgie gesehen. Es sei denn, Sie bezeichnen ein Mädchen, das von zwei Typen gevögelt wird, als Orgie."

Bemerkenswert ist nicht die Chronik vorgeblicher Exzesse, sondern viel eher, wie wenig dieser Film, der die inhaltliche und zeitliche Mitte zwischen *Pull My Daisy* und *Candy Mountain* markiert, in seinem inneren Design von den übrigen Arbeiten Franks abweicht: Man findet die nomadisierende Kamera, die, wie auch in *About Me: A Musical* oder dem Musikvideo zu Patti Smiths "Summer Cannibals", ihre Protagonisten immer wieder verliert und sich der Intuition eines zweckfreien Dérive überlässt. Man verirrt sich im akustischen Labyrinth einer nach komplexen Schaltplänen gefertigten Klang-Partitur, die Stimmengewirr, Konversationsfetzen, den Lärm startender Flugzeuge und brutal zerhackte Teilkörper von Stones-Songs zu einer Art Brut verdichtet.

Das eindringlichste Bild in *Cocksucker Blues* zeigt die Gladiatoren beim Gang durch endlose Korridore, die zur Bühne führen. Ein Motiv, das auch in dem ein Jahr früher entstandenen Film *About Me: A Musical* auftaucht. Hier ist es allerdings eine Chain Gang, die in einem Gefängnis, durch Sperrgitter hindurch, an mürrisch blickenden Wächtern vorbei einen langen Gang beschreitet.

Der Korridor und die Glühbirne, die ein nacktes, ungeschütztes Licht auf das Geschehen wirft: Das sind zwei visuelle Chiffren, die in unterschiedlichen Konstellationen und seriellen Anordnungen im Werk Robert Franks immer wieder auftauchen. Bei *Cocksucker Blues* dröhnt im Hintergrund eine Kakophonie aus unspezifischen Lauten – archaisches Rauschen, das in der Geräuschamplitude geheime Botschaften zu verstecken scheint. In *About Me: A Musical* wird die Passage durch den Korridor von einem quasi evangelischen Close-Harmony-Acapella-Gesang gerahmt: Hölle und Himmel, Deklination des Gegensätzlichen unter dem Zauberbann einer übergeordneten Bildmetapher.

Cocksucker Blues

Frank's work. In *Cocksucker Blues* a cacophony of unspecified sounds drones in the background—archaic roaring that seems to hide secret messages in the amplitude of sound. In *About Me: A Musical,* the passage down the corridor is framed by an, as it were, close-harmony Evangelical a cappella singing: heaven and hell, declination of counterparts under the magic spell of a higher-order pictorial metaphor.

　　　William Burroughs once described his novel, "Naked Lunch" as "a plan, instructions, which enable different kinds of experiences in that they open the door at the end of a long corridor."[11] In Robert Frank's corridors there are no doors leading to the outside. One does not see the light at the other end of his tunnels, but instead is catapulted into other scenarios through the hard (film) cuts. Frank smashes genre, plot, and symbolic content to lend a fragmented aesthetic form to the astonishment felt at the desolation of the mortal realm. There is no liberation at the end, but rather, "consumimur igni," consumption by fire: the phantoms' dance, imploding awareness, particle dusting at the edge of perception—fire walk with me!

[1] France 1978

[2] Quoted from: Roberto Ohrt, "Phantom Avantgarde – Eine Geschichte der Situationistischen Internationale und der modernen Kunst," Hamburg 1990, p. 34.

[3] Jack Sargeant, "The Naked Lens. An Illustrated History of Beat Cinema," London 2001, p. 18.

[4] William Anthony Nericcio, "The Aesthetic Triptych of Jack Kerouac" (www-rohan.sdsu.edu/dept/english/textmex/RobertFrank/frankworking.html - 22k).

[5] Allen Ginsberg, "Being the Notebook of Allen Ginsberg," quoted from: Hans-Christian Kirsch, "Dieses Land ist unser," Munich 1993, p. 33.

[6] John Clellon Holmes, Vorstudie zu dem Roman "The Horn," as quoted by Kirsch, p. 162 f.

[7] Jack Kerouac, "On the Road," Penguin Books, 1991 (orig. 1955), p. 173.

[8] Kirsch, p.65.

[9] Allen Ginsberg, "Robert Frank to 1985—A Man," in: Anne W. Tucker/ Philip Brookman, "Robert Frank: New York to Nova Scotia," exhibition catalogue, Museum of Fine Arts, Houston. Little, Brown and Co., Boston 1986, p. 74.

[10] Kerouac, "On the Road", p. 173.

[11] Quoted from: Barry Miles, "William S. Burroughs – Eine Biographie," Hamburg 1994, p. 121.

William Burroughs hat seinen Roman "The Naked Lunch" einmal als „einen Plan, eine Anleitung" bezeichnet, „die andersartige Erfahrungen ermöglicht, indem sie die Tür am Ende eines langen Korridors öffnet."[11] In den Korridoren von Robert Frank gibt es keine Türen, die nach draußen führen. In seinen Tunneln sieht man nicht das Licht am anderen Ende, sondern wird durch harte (Film)schnitte in andere Szenarien katapultiert. Frank zerschlägt Genre, Plot und Symbolgehalt, um dem Erstaunen über die Ödnis des Reichs der Sterblichen eine zersplitterte ästhetische Form zu verleihen. Am Schluss steht nicht Befreiung, sondern das „consumimur igni", die Verzehrung durch das Feuer: Tanz der Phantome, implodierendes Bewusstsein, Partikelzerstäubung am Rande der Wahrnehmung – fire walk with me!

[1]   Frankreich, 1978

[2]   zitiert nach: Roberto Ohrt: "Phantom Avantgarde – Eine Geschichte der Situationistischen Internationale und der modernen Kunst", Hamburg 1990, S. 34

[3]   Jack Sargeant: "The Naked Lens. An Illustrated History of Beat Cinema", London 2001, S. 18

[4]   William Anthony Nericcio:"The Aesthetic Triptych of Jack Kerouac" (www-rohan.sdsu.edu/dept/english/textmex/RobertFrank/frankworking.html - 22k)

[5]   Allen Ginsberg: "Being the Notebook of Allen Ginsberg", zit. nach: Hans-Christian Kirsch: "Dieses Land ist unser", München 1993, S. 33

[6]   John Clellon Holmes: Vorstudie zu dem Roman "The Horn", zit. nach: Kirsch, S. 162 f

[7]   Jack Kerouac: "Unterwegs", Reinbek bei Hamburg 1984, S.150

[8]   Kirsch, S.65

[9]   Allen Ginsberg: "Robert Frank to 1985 – A Man", in: Anne W. Tucker/ Philip Brookman: "Robert Frank: New York to Nova Scotia", Boston 1986, S. 74

[10] Kerouac: "Unterwegs", S. 150

[11] zitiert nach: Barry Miles: "William S. Burroughs – Eine Biographie", Hamburg 1994, S. 121

About Me: A Musical

Gegenwart

Kent Jones

Wie nähert man sich einem Video, das auf so bewegende Weise unmittelbar ist wie
The Present? Man könnte seine verschiedenen Strategien und Qualitäten herunterdeklinieren, aber das
wäre ein armseliges Unterfangen vor einem Werk von solch unsentimentaler Kraft und Einfachheit. Vor
allem Einfachheit. Nichts, aber auch gar nichts in den 27 Minuten wirkt ausgedacht oder aufgeblasen
für den Moment. Jede Entscheidung, jede Bewegung, sieht aus, als wäre man bei ihr angekommen im
Verlauf einer konzentrierten Suche nach einem unmöglichen Gegenstand. Nämlich: was es ausmacht,
am Leben zu sein.

Robert Frank war darin immer schon sehr gut. Seine Fotografien/Filme/Videos lassen
sich so schwer unterteilen und kategorisieren, weil sie alle derselben Quelle, demselben Impuls zu ent-
stammen scheinen. Sie haben eine bemerkenswerte Balance zwischen großer Sorgfalt und einer selbst-
verständlichen Unbekümmertheit, die das ganze Werk Franks auszeichnet. Es zeigt den Künstler als
menschliches Wesen, nicht als Maestro, Demiurg oder Philosophenkönig. In "The Americans" ist die
Position weder mitfühlend noch kritisch, nicht zudringlich und auch nicht voyeuristisch. Der Künstler,
scheint es, ist einfach da. Es geht niemals darum, ein scharfes, verdichtendes Bild zu finden in der Art
von Evans oder Lange, oder wie Cartier-Bresson den „richtigen Augenblick" zu treffen. Frank ist einfach
dabei, wenn es unten im Süden ein Begräbnis gibt, oder einen Unfall an der Straße im Westen. Er ist
nicht gerade ein emphatischer Zeuge und Teilnehmer: In seinen Bildern gibt es ein seltsames Gefühl des
Alleinseins, eine Vereinzelung, die zu sagen scheint: „Kümmert euch nicht um mich – ich mache meine
Sache und Ihr die Eure."

Ein Film wie *Candy Mountain*, in dem ein unsympathischer Protagonist ständig auf nette
Leute trifft und anheimelnde Landschaften durchquert, macht das nur noch deutlicher. Es ist einer
der unterschätztesten Filme der achtziger Jahre, voller Kraft. Die Geschichte sieht ein wenig nach einer
frühen Warnung vor der drohenden Globalisierung aus. Ein armseliger, ehrgeiziger Typ fährt an das
Ende der Welt, um einen legendären Gitarrenbauer aufzusuchen, nur um festzustellen, dass der schon
von den Japanern eingekauft wurde. Gegen einen Haufen Geld verbrennt er seine Gitarren, sodass
schließlich nur dreißig davon übrigbleiben werden, die dann eine Menge Wert sein werden. Jedoch ist
es nicht so, daß *Candy Mountain* wegen einer Botschaft nachwirkt. Es sind die Bilder und Eindrücke:

Presence

Kent Jones

How to approach a "piece of video" as movingly direct as *The Present...* Ticking off its various strategies and properties seems like a paltry response to a work of such unsentimental force and simplicity. Simplicity most of all. Absolutely nothing in the entire twenty-seven minutes feels assumed or cooked up for the occasion. Every choice, every move, feels *arrived* at, resulting from a hard-working effort to get at an impossible subject. Namely: what it feels like to be alive.

Robert Frank's always been pretty good at that. If it's impossible to break his photographs/films/videos down into separate categories, it's because they all seem to flow from the same source, the same impulse. There's a remarkable balance between great care and (stubbornly) imperturbable ease that runs throughout Frank's body of work, the strong sense of the artist as human being rather than maestro, demiurge or philosopher king. In "The Americans", the stance is neither affectionate nor critical, not inquisitive, and not voyeuristic. Rather, there's the feeling of an artist simply being there. It's never a matter of getting a sharp, encapsulating image in the manner of Evans or Lange, or hitting on the "right moment" à la Cartier-Bresson. Frank is simply present at the funeral down south or the accident on the western roadside. He is not exactly the model of an empathic participant or observer: there's a funny feeling of aloneness in his images, a kind of solitude that always seems to be saying "Don't look at me - just let me go about my business and I'll let you go about yours."

Watching a film like *Candy Mountain*, with its unlikeable protagonist crossing paths with one amenable person and homey landscape after another, only reinforces the point. *Candy Mountain*, one of the most undervalued films of the 1980s, has a wonderful kick to it. The story appears to be an early cautionary tale about looming globalization: a miserable, ambitious small-timer journeys to the end of the world in search of a legendary guitar-maker, only to find that he's already been bought by the Japanese. In exchange for a bundle of money, he's burning his guitars so that only thirty will be left around the world, thus increasing their value. But you don't come away from *Candy Mountain* thinking about a message. Instead, you come away with images and sensations: a lonely encounter with a loveable old Hank Snow fan, the Northway from New York to Canada in blazing autumn color, the seascapes of Nova Scotia, homey diners and bars. Few movies have ever given such presence to people and places, incorporating them into a barebones narrative in a jokey, no sweat fashion that suggests vaudeville, the

eine einsame Begegnung mit einem liebenswürdigen alten Fan von Hank Snow; der Northway von New York nach Kanada in prächtigen Herbstfarben; die Meerblicke in Nova Scotia; intime Diners und Bars. Wenige Filme geben Menschen und Plätzen eine derartige Präsenz, lassen sie mit sich allein, so wie sie sind, zusammengehalten nur von einer dürren Narration, in einer witzigen, unangestrengten Weise, die an Vaudeville denken läßt. Diese Praxis, eine ausreichend flexible erzählerische Struktur über die Wirklichkeit zu legen, war eine zentrale Strategie von Wenders in den frühen und mittleren siebziger Jahren, in der Zeit seiner besten Werke. Aber der gänzlich unsentimentale Frank ist Welten entfernt von dem ultrasensiblen, mit historischer Erfahrung belasteten Auteur von *Im Lauf der Zeit* oder *Der amerikanische Freund.* Wenders folgt dem Weg von Godard und Straub (Erstes Gebot: Du sollst der Wirklichkeit keinen Stempel aufdrücken), während dieses lose Erzählen bei Frank eine Sache des Temperaments zu sein scheint. Zwar hat Rudy Wurlitzer an *Candy Mountain* mitgeschrieben (die Partnerschaft endete stürmisch, wie die mit Alfred Leslie), aber der Film ist doch durch und durch Frank. Aus der Distanz ist das Leben tatsächlich beschissen. So recht aus dem Hier und Jetzt aber ist es immer schön, geheimnisvoll, lebendig. Am Ende der Reise in *Candy Mountain* könnte der mickrige Antiheld (Kevin O'Connor) seine Enttäuschung auch dadurch überwinden, daß er einfach noch ein paar Schritte macht. (Er ist in Nova Scotia, nicht zu vergessen! Man könnte sich gut vorstellen, wie er an Franks würfelspielenden Freund gerät, mit dem *The Present* aufhört. „Ich habe verloren. Und? Das ist die Frage.")

Ein atemberaubender Moment: Schnitt auf drei schwarze Krähen, die zwischen Grashalmen und Unkraut, das aus dem Schnee ragt, herumpicken. Töne vom Leben draußen im tiefen Winter. „Ich denke mir, ich sollte jeden Tag etwas drehen", sagt Robert Frank in seiner ausdruckslosen Stimme mit Schweizer Akzent. „Aber es wird besser sein ... Material ... von Menschen zu haben", fügt er hinzu. „Jeden Tag will ich ein kleines Stück Video machen. Und ich finde, daß Menschen ..." Eine Pause, und plötzlich fliegen die Krähen aus dem Bild, alle auf einmal. „... sehr gut sind ..." Zoom hinaus auf eine verschneite, leicht hügelige Landschaft, am Rand des Bildes liegt ein alter Reifen. „... und sehr expressiv." Schnitt auf einen Mann in einem karierten Hemd, der vor einem Fenster in Nova Scotia sitzt und über die Hunde in der Gegend redet.

Warum berührt mich diese Vignette so? In erster Linie wegen Franks untrüglichem Auge – durchdringend, schnell, ruhig. Die entspannten schwarzen Krähen ergeben eine schöne Dreiecksgruppe vor dem weißen Schnee, aber durch das unscheinbare braune Gras bleibt das Bild unprätentiös. Wie immer bei Frank ist das Bild vollständig präsent, gebunden an den Moment seiner Erscheinung in der Wirklichkeit, einfach vorgefunden. Zum zweiten wird die entspannte, ganz dem Augenblick hingegebene Ästhetik auf ein Spiel mit Bild und Narration ausgeweitet, weil Frank eine schöne Verbindung herstellt. Er spricht über Menschen, während er anscheinend auf Krähen blickt, und trifft damit etwas, was seine Karriere von Beginn an geprägt hat – eine künstlerische Praxis, die sich an den Rhythmen und Gewohnheiten des Lebens ausrichtet, nicht wie es gelebt werden sollte, sondern wie es gelebt *wird.* Die Pause zwischen dem Abflug der Krähen und Franks Menschenbejahung ist unwiderstehlich, perfekt gesetzt, wagemutig affirmativ. Wenn man sich die Sache dann noch genauer ansieht (und ich habe *The Present* viele, viele Male gesehen), haben die Überlegung, die intellektuelle wie künstlerische Leistung hinter diesem Moment ihren eigenen Charme. Anscheinend blickt Frank durch ein Fenster auf die Krähen und denkt dabei laut, wahrscheinlicher aber ist es, daß der Moment perfekt konstruiert ist, um den Anschein einer spontan sich entwickelnden Wirklichkeit zu geben (wodurch wurden die Krähen aufgeschreckt? ein Geräusch? warum ist es dann auf der Tonspur nicht zu hören?). Die Bescheidenheit

better to leave them alone, very much as they are. This practice of grafting a suitably flexible narrative structure onto the Real World was a key Wenders strategy in the early and mid-1970s, when he was doing his best work. But the completely unsentimental Frank is a world away from the historically troubled, ultra-sensitive auteur of *Im Lauf der Zeit* or *Der Amerikanische Freund.* Whereas Wenders is following in the path of Godard and Straub (Commandment #1: Thou shalt alter reality as little as possible), for Frank it feels like a matter of temperament. *Candy Mountain* may have been co-authored with Rudy Wurlitzer (like Alfred Leslie, another stormy partnership that ended badly), but it feels like Frank through and through. From the long view, life does indeed suck. From the right here and now, it's always beautiful, mysterious, lively. When Kevin O'Connor's crummy anti-hero gets to the end of the road in *Candy Mountain*, he might find an antidote to his discouragement just around the corner from the end of his movie (right there in Nova Scotia, come to think of it). Easy to imagine him running into Frank's dice-throwing friend who closes *The Present.* "I lost. But so what? That's the question."

A breathtaking moment: cut to three black crows pecking at something betweeen blades of grass and weeds sticking up through the snow. Sounds of outdoor life in mid-winter. "I think every day I should have some footage," says Robert Frank in his deadpan, Swiss-accented voice. "But it will be better...to have footage...of people," he adds. "Every day, I want to make a little piece of video. And I find that people..." A pause, and the crows suddenly fly out of the frame, all at once "...are very good..." Zoom out to reveal a snowy, nicely disshevelled landscape, with an old tire lying in the corner of the frame. "...and very expressive." Cut to a man in a plaid shirt, sitting by a Nova Scotia window, discussing the local dogs.

Why does this little vignette move me so? First of all, because of Frank's unfailing eye— limpid, quick, calm. The laid-back black crows are grouped in a nice triangle formation against the white snow, and the unpicturesque brown grass dilutes the potential preciousness: as always with Frank, the image is strictly present tense, fused to the moment of its occurrence in reality, apparently happened upon. Secondly, the sense of relaxed, no-sweat, in-the-moment aesthetics extends to the byplay between image and narration, as a nice juxtaposition is set up: Frank is talking about people as he's supposedly looking at crows, getting at something he's cultivated from the beginning of his career, which is an artistic practice wedded to the rhythms and habits of life, not as it's supposed to be lived or as it should be lived, but as it *is* lived. The pause before the crow trio flies away in unison and Frank's thumbs up on people is irresistible, perfectly timed, thrillingly affirmative. On another level, if you're looking at it closely (and I've seen *The Present* many, many times), the calculation, brainwork, and artistry behind the moment has its own charm. Frank may be looking at the crows through a window and thinking out loud, or (more likely) the moment has been perfectly constructed to give the appearance of spontan- eously generated reality (what was it that drove the crows away? An offscreen noise? If so, why isn't it on the track?). As has often happened with Frank, the modesty of his viewpoint as an artist (determinedly small-scale, minoritarian, unglamourous) has obscured the fact that he's pioneered many aesthetic practices that have come into vogue over the years. This kind of careful re-constitution of reality now seems to be Kiarostami's domain, but Frank has been taking it through far less lofty realms for years now. Where Kiarostami is looking at Nature, Existence (or is that The Nature of Existence), etc. with his artfully constructed artlessness, Frank is never stepping back to look at the big picture, but putting everything on the level of dailiness, what could be called "practical reality"—he winds up giving us the big picture anyway, but he allows it to piece itself together. Connections are made amd metaphors are

The Present

seines Standpunkts als Künstler (bewußt klein, minoritär, unglamourös) hat häufig die Tatsache verdeckt, daß Frank eine Reihe von ästhetischen Strategien vorweggenommen hat, die mit der Zeit in Mode kamen. Diese Art der sorgfältigen Nachstellung der Wirklichkeit scheint inzwischen die Domäne von Kiarostami zu sein, aber Frank hat dieses Prinzip jahrelang auf weniger hehre Themen angewendet. Wenn Kiarostami mit seiner kunstvoll konstruierten Kunstlosigkeit auf die Natur oder die Existenz blickt (oder vielleicht sogar auf die Natur der Existenz?), macht Frank niemals den Schritt zurück auf diese allgemeine Ebene, sondern bleibt immer auf einer Ebene der Täglichkeit, die man „praktische Realität" nennen könnte. Am Ende gibt es trotzdem einen Gesamteindruck, aber er läßt es zu, daß sich dieser wie von selbst zusammensetzt. Verbindungen und Metaphern werden so natürlich hergestellt, wie der Mensch atmet: und so folgt der nächste Gedanke, der nächste Eindruck, das nächste Begreifen, der nächste Moment des Vergessens, Träumens, freien Assoziierens. Oder Erinnerns.

Es gibt noch andere Gründe, diesen Moment zu lieben, vor allem, weil er Teil dieses besonderen Werks ist. Wenn Sie *The Present* gesehen haben, werden Sie wissen, daß er auf der einen Seite eine Klage ist. Ich möchte es keine Trauerarbeit nennen, denn das hieße, es mit einem dämlichen Präzisionsklischee zu versehen. Aber Franks Sohn Pablo, der schon tot ist, als sein Vater mit diesem Video beginnt (ein Foto an einer Wand mit Bildern, in einem der vielen Fragmente in *The Present*: Franks Sohn, daneben die Worte Pablo ... Gone, und auf der Tonspur ein Country-Song "Well, goodbye, Mr. Reporter, I'm sorry for what I done"), kommt immer wieder. *The Present* hat eine archäologische Struktur, die an das Wühlen und Kramen in einem alten Haus gemahnt, an eine ziellose Reise durch die Vergangenheit. Oder, einfach auf das Leben angewandt: Wir sind immer in einer Vergangenheit hineingehalten, wie Fitzgerald sagte, der aber ein großes, bedeutsames Subjekt meinte (Amerika!), während Frank auf der lokalen Ebene arbeitet – natürlich gehen wir immer voran, und natürlich blicken wir immer zurück. Was bleibt uns übrig? Wir sehen Pablos Gesicht auf Fotos, wir hören eine Erinnerung an ihn, die zu einem wunderbaren Bild von fallendem Schnee an der Bleecker Street (wieder eine dieser schönen, einfachen Verbindungen), wir sehen seine Blumen (und des Vaters Fotografien dieser Blumen), wir sehen die Unordnung in seiner Wohnung (Frank auf der Tonspur: „Wie kann ich meine Gedanken ordnen?"). Wir lesen die kaum zu ertragende Nachricht, die ihm der Vater nach seinem Tod schrieb („Ich wünschte, du könntest deine Blumen sehen. Von Vater, mit einem Kuss.") Frank und seine brillante Cutterin und Komplizin Laura Israel gestalten dies alles so nahtlos und gleichzeitig so wunderbar lose, daß wir innerhalb dieser wie unbeaufsichtigt wirkenden Momente genügend Raum für unsere Assoziationen haben. An einer früheren Stelle in *The Present* erwähnt Frank, daß gerade der Geburtstag seiner Tochter Andrea ist – auch sie ist tot, gestorben bei einem Flugzeugabsturz vor zwanzig Jahren.

generated as naturally as breathing, and then we're on to the next thought, the next sensation, the next realization, the next instant of forgetting, dreaming, free-associating. Or remembering.

There are other reasons to love this moment, and they have to do with the fact that it is part of this particular piece. If you've seen *The Present*, you will know that it is, in one sense, a lament. I won't call it a work of mourning, because that would be to tag it with a bullshit, precision-tooled cliché. But Frank's son Pablo, dead before his father started making this video (a photo on a gallery wall, glimpsed in one of *The Present*'s many fragments: Frank's son, framed by the words "Pablo...Gone" and followed by a country song on the track - "Well, Goodbye Mr. Reporter, I'm sorry for what I done"), keeps coming back. *The Present* has an achronological structure which suggests rummaging, moseying through an empty house and letting your mind wander, or taking a leisurely journey through the past. Or, just living: we're always borne back into the past, as Fitzgerald said, but where he was addressing a grand, pretentious subject (America!), Frank is working at the local level—of course we're always going to go forward, and of course we're always going to look back. What else can we do? We see Pablo's face in photographs, we hear a remembrance of him read over a lovely image of snow falling on Bleecker Street (another beautifully hand-made juxtaposition), we see his flowers (and his father's photographs of his flowers), we look at the clutter of his apartment (Frank on the track: "How can I sort out my thoughts?"). We read the heartbreaking note his father has written him after he's gone ("I wish that you could see your flowers...From Dad, with a kiss"). And the way Frank and his obviously brilliant editor and partner in crime Laura Israel construct this piece, so seamless and yet so lovably ragged, we have the space to generate associations between moments that are left just untended enough. Earlier in *The Present*, Frank says that it's his daughter Andrea's birthday—also gone, killed in a plane crash over twenty years ago. "I wonder what she's thinking," he wonders. Perhaps Pablo and Andrea are merely dead, but not gone. Not there, but always present. So, in this movie in which death is so ubiquitous, and so real, the sight of three black crows against a white background has a special lilt. It may seem like it's stretching the point to mention the piece's other death—Frank's old friend Werner, the third black crow—but maybe that would please Frank after all. The world has a way of offering metaphors at the most unlikely moments, in the least likely settings.

"It's gonna be a crows movie!" announces Frank—the moment in question marks one of many appearances of the black birds, and prompts a funny discussion with a neighbour ("You feed them *too?*" asks Frank's wife June). There are other animals—a dog that keeps looking out the window ("What does he *see?*" "I don't *know*, Robert."), a horse ("What kind of animal is this?" asks Frank, trying to pretend he's the first man after the act of creation, or something like that—"This animal is called…" and then a cut), more crows in another snowbound convocation, this time with off-camera animals braying in the distance. Like everything else in *The Present*, these visits to the animal kingdom are events. There is no hierarchy among the events, nothing is more important or urgent than anything else, and they come in all shapes and sizes: a fly dropping dead; a dying tree on Bleecker Street ("I remember every goddamned twig"); a woman brushing her lustrously dark hair, her face out of frame, against a white background (like the crows against the snow); a cut from a hissing wood stove to a poster of the muscular substructure of the human face; the resolution to make a new piece of video every day; a sudden eruption of useless blathering nonsense, for no good reason. "We were celebrating the new jacket," Frank says at one point. Later, near the end of the film: "I've asked my friend Yuichi to come…we'll see what *that* visit will be."

„Ich wüßte gern, was sie denkt", fragt er sich. Vielleicht sind Pablo und Andrea bloß tot, aber nicht vergangen. Nicht da, aber immer gegenwärtig. In diesem Film, in dem der Tod so allgegenwärtig ist, und so real, hat der Anblick von drei schwarzen Krähen vor weißem Hintergrund eine besondere Färbung. Vielleicht ist es ein wenig überzogen, jetzt noch einen weiteren Todesfall in diesem Film zu erwähnen – Franks alter Freund Werner, die dritte Krähe –, aber vielleicht würde gerade dies Frank gefallen. Die Welt produziert Metaphern durch die unwahrscheinlichsten Orte und Zusammenhänge.

„Das wird ein Krähenfilm", kündigt Frank an. Der besagte Moment liegt in einer langen Reihe von Begegnungen mit Krähen. Es entsteht eine lustige Diskussion daraus („Sie füttern sie auch?", fragt Franks Frau June.). Es gibt noch andere Tiere – einen Hund, der aus dem Fenster blickt („Was sieht er?" „Ich weiß es nicht, Robert."), ein Pferd („Was ist das für ein Tier?", fragt Frank, als wäre er der erste Mensch nach dem Schöpfungsakt. „Dieses Tier heißt..." Und dann kommt ein Schnitt.), weitere Krähen bei einer Versammlung im Schnee, in diesem Fall mit weiteren Tieren, deren Laute deutlich zu hören, die aber nicht im Bild sind. Diese Besuche im Reich der Tiere sind Ereignisse in *The Present*, wie alles andere. Es gibt zwischen ihnen keine Hierarchie, nichts ist wichtiger oder dringender als anderes, sie kommen in allen Formen und Größen: eine Fliege, die tot zu Boden fällt; ein sterbender Baum an der Bleecker Street („Ich erinnere mich an jeden gottverdammten Zweig"); eine Frau, die ihr verführerisches dunkles Haar kämmt, das Gesicht ist nicht im Bild, vor einem weißen Hintergrund (wie die Krähen vor dem Schnee); ein Schnitt von einem zischenden Holzofen auf ein Poster der muskulären Substruktur im menschlichen Gesicht; der Beschluß, jeden Tag ein neues Stück Video herzustellen; ein Ausbruch blödelnden Unsinns, einfach so. „Wir feierten die neue Jacke", sagt Frank an einer Stelle. Später, gegen Ende des Films: „Ich habe meinen Freund Yuichi eingeladen zu kommen – wir werden sehen, was *dieser* Besuch bringt."

Alles in *The Present* erscheint gleichermaßen gefunden (also in einen Zusammenhang gesetzt, erinnert) und gerade geschehend. Wir wissen nie, wohin es als nächstes geht, und wann – die Chronologie ist ungewiß, und Frank wechselt umstandlos zwischen Nova Scotia, Bleecker Street, Zürich, einem Hotelzimmer irgendwo, einer Galerie an einem anderen Ort. Wenn man genau hinschaut, gibt es einen erzählerischen Rahmen. „Ich bin froh, dass ich meine Kamera gefunden habe", sagt er, die ersten Worte im Film, und sofort ist er auf der Suche nach einer Geschichte, die sich irgendwo in der Alltäglichkeit des Hauses versteckt hält. Es ist aber nicht so sehr eine Geschichte, die er findet, sondern ein Ausgangspunkt, eine Gewohnheit. „Ich sehe beim Fenster hinaus", sagt Frank, während wir die Landschaft des Cape Breton vor seinem Fenster sehen. „Und dann ist da ... Erinnerung." Als Yuichi gegen Ende des Films zu Besuch kommt, bittet Frank ihn, das Wort "Memory" von einem Stück Glas (Wand? zu schrubben – es war zwanzig Jahre an dieser Stelle, ein schwarzer Schriftzug, mit Fingern gezeichnet. Wenig überraschend, ist die Erinnerung schwer wegzukriegen. Lachen sie über diese Bemerkung, weil sie begreifen, daß dies für das Ende des Videos ein wenig zu glatt wäre? Oder hat Frank einfach entschieden, über diese kitschige und willkommene Metapher ein Stück Video zu drehen, und später zu entscheiden, an welche Stelle es kommen sollte?

Ist es „Erinnerung", oder ist es „Erinnern"? Oder handelt es sich um Erfahrung (in diesem Fall auch um die Erfahrung des Filmens), die gerade zur Erinnerung wird? *The Present* ist eine Sammlung von Fragmenten, solange man den Film nicht darauf reduziert (und Frank auf die Rolle eines Systemkünstlers). Wie bei seinen alten Kumpels in der Beat Generation sind die Ideen des Automatischen, des Spontanen und Intuitiven nur insofern sinnvoll, als sie die Kunst mit dem Lebensprozess verbinden.

Everything in *The Present* feels at once caught—thus framed and, in a sense, remembered—and happening…in the present. We never know where we will be dropped next, or when—chronology is uncertain, and Frank shifts effortlessly between Nova Scotia, Bleecker Street, Zurich, a hotel room somewhere, a gallery somewhere else. If you pay close attention, you'll find a framing device. "I'm glad I found my camera," he says, the first words in the film, and right away he's in search of a story, lurking somewhere in the dailiness of his house. And it's not so much a story that is found as a touchstone, or a habit. "I look out the window," says Frank, as we look out at the Cape Breton landscape from his window, "and then it's…memory." And when Yuichi comes to visit near the end of the film, Frank asks him to scrub the word "memory" off a piece of glass: it's been there for twenty years, finger-painted in black. Predictably, memory is hard to erase. Are they laughing over this remark because they know this will make a too-tidy ending for the video, or did Frank just decide that it was fitting to make his daily piece of video over a corny and readily available metaphor, and then decide on its placement later?

Is it "memory," or is it "remembering?" Or, is it experience—and in this case, filming is a part of experience—in the process of becoming memory? In a sense, *The Present* could be considered a collection of fragments, but that would be reductive, making Frank into a systems artist. Like his old pals in the Beat generation, the ideas of the automatic, the spontaneous and the intuitive are meaningful only to the extent that they merge the making of art with the process of living: they effaced the model of the meditative, "ivory tower" artist, the better to work within and through experience itself—partly political, partly temperamental, partly spiritual and partly generational. To see the spontaneity—sometimes the *impression* of spontaneity—in Frank's (or Kerouac's) work as an end in itself, as opposed to one aspect of the art, is to misunderstand the work, to pre-judge it according to inapplicable criteriae and thus avoid it altogether.

I said earlier that I see no difference whatsoever between Frank's photographs, his filmed images, and his video images. Nor between his "fictions," like *Candy Mountain*, and his "documentaries," like *The Present* or *One Hour*. In each case, the image is, or appears to be, happened upon. And there's something else, too. What is it that Frank keeps happening *upon*, again and again, throughout his career, in his memento pieces, his little stories, his landscapes, his impromptu portraits, his moments? It has something to do with the aforementioned solitude. In every Frank image I've ever seen—the animal soon-to-be-named "horse" in *The Present*, O'Connor driving north and sharing the frame with a colorful autumn landscape in the oddest composition in *Candy Mountain*, that gorgeous shot of sunflowers with "Les Filles" scrawled across it, the South Carolina mourners in "The Americans"—there's a fiercely powerful sense of the elemental freedom in aloneness. Often it's reflected in the relationship between Frank himself and the landscape. Take the famous photo from "The Americans" of Highway 285. There's no cliché here—The Freedom of the Open Road, the Terror of the Open Road. It feels too dark for the former, hardly ominous enough for the latter. In one sense, it is a classically composed photograph. In another, more pressing sense, it is a moment of communion with the idea of solitude itself. Frank exposes for the darkness on the horizon, but it's a nice darkness—not sweet, but calm, restful, comforting even. It's about a million miles from the tabloid blackness of Weegee, the suave darknesses of a Callahan or a Minor White, the bewitching blacks of a Weston, or the hard, slatelike range of grays in Evans. The various darknesses of the Butte, Montana billiard table or the Salt Lake City School of Art, surrounding Kerouac's beloved lonely elevator girl or behind the blonde at the

The Present – Andrea Frank

Sie überwanden die Rolle des meditativen Elfenbeinturm-Künstlers, indem sie in und mit der Erfahrung arbeiteten – politisch, temperamentvoll, spirituell und generationenbewußt. Spontaneität (manchmal nur der *Eindruck* davon) ist im Werk von Frank (oder Kerouac) kein Selbstzweck, sondern ein Teil der Kunst. Wer das nicht sieht, wendet die falschen Kriterien an, und verfehlt das Werk insgesamt.

Ich habe schon gesagt, daß ich zwischen Franks Fotografien, seinen gefilmten Bildern und seinen Videobildern keinen Unterschied, wie auch immer, sehe. Ebensowenig zwischen seinen „Spielfilmen", wie *Candy Mountain*, und seinen „Dokumentarfilmen", wie *The Present* oder *One Hour*. In jedem Fall ist das Bild wie eine zufällige Begegnung, oder es wirkt zumindest so. Dazu kommt noch etwas anderes. Worauf stößt Frank immer wieder, in seiner ganzen Karriere, in seinen Memento-Stücken, seinen kleinen Geschichten, seinen Landschaften, seinen improvisierten Porträts, seinen Momenten? Es hat etwas mit der schon erwähnten Einsamkeit zu tun. In jedem Frank-Bild, das ich jemals gesehen habe – das Tier, das man „Pferd" nennen würde in *The Present*; O'Connor auf seiner Fahrt in den Norden vor einer farbenprächtigen Herbstlandschaft in der seltsamsten Kadrierung in *Candy Mountain*; das großartige Bild der Sonnenblumen, über das „Les Filles" gekritzelt ist; die Trauernden in South Carolina aus "The Americans" – immer gibt es einen unbezwingbaren Sinn für die grundlegende Freiheit des Alleinseins. Häufig spiegelt sich dies in der Beziehung zwischen Frank selbst und der Landschaft wider. Zum Beispiel das berühmte Bild des "Highway 285" in "The Americans". Es gibt hier kein Klischee – die Freiheit, der Schrecken der offenen Straße sind nicht enthalten, das Bild ist zu dunkel für erstere Vorstellung, aber nicht unheilvoll genug für die zweitere. Einerseits ist es eine klassisch komponierte Fotografie. Anderseits aber, und das ist der wichtigere Aspekt, ist es ein Moment der Begegnung mit der Vorstellung von Einsamkeit selbst. Frank zielt auf die Dunkelheit am Horizont – aber es ist eine angenehme Dunkelheit, keine süße, sondern eine ruhige, friedliche, ja tröstliche. Das ist Welten entfernt von der Schlagzeilen-Schwärze eines Weegee, den sanften Dunkelheiten eines Callahan oder Minor White, dem betörenden Schwarz von Weston, oder den harten Schiefergrautönen bei Evans. Die verschiedenen Dunkelheiten an einem Billardtisch in Butte, Montana oder in der Salt Lake City School of Art, rund um Kerouacs geliebtes einsames Liftmädchen oder hinter der Blondine bei der Hollywoodpremiere sind nicht bedrohlich, sondern fast behaglich – wie diese schwarzen Krähen in *The Present*. Sie sind Räume, in denen man sich zurücklehnen und Kraft sammeln kann, vielleicht auch Räume, in denen man auf das Vergessen warten kann, in denen man sich ein paar Minuten ausruht, bevor man in den Kampf zurückkehrt, in denen man vielleicht an die Ewigkeit denken kann. Es ist eine der großen Leistungen, dass Frank den beängstigenden Teil von Amerika freilegt, den religiösen Wahn

Hollywood premiere, strike me as wholly unthreatening and even cozy—just like those black crows in *The Present*. They are spaces in which to repose, to re-gather momentum, perhaps to await oblivion, perhaps to take a few minutes before getting back into the fray, perhaps to contemplate eternity. It's one of the great achievements of "The Americans" that Frank zeroes in on the scary part of America, the religious mania and the deathly political paranoia, the poverty and the exhaustion, but also finds the salvation of potential solitude in its anonymity and famously wide open spaces. And its shadows.

The New York City rodeo rider, hidden behind his Stetson, rolling a cigarette. The blurred Hollywood starlet looking away from her fans. The pregnant woman staring into the dirt in Belle Isle, her arms folded. The plain-faced blonde behind the two old men leaning against the tree somewhere in North Carolina, raising her abstracted gaze toward Frank's camera. And, most touchingly of all to these eyes, that elevator girl staring heavenward as the frame tilts with her and against her fancy passengers. And that beautiful girl in Reno, tightly encircled in her boyfriend/new husband's arms, allowed to resist the scenario of True Love Forever for one precious moment before Frank's camera. There's the same sense of shapely singularity and solitude in Frank's nameless, silent pony-tailed friend in *The Present,* approaching the camera and getting out his own camera to start shooting—did Frank have to do multiple takes to rid him of his self-consciousness, to get that wonderful mixture of deter-mination, boredom, (feigned) nonchalance, and intelligence in his gestures and expressions? And let's not forget that horse, standing still, looking guardedly at the camera. Or the dog, fixated on the mythical object out the window.

In a very real way, the life-tested solitude I prize so much in Frank's work is a matter of context. And sequencing. Early on, Frank embraced the idea of sequential as opposed to singular images. So why the beef with Steichen over *The Family of Man*? First of all, because Frank has always been a resolutely anti-cliché artist. But even more than that, the clichés of universal meaning in that show—suffering, hope, endurance, etc, etc, etc.—run against the grain of Frank's art, and what I will presume is his philosophical stance. Namely, that real freedom is an elusive state, available in the far corners of life, far from the madness of the glorious and all-consuming center. And that the minute you start grouping images together according to a Theme, you're lost. Because in Frank the solitude doesn't just belong to the people in the image, or to the shadows in the image, or to the man behind the camera, but finally to the images themselves. The move from the hotel room on a foggy afternoon, that woman brushing her hair, the bed, to a coin placed in a filthy outsretched hand, shadows on a New York sidewalk, the lower east side before sunset, to the dice-wielding friend in Nova Scotia, has the same air-filled freedom/intelligence/wisdom as the darkened Salt Lake School of Art, to the smiling lady from South Carolina happily resting in a chair with the sunset and a providential telephone pole behind her, to the starched mourners filing past the body, to the toppled flower arrangement at the fogswept Chinese cemetery in San Francisco, to the Stephenson fan hidden behind his tuba. Each is an image to be sure, allowed to retain its identity as a moment.

Frank leaves me feeling at peace with myself, and for that I feel grateful. I'm sure Andrea and Pablo feel the same. Wherever they are.

und die tödliche politische Paranoia, die Armut und die Erschöpfung, aber auch die Rettung durch eine mögliche Einsamkeit in seiner Anonymität und in seinen weiten, offenen Räumen. Und in seinen Schatten.

Der New Yorker Rodeo-Reiter, der, hinter seinem Stetson verborgen, eine Zigarette dreht. Das verwischte Hollywood-Starlet, das von den Fans wegblickt. Die schwangere Frau, die in Belle Isle in den Dreck starrt, die Hände verschränkt. Die unscheinbare Blondine hinter den beiden alten Männern an einem Baum irgendwo in North Carolina, die ihren zerstreuten Blick auf Franks Kamera richtet. Und, für mich besonders anrührend, das Liftmädchen, das himmelwärts blickt, während das Bild mit ihr und ihren feinen Passagieren kippt. Und dieses schöne Mädchen in Reno, gefangen im Arm ihres Freunds und frischgebackenen Ehemanns – vor Franks Kamera kann sie für einen kostbaren Moment dem „Bis der Tod euch scheidet" entkommen. In *The Present* gibt es eine ähnlich konturierte Vereinzelung und Einsamkeit in der Figur eines namenlosen Freundes von Frank, ein Mann mit zusammengebundenem Haar, der seine eigene Kamera herausnimmt, während er auf die von Frank zugeht. Musste Frank diese Szene mehrmals drehen, um diesen Mann in jenen wunderbaren Zustand aus Entschlossenheit, Langeweile, (vorgeschützter) Nonchalance und Intelligenz zu versetzen, in dem er ganz unmittelbar zu werden scheint? Nicht zu vergessen das Pferd, das einfach dasteht, und reserviert in die Kamera blickt. Oder der Hund, der auf das mythische Objekt draußen vor dem Fenster fixiert ist.

In einem sehr konkreten Sinn ist die im Leben bewährte Einsamkeit, die ich in Franks Werk so rühme, eine Frage des Kontexts. Und der Sequenz. Schon früh hatte Frank etwas übrig für Bilderfolgen anstatt einzelner Bilder. Warum kam es also zu dem Gemecker mit Steichen wegen *The Family of Man*? Vor allem, weil Frank als Künstler immer resolut gegen die Klischees vorging. Mehr noch, die Klischees einer universalen Bedeutung in dieser Schau – Leiden, Hoffnung, Geduld etc. etc. etc. – gehen Frank gegen den Strich, auch in philosophischer Hinsicht. Ich denke, er hält wirkliche Freiheit für etwas Flüchtiges, in den entlegenen Winkeln des Lebens Verborgenes, weit entfernt von dem Wahnsinn, mit dem im Zentrum alles überstrahlt und vereinnahmt wird. In dem Moment, in dem du Bilder zu einem Thema versammelst, bist du auf dem Holzweg. Denn bei Frank gehört das Alleinsein nicht nur den Leuten im Bild, oder den Schatten im Bild, oder dem Mann hinter der Kamera, es ist eine Eigenschaft der Bilder selbst. Der Schwenk aus einem Hotelzimmer an einem dämmerigen Nachmittag; die Frau, die ihr Haar bürstet; das Bett; eine Münze, die in einer schmutzigen, ausgestreckten Hand liegt; Schatten auf einem Gehsteig in New York; die Lower East Side im Sonnenuntergang; der Freund mit den Würfeln in Nova Scotia – all das hat dieselbe, frische Freiheit/Intelligenz/Weisheit wie die schattige Salt Lake School of Art, die lächelnde Lady, die während eines Sonnenuntergangs in South Carolina glücklich in ihrem Sessel sitzt, hinter dem vorsichtshalber ein Telefon ist, die steifen Trauergäste, die sich hinter einem Toten einreihen, das fragile Blumenarrangement auf dem nebligen chinesischen Friedhof in San Francisco, der Fan von Stephenson hinter seiner Tuba. Jedes einzelne davon ist ein Bild, das seine Identität im Moment bewahren darf.

Frank hinterlässt in mir ein Gefühl des Friedens mit mir selbst. Dafür bin ich ihm dankbar. Ich bin sicher, Andrea und Pablo fühlen das gleiche. Wo immer sie sind.

Take a picture of my baby:
Robert Frank und die Dramaturgie des Scheiterns

Michael Barchet / Pia Neumann

> I'm always looking outside,
> trying to look inside. Trying to say something that's true.
> But maybe nothing is really true.
> Except what's out there.
> And what's out there is always changing.[1]

Robert Franks Filme bewegen sich auf schwierig zu kartografierendem Gelände. Ihr Terrain liegt an den Rändern sehr divergenter Regionen kultureller Produktion und Wahrnehmung, die zum Teil weder aneinander grenzen noch über einen gemeinsamen Kanon von Sitten und Gebräuchen verfügen. In Franks Filmen zeigen sich Verfahren und Repräsentationsmuster des Dokumentarfilms und Spielformen des experimentellen Theaters, aber auch Erzähltechniken des Spielfilms und die Intimitäten des Amateurvideos. Für die Navigation in diesen höchst widersprüchlichen medialen Szenarien stellen Franks Filme nur sehr ungenaue, manchmal sogar bewusst irreleitende Landkarten und Wegweiser bereit. Allerdings weisen viele stilistische und thematische Merkmale seiner Filme – und auch das eingangs aufgeführte und in der Literatur zu Frank oft zitierte Statement aus seinem Video *Home Improvements* (1985) – darauf hin, dass der in Franks Arbeiten so obsessiv umspielte Begriff der „Wahrheit" nicht allein als Metapher des fundamentalen Zweifels an der Möglichkeit authentischer künstlerischer Subjektivität zu verstehen ist, sondern die Notwendigkeit des filmischen Blicks nach „draußen" mit einer Art verzweifelter Hoffnung besetzt. Dies deutet auf eine Privilegierung oder zumindest auf eine Zentralität dokumentarischer Herangehensweisen hin.

Allerdings zeigen sich diese Herangehensweisen in Franks Filmen als vielfach gebrochene und reflektierte Befragung ihrer Bedingungen, die ihren Gebrauch als Instrumentarien der filmischen Vergewisserung von Welt immer wieder und buchstäblich mutwillig beschädigt. Es scheint, als ob die Filme Franks sich verschiedener Stilistiken und Arbeitsweisen des Dokumentarischen bedienen, um die Grenzen ihrer Reichweite zu erforschen. Vor allem in der Montage der Filme spielen diese intuitiv und wenig systematisch vorangetriebenen Forschungen oft filmische Beobachtung, kontrollierte Erzählkonstruktionen und den Eigensinn improvisierter Performances gegeneinander aus. Obwohl die aus

Take a Picture of My Baby:
Robert Frank and the Dramaturgy of Failure

Michael Barchet / Pia Neumann

> I'm always looking outside,
> trying to look inside. Trying to say something that's true.
> But maybe nothing is really true.
> Except what's out there.
> And what's out there is always changing.[1]

Robert Frank's films travel through terrain that is difficult to map. Their territory lies at the peripheries of divergent regions of cultural production and perception, which neither border one another nor share a common canon of customs and habits. Present in Frank's films are methods and representational patterns from documentary film, forms of acting from experimental theater, and also narrative forms from feature films and the intimacies of amateur video. Frank's films offer only extremely imprecise, at times even consciously misdirecting maps and road signs for navigation in these highly contradictory media scenarios. Many stylistic and thematic characteristics of his films, though— including the quotation offered here at the beginning from his video *Home Improvements* (1985), which is often cited in the literature about Frank—point out that the concept of "truth," so obsessively tossed around in his works, is not to be understood merely as a metaphor of the fundamental doubt in the possibility of understanding authentic artistic subjectivity; it also fills the cinematic gaze "outward" with a type of desperate hope. This indicates a privileging or at least a centrality of documentary approaches.

Admittedly, in Frank's films these methods for approaching issues are revealed as multiply broken and reflected interrogations of their conditions, which continually and literally wantonly destroy their use as instruments for the cinematic ascertainment of the world. Frank's films seem to use various documentary styles and modes of operation in order to explore their outer limits. It is primarily in the montage of the films that this intuitive and not very systematically carried out research often plays out cinematic observation, controlled narrative constructions, and the obstinacy of improvised performances against each other. Although the weaves of text arising from this method are very loose, ambivalent, and *in principle* remain open, a rhetorical topos continually comes to the fore of a privileged legibility—

diesem Verfahren entstehenden Textgeflechte sehr locker, ambivalent und *prinzipiell* offen bleiben, rückt doch ein rhetorischer Topos immer wieder in den Vordergrund einer privilegierten Lesbarkeit – die filmische Rhetorik des Scheiterns. Dieser möchten wir in einer Auseinandersetzung mit einigen Passagen aus Robert Franks Filmen *Last Supper, About Me: A Musical, C`est vrai!* und *Me and My Brother* nachgehen.

Ziel ist dabei, diese Rhetorik als Bedingung der *filmischen* Konstruktion einer Autorenpersona zu verstehen, deren unablässig vorgetragener Zweifel an ihrer eigenen Kontrolle über die Diegese starke Züge der Fiktionalisierung trägt und gerade daraus plausible Positionen authentischen Ausdrucks schöpft. Dabei scheint es, dass gerade die an Franks Filmen so oft festgestellte Verschränkung von „Leben und Werk" die deutlichsten Zeichen der Fiktion dort aufscheinen lässt, wo sie am engsten an autobiografische Szenarien gekettet ist und ihre Referenz zum Leben des Filmemachers im Vordergrund steht.

Es kann in diesem Kontext weniger darum gehen, der einschlägigen Filmkritik ihre hingebungsvolle Verwechslung von Filmemacher und Autor vorzuwerfen. Vielmehr erscheint es wichtig, herauszuarbeiten, wie die Filme Franks diese Verwechslung einfordern und wozu sie gebraucht wird. So ist die Figur des Künstlers, der auf der „Suche nach Wahrheit und nach einer Sprache, sie auszudrücken,"[2] die „Nähe zum Chaos"[3] riskiert, um die Bedingungen der eigenen Subjektivität immer wieder zu hinterfragen, so deutlich als Zentralfigur des romantischen Kunstbegriffs erkennbar, dass sie sofort in den Verdacht der Projektion geraten muss. Dies bedeutet allerdings nicht, diese Figur als Produkt von Verfälschung oder Lüge zu begreifen. Es könnte sich vielmehr um eine taktische Reduktion von Komplexität handeln, bei der die ästhetischen Idiosynkrasien der Filme Franks den Begriff des authentischen Künstlers für die Diegese der Kunst gerade dadurch retten, dass sich eine Autorenfigur immer wieder in Szenarien verstrickt, die durch das Scheitern an den Bedingungen künstlerischen Sprechens charakterisiert sind.

Ästhetik des Scheiterns

„Aesthetics of Failure" nennt Paul Arthur in einem einflussreichen Artikel einen rhetorischen Gestus, den er in einer Reihe von amerikanischen Dokumentarfilmen der späten 80er Jahre beobachtet. Ausgehend von der Situation einer historisch einmaligen Hybridität dokumentarischer Verfahren und eingebettet in die Paradigmen post-moderner Subjektkritik einerseits und des Gefühls einer Erschöpfung stilprägender dokumentarischer Ansätze (etwa der in den 60er Jahren formierte beobachtende Dokumentarfilm) andererseits, vermerkt Arthur eine eigentümliche Form der Selbstreflexion dokumentarischer Repräsentationsansprüche und Verfahrensweisen:

"A particular structural gambit has emerged in a group of films including Ross McElwee's *Sherman's March*, Tony Buba's *Lightning Over Braddock*, Michael Moore's *Roger and Me*, and Nick Broomfield's *Driving Me Crazy* (...) by which the dramatization of inadequacy or failure to complete a standard documentary project, the cohesive inscription of a given subject, serves as a heightened guarantee of authenticity."[4]

Während das Scheitern eines dokumentarischen Projekts als Sujet eines Dokumentarfilms dabei eine dünne, aber recht prominente Traditionslinie dokumentarischer „Anti-documentaries" fortsetzt[5], zeigt sich dieser performative Zweifel an der Gattungsform in den von Arthur aufgeführten Filmen in der Gestalt einer ungewohnten diegetischen Figur: jener des Dokumentarfilmers, dessen Film zum Dokument des Scheiterns an dem Projekt wird, das seinem Film zugrunde liegt. Dargestellt von den

the cinematic rhetoric of failure. We would like to look into this through a closer investigation of several passages from Robert Frank's films: *Last Supper, About Me: A Musical, C`est vrai!* and *Me and My Brother*.

The reason for doing this is to understand this rhetoric as a condition for the *cinematic* construction of an author persona whose incessantly expressed doubt of their control over the diegesis carries strong traits of fictionalization and from that creates plausible positions of authentic expression. In this, it seems that it is this crossing of "life and work," so often detected in Frank's films, which allows the most distinct signs of fiction to appear there, where they are most closely linked to autobiographical scenarios and where they foreground their reference to the life of the filmmaker.

In this context, concern is less with reproaching relevant film critiques for their steadfast confusion of filmmaker and author. It appears much more important to work out how Frank's films call for this confusion and what it is used for. Thus, the figure of the artist, who in the "search for truth and for a language to express it,"[2] risks "proximity to chaos,"[3] in order to constantly question the conditions of his or her own subjectivity, is so clearly recognizable as the central figure in the romantic concept of art, that he or she must immediately come under suspicion of projection. However, this does not mean understanding this figure as a product of distortion or lies. Much more likely is a tactical reduction of complexity in which the aesthetic idiosyncrasies of Frank's films rescue the concept of the authentic artist for the diegesis of art by having an author figure constantly involved in those scenarios that are characterized by failure in the conditions for artistic articulation.

The Aesthetics of Failure

In an influential article, Paul Arthur dubs a rhetorical gesture that he observed in a series of American documentary films of the late 1980s, as the "Aesthetics of Failure." He begins with the situation of a unique historical hybrid of documentary method, embedded in the paradigm of post-modern subject critique, and the feeling of an exhaustion of the style-defining documentary approaches (such as the observational documentary film arising in the 1960s). From this, Arthur records a unique form of the self reflection of documentary representational claims and modus operandi:

"A particular structural gambit has emerged in a group of films including Ross McElwee's *Sherman's March*, Tony Buba's *Lightning Over Braddock*, Michael Moore's *Roger and Me*, and Nick Broomfield's *Driving Me Crazy* ... by which the dramatization of inadequacy or failure to complete a standard documentary project, the cohesive inscription of a given subject, serves as a heightened guarantee of authenticity."[3]

Whereas a documentary project's failure as the subject of a documentary film extends a thin but entirely prominent line of "anti-documentaries,"[5] this performative doubting of the genre is shown in the films presented by Arthur in the gestalt of an unfamiliar diegetic figure: that of the documentary filmmaker whose film becomes the documentation of failure of the project on which the film is based. Presented by the filmmakers and narrated as a contemplative observation of their own modus operandi, figures such as Ross McElwee in *Sherman's March* and Michael Moore in *Roger and Me* personify the failure of their own projects. McElwee is not even able to start his historical documentary film, which should be about the Civil War march of northern general William Tecumseh Sherman through the American south. Instead, he becomes distracted in the apparently private obsession of film as an autobiographical medium—which becomes the material of his film. Moore is also unable to entice

Filmemachern selbst und erzählt als reflexive Beobachtung der eigenen Vorgehensweisen, personifizieren Figuren wie Ross McElwee in *Sherman's March* und Michael Moore in *Roger and Me* das Scheitern ihrer eigenen Projekte. McElwee gelingt es nie, seinen historiografischen Dokumentarfilm, der den Marsch des Nordstaaten-Generals William Tecumseh Sherman durch den amerikanischen Süden während des Bürgerkriegs zum Thema haben sollte, auch nur anzufangen. Er verzettelt sich stattdessen in der scheinbar privaten Obsession von Film als autobiografischem Medium – was zum Material seines Films wird. Auch Moore schafft es nicht, Roger Smith, den Vorstandsvorsitzenden des Autokonzerns General Motors, zu einem Drehtermin nach Flint/Michigan zu locken, um das Zusammentreffen des Chairmans mit den von ihm entlassenen Arbeitern zu filmen. Moores vergebliche Versuche, Smith vor die Kamera zu bekommen, bilden zusammen mit allerlei scheinbar zufälligen Abschweifungen das Material seiner dokumentarischen Groteske. Der definierende Kunstgriff dieser Filme ist die Verdoppelung des Dokumentarfilmers als Autor mit persönlicher Handschrift und als Figur in der dokumentarischen Erzählung selbst, die an der pragmatischen Umsetzung ihres Projekts mehr oder minder aufschlussreich scheitert.

Diese Figuration des Scheiterns an der Durchführbarkeit eines Unternehmens, aber auch das Element der Verdoppelung von Autor und Figur zeigt sich mehrfach in den Filmen Robert Franks. Wenn auch kaum vergleichbar mit der selbstironischen Figur des Dokumentaristen als wagemutigem Clown, den Michael Moore ja mittlerweile zum Markenzeichen entwickelt hat, oder mit dem offensiven Narzissmus, den Nick Broomfield in mehreren Filmen als Signatur zu etablieren versucht hat, finden sich in vielen Filmen Franks dennoch strukturanaloge Konstruktionen. So thematisieren seine Arbeiten nicht nur immer wieder und auf verschiedenen Ebenen das Scheitern ihrer experimentellen Anordnungen, sie inszenieren zudem oft den Fehlschlag oder die Unfähigkeit, sich an Vorgaben zu halten, als Rahmenhandlung. Besonders deutlich wird dies in *About Me: A Musical* (1971) und *C`est vrai! (One Hour)* (1990).

Dies wird in der nahezu identischen Anlage der „Rahmenfiktion" bei Franks *About Me* und McElwees *Sherman's March* besonders auffällig. Der Sprecher, der sich in *About Me* aus dem Off einer ungeklärten, aber offenbar ziemlich allmächtigen Kontrollposition zu Wort meldet und dessen Diktion sehr nach der Stimme Robert Franks klingt, berichtet, dass er eigentlich einen Film über amerikanische Musik machen sollte, dann aber entschieden habe, stattdessen einen Film über sich selbst zu machen. "Fuck the music", erklärt er trotzig, um dann zu schildern, dass er eine Schauspielerin namens Lynn Reyner angeworben habe, die ihn im Film darstellen soll. So entschieden diese Geste sich als Abweichung und Rebellion gegen Verpflichtungen des Künstlers gegenüber normativen Erwartungen gibt, so deutlich wird das Scheitern dieses rebellischen Akts im weiteren Verlauf des Films: *About Me* ist weit deutlicher als Meditation über amerikanische Musik und nicht zuletzt auch über das Genre des Musicals zu verstehen, denn als Auskunft über jenes ziemlich ortlose „Ich", das da spricht.

In ähnlicher Weise beginnt *Sherman's March* nahezu zwanzig Jahre später mit einer Szene der Aufkündigung des eigentlichen Projekts, führt jedoch weit weniger aggressiv, dafür um einiges subversiver die Figur des unentschiedenen Filmemachers ein, dessen scheinbar ziellose Reise durch den Süden die Zuschauer dann mitverfolgen dürfen. Dass auch dieser Film sehr viel mehr über die Narben der historischen Verletzungen zu sagen hat, die den amerikanischen Süden konstituieren, als über jenes scheinbar so selbstgefällige Ich, das ständig am Puls der eigenen Befindlichkeit fühlt, ist eine weitere Parallele der performativen Metapher des Scheiterns. Dass McElwee in *Sherman's March* an einem Punkt sein filmisches Credo damit formuliert, er „würde sein Leben filmen, um ein Leben zu haben,

Roger Smith, the head of the automobile manufacturer General Motors to Flint, Michigan for filming, in order to film the meeting of the chairman with the workers whom he fired. Moore's supposed attempts to get Smith in front of the camera, together with a grab bag of seemingly chance digressions, form the material for his grotesque documentary. The defining trick of these films is the doubling of the documentary filmmaker as an author with a personal writing style and a character in the documentary narrative itself, who fails in the pragmatic realization of his project in a more or less insightful way.

This figuration of failure in the feasibility of an enterprise, and also the element of doubling of author and character, appear often in Robert Frank's films. Although hardly comparable with the self-ironic figure of the documentary filmmaker as a daring clown, which Michael Moore has meanwhile developed as a trademark, or with the offensive narcissism, which Nick Broomfield attempted to establish as a signature in several films, there are nonetheless structurally analogous constructions in many of Frank's films. Thus his works not only constantly thematize the failure of their experimental arrangements at various levels, but they additionally stage their failure or inability to stick with guidelines as a framing structure. This is particularly clear in *About Me: A Musical* (1971) and *C`est vrai! (One Hour)* (1990).

It is especially obvious in the almost identical construction of the "framing fiction" in Frank's *About Me* and McElwee's *Sherman's March*. The speaker, speaking in *About Me* from the off, an undeclared but obviously rather omnipotent position of control, and whose diction sounds very much like Robert Frank's voice, reports that he should actually be making a film about American music, but has decided instead to make a film about himself. "Fuck the music," he defiantly explains, to then describe how he has recruited an actress named Lynn Reyner to represent him in the film. Equal to the defiance of this gesture as a deviation from and rebellion against the artist's responsibilities in light of normative expectations, is the clarity of its failure as the film proceeds. *About Me* is much more clearly understood as a meditation on American music and, not least, as also being about the genre of the musical, rather than as information about that rather dislocated "I" that speaks here.

Sherman's March begins in a similar way nearly twenty years later with a scene announcing the actual project; however, it introduces, in a much less aggressive yet that much more subversive way, the figure of the indecisive filmmaker, whom the viewer is invited to accompany on his apparently aimless journey through the south. The fact that this film has much more to say about the scars left from historical injuries that constitute the south of the U.S. rather than about the apparently so smug I, which constantly measures the pulse of its own state of being, is a further parallel of the performative metaphor of failure. The fact that Mc Elwee formulates his cinematic credo in *Sherman's March* with the point, that he would film his life, "in order to have a life to film," [6] would, additionally, be a perspective of the author persona of Robert Frank that could be further investigated in another study.

For the present context, however, it seems more productive to look into the topos of failure in Robert Frank's films in the dramaturgy of *C`est vrai!*. *C`est vrai!* is laid out as an experimental *tour de force*, which is found in that tradition of experimental film that is situated as closely as possible to the scientific concept of research: the experimental set-up—reflective and precisely defined in terms of its parameters—forms the frame and necessary conditions for an almost empirical questioning of its possibilities. Cinematic experiments have often concentrated on an element of film aesthetics in order to investigate its place in the order of the filmic real in the greatest possible number of declinations. In *C`est vrai! (One Hour)*, this element is the established sequence: a one-hour cinematic sequence, which is not broken by a single cut, which aligns filmic and filmed time, at least at the level of plot duration.

das er filmen kann"[6] wäre zudem eine Perspektive auf die Autorenpersona Robert Franks, der man an anderer Stelle nachgehen könnte.

Für den vorliegenden Kontext jedoch scheint es ergiebiger, dem Topos des Scheiterns in den Filmen Robert Franks in der Dramaturgie von *C`est vrai!* nachzugehen. *C`est vrai!* ist angelegt als eine experimentelle *tour de force*, die sich in jene Tradition des Experimentalfilms stellt, die sich in grösstmöglicher Nähe zum wissenschaftlichen Begriff der Forschung situiert: Die reflektierte und in ihren Parametern genau definierte Versuchsanordnung bildet den Rahmen und die Bedingung für eine nahezu empirische Befragung ihrer Möglichkeiten. Nicht selten haben sich filmische Experimente dabei auf ein filmästhetisches Element konzentriert, um dessen Platz in der Ordnung des filmisch Realen in möglichst vielen Deklinationsformen zu erforschen.

In *C`est vrai! (One Hour)* ist dieses Element die Plansequenz: Eine einstündige filmische Sequenz, die durch keinen Schnitt unterbrochen wird, die also filmische Zeit und gefilmte Zeit zumindest auf der Ebene der Plot-Dauer zur Deckung bringt.

Eine Eigentümlichkeit dieser forcierten Reduktion auf ein zentrales Konzept besteht darin, einen spezifischen hermeneutischen Code beim Zuschauer abzurufen: zum einen eine Hermeneutik des Misstrauens, die jede Abfolge des Laufbilds und der Tonwelt immer auf ihre Konsistenz mit dem Konzept hin überprüft – wird hier wirklich nicht geschnitten? Ist das wirklich „wahr"? Zum anderen wird alles Sicht- und Hörbare zur Registratur der Deklination und zum Gegenstand des Staunens über die ausgeklügelte Logistik des Drehaktes. Dies bildet unter anderem den Horizont für die Wahrnehmung von beobachtetem Straßenleben, für scheinbar ziellose Fahrten mit handgehaltener Kamera, bei der sich kein Element finden lässt, das einer filmischen Beobachtung wert wäre; für offensichtlich inszenierte Sequenzen, wie etwa das Alltagsgespräch zweier Frauen beim Mittagessen, deren sorgfältige Vermeidung des Blicks in die Kamera, was den Eingriff des Films in die Wirklichkeit des Pro-Filmischen als physisch geschaffene Situation der Darstellung von Alltag kennzeichnet und eben nicht als Produkt der kreativen Geografie der Montage. All dies bleibt jedoch Gegenstand einer gewissermaßen abgelenkten oder zumindest verdoppelten Aufmerksamkeit, denn die „Wahrheit", die der Film im Titel führt, bezieht sich nicht allein auf den Gehalt der filmischen Szenen, vielmehr auf die kohärente und vom Zuschauer überwachte Umsetzung des Konzepts. Die ständige und zunehmend zornige Unzufriedenheit mit den Ergebnissen des Projekts, die ein junger Mann ausspricht, der auch die logistische Funktion eines Aufnahmeleiters übernimmt, verlegen die Diskussion um die Begrenzung der Reichweite konzeptueller Geschlossenheit in das Szenario des Films hinein, und die Frage nach ihrem Status als inszeniertes, improvisiertes oder spontan entstehendes diskursives Element wird im geschlossenen raum/zeitlichen Gefüge der Plansequenz abgebildet.

Nach etwa zwei Dritteln der Laufzeit des Films, der bis dahin die Anordnungen seines Versuchs strikt eingehalten, immer wieder spektakulär vorgezeigt hat und mit erstaunlicher Effektivität und Disziplin auf das Durchspielen seiner Möglichkeiten gesetzt hat, befindet sich das Kamerateam einmal mehr in dem Lieferwagen, der als Transportmittel und *dolly* dient. Mit einem Mal schlägt das Bild um ins Schwarze. Auf der minutenlang weiter laufenden Tonspur ist von technischen Problemen mit der Kamera die Rede, die man jetzt gegen eine andere austauschen müsste und die dort sprechende Stimme ist durch ihre eigentümliche Inflektion, die Spuren des schweizerdeutschen Dialektes im Englischen als die Stimme Robert Franks erkennbar. Diese Verweigerung des Bildes formuliert den Bruch und damit das Scheitern des konzeptuellen Projekts: In der Folge wird die zweite Kamera ihren eigenen Film

One particularity of this forced reduction to a central concept consists of calling up a specific hermeneutic code in the viewer: for one, a hermeneutics of mistrust that tests every sequence of the running picture and the sound for its consistency with the concept—has there really been no cut made here? Is that really "true"? Another particularity is that everything that is visible and audible registers the declination and becomes an object of amazement because of the cleverly devised logistics of the act of filming. Among other things, this creates the horizon for perceiving observed street life; for apparently aimless journeys with the handheld camera, in which no element worthy of cinematic observation can be found; for obviously staged sequences, such as the everyday conversation of two women during lunch, whose gazes carefully avert the camera thus characterizing the intervention of the film into the reality of the pro-filmic as a physically created situation for the presentation of everyday life and not as a product of the creative geography of montage. All of this, however, remains an object of a certain diverted or at least doubled attention, since the "truth" that the film carries in the title refers not only to the content of the cinematic scenes, but even more so to the coherent and viewer-monitored realization of the concept. The constant and increasingly furious dissatisfaction with the results of the project, as spoken by a young man who also takes on the logistic function of head of recording, transfers the discussion of the limitation of the range of conceptual unity to the scenario of the film, and the question of its status as a staged, improvised, or spontaneously arising discursive element is depicted in the closed space/time structure of the established sequence.

Approximately two thirds of the way through the film—which until that point keeps strictly to the experiment's arrangements and has again and again, with amazing effectiveness and discipline, spectacularly displayed and been determined by the playing out of its possibilities—the camera team is once again found in the delivery wagon which serves both as a means of transportation and a dolly. All at once, the screen turns black. On the soundtrack, which continues to run for another few minutes, there is talk of technical problems with the camera, which now must be exchanged for another, and the voice speaking is recognizable through its characteristic inflection, the traces of the Swiss-German dialect in the English, as the voice of Robert Frank. This refusal of the image formulates the break and thereby the failure of the conceptual project. As a result, the second camera begins its own film, forcing a cut—regardless of the fact that we are dealing with an entirely technical insertion and not a sense-producing montage. Between the established sequence shot until that point and the second one inserted here, there could be either seconds or months of pro-filmic time—the aesthetic of virtuosity, which had dominated the visual protocol until now, is devalued, since a conceptual break is the only thing that cannot possibly happen. It reveals the project's failure at the hands of the notoriously treacherous detail of technology and denounces the entire concept as a mechanical procedure that pulls its concept of truth from mere contingent rules, the crossing of which would be coincidental, uncontrolled, and without expression if the technical failure should prove a fake.

The mistrust of the stringently tight concept, which contains clear rules and limited messages, expresses itself here almost menacingly; the *tour de force* has functioned amazingly well, a thoroughly successful form has been violently brought to an end. Even if there is no sign that the unity of the established sequence will be abandoned in what follows, nothing and no one can guarantee that the "technical failure" of the camera was not part of a staged scene planned to culminate precisely in this moment of failure. If previously, coincidence and staging, spontaneous behavior and logistics, observation and improvisation took place in a world whose clearly marked discursive parameters were

beginnen und dies zwingt zu einem Schnitt – auch wenn es sich nur um ein ganz und gar technisches Anheften und keine sinnproduzierende Montage handelt. Zwischen der bis dahin gedrehten Plansequenz und der zweiten hier einsetzenden könnten Sekunden oder Monate pro-filmischer Zeit liegen – die Ästhetik der Virtuosität, die bis dahin das Protokoll der Seherfahrung dominiert hatte, entwertet sich selbst, da der Konzeptbruch das einzige ist, was ihr nicht passieren darf. Sie zeigt das Scheitern des Projekts an der notorischen tückischen Kleinigkeit der Technik und denunziert das gesamte Konzept als mechanistisches Verfahren, das seinen Begriff der Wahrheit allein aus kontingenten Regeln bezieht, deren Überschreitung selbst dann zufällig, unkontrolliert und ohne Ausdruck wäre, wenn das technische Versagen fingiert sein sollte.

Das Misstrauen gegenüber dem stringenten, geschlossenen Konzept mit klaren Regeln und Aussagehorizonten äußert sich hier nahezu tückisch, denn die *tour de force* hatte erstaunlich gut funktioniert; hier wird eine durchaus gelungene Form gewaltsam zum Scheitern gebracht. Auch wenn es kein Anzeichen dafür gibt, dass die Geschlossenheit der Plansequenz im weiteren aufgegeben würde, kann nichts und niemand garantieren, dass das „technische Versagen" der Kamera nicht Teil einer Inszenierung ist, die genau auf diesen Moment des Versagens hin geplant war. Wenn zuvor Zufall und Inszenierung, spontanes Handeln und Logistik, Beobachtung und Improvisation in einer Welt stattgefunden haben, deren klar markierte diskursive Parameter ihre eigenen Reichweiten und Grenzen genau kannten und damit auch für die Zuschauer kontrollierbar waren, so formuliert das Scheitern des Projekts an seiner Technik die Fiktionalität aller Authentizitätskriterien, die auf unhintergehbaren und in diesem Sinne technischen Regeln beruhen. Regeln haben keine Existenz außerhalb der Verträge, die ihre Einhaltung sichern. Wenn diese Verträge einseitig gebrochen werden, wenn also die Forderung an den Zuschauer, sich der Erfahrung eines filmischen Konzepts zu unterwerfen, nicht mehr der Selbstbeschränkung eines Autors entspricht, seine Möglichkeiten auf die Vorgaben dieses Konzepts zu beschränken, dann bleibt nichts als die fundamentalistische Behauptung, dass jeder Versuch einer „Wahrheit im außermoralischen Sinn" zum konstituierenden Scheitern verurteilt ist.

Die Partitur der Fallhöhe

Erst in den letzten beiden Minuten von Franks *About Me: A Musical* (1971) ist Zeit für Antworten. Zuvor war die Befragung von „Robert Frank", jener fiktionalen Figur, die von der Schauspielerin Lynn Reyner verkörpert wird[7], einigermaßen ergebnisoffen. Es ist, als hätten gerade der aggressive, inquisitorische Ton, mit dem ein unterschiedlich besetztes Komitee die Frau namens Robert Frank zuvor konfrontiert hat und die Stilisiertheit der *mise-en-scène* immer wieder nur die Unmöglichkeit einer authentischen Auskunft inszeniert. Die gelegentlichen Aussagen jener männlichen Off-Stimme, die in der ersten Person in wütendem Ton über künstlerische Entscheidungen und Lebensumstände eines Mannes spricht, der über die Diegese dieses Films zu herrschen scheint, haben zur Aufklärung nicht viel beigetragen, eher zusätzliche Verwirrung gestiftet.

Erst jetzt, als die Kamera sich aus dem klaustrophoben Szenario eines zwar durchaus reizvollen, aber undurchsichtigen Spiels mit den unbekannten Regeln diverser Performances in das normativ gesicherte, weil recht genau vermessene und vom Gestänge zeitgenössischer Konventionen gehaltene ästhetische Terrain des Dokumentarischen begibt, werden Fragen, Adressierung und Referenzen deutlich.

acutely aware of their own range and borders and were thereby also controllable for the viewers, the technical failure of the project formulates the fiction of all criteria for authenticity that rest on technical rules that cannot be deceived. Rules have no existence outside of the contracts that assure that they will be kept. When these contracts are one-sidedly broken, when the demand made of the viewers to subject themselves to the experience of a cinematic concept no longer corresponds with an author's self restraint to limit possibilities to the guidelines of the concept, then nothing remains other than the fundamental claim that sentences every attempt at "truth in an extra-moral sense" to constitutional failure.

A Score for the Extent of the Dramatic Hero's Fall

It is first in the final two minutes of Frank's *About Me: A Musical* (1971) that there is time for answers. Prior to that, the questioning of "Robert Frank," the fictional character embodied by the actress Lynn Reyner,[7] was somewhat open in terms of results. It is as though precisely the aggressive, inquisition-like tone with which a committee comprised of different persons had confronted the woman named Robert Frank and the stylized nature of the *mise-en-scène* had again and again merely staged the impossibility of any authentic information. The occasional statements of that male off-camera voice, which speaks in an angry tone about artistic decisions and the living conditions of a man who appears to have control over the diegesis of this film, did not contribute much to the explanation, but instead actually caused additional confusion.

Not until this stage in the film do questions, addresses, and references become clear, as the camera leaves the claustrophobic scene of a stimulating, although impenetrable game with unknown rules of diverse performances to enter the aesthetic terrain of the documentary, which is normatively secure because it is so very precisely measured and held away from the linkages to contemporary conventions.

In a rapid montage, we see talking heads answering a question that we have not heard but which can nonetheless be deduced from the answers. Someone has asked: what would *you* shoot a film about? The answers are valuable as historical documentation, not only because the selection of those asked suggests a cross section of various ethnicities, genders, ages, and social classes of New York's population in the early 1970s (in the form of a random sampling), but also because many of the answers can be understood as an echo of a historically contemporary community. A woman with sunglasses and a scarf on her head says that she would film the unrest that has broken out in the country; several people would film New York's descent into chaos; a woman with a pearl necklace and fashionable hat says that she would make a film about Central Park; a young man would make a film about sports, and an older woman would concentrate on measures to get young people back on track—all answers expressed in the tradition of the social documentary concerned with society's problems or the entirely related gesture of documentary reporting.

The final character that the film lets get a word in, plays a Russian folk tune on a type of flute that sounds, however, like a musical saw. Its melody, to which the flute player dances on a street corner, is only able to break through the noise of the traffic with the help of a microphone; before, he states emphatically that naturally he would only make a film about himself: *Life Dances On,* a perfect ending for a musical about the autobiography, perhaps even a happy ending. *About Me* makes clear here that it is possible to rely on chance, on everyday urban life's situational abundance, on the vitality of

In einer raschen Montage sehen wir sprechende Köpfe, die eine Frage beantworten, die zwar nicht zu hören, aber aus den Antworten zu erschließen ist. Worüber *sie* denn einen Film drehen würden, hat man wohl gefragt. Die Antworten sind von zeitdokumentarischem Wert. Nicht nur, weil die Auswahl der Befragten einen nach Ethnie, Geschlecht, Alter und sozialer Schicht repräsentativen Querschnitt durch die Bevölkerung New Yorks in den frühen 70er Jahren (in Form einer per Zufallsprinzip zusammengestellten Stichprobe) suggeriert, sondern auch, weil viele der Antworten sich als Echo historischer Zeitgenossenschaft verstehen lassen: Die Unruhen, die im Land ausgebrochen seien, würde sie filmen, antwortet eine Frau mit Sonnenbrille und Kopftuch; über das Versinken von New York City im Chaos würden sie einen Film drehen, meinen mehrere; über Central Park, meint eine Dame mit Perlenkette und modischem Hut; über Sport, meint ein junger Mann, und über Maßnahmen, die Jugend wieder auf den rechten Weg zurück zu führen, meint schließlich eine ältere Lady – allesamt Antworten, aus denen entweder die Tradition des sozial-dokumentarischen Films spricht, der sich mit gesellschaftlichen Problemen befasst, oder der ihm durchaus verwandte Gestus der Reportage.

Die letzte Figur, die der Film zu Wort kommen lässt, spielt eine russische Volksweise auf einer Art Flöte, die allerdings klingt wie eine singende Säge. Seine Melodie, zu der der Flötenspieler an einer Straßenecke tanzt, setzt sich nur mit Hilfe des Mikrofons gegen den Verkehrslärm durch; zuvor hat er emphatisch betont, dass er selbstverständlich nur einen Film über sich selbst machen würde: *Life Dances On.* Ein perfektes Ende für das Musical der Autobiografie, vielleicht sogar ein glückliches. Denn – so gibt *About Me* hier zu verstehen – auf den Zufall ist Verlass, auf die situative Fülle des urbanen Alltags, die Lebendigkeit gelebter Identität, das Potential der Straße und der Idiosynkrasie. Jene Utopie des Wandels in der Kontingenz, echter Energie und Fülle im ganz und gar Künstlichen und Überformten, von der gerade das Musical schon immer lebte, vor allem aber die Utopie des „richtigen Moments", der zwar selten länger als eine Szene dauert, dessen sich die aufmerksame und kulturell bewegliche Kamera aber dennoch bemächtigen kann.

Utopien existieren in kleinen, filmischen Beobachtungen zugänglichen Inseln im Diskurs der Entfremdung, der Masken und Prätentionen. Die Enge und Zirkularität der Versuche, sie durch experimentelle Anordnungen hervorzubringen, die pornografische Drehsituation aufzusuchen wie in

About Me: A Musical

lived identity, on the potential of the street and on idiosyncrasy. That utopia of transformation in the contingency of true energy and abundance within that which is utterly artificial and overly formed, from which the musical in particular has always survived, but primarily that utopia of the "right moment," which seldom lasts longer than a scene, but which the attentive and culturally flexible camera can nonetheless empower.

Utopias exist in small, cinematic observations of accessible islands in the discourse of alienation, masks, and pretensions. The narrowness and circularity of the attempt to evoke them through experimental arrangements, to seek out pornographic situations for filming such as in *Me and My Brother*, the absurd epic theater of *Last Supper*, which is also meant to be understood as a repetition of Beckett's modern "End Game," even the rampage through the cultural unawareness of the Ruhrgebiet in *Hunter*, are all clearly identified through a rhetoric of necessity, which is almost eye-catching in its violence. "To do what is necessary," is to create situations in which the decisive moment is *not* possible, for it is precisely this, which creates the conditions for its perceptibility.

The necessity of the intervention is legitimated less through the idea that perhaps the pressure of the pro-filmic—and thereby synthetic situation—evinces truths that draw their authenticity from the reflective conditions of their produced state (such as the Cinéma Vérité from Rouch and Morin would have believed), but rather, are there much more to establish the staged situation as the height and the framework of the fall within the film-aesthetic structure, which is what establishes the observation as a difference that makes sense.

Alone the tourist's, or even the journalist's gaze at the real is not sufficient. The broken-ness and contingency of the utopia of everyday life can only be had as deviation, marginality, and selection; in addition, the tourist as well as the journalist consistently simply reproduce the conditions for the sights. To make these conditions visible and traceable, not to merely question them, but rather to be present at their construction in that they accompany the reception of the film as a permanent question, could be described as one of the most important sources of the pleasure in the text that can be found in Robert Frank's films.

The Prohibition

"The sign says walk," assures the voice from off-camera, but what we see are the red blinking letters of a traffic sign that orders the opposite: "Stop. Do not enter."

It is seldom that Robert Frank's films formulate their program so clearly and boldly as in this sequence from *Me and My Brother*. Previously, the streaks of light from car headlights had sketched ornaments of movement on the dark screen while the noise of starting car motors, screeching tires, and speeding vehicles broke into the silence before the start of the film. Dynamic, energetic promises of escape, movement, possibly adventure, and perhaps even danger are what the film achieves here. The shaky pan of the camera, the hesitant and seemingly indecisive zoom lifts the blinking traffic sign from the dark of the night and displays it before our eyes as booty. For a long time, the camera does not lose sight of this sign, even if the blinking writing often injures the border of the cadre and its legibility fights with the impatience of the handheld camera.

Standing in contrast to the unrest of the images is the control and modulation of the voice from off-camera. The "fidelity" or naturalness with which it is rendered, and its audible efforts to

Me and My Brother, das absurd-epische Theater von *Last Supper*, der sich auch als Wiederholung des modernistischen Endspiels von Beckett zu verstehen gibt, selbst der Beutezug durch das kulturelle Unbewusste des Ruhrgebiets in *Hunter*, sind allesamt klar ausgewiesen durch eine in ihrer Gewalttätigkeit fast plakativen Rhetorik der Notwendigkeit: „Zu tun, was notwendig ist", um Situationen herzustellen, in denen der entscheidende Augenblick *eben nicht* möglich ist, denn erst dies schafft die Bedingungen seiner Wahrnehmbarkeit.

Die Notwendigkeit der Intervention ist weniger durch die Vorstellung legitimiert, dass etwa der Druck der pro-filmischen – also synthetischen Situation – Wahrheiten hervorbringt, die ihre Authentizität aus den reflektierten Bedingungen ihrer Produziertheit beziehen (wie etwa das Cinéma Vérité von Rouch und Morin geglaubt hatte), sondern vielmehr dazu da, um innerhalb des filmästhetischen Gefüges die inszenierte Situation als Fallhöhe und Rahmen zu etablieren, die die Beobachtung erst als sinntragende Differenz etablieren.

Der touristische oder auch der journalistische Blick auf das Reale allein kann nicht genügen. Die Gebrochenheit und Kontingenz der Utopien des Alltäglichen ist nur als Abweichung, Marginalität und Aussonderung zu haben; zudem reproduziert der Tourist wie der Journalist immer nur Bedingungen der Sehenswürdigkeit. Diese Bedingungen sichtbar und spürbar zu machen, sie nicht nur zu befragen, sondern ihrer Konstruktion beizuwohnen, indem sie als permanente Frage die Rezeption des Films begleitet, könnte als eine der wichtigsten Quellen der Lust am Text bezeichnet werden, die man in Robert Franks Filmen finden kann.

Das Verbot

"The sign says walk", versichert die Stimme im Off, aber zu sehen ist die rot blinkende Leuchtschrift eines Verkehrszeichens, die das Gegenteil befiehlt: "Stop. Do not Enter."

Nur selten formulieren die Filme Robert Franks ihre Programmatik so deutlich und plakativ, wie diese Sequenz aus *Me and My Brother*. Zuvor hatte das Streiflicht von Autoscheinwerfern Ornamente der Bewegung auf die dunkle Leinwand gezeichnet, während in die Stille vor dem Film die Geräusche startender Automotoren, quietschender Reifen und beschleunigender Fahrzeuge eingefallen waren. Dynamische, energiegeladene Versprechen des Aufbruchs, der Bewegung, womöglich des Abenteuers und vielleicht sogar der Gefahr sind es, die der Film hier leistet. Der wackelige Kameraschwenk, der zögernde und scheinbar unentschiedene Zoom hebt das blinkende Verkehrszeichen aus dem Dunkel der Nacht und stellt es als Beutestück vor unseren Augen aus. Die Kamera verliert dieses Zeichen eine ganze Weile lang nicht mehr aus dem Auge, auch wenn die blinkende Schrift öfter die Grenze der Kadrage verletzt und ihre Lesbarkeit mit der Ungeduld der handgehaltenen Kamera streitet.

Im Gegensatz zur Unruhe des Bildes steht die Kontrolliertheit und Modulation der Stimme aus dem Off. Die "Fidelity" oder Naturtreue, mit der sie wiedergegeben ist, und ihr hörbares Bemühen darum, verstanden zu werden, konstituieren den Hörraum des Studios, der kontrollierten Situation der Aufnahme und ihre Autonomie vom Bild. Nicht nur dadurch gehört diese Stimme zur Sphäre der Fiktionen. Sie adressiert zudem eine noch unsichtbare Filmfigur und führt damit ein in den Raum einer erzählten Geschichte und sie spricht zu den Zuschauern im Kino. Den hier angesprochenen Julius werden wir als Bruder von Peter Orlovsky in zwei Fassungen erfahren: Als Objekt dokumentarischer Beobachtung – und als fiktionale Figur, die von einem Schauspieler dargestellt wird. Die Rhetorik

Me and My Brother

be understood, are constituted by the sound room in the studio, the controlled recording situation, and its autonomy from the picture. And it is not only through this that the voice belongs to the sphere of fiction. Additionally, it addresses a film character who is not yet visible and thus introduces a narrated story into the space and speaks to the viewers in the cinema. We will experience Julius, who is spoken to here, in two versions as Peter Orlovsky's brother: as the object of documentary observation—and as a fictional character who is played by an actor. The rhetoric of the request, however, that can be found in the speaker's attempts to set Julius in motion, to talk him into coming along, into participating, or at least to even watch are a clear appeal to the viewer at the beginning of the film. The promised sex in front of the camera outlines more precisely the enticement of that prohibition that the traffic sign formulates and from which the cinema has lived for as long as it has existed: "The sign says walk"—but over the sound of the words, the seeds of a fiction and the anticipation of the attraction, the writing of the prohibition blinks, both a warning and a temptation.

A great deal speaks for reading this sequence not only as an allegory of the situation in the cinema, but also as a metaphor of the reflexive style of Robert Frank's films. It also contains the attitude that they give rise to in their viewers: follow the promise of the sign, but do not await entry into a world—neither one that is represented with documentary means, nor one constructed with the means of cinematic fiction—because the reality of film can't be deceived. Thus, viewing Frank's films means being challenged to participate in a (usually thoroughly serious) game of being called upon to produce cinematic norms and conventions, whose rules are never fully unified and whose aims remain unclear; it means being a witness to scenes, situations, and plots without receiving information and knowledge about the world. It also means abandoning the cinematically visible and audible elements—the reality of film, with a sense that most of the conventional compensations that cinema has invented are subjected here to a ban on being confused with the emotional truths of fiction or the empirical truths of documentary rhetoric of the world.

The Utopia of Vanishing

Possibly the most touching moment in *Last Supper* is the scene in which an Afro-American woman holds her child, wrapped in a romper suit, in front of the camera's lens and repeatedly demands the camera man to "[T]ake a picture of my baby." Here as well, the degree of the peaks and falls are decisive: first the plunge of a techno-aesthetic difference. The professionally, richly contoured

der Aufforderung allerdings, die in den Versuchen des Sprechers steckt, diesen Julius in Bewegung zu setzen, ihn zu überreden mitzukommen, teilzunehmen, oder wenigstens erstmal zuzusehen, sind ein deutlicher Appell an die Zuschauer am Anfang eines Films. Der Sex vor der Kamera, der versprochen wird, umreißt jene Verlockung des Verbotes genauer, die das Verkehrszeichen formuliert und von dem das Kino lebt, seitdem es existiert. "The sign says walk" – aber über dem Klang der Worte, dem Keimen einer Fiktion und der Vorlust der Attraktion blinkt warnend und verlockend zugleich die Schrift des Verbotes.

Vieles spricht dafür, diese Sequenz nicht nur als eine Allegorie auf die Kinosituation, sondern auch als Metapher für die reflexive Stilistik der Filme Robert Franks zu lesen. Darin enthalten ist auch die Haltung, die sie ihren Zuschauern nahe legen: Folge dem Versprechen der Zeichen, aber erwarte dir keinen Zutritt zur Welt – weder einer mit dokumentarischen Mitteln repräsentierten noch einer mit den Mitteln der filmischen Fiktion konstruierten, denn die Wirklichkeit des Films ist unhintergehbar. So bedeutet das Sehen von Franks Filmen zur Teilnahme an einem (zumeist überaus ernsten) Spiel mit filmischen Normen und Konventionen aufgefordert zu werden, dessen Regeln sich nie völlig erschließen und dessen Ziele unklar bleiben; es bedeutet Zeuge zu werden von Szenen, Situationen und Handlungen, ohne dadurch in den Besitz von Auskunft und Wissen über die Welt zu kommen. Es bedeutet auch, sich filmisch Sicht- und Hörbarem – der Wirklichkeit des Films – auszusetzen mit dem Gefühl, dass die meisten konventionellen Kompensationen dafür, die das Kino erfunden hat, hier dem Verbot unterliegen, sie mit den emotionalen Wahrheiten der Fiktion oder den empirischen Wahrheiten der dokumentarischen Rede über die Welt zu verwechseln.

Die Utopie des Verschwindens

Der vielleicht anrührendste Moment in *Last Supper* ist die Szene, in der eine Afro-Amerikanerin ihr im Strampelanzug verpacktes Kind vors Kameraobjektiv hält und wiederholt vom Kameramann verlangt: "Take a picture of my baby." Auch hier sind Fallhöhen entscheidend: zunächst das Gefälle einer techno-ästhetischen Differenz. Die professionelle, reich konturierte und abgestufte Ästhetik des filmischen Bildes, das die Szenen jener Party zeigt, die den Hauptschauplatz des Film ausmacht, gegen die ausgewaschene, grob gerasterte, verzerrte Bildoberfläche des *home video* samt Datumsleiste, auf der sich diese Szene zeigt.

Last Supper

and layered aesthetic of the cinematic image, the scene of the party which constitutes the main scene of the film, against the washed-out, roughly screened, distorted pictorial surface of the *home video* including date line, on which this scene is shown.

At least related to this difference is the topos of those elementary, cultural, and mental functions that are constantly assigned to photography and cinema. The safety, storage, and rescue of fleeting truth from its unavoidable decay is a defining narrative in the cultural history of desire of the photo-filmic apparatus. The servant's cinematic authorship, a function without expression, established by the address of the mother, sketches a horizon showing the impossible desire for immortality and duration as the pragmatic truth of the recording medium. This scene is particularly moving because of its triviality, shocking through the plausibility of its version of picture making for others: the character previously so endlessly orbited in the party scene—the father, husband, artist, famous man, friend, employer—whose absence and refusal to show himself become the negative of an insatiable longing, a longing for a praxis without the compulsion of expression, which becomes absorbed in the function of the apparatus and therefore knows, demands, and legitimates clear rules such as recognition, identification, technical norms, professionalism, and craftwork. The longing is thus for a practice of making pictures outside of art, constituted solely through the desire of use, and whose power over the symbols is freed of the compulsion for expression, because it is concerned solely with preserving, securing, and overcoming transience.

[1]   Robert Frank in *Home Improvements*.

[2]   Philip Brookman, "Fenster auf eine andere Zeit. Autobiographische Fragen," in: *Robert Frank: Moving Out*, Zurich 1995, p. 42.

[3]   John Hanhardt, "Kenner des Chaos. Die Filme und Videos," in: *Moving Out*, Zurich 1995.

[4]   Paul Arthur, "Gilding the Ashes. Toward a Documentary Aesthetics of Failure," *Motion Picture* 6/1 (1991): 24-27; here: 24.

[5]   See, i.e., Alain Resnais, *Nuit et Brouillard*, which thematizes the fundamental failure of a documentary grasp of history in the representation of the Holocaust, or Luis Bunuel's *Land without Bread*, whose documentary gaze at the living conditions in a Spanish mountain village is revealed as a grotesque exaggeration of social documentary discussion of the victim.

[6]   "I'm filming my Life in Order to Have a Life to Film", Ross McElwee in *Sherman's March*. C.f. Arthur: 24.

[7]   Here as well, it is difficult not to follow the path of "double occupation" as Frank's dramaturgical strategy. There is also this doubling of a character in *Me and My Brother*, and even the parody of the speaking and gesture of the absent father in *Last Supper* could be read as an act of replacement and doubling.

Mit dieser Differenz mindestens verwandt ist der Topos jener elementaren kulturellen und psychischen Funktionen, die der Fotografie und dem Kino immer wieder zugeschrieben werden: Die Sicherung, Aufbewahrung, Rettung der flüchtigen Wirklichkeit vor ihrem unvermeidlichen Verfall ist eine definierende Erzählung in der kulturellen Sehnsuchtsgeschichte der foto-filmischen Apparatur. Die durch die Adressierung der Mutter hergestellte filmische Autorenschaft des Dienenden, einer Funktion ohne Ausdruck, zeichnet einen Horizont, der das unmögliche Begehren nach Unvergänglichkeit und Dauer als die pragmatische Wahrheit des Aufzeichnungsmediums zeigt. Rührend ist diese Szene gerade durch ihre Trivialität, erschreckend durch die Plausibilität ihrer Version des Bildermachens für andere. Die zuvor im Szenario der Party so endlos umkreiste Figur – der Vater, Ehemann, Künstler, berühmte Mann, Freund, Arbeitgeber –, dessen Abwesenheit und Verweigerung sich zu zeigen wird zum Negativ einer unerfüllbaren Sehnsucht. Sehnsucht nach einer Praxis ohne den Zwang zum Ausdruck, die in der Funktion des Apparats aufgeht und daher klare Regeln wie Wiedererkennbarkeit, Identifikation, technische Normen, Professionalität und Handwerk kennt, einfordert und legitimiert. Die Sehnsucht nach einer Praxis des Bildermachens außerhalb der Kunst also, die allein durch das Begehren des Gebrauchs konstituiert ist und deren Macht über die Symbole vom Zwang zum Ausdruck befreit ist, weil es allein um Aufbewahren, Sichern und den Sieg über die Vergänglichkeit geht.

1. „Ich mache immer dieselben Bilder – ich versuche immer, im Draußen das Drinnen zu sehen. Ich versuche, etwas zu sagen, das wahr ist. Aber vielleicht ist nichts wirklich wahr. Außer dem, was dort draußen ist. Und was dort draußen ist, verändert sich laufend." Robert Frank in *Home Improvements*. Übersetzung in John Hanhardt. „Kenner des Chaos. Die Filme und Videos," in "Robert Frank: Moving Out". Zürich, 1995: S. 51.
2. Philip Brookman. „Fenster auf eine andere Zeit. Autobiographische Fragen", in: "Robert Frank: Moving Out". Zürich, 1995: S. 42.
3. John Hanhardt. „Kenner des Chaos. Die Filme und Videos", in: "Moving Out". Zürich, 1995.
4. Paul Arthur. "Gilding the Ashes. Toward a Documentary Aesthetics of Failure," in "Motion Picture" 6/1 (1991): 24-27; hier: 24.
5. Siehe etwa Alain Resnais. *Nuit et Brouillard*, der das fundamentale Scheitern dokumentarischen Zugriffs auf Geschichte an der Repräsentation des Holocaust thematisiert oder Luis Bunuels *Land without Bread*, dessen dokumentarischer Blick auf die Lebensbedingungen in einem spanischen Bergdorf sich als groteske Überzeichnung sozialdokumentarischer Rede über die Opfer zeigt.
6. "I'm filming my Life in Order to Have a Life to Film" Ross McElwee in *Sherman's March*. C.f. Arthur: 24.
7. und auch hier fällt es schwer, nicht dem Pfad der „Doppelbesetzung" als dramaturgische Strategie Franks zu folgen. Auch in *Me and My Brother* findet sich diese Verdoppelung einer Figur; und selbst die Parodie auf das Sprechen und die Gestik des abwesenden Vaters in *Last Supper* könnte als Akt der Ersetzung und Verdoppelung gelesen werden.

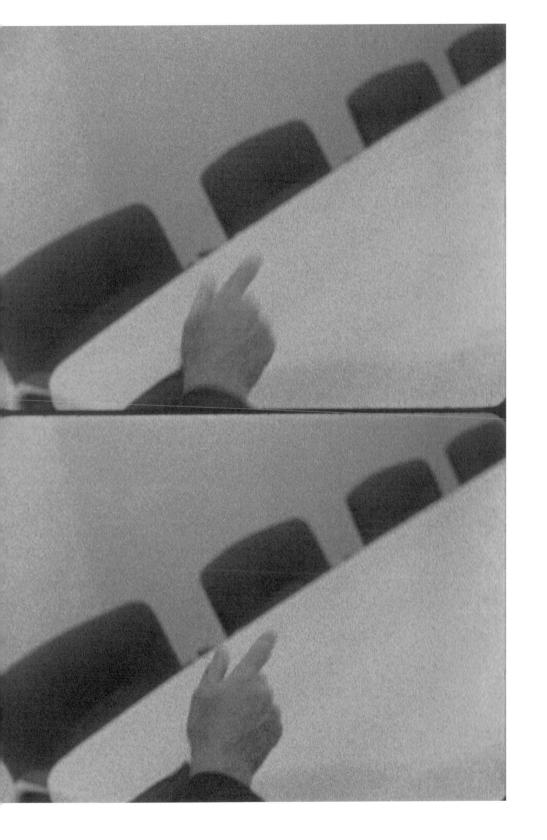

I HAVE COME HOME AND I'M LOOKING THROUGH THE WINDOW, OUTSIDE IT'S SNOWING, NO WAVES AT ALL. THE BEACH IS WHITE, THE FENCE POSTS ARE GREY. I AM LOOKING BACK INTO A WORLD GONE FOREVER. THINKING OF A TIME THAT WILL NEVER RETURN. A BOOK OF PHOTOGRAPHS IS LOOKING AT ME. TWENTY-FIVE YEARS OF LOOKING FOR THE RIGHT ROAD. POST CARDS FROM EVERYWHERE. IF THERE ARE ANY ANSWERS I HAVE LOST THEM. THE BEST WOULD BE NOT WRITING AT ALL.

(ROBERT FRANK, THE LINES OF MY HANDS, 1971)

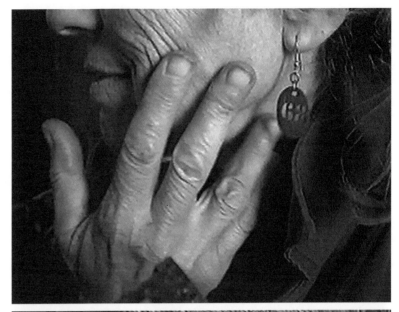

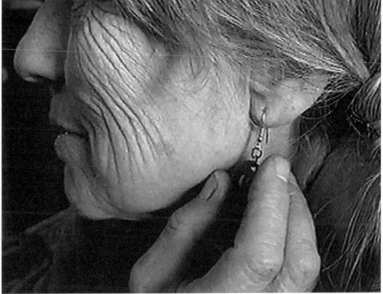

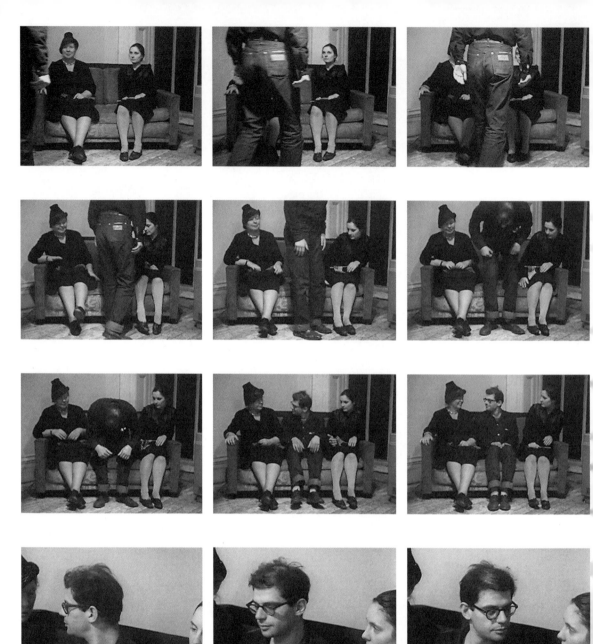

A LOT HAS CHANGED SINCE I ASSISTED WALKER ON HIS TOOLS SERIES. BACK THEN, I ADMIRED HIS ABILITY TO ACHIEVE THIS EXTRAORDINARY PRECISION WITH VERY BASIC TECHNICAL EQUIPMENT (SHAKY TRIPOD AND SO ON). IT WAS IMPRESSIVE, BUT THERE WAS A COLDNESS TO IT. WALKER EVANS CHOSE HIS TOOLS WITH THE EXPERIENCE AND THE TASTE OF THE ELITE. IN MY ROOM IN MABOU, FAMILIAR OBJECTS ARE JUST LYING AROUND, AND I JUST HAVE TO WAIT FOR THE RIGHT LIGHT. THAT'S ENOUGH FOR ME.

(UTE ESKILDSEN, "IN CONVERSATION WITH ROBERT FRANK;" IN: "HOLD STILL_KEEP GOING," 2000)

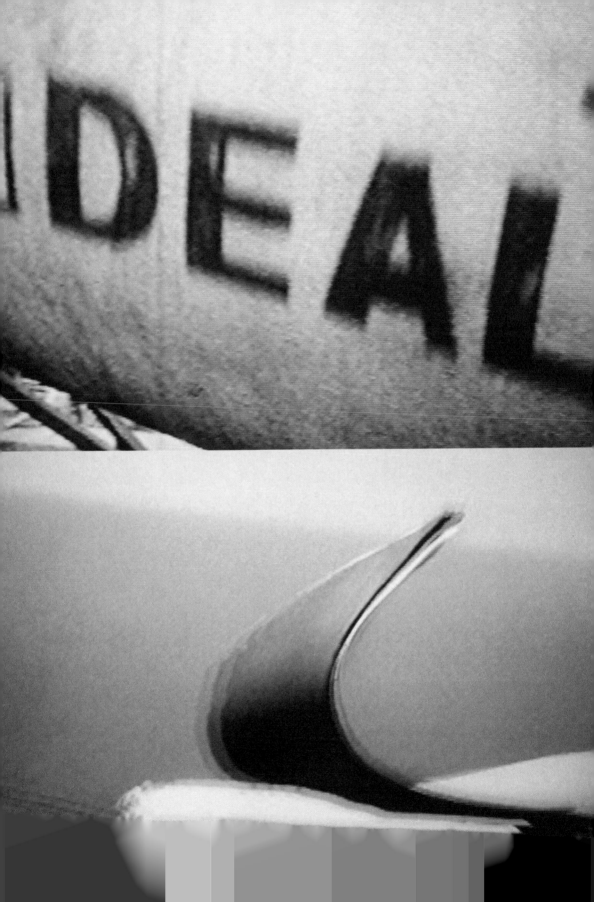

THE TRUTH IS SOMEWHERE BETWEEN THE
DOCUMENTARY AND THE FICTIONAL, AND THAT IS
WHAT I TRY TO SHOW. WHAT IS REAL ONE
MOMENT HAS BECOME IMAGINARY THE NEXT.
YOU BELIEVE WHAT YOU SEE NOW, AND THE
NEXT SECOND YOU DON'T ANYMORE.

(ROBERT FRANK, SCRIPTBOOK: ME AND MY BROTHER)

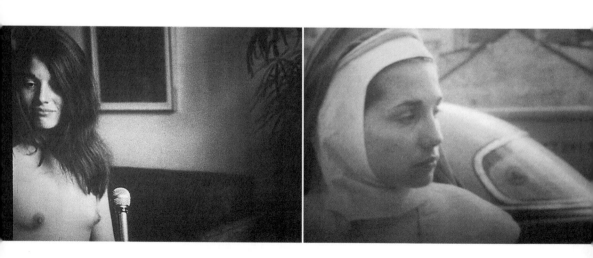

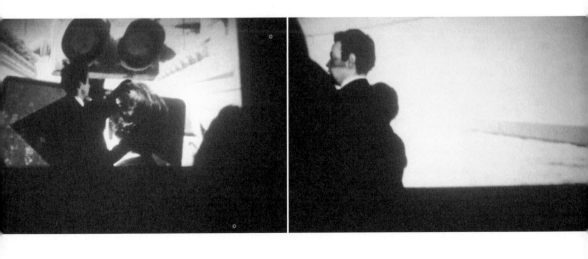

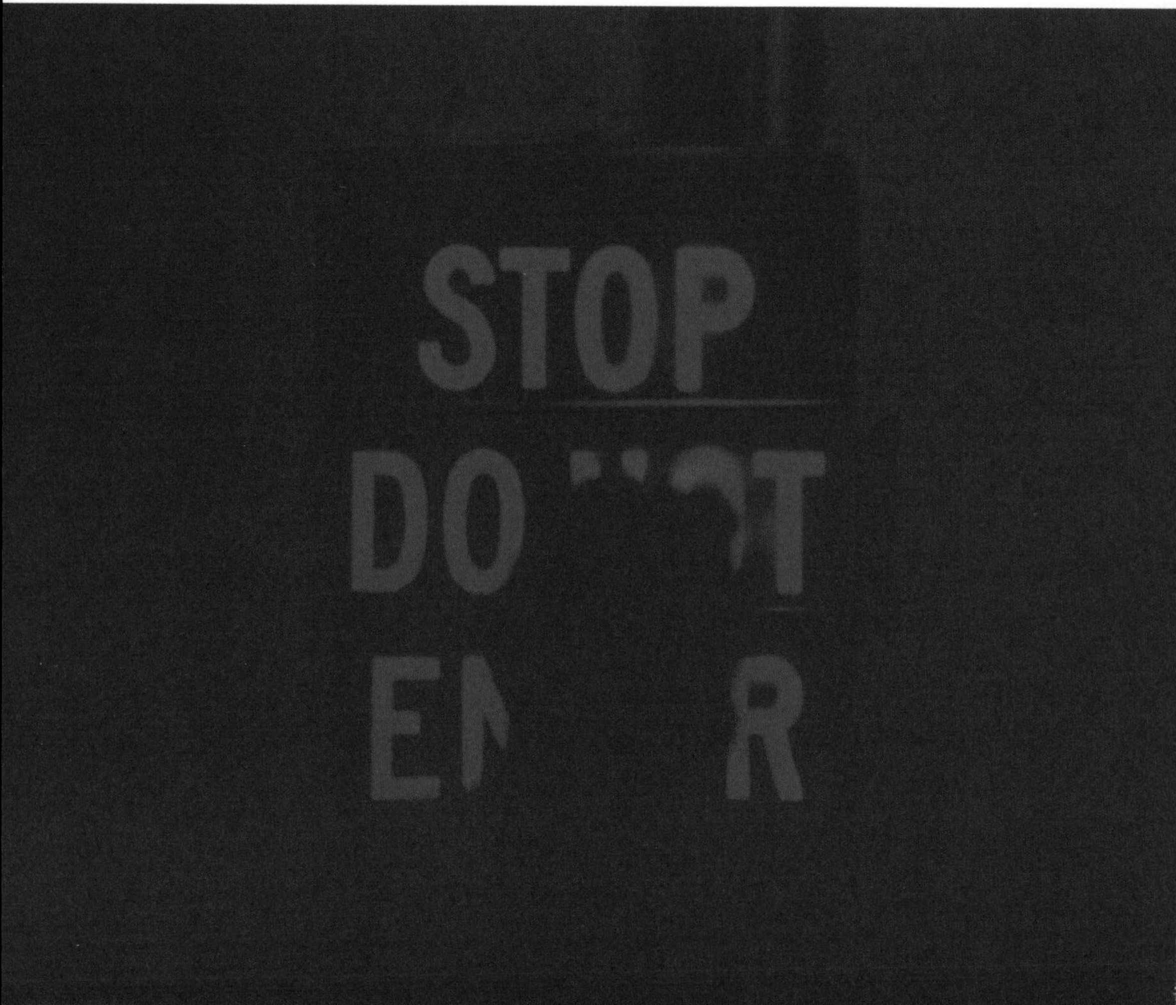
STOP

DO NOT
ENTER

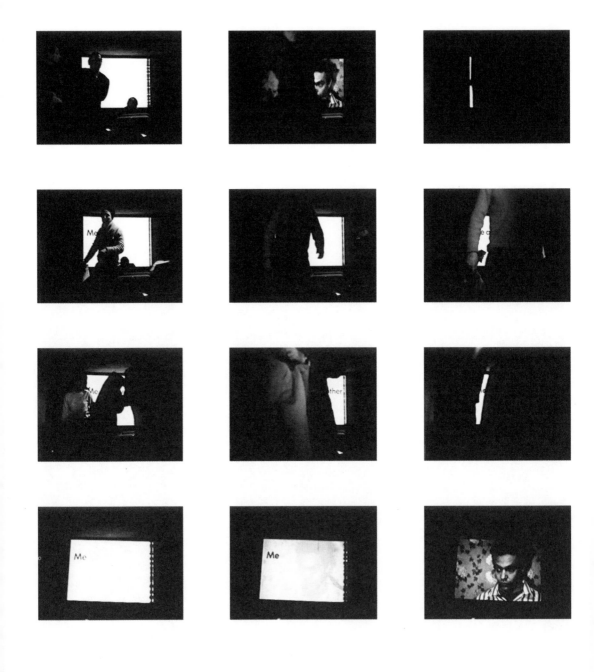

AT A PARKING LOT
FOOD & DRUGS

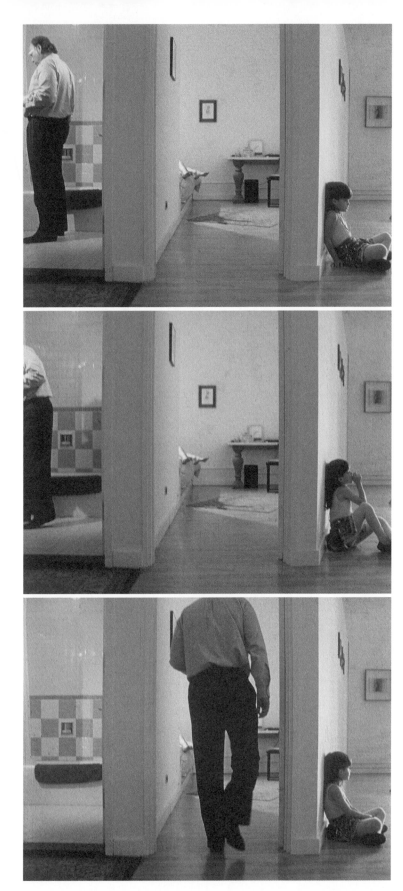

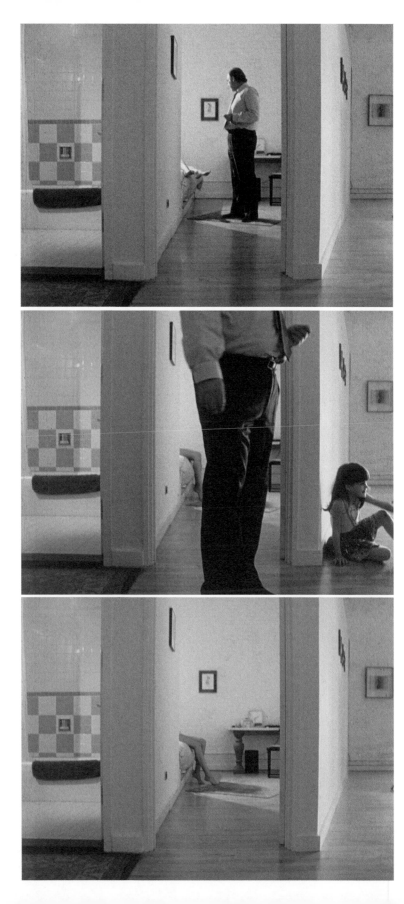

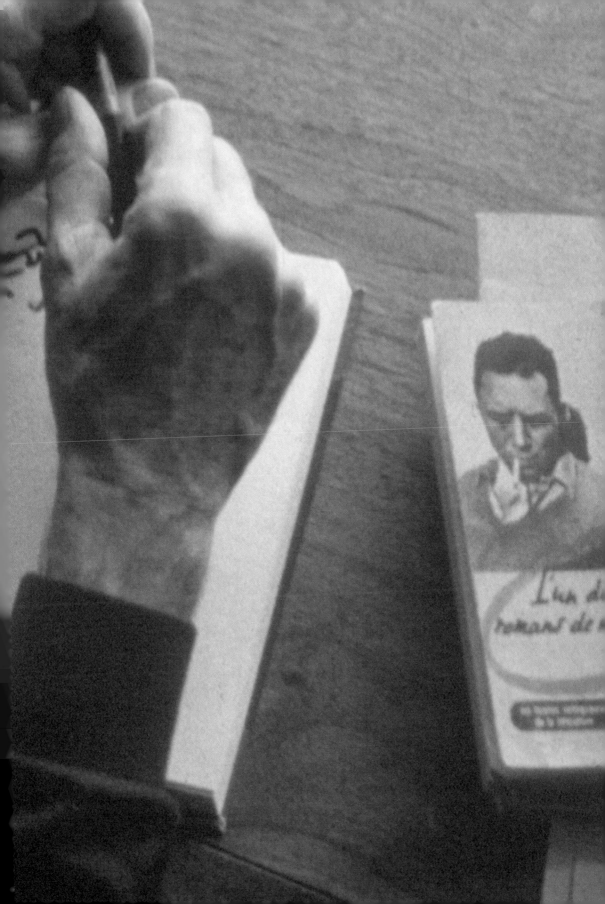

w... The ice is breakir
be out there. The hills

Yes it's later now... T
The boats will be out

ng up, the water will be
will look green again.

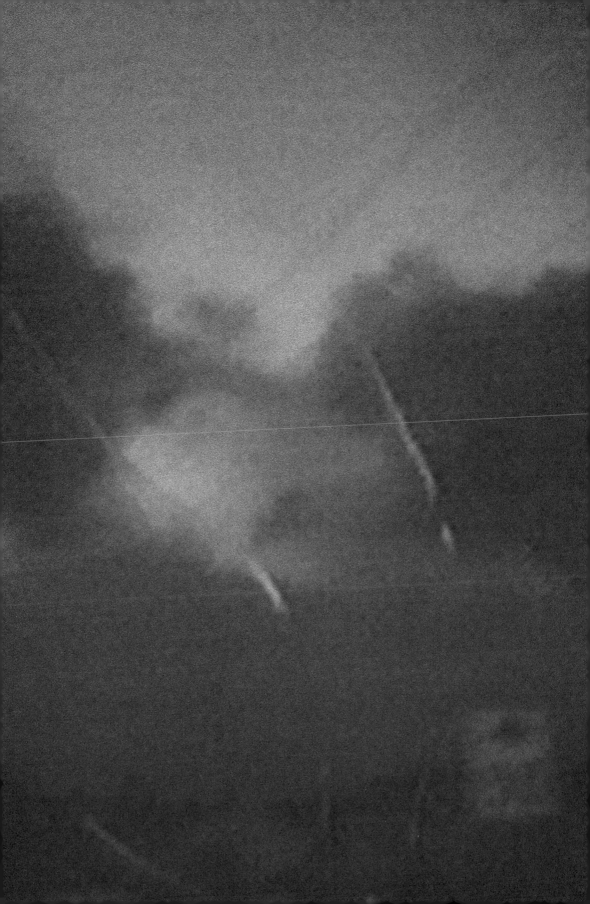

IN MAKING FILMS I CONTINUE TO LOOK AROUND ME, BUT I AM NO LONGER THE SOLITARY OBSERVER TURNING AWAY AFTER THE CLICK OF THE SHUTTER. INSTEAD I'M TRYING TO RECAPTURE WHAT I SAW, WHAT I HEARD AND WHAT I FEEL. WHAT I KNOW! THERE IS NO DECISIVE MOMENT, IT'S GOT TO BE CREATED. I'VE GOT TO DO EVERYTHING TO MAKE IT HAPPEN IN FRONT OF THE LENS: SEARCHING_ EXPLAINING_ DIGGING_ WATCHING_ JUDGING_ ERASING_ PRETENDING_ DISTORTING_ LYING_ JUDGING_ RECORDING_ TRYING_ TRYING_ TRYING_ RUNNING_ TELLING A TRUTH_ RUNNING_ CRAWLING_ WORKING TOWARDS THE TRUTH_ UNTIL IT IS DONE (ROBERT FRANK, THE LINES OF MY HAND, 1971)

THE ONLY THING I'M INTERESTED IN THESE DAYS
IS WHAT I DID LAST. IF SOMEONE TALKS ABOUT
MY PAST, I DON'T LIKE TO GO ALONG WITH IT.
I DON'T CORRECT EITHER, WHATEVER PEOPLE
MIGHT SAY ABOUT INFLUENCES AND
DEVELOPMENTS. IT DRAWS YOU BACK IN THE
SAME OLD WATERS THAT YOU HAVE ALREADY
CROSSED. (ROBERT FRANK IN "CINEMA: BILD FÜR BILD," ZURICH 1984)

THE FILMS I HAVE MADE ARE THE MAP OF MY
JOURNEY THRU ALL THIS... LIVING. IT STARTS
OUT AS "SCRAP BOOK FOOTAGE." THERE IS NO
SCRIPT, THERE IS PLENTY OF INTUITION. IT
GETS CONFUSING TO PIECE TOGETHER THESE
MOMENTS OF REHEARSED BANALITIES,
EMBARRASSED DOCUMENTATION, FEAR OF
TELLING THE TRUTH AND SOMEWHERE THE
FEARFUL TRUTH SEEMS TO ENDURE. I WANT
YOU TO SEE THE SHADOW OF LIFE AND DEATH
FLICKERING ON THAT SCREEN. JUNE ASKS ME:
WHY DO YOU TAKE THESE PICTURES?
BECAUSE I AM ALIVE... (ROBERT FRANK, SEPT. 1980)

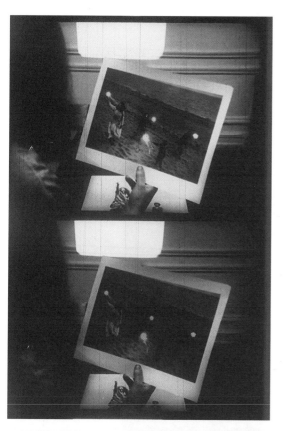

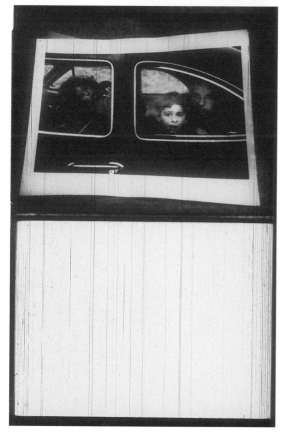

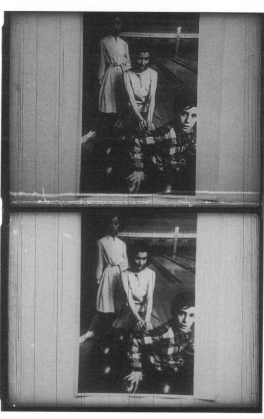

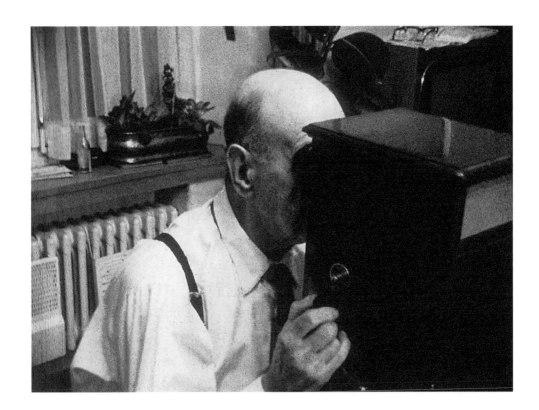

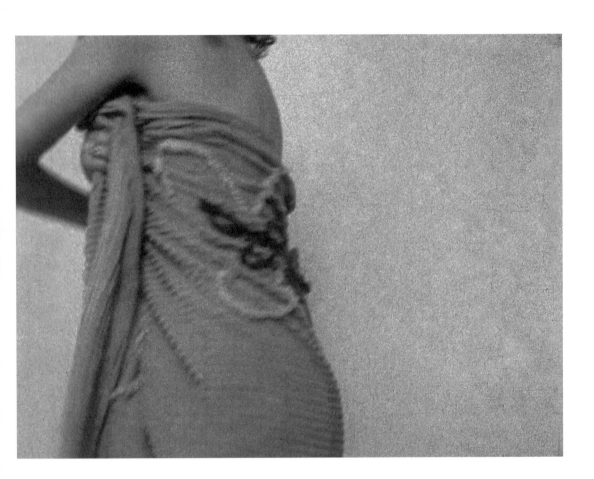

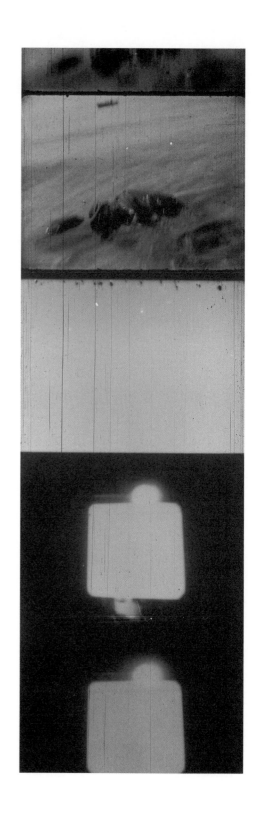

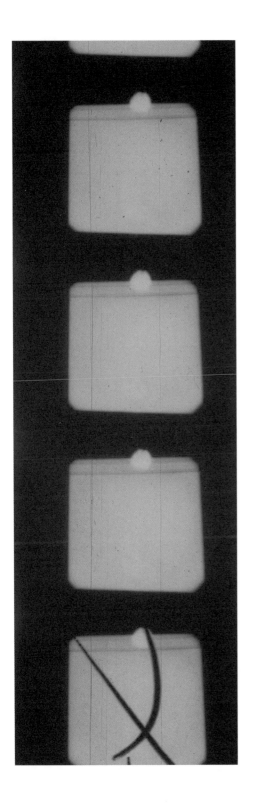

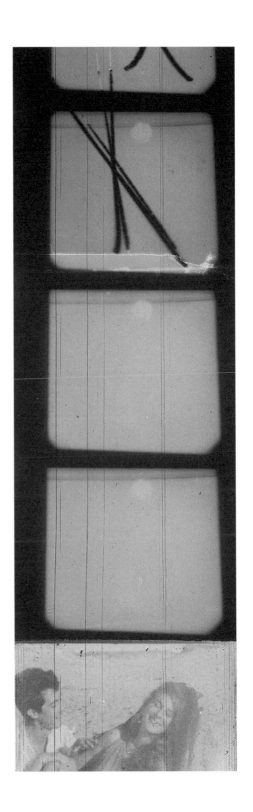

1959

Pull My Daisy

All und Alltag   1958 hatte Robert Frank begonnen, durch Busfenster das Leben des anonymen New York zu fotografieren. Ein Jahr danach beginnen sich die Bilder tatsächlich zu bewegen, und das Fenster wird geöffnet. Davor erfasst die Kamera in ruhigen Schwenks Wände, ein Bild, Kasten und Kühlschrank, eine Aufsicht zeigt einen Tisch mit Stühlen. Diese Wohnung wird für die nächste halbe Stunde als Schauplatz und Bühne dienen. Dann geht eine Tür auf, und im angrenzenden Zimmer flutet Licht durchs Fenster.

Der visuellen folgt die verbale Overtüre mit einem gigantischen Zoom: "Early morning in the universe" lauten die ersten Worte, die Jack Kerouac aus dem Off spricht, als fiele der Blick auf die Szenerie aus einer anderen Galaxis. Aber schnell wird der Zuseher in die häusliche Konkretion geholt – "The wife is getting up. Opening the windows" – und mit den Koordinaten des Erdendaseins versorgt, das in einem Loft in der "Bowery. Lower East Side" stattfindet. Dieser Sturzflug aus dem All in die Alltäglichkeit hat keinerlei filmische Entsprechung – und doch definiert er die beiden Pole, die Franks erste filmische Arbeit mit jener Spannung versorgen, von der sie lebt. *Pull My Daisy* ist ein *domestic drama*, das sein Pathos und seine Ironie aus dem Umstand bezieht, dass sich diese Häuslichkeit in all ihrer Banalität gleichzeitig auch "in the universe" vollzieht: Die Sterne, nach denen zu greifen Wollust und Wahnsinn ist, sind einerseits unendlich weit entfernt und liegen dennoch gleich vor der Haustür.

Entscheidend ist, dass der Film den Gegensatz von Profanität und Poesie analog zur Geschlechter-polarität inszeniert. "The wife", dargestellt von der Schauspielerin Delphine Seyrig, ist zwar "a painter", also – im Unterschied zu ihrem Mann, dem Eisenbahner Milo (der Maler Larry Rivers) – eindeutig die fürs Künstle-rische zuständige Person in dem Haushalt, den sie auch führen muss; zugleich wird sie den ganzen Film über als Kontrastfigur zur bohème-haften Welt der Beat-Poets eingesetzt, aus denen sich Milos Freundeskreis rekrutiert.

Schon aufgrund seiner Position im "richtigen Leben", als Kumpel und Kollege von Allen (Ginsberg), Gregory (Corso) & Peter (Orlovsky), ist Kerouac Partei. Im Film genießt er fast uneingeschränkte Autorität: Er ist allwissender Erzähler (dessen Worte die Bilder immer wieder vorausnehmen), Kommentator, Synchronsprecher und Improvisator, dessen poetische Wortkaskaden mit dem Soundtrack der Jazz-Komposition wetteifern. Aber so sehr sich die Beat-Bubenbande in ihrem heroischen Kampf – "struggling to be poets" – auch müht, den Gegensatz zwischen Kunst und Leben aufzuheben, der Schnitt zwischen den Bereichen bleibt be-stehen. Unmittelbar nachdem Milos Frau ihrem Gatten eine geklebt hat, beginnt ein Kameraschwenk durch die Wohnung, deren banale Einrichtung Kerouac aus dem Off poetisch-mythologisch hochjazzt. Die Sakralisierung der Profanität, die in Allens Fragen anklingt – "Is the world holy? Is the baseball holy?" – und unübersehbar eine Referenz an Ginsbergs vier Jahre zuvor entstandene "Footnote to Howl" ist, bleibt ein prekäres Unterfangen. Am Ende steht, ganz konventionell, der Auszug der Bubenbande aus der vom zänkischen Eheweib verwalteten Wohnung. Milo versetzt dem Schaukelstuhl einen Tritt und folgt dem Ruf seiner Kumpane. *Klaus Nüchtern*

Space and Everyday Space   In 1958, Robert Frank began to photograph life in the anonymity of New York City through bus windows. One year after that, his photos began to move and the window was opened. But first his camera filmed walls, a picture, furniture, and a refrigerator in slow pans, one view shows a table and some chairs. For the next thirty minutes this apartment becomes a stage and venue. Then a door opens, and the adjoining room is flooded with sunlight.

This visual overture is followed by one of a verbal nature which includes a colossal zoom: "Early morning in the universe" are the first words spoken by Jack Kerouac off-camera, as if the camera showed a scene from a different galaxy. But the viewer is promptly brought back into the domestic concretion—"The wife is getting up. Opening the windows"—and is given the coordinates of an earthly existence in a Bowery loft on New York's Lower East Side. This power dive from space into everyday space has no correspondence in film—but at the same time it defines the poles providing Frank's first cinematic work with the tension from which it lives. *Pull My Daisy* is a domestic drama which takes its pathos and irony from the circumstance that this domesticity, in all its banality, also exists "in the universe." The stars one reaches for in lust and lunacy are on the one hand infinitely far away, and on the other they lie just beyond the door.

The decisive aspect is that this film presents the opposites of profanity and poetry as being analogous to the polarity of the sexes. "The wife," played by actress Delphine Seyrig, is "a painter"; in other words, in addition to running the household she is clearly the one responsible for artistic matters, as opposed to her husband, railway worker Milo (played by painter Larry Rivers). At the same time she functions throughout the film as a contrast to the Bohemian world of the Beat poets, to which Milo's friends belong

Due to his "real-life" position as buddy and fellow writer of Allen (Ginsberg), Gregory (Corso) and Peter (Orlovsky), Kerouac is unable to be objective. Enjoying almost unlimited authority in the film, he is an omniscient narrator (whose words always anticipate what the images show), commentator, dubbing speaker, and improviser whose cascades of lyricism compete with jazz composer David Amram's soundtrack. But regardless of the Beat boy band's heroic efforts—"struggling to be poets"—at removing the barrier between life and art, it remains intact. Just after Milo's wife gives her husband a firm smack, a pan through the apartment begins, the banal furnishings jazzed up poetically and mythologically by Kerouac's off-camera voice. The sanctification of the secular in Allen's questions—"Is the world holy? Is the baseball holy?" (an obvious reference to Ginsberg's "Footnote to Howl," written four years previously)—remains a precarious undertaking. Quite conventionally, the boy band moves out of the apartment presided over by the quarrelsome and nagging woman at the film's end. Milo gives the rocking chair a kick and follows his buddies' call. *Klaus Nüchtern*

USA 1959, 16 mm, black and white, 28 min. directed by: Robert Frank, Alfred Leslie. script: based on the third act of the play "The Beat Generation" by Jack Kerouac. cinematography: Robert Frank. editing: Leon Prochnik, Robert Frank, Alfred Leslie. music composed by: David Amram. musicians: David Amram, Sahib Shahab, a.o. "The Crazy Daisy" sung by: Anita Ellis, text by: Allen Ginsberg, Jack Kerouac. production: G-String Enterprises, Walter Gutman. world premiere: 11. 11. 1959, Cinema 16, New York. cast: Mooney Peebles (Richard Bellamy), Allen Ginsberg, Peter Orlovsky, Gregory Corso, Larry Rivers, Delphine Seyrig, David Amram, Alice Neel, Sally Gross, Denise Parker, Pablo Frank. awards: Best American Experimental Film (Cinemages Magazine 1959), 2nd Independent Film Award (Film Culture Magazine 1960)

1961

The Sin of Jesus

Drama der Autonomie   Psychologie und Theodizee, nach einer Geschichte von Isaac Babel. Eine Frau auf einer Hühnerfarm verbringt ihre Tage an der Eiersortiermaschine. "I'm the only woman here." Sie ist schwanger, der Mann liegt im Bett herum, sein Freund drängt ihn dazu, mit ihm fortzugehen. Während sie arbeitet, spricht sie zu sich selbst, in einem Tonfall, der sich der hermetischen Musik von Morton Feldman angleicht, introvertiert und durchlässig zugleich, verloren an die Monotonie des Daseins ("feeding, cleaning, soiling – it doesn't matter"). Sie zählt die Eier wie die Tage. Selbst außerordentliche Ereignisse geraten in den Strom dieses melancholischen Solipsismus. Die Erscheinung Jesu in der Scheune ist die Reaktion auf ein Schuld-gefühl, das sich eine Instanz sucht, bei der eine Gegenklage eingereicht werden kann.

      "I'm troubled", sagt die Frau. Die Scheune erscheint ihr wie eine Kirche, die Farm ist ihre Welt, der Acker und die Bäume sind der Kosmos. Das Gegacker der Hühner draußen hört nicht auf, drinnen aber erscheinen ihr Engel. "I'm alone", sagt sie zu Jesus. "Is that how you made me?" Mit dieser Frage macht sie sich selbst zum Objekt, distanziert sie sich von ihren Handlungen, sucht sie nach einem Gegenüber, das sie von sich selbst entlasten kann. Jesus verspricht ihr einen Engel, in dessen Gegenwart sie ihr Alleinsein als Glück empfinden kann. Die zerbrechlichen Flügel mit ihren langsam zu Boden schwebenden Federn sind der Alltagsrest in diesem Phantasma, sie sind auch das Motiv, das den Tod zurückbringt. Die Frau erdrückt den Engel Alfred, mit ihrem Unglück wendet sie sich erneut an einen Schöpfer: "Who made my body a burden? Who made my soul lonely and stupid?" Die Kreatur befindet sich in einer ausweglosen Lage, die Frank mit mehreren Kreisschwenks betont. Die Einsamkeit (der Psychotikerin? der Hysterikerin?) ist erdrückend, diese Situation erst gibt ihr die Berechti-gung, ihren Fall auf der Ebene der Gattung zu verhandeln, als ein religiöses Drama, in dem die Heilsgeschichte („Seht auf diesen Mann", heißt es von Jesus in der Bibel) und die menschliche Unheilsgeschichte ("Look at me", ruft die Frau) aneinander gemessen werden. In Abwehr der Zudringlichkeit der Männer und im Aufbegehren gegen deren (unschuldig verschuldete) Abwesenheit entwickelt die Frau einen Sinn für ihre individuelle Existenz: "I don't wanna know", ruft sie in die Welt, zum ersten Mal ist sie damit nicht "außer sich", sondern wieder an ihrem Ort, einer Hühnerfarm. Dass Jesus noch einmal erscheint, als "simple God", der um Vergebung bittet, ist nur mehr Epilog in einem Drama der Autonomie, das über alle seelischen Abgründe hinweg verläuft. Die Theodizee, die Rechtfertigung Gottes für seine Schöpfung, unterbleibt, weil das Geschöpf sich gerade im Selbstverlust als ganz bei sich begreift. In diesem Gedanken liegt ein Rest der christlichen Erlösungslehre, deren Säkularisierung in *The Sin of Jesus* durch das Unbehagen der Geschlechter provoziert wird. *Bert Rebhandl*

      Drama of Autonomy   Psychology and theodicy, based on a story by Isaac Babel. A woman on a chicken farm spends her days working at the egg-sorting machine. "I'm the only woman here." She is pregnant, her husband spends his days lying in bed, and his friends encourage him to go out on the town with them. The woman talks to herself as she works, in a cadence resembling the hermetic music of Morton Feldman, simultaneously introverted and permeable, lost in the monotony of human existence ("feeding, cleaning, soiling—it doesn't matter"). She counts the passing days in the same way she counts eggs. Even extraordinary events go under in the stream of this melancholy solipsism. The appearance of Jesus Christ in the barn is a reaction to a guilty conscience looking for some place to file a countersuit.

"I'm troubled," says the woman. The barn seems to her like a church, the farm is her world, the ploughed field and the trees represent the cosmos. The hens' cackling outside never ceases, but angels appear to her inside. "I'm alone," she says to Jesus. "Is that how you made me?" She turns herself into an object with this question, distancing herself from her own actions. She is searching for a counterpart who can liberate her from herself. Jesus promises her an angel in whose presence her solitude will be as happiness. The fragile wings, their feathers wafting to the ground, are all that is left of everyday existence in this phantasm, and they also represent the motif with which death returns. The woman smothers Alfred the angel, she turns to her Creator again with her misfortune: "Who made my body a burden? Who made my soul lonely and stupid?" This poor creature is caught in a hopeless situation, as Frank emphasizes with several 360-degree pans. The solitude (of a psychotic woman? a hysterical woman?) is overwhelming, it justifies her regarding her situation in terms of a genre, as a religious drama in which the story of salvation ("Look at this man," said Jesus according to the Bible) and the story of human suffering ("Look at me," cries the woman) are compared. By resisting the audacity of men and rebelling against their (innocent) absence, the woman develops a sense of her own personal existence: "I don't wanna know," she shouts at no one in particular; for the first time she is not "beside herself" but back at her accustomed place, the chicken farm. The fact that Jesus appears to her once again, this time as a "simple God" who asks for forgiveness, is only the epilogue in a drama of autonomy which goes beyond any and all psychological chasms. The theodicy, God's justification for his creation, is omitted because this creature has just begun to regard itself as being whole through the loss of self. This idea contains a trace of the Christian doctrine of salvation, its secularization in *The Sin of Jesus* provoked by the discomfort plaguing male-and-female relations.
Bert Rebhandl

USA 1961, 35 mm, black and white, 37 min. directed by: Robert Frank. script: Howard Shulman, Mimi Arscher, based on the story by Isaac Babel. cinematography: Gert Berliner. editing: Robert Frank, Ken Collins. music: Morton Feldman. sound: Philip Sterling. production: Off-Broadway Productions, Jerry Michaels, Walter Gutman. world premiere: 19. 6. 1961 Spoleto Film Festival, USA: 10. 12. 1961 Cinema 16, Murray Hill Theatre New York. cast: Julie Bovasso, John Coe, Roberts Blossom, St. George Brian, Telly Savalas, Mary Frank, Jonas Mekas

1963

OK End Here

On sundays your eyes are grey   Sonntagsstimmung. Ein junges bürgerliches Paar schlägt sich die Zeit tot mit ziellosen Handlungen, gelangweilt voneinander und von seiner Umgebung. Gesten und Bewegungen, die ins Leere laufen. Sprachlosigkeit. Bemühungen, die herrschende Kluft zu überbrücken, um dann aber doch gleich wieder auseinanderzudriften.

Sie: „Talk to me." Er: "When a woman says to a man: Talk to me, it's like saying: Do you still love me?" Besuch kommt. Kleine Eifersüchteleien ohne große emotionale Gesten. Ein Spaziergang durch die Straßen. Abends im Restaurant. Rückkehr ins Apartment.

Robert Franks Kurzfilm über den Stillstand einer modernen Beziehung, inszeniert 1963, scheint in Erzählhaltung und Ästhetik unmittelbar von der französischen Nouvelle Vague und den Filmen Michelangelo Antonionis beeinflusst zu sein. Der Film oszilliert zwischen streng formal komponierten Einstellungen und semidokumentarischen Aufnahmen. Im Apartment pendelt der Kamerablick zwischen den beiden Hauptfiguren, die sich – ähnlich wie bei Antonioni – oft nur angeschnitten, meist am jeweils äußersten Rand des Bildes befinden, räumlich voneinander getrennt durch Wände, Türen, Spiegelungen oder Wohnungsinventar.

Wie sich die Protagonisten eher halt- und absichtslos durch den Tag gehen lassen, so bewegt sich auch die Kamera durch deren Welt. Mitunter verlässt sie die Personen, um den Raum zu durchmessen oder über Möbel und Gegenstände zu streifen, ein vagabundierender Blick, der sich in Nebensächlichkeiten zu verlieren scheint, damit aber die herrschende Atmosphäre von Gewohnheit, Entfremdung und Teilnahmslosigkeit einfängt.

Noch deutlicher wird dieser „dokumentierende" Akzent gegen Ende, als sich die beiden mit Bekannten in einem Restaurant treffen. Während sich die offen geäußerten Gefühle eines rezitierten Liebes- und Abschiedsbriefes im Lärm des Lokals verlieren, folgt die Kamera dem allgemeinen Desinteresse und wendet sich ebenso von der Vortragenden ab wie ihre Tischnachbarn, schenkt ihre Aufmerksamkeit mehr und mehr den anderen Gästen im Lokal. Begrüßungen, Handbewegungen, Blicke. Filmische Momentaufnahmen eines urbanen Lebens, ganz im Stil von Robert Franks berühmtem Fotozyklus "The Americans" aus den fünfziger Jahren.

Fotografisch komponiert auch sind jene Einstellungen, die die Protagonisten auf ihrem Weg durch die Stadt zwischen Wohnung und Restaurant begleiten. Beinahe geometrisch streng gekennzeichnete leere Plätze mit markanten kubischen Gebilden, einsame Arkaden mit geradlinigen Säulenreihen. Bei Antonioni dienen solche (Stadt-) Landschaften meist der Visualisierung der inneren Gefühlswelten seiner Protagonistinnen – und auch in *OK End Here* scheint der Weg durch die Architektur erste Klarheit in den Erkenntnisprozess der Hauptdarstellerin zu bringen, der sich am Ende äußern wird, ohne jedoch eine Konsequenz zu zeitigen: "I don't love you. I love what is familiar. You are not familiar to me." *Isabella Heugl, Gerald Weber*

On sundays your eyes are grey   A Sunday mood. A young, well-to-do couple aimlessly wiles away their day, bored with each other and their surroundings. Gestures and movements that come to nothing. Nothing to say, nothing to talk about. Attempts are made to bridge the gaping space, after which they drift apart again. She: "Talk to me." He: "When a woman says to a man: Talk to me, it's like saying: Do you still love me?" A visitor arrives. Little jealous squabbles without any grand emotional gestures. A walk through the streets. Dinner at a restaurant that evening. Then they return to their apartment.

Robert Frank's 1963 short film about inertia in a modern relationship seems to have been directly influenced by the French Nouvelle Vague and Michelangelo Antonioni's films with regard to narrative style and aesthetics. It alternates between semi-documentary scenes and shots composed with rigid formality. In the apartment, the camera goes from one main character to the other. Similar to Antonioni's characters, they are often only partially visible, usually at the edge of the frame, or are physically separated by walls, doors, reflections, or furniture.

The camera moves through the protagonists' world in the same way that they spend their day, with neither rhyme nor reason. At times it even abandons them to survey the room or skim over pieces of furniture or other objects, a roaming gaze, which seems to lose itself in things of little importance, while at the same time capturing the dominant atmosphere of routine, alienation, and apathy.

This "documentary" aspect becomes even more obvious near the end when the two meet friends in a restaurant. While the openly expressed emotions in a lover's farewell letter read aloud are lost in the background noise, the camera reflects the general lack of interest and turns away from the speaker, as do the others at the table, paying more and more attention to the other diners. Greetings, hand movements, glances: these cinematic snapshots of urban life are very much in the style of Robert Frank's well-known volume of photographs "The Americans", which was made in the 1950s.

Even the shots showing the protagonists on their way through the city from their apartment to the restaurant are composed photographically. Empty spaces with prominent cubic structures and isolated arcades with straight lines of columns are characterized by almost geometric rigidity. In Antonioni's films, such (urban) landscapes are normally employed to visualize the protagonists' emotions. In *OK End Here*, the path through architectural structures is the first element to introduce some clarity into the main characters' learning process. At the film's end it will be expressed, although without demonstrating any kind of consistency: "I don't love you. I love what is familiar. You are not familiar to me." *Isabella Heugl, Gerald Weber*

USA 1963, 35 mm, black and white, 32 min. directed by: Robert Frank. script: Marion Magid. cinematography: Gert Berliner. editing: Aram Avakian. production: September 20 Productions, Edwin Gregson. world premiere: September 1963, Bergamo Filmfestival, Italy, 14.9.1963 First New York Film Festival, Lincoln Center. cast: Martino La Salle, Sue Ungaro, Sudie Bond, Anita Ellis, Joseph Bird, a.o. awards: First prize, Bergamo Filmfestival 1963

1965-1968

Me and My Brother

Chaos-Theorie   Den Schlüssel dazu, wie die Möbiusschleife der Docu-fiction in der Arbeit Robert Franks auf den Punkt zu bringen ist, muss man hier suchen – an *Me and My Brother* führt diesbezüglich kein Weg vorbei. Keiner der Filme dieses Künstlers erstattet variantenreicher (und, typischerweise, komplizier-ter) Bericht von den sich unentwegt multiplizierenden Problemen, die die Engführung des „Wirklichen" im Filmischen mit sich bringt. Am Ziel der Klärung solcher Fragen scheitert dieser Film (weil sein Autor klug genug ist, zu wissen, dass er daran scheitern muss), aber er vollzieht dieses Scheitern mit außerordentlichen Ideen, mit großem Formwillen und hoher visueller Energie.

Jemand, der Filme macht, setzt sich einer Selbstbefragung aus. Frank fiktionalisiert (hier und anderswo) das eigene Leben, um sich über die Fiktion seiner selbst zu vergewissern. Alles, was Franks Kunst bis dahin definiert hat, taucht in diesem Film, neu konfiguriert, wieder auf: der Blick auf Amerika, „von außen"; die poetische Libertinage der Beats; das Marginale als das Zentrale (repräsentiert in der „realen" Figur des Julius, des katatonischen Bruders Peter Orlovskys, der die Poetenbande hier auf Tourneen und durchs Leben begleitet). Die Erzählung schlägt absonderliche Haken: Was bereits *Me and My Brother* zu sein scheint, entpuppt sich als – eher kunstarmer – Film-im-Film, zur Schau gestellt in einem Billigkino; später übernimmt ein Schauspieler, der Julius nicht im geringsten ähnlich sieht, dessen Rolle, ohne den „echten" Julius, der sich hier natürlich auch nur selbst spielt, aus dem Bild oder dem Film drängen zu können.

Nebenbei simuliert Frank, passend zu seinen vielen Städtebildern, urbane Wirklichkeit auch im Formalen: etwa die Unmöglichkeit, die Konzentration auf ein Sujet länger als ein paar Sekunden zu halten. *Me and My Brother* verdreht Gegensätzliches geschickt ineinander, spielt Gefälschtes gegen Authentisches aus, Pornographie gegen Poesie, Schauspiel gegen Dasein, Beat-Zynismus gegen Hippie-Romantik, Farbloses gegen Gefärbtes: Der radikale Wildwuchs ist das Programm dieses Films, die mögliche Simultaneität verschiedener narrativer Ebenen seine formale Basis. Das Kino wird studienhalber zersetzt, *de-composed,* es verwest, mitten im Leben. Franks erste lange Filmarbeit feiert die Wiederkehr des poetischen Essays als Assemblage, die Affirmation des Underground als wüste filmanalytische Collage.

Die Konfusion dieses Films hat Methode: Er ist so reich an Text, Zitaten, Musiken und Assozia-tionen, dass man ihm auf seinem Weg durch das Dickicht von Psyche, Kino und Metropole kaum folgen kann. Aber das muss so sein, alles andere wäre nur ein Kompromiss: Wenn das Kino mit dem Erzählen Ernst machen wollte, müsste es seine Konsumenten hinter sich lassen. Kein Zutritt. Die Leuchtschrift eines Schilds in schwarzer Nacht, irgendwo in der großen Stadt, verkündet gleich zu Anfang das (ironische) Credo dieser Arbeitshypo-these: „Stop", verkündet es – und: „Do not enter". *Stefan Grissemann*

Chaos Theory   The key to explaining the Möbius strip of docu-fiction in Robert Frank's work comprehensively must be searched for here—there is no getting around *Me and My Brother*. None of this artist's films allow a more varied (and, typically, more complicated) report on the constantly multiplying problems which accompany the narrowing of the "real" in the filmic. This film fails to achieve such clarification (because its maker is smart enough to know that such failure is inevitable), but its failure is realized by means of extra-ordinary ideas, with great desire to give form and a high degree of visual energy.

Someone who makes films exposes him or herself to self-examination. Frank fictionalizes his own life (both here and in other works) to obtain, via fiction, certainty about himself. Everything which had defined Frank's art up to that point turns up in this film, newly configured: the look at America, "from the outside"; the poetic libertinage of the Beats; the marginal in a central role (represented by the "real" figure of Julius, Peter Orlovsky's catatonic brother who accompanies the band of poets on tour in the film and through life). The story contains bizarre twists and turns: What *Me and My Brother* seems to be is revealed early on as a—rather artless—film-within-a-film being shown at a rundown movie theater. An actor who fails to resemble Julius in the slightest, later assumes his role without being able to drive the "real" Julius (just playing himself, of course) from the scene or the film.

At the same time, Frank, fittingly in light of his many images of cities, simulates urban reality in formal aspects, such as with the impossibility of concentrating on a single subject for more than a few seconds. *Me and My Brother* skillfully weaves together opposites, plays counterfeits against the authentic, pornography against poetry, acting against being, Beat cynicism against hippie romanticism, monochrome against colored: Radical overgrowth is this film's program, the potential simultaneity of various narrative levels its formal basis. Cinema is dissected for study purposes, "de-composed," surrounded by life as it rots. Frank's first feature-length film work celebrates the return of the poetic essay as assemblage, the affirmation of the underground as a wild cinematic analysis in the form of a collage.

There is a method to this film's madness: It is so rich in text, quotes, music, and associations that keeping up with it through the underbrush of psyche, film, and urbanity is barely possible. But that is necessary; anything else would be nothing more than a compromise: If film were to take storytelling seriously, it would leave its consumers behind. No admittance. An illuminated sign shining through a black night, somewhere in a big city, announces at the very beginning the (ironic) creed of this working hypothesis: "Stop," it announces, and "Do not enter." *Stefan Grissemann*

USA 1965-1968, 35 mm, colour & black and white, 91 min. (re-edited 85 min.). directed by: Robert Frank. script: Robert Frank, Sam Shepard. poetry: Allen Ginsberg, Peter Orlovsky. cinematography: Robert Frank. editing: Robert Frank, Helen Silverstein, Bob Easton, Lynn Ratener. production: Two Faces Company, Helen Silverstein. world premiere: 1. 9. 1968 Filmfestival Venice, Italy. cast: Julius Orlovsky, Joseph Chaikin, John Coe, Allen Ginsberg, Peter Orlovsky, Virginia Kiser, Nancy Fisher, Cynthia McAdams, Roscoe Lee Browne, Christopher Walken, Seth Allen, Maria Tucci, Jack Greenbaum, Otis Young, Lou Waldon, a.o.

1969

Conversations in Vermont

Familienalbum   „Dieser Film handelt von der Vergangenheit, die neunzehn Jahre zurückreicht zu jener Zeit, als Mary und ich geheiratet haben. (...) Dieser Film handelt also von der Vergangenheit und von der Gegenwart. Die Gegenwart kommt in Form von Filmaufnahmen zurück, die ich dort aufgenommen habe, wo meine Kinder jetzt zur Schule gehen. Das heißt, sie haben New York verlassen und leben nun an einem anderen Ort. (...) Vielleicht ist das ein Film übers Älterwerden. (...) Eine Art Familienalbum. Ich weiß nicht ... Er handelt von ....“

Conversations in Vermont aus dem Jahr 1969 gilt als der erste autobiografische Film von Robert Frank. Wenn man ihm ein Thema geben will, so erzählt er von der Beziehung eines Vaters zu seinen beiden halbwüchsigen Kindern. Er beschreibt den vom Vater ausgehenden Versuch, sich über eine gemeinsame Geschichte zu verständigen, einen Raum für gemeinsames Erinnern aufzumachen. Und er zeigt die Brüchigkeit dieses Unterfangens, die bereits im oben zitierten Prolog anklingt: Längst schon haben die Kinder ihre eigene Vergangenheit, führen ihr eigenes Leben. Dabei ist die Familiengeschichte scheinbar bestens dokumentiert. Begleitet von Franks Stimme fällt der Blick der Kamera zu Beginn des Films auf Fotos, rückt neben anderen (weltberühmten) Aufnahmen immer wieder auch Familienfotos ins Bild. Ein Teil dieser Fotografien ist mit im Gepäck, wenn Frank später wie ein scheuer Besucher mit seinem Kameramann Ralph Gibson in der alternativen Schule eintrifft, in der seine Kinder, Andrea und Pablo, leben.

Doch die Bilder eignen sich nur bedingt als Kommunikationsmittel. Auch davon erzählt der Film, der Sehen, Gesehenwerden und Sprechen kaum merklich voneinander absetzt. Fragen gehen ins Leere, auf beiden Seiten machen sich Unsicherheiten bemerkbar. Das Fleisch sei frisch, sagt die Tochter ein wenig ungehalten, nachdem der Vater die Einladung, zum Essen zu bleiben, zunächst ausschlägt. Und: „Man hat mir schon früher eine Filmkamera vor die Nase gehalten.“

Denn in den Fotos – wie im Film – überlagern einander beständig ein professionelles und das persönliche Interesse („Ich glaube, der Take mit Pablo war gut.“), eine private und eine veröffentlichte Geschichte. Geredet wird schließlich über das, was den Fotografien entgangen ist – oder was sie erst auf den zweiten Blick preisgeben. Währenddessen läuft die Kamera. Der Vater ist trotz allem ein Bildermacher geblieben. Mitunter wirken seine Bilder wie gestohlene Momentaufnahmen, die kommentarlos kostbare kleine Beobachtungen bewahren: Junge und Mädchen beim gemeinsamen Ausmisten im Pferdestall. Sonniges Gegenlicht, in dem der schwere Staub tanzt. Routinierte Handgriffe. Auch daran wird man sich irgendwann erinnern. *Isabella Reicher*

Family Album   "This film is about the past, which goes back nineteen years when Mary and I got married. ... As I said—this film is about the past and the present. The present comes back in actual film-footage which I took where my children now go to school. That means they left New York and they live in a different place now. ... Maybe this film is about growing older ... some kind of a family album. I don't know ... it's about ..."

Conversations in Vermont, produced in 1969, is considered Robert Frank's first autobiographical film. If defining a theme for it were necessary, one could say it tells the story of a father's relationship with his

two teenaged children. It also describes the father's attempt to communicate with them by means of a shared story, to open up a space for joint memory. And it shows the fragility of such an undertaking, which is intimated in the prologue quoted above. The children have long since found their own past and now lead their own lives. The records of the family's history are apparently quite complete. Accompanied by Frank's voice, the camera is trained on a number of photographs at the film's beginning: Family pictures enter the scene along with other (world-famous) stills. Some of these photographs are in Frank's luggage when, resembling a bashful visitor, he later arrives along with his cameraman Ralph Gibson, at the alternative boarding school where his children Andrea and Pablo live.

But these photos possess only limited value as means of communication. That is another theme dealt with by this film, which barely distinguishes between seeing, being seen, and talking. Questions hang in the air, unanswered. There is uncertainty perceptible in both those asking and those being asked. "The meat is fresh," says the daughter with some annoyance, after her father at first refuses an invitation to stay for dinner. Then, "I've had movie cameras in front of me before."

In the photographs—and the film—there is continuous overlap of professional and personal interests ("I think we made a good take with Pablo"), private and publicized history. All talk eventually revolves around what the pictures failed to capture—or what they reveal only after a second look. And the camera is running the entire time. Despite everything, the father has remained a creator of images, some of them resembling stolen snapshots which preserve precious moments without comment, such as boys and girls shoveling out a stable together. Heavy dust swirling, backlit by the sun. Routine hand motions. All that, too, will be recalled some time in the future. *Isabella Reicher*

USA 1969, 16 mm, black and white, 26 min. part of a twelve-piece TV-serial for KQED-TV in San Francisco. directed by: Robert Frank. cinematography: Ralph Gibson. editing: Robert Frank. sound: Robert Frank. production: Dilexi Foundation, Robert Frank. world premiere: TV Los Angeles. cast: Robert, Pablo and Andrea Frank

1969

Liferaft Earth

Hungern für DieGanzeWelt   Zu Beginn von *Liferaft Earth* kommt ein Zeitungsbericht über ein lokales Ereignis in Hayward, Kalifornien ins Bild: „Eingezwängt in ein durch Plastikmaterial abgegrenztes Terrain zwischen Restaurant und Supermarkt verbrachten 100 Anti-Bevölkerungs-Protestler ihren zweiten Hunger-Tag … Die sogenannte Hunger-Show – die eine Woche dauern wird – soll die gefährdete Zukunft der Menschheit dramatisieren: Überbevölkerung und Nahrungsmangel."

Der Film begleitet die Menschen auf diesem „Rettungsboot Erde", vom 11. bis 18. Oktober 1969. Gleich nach den ersten Einstellungen auf die TeilnehmerInnen (sie machen Yoga, meditieren) steht Robert Frank vor seiner Kamera: unsicher, im Gegenlicht kaum zu erkennen. Er beteuert, wie wichtig es ihm ist, diesen Film für Stewart Brand zu machen. Später ist noch ein Teil dieses Kommentars eingeschnitten: Frank fühlt sich schlecht, weil er bei heftigem Regen das Floß verlassen hat, er hat sich dann aber entschlossen, zurück zu gehen.

Steward Brand ist der – wie es heißt – am wenigsten anerkannte, aber wichtigste Vordenker Amerikas: Er war u. a. Mitbegründer der „Bibel der Alternativen": des "CoEvolution Quarterly", Herausgeber des Bestsellers "Whole Earth Catalog" (1968–85: ein enzyklopädischer Zugang zu Werkzeugen und Ideen) und 1985 Mitbegründer / Architekt des Whole Earth Lectronic Link (WELL), der legendären Site für elektronische Kommunikation noch vor der www-Ära. 1968 fahndete Brand mit einer Medienkampagne nach einem Bild der ganzen Erde. Eine der ersten Aufnahmen des Planeten, die die Nasa aus ihrem Apollo-Programm zur Verfügung stellte, wurde das Logo des "Whole Earth Catalog". Viele Brand-Fans sind überzeugt, dass dieses Weltlogo die internationale ökologische Bewegung konzeptuell mitbegründete.

Die inflationäre Vermarktung der Bilder aus Woodstock (15. – 17. 8. 1969) hat den so direkten, ruhigen Blick überlagert, den Frank auf diese neuen Nomaden richtete. Es fällt auf, wie unprätentiös er die Kamera zu einer Strategie der präzisen Aufzeichnung verwendet. Die freiwilligen AußenseiterInnen der Überflussgesellschaft zelebrieren ihren Protest mit großem Ernst. Natürlich ist uns bewusst, dass normal ernährte Menschen nach sieben Fastentagen noch nicht lebensbedrohend geschwächt sind – und dieses Hungern gegen den Hunger hat auch etwas Naives. Frank lässt die Menschen diesen Aspekt vor seiner Kamera relativieren.

Die Streikenden lagern auf Schlafsäcken und Decken. Die Kamera umkreist sie in langen, handgehaltenen Einstellungen. Assoziationen zu Schlüsselbildern unserer Zivilisation drängen sich auf: Flüchtlingslager, Gefangene, Überlebende nach der großen Katastrophe – und auch Installationen von Ilya Kabakov oder Christian Boltanski kommen einem in den Sinn. Am letzten Tag verlangsamt das Fasten die Bewegungen, so lässt auch der Film den Menschen mehr Zeit. Lange schauen sie direkt in die Kamera.

Eine Frau sagt mit dem freundlichsten Lächeln: "You fucking media whores" – und dann: „Jetzt kann ich aber kaum noch aufrecht stehen." *Birgit Flos*

Fasting for the Whole Earth   *Liferaft Earth* begins with a newspaper report from Hayward, California: "Sandwiched between a restaurant and supermarket, 100 antipopulation protesters spent their second starving day in a plastic enclosure.... The so-called Hunger Show, a week-long starve-in aimed at dramatizing man's future in an overpopulated, underfed world...."

This film accompanies the people on this "life raft" from 11 to 18 October 1969. Right after the first shots of the participants (who are doing yoga and meditating), Robert Frank is shown standing in front of his camera: uncertain, barely recognizable in the backlighting. He declares how important it is to him to make this film for Stewart Brand. Part of this statement was used again later: Frank feels bad because he left the raft when the weather turned foul, but then he decided to get back on.

Steward Brand is—it is said—considered the least recognized but most important visionary thinker in America: He was a co-founder of the "bible of the alternative community," the "CoEvolution Quarterly"; publisher of the bestselling *Whole Earth Catalog* (1968-85: an encyclopedic guide to tools and alternative ideas) and in 1985 co-founder and architect of the Whole Earth Lectronic Link (WELL), the legendary Internet site for electronic communication which predated the advent of the WWW era. In 1968, Brand launched a media campaign to search for a photograph of the entire Earth. One of the first pictures of the planet, provided by NASA from its Apollo program, became the *Whole Earth Catalog*'s logo. A number of Brand fans are convinced that this international logo represented the conceptual foundation of the international ecological movement.

The boom in the marketing of images from Woodstock (15 to 17 August 1969) overpowered Frank's quiet, direct gaze at these modern nomads. The unpretentious manner in which the camera is used in a strategy of precise documentation is outstanding. These voluntary outsiders of consumer society held their protest with a great deal of sincerity. Of course we are aware of the fact that seven days of fasting does not represent a danger to normally well-fed individuals—and this idea of fasting against hunger is somehow naïve. Frank gave the protestors an opportunity to justify this aspect on camera.

The hunger strikers lie on sleeping bags and blankets. The handheld camera circles them in long shots. Associations with key images of our civilization occur: refugee camps, prisoners, survivors of a great catastrophe—the installations of Ilya Kabakov and Christian Boltanski also come to mind. On the last day, as the protestors' movements slowed, the camera gave them additional time. They stare directly into it with enduring gazes.

With her most friendly smile a woman says, "You fucking media whores," and then: "I can't stand up much longer." *Birgit Flos*

USA 1969, 16 mm, color & black and white, 37 min. directed by: Robert Frank. cinematography: Robert Frank. editing: Susan Obenhaus. sound: Danny Lyon. production: Sweeney Productions; Portola Institute, Robert Frank. cast: Robert Frank, Danny Lyon, Hugh Romney, Stewart Brand, participants in "The Hunger Show"

1971

About Me: A Musical

Eine Subjektkomposition. Das Selbstporträt von Robert Frank entsteht aus einer Themen-verfehlung, für deren Willkür er persönlich die Verantwortung übernimmt: "My project was to make a film about music in America." Und dann, großartig abschätzig: "Well, fuck the music. I just decided to make a film about myself." Es wird dann trotzdem ein Film über Musik, in dem jedoch ständig Fragen der künstlerischen Äußerung verhandelt werden, und die Erinnerung wie ein Kaleidoskop funktioniert. Die interessanteste Entäußerung betrifft eine Schauspielerin namens Lynn Reyner, die Frank selbst einführt als "the young lady that's playing me". Sie tritt in mehreren (viragierten, verfremdeten) Szenen auf, spielt eine Interviewsituation durch, in der sie für Frank spricht und einige Stationen seines Lebens aufzählt. Eine Frage nach der Politik bleibt unbeantwortet, die Theatralität gibt diesen Auftritten den Charakter eines Workshops. Die Gegenkultur der späten sechziger Jahre ist nicht ausdrücklich, aber deutlich präsent. Kollektive Situationen sind die Regel, es gibt kein „Ich", das außerhalb der Welt in Reflexionsdistanz existiert. Frank begreift sich enzyklopädisch, die Tempelmusiker im indischen Benares spielen ebenso eine Rolle in seinem *About Me* wie "hope freaks" in New Mexiko oder, in einer besonders intensiven Szene, schwarze Häftlinge in einem texanischen Gefängnis. Sie singen ein "soulful piece", in einem ungemein wehmütigen Chor, danach gibt jeder einzeln seine Lage bekannt: "life", "a hundred years". Frank, der Einwanderer, begreift seine Geschichte als kollektive. Er sieht ebenso von sich ab (die erste Aufnahme der Schauspielerin, die ihn spielt, ist ein Outtake), wie er narzisstisch alles auf sich bezieht. Mit den Worten "It's great, but who gives a shit?", kommentiert er die Präsenz seiner Frau, die im Fenster der gemeinsamen Loft in der New Yorker Bowery Geige spielt. "Well, I do." Die Zerrüttungen des Lebens werden angedeutet. Die Skepsis gegenüber der Fotografie ist virulent, bricht sich aber in einer Aufnahme aus der Wohnung der Eltern, die voller Bilder ist, zwischen denen die blinde Mutter herumgeht. „Das bin ich", sagt Frank, durch einen altmodischen Apparat ist er selbst als Kleinkind zu sehen. Eine Befragung von Passanten schließt den Kreis: „Wenn Sie eine Kamera hätten und einen Film, was würden Sie drehen?" Natürlich etwas über die Probleme des Landes, antworten die meisten, und Frank sieht sich einmal mehr isoliert in seiner durch Repräsentationsfragen gebremsten Selbstbezüglichkeit. Dann aber antwortet ein Straßenmusiker: "About myself", und schon spielt er einen Klassiker. "Those were the days, my friend." Das ist ein explizites Echo auf die Szene, in der die Frank-Darstellerin einen Stapel Fotos auf das Bett wirft, und verächtlich sagt: "That's my past." Werke und vergangene Tage. *Bert Rebhandl*

An exposition of the subject Robert Frank's self-portrait embodies his failure to adequately develop a certain theme, and he assumes personal responsibility for its random nature: "My project was to make a film about music in America." And then, with marvelous disdain: "Well, fuck the music. I just decided to make a film about myself." In any case the result was a film about music that repeatedly poses questions concerning artistic expression and presents the function of memory similar to a kaleidoscope. The most interesting revelation came from an actress named Lynn Reyner, whom Frank himself introduces as "the young lady that's playing me." She appears in several colored and visually distorted scenes, and rehearses an interview in which she speaks for Frank, relating some of the important events in his life. One political question remains unanswered, and the theatrical nature of these scenes makes them reminiscent of a workshop. The counter-

culture of the late 1960s is definitely present, though not explicitly. Collectivity is the norm; there is no "I" except within this particular world. Frank is being encyclopedic; the role played by temple musicians in Benares, India is equally important as that of "hope freaks" in New Mexico or, in an especially intense scene, Black inmates in a Texas prison. The latter sing a "soulful piece" in an extraordinarily melancholic chorus, after which each individual reveals his sentence: "life," "a hundred years." Frank, the immigrant, regards his story as a collective one. He disregards himself (the first scene with the actress who plays him is an exception) to the same extent that he narcissistically relates everything to himself. He comments on the presence of his wife who plays a violin at the window of their loft in New York's Bowery with the words "It's great, but who gives a shit?"— "Well, I do." The scars left by life are implied. While his skeptical view of photography is virulent, it is refracted in a picture of his parents' apartment, filled with other pictures among which his blind mother walks. "That's me," says Frank when an old-fashioned film projector shows him as a small child. An interview of passers-by completes the circle: "If you had a camera and some film, what would you shoot?" Something about the country's problems is naturally the most common reply, and once again Frank sees himself isolated in his self-referentiality, which is curbed by issues of representation. Then a street musician answers, "About myself," and starts playing a classic number. "Those were the days, my friend." This is an explicit echo of the scene in which the actress playing Frank throws a stack of photographs onto the bed and says with disgust, "That's my past." Photographic works and days long gone. *Bert Rebhandl*

USA 1971, 16 mm, black and white, 30 min. directed by: Robert Frank. script: Robert Frank. cinematography: Danny Seymour, Robert Frank. editing: Robert Frank. sound: Robert McNamara. production: American Film Institute (support), Robert Frank. cast: Lynn Reyner, Jaime deCarlo Lotts, Robert Schlee, Sheila Pavlo, Bill Hart, Vera Cochran, Sid Kaplan, June Leaf, Allen Ginsberg, Danny Lyon, Peter Orlovsky

1972

Cocksucker Blues

Camera? Rolling: Bilder in Bewegung   Was haben sich die Rolling Stones erwartet, als sie Frank 1972 mit einem Film über ihre Kanada/US-Tournee beauftragten? Ein Frank-Foto von 1950 wurde für das Cover von "Exile on Main Street" verwendet. Vielleicht erhofften sie sich eine avantgardistische Hommage? Mit *Cocksucker Blues* waren sie so unzufrieden, dass sie den Vertrieb des Films verhinderten. Frank gelang es später, die Rechte zurück zu kaufen. *CSB* kursierte jahrelang nur in Raubkopien und durfte angeblich nur einmal im Jahr in Anwesenheit von Frank projiziert werden. All das produziert Erwartungen: Ja, es kommen die Szenen im Stones-Privatjet vor, in denen Nebenpersonen mit diversen Groupies Sex haben. Es wird Kokain geschnupft und Heroin gespritzt. Ja, es gibt eine autoerotische Szene, bei der sich in der Spiegelbildauflösung Jagger selbst als Kameramann outet. Frank montierte die heiße Nummer ziemlich an den Anfang des Films, vielleicht, um Erwartungen schneller zu ernüchtern. Vermutlich hatte Frank durch seine Nähe zu Künstlern der Beat-Generation, zu Kerouac, Ginsberg und Burroughs, anarchistischere Erfahrungen gemacht als mit den Stones.

In seinem *One plus One* zeigte Godard die Stones 1968 als Workaholics; durch Stellwände sauber voneinander getrennt, erarbeiten sie ihr "Sympathy for the Devil". In *Gimme Shelter* von den Maisles Brothers überprüfen sie ernst und betroffen die Bilder des Katastrophenkonzerts von Altamont inklusive tödlicher Messerstecherei auf der Moviola. In *CSB* gibt es nur ca. 15 Minuten Konzert. Alles andere spielt sich in den Proberäumen, in Hotelzimmern ab, in Vorbereitung, im Warten. Nach ein paar Minuten denkt man: Diese trashige Handkamera ist nicht auszuhalten. Sie umkreist die Menschen, toleriert jede „Störung"; sie lauert den Stars nicht auf, sondern lässt sie verschwinden, vergisst sie und nimmt sie wie nebenbei wieder ins Bild: pure Filmbewegung. Die Bewegung geht fast ausschließlich von der Kamera aus, sie infiziert das Filmbild, sie allein schafft diese unglaubliche filmische Energie.

Ich habe *CSB* auf einer Videokopie gesichtet, auf der die Kontraste von den vielen Kopiervorgängen ausgewaschen waren. Ähnlich der Ton: eine Collage, in der nur passagenweise eine Musikphrase erkennbar wird, oder Sätze, die man plötzlich versteht, bevor sie wieder in den allgemeinen Geräuschpegel abtauchen. Ein grandioses "work in progress". Die Verschleifungen, die dem Film eine geradezu haptische Qualität geben, wären mit keiner Software zu erreichen: The Stones Rolling (so ein Zwischentitel in Godards *One plus One*).

Vor der handgeschriebenen Titelkarte *Cocksucker Blues* kommt ein Hinweis: "Except for the musical numbers the events depicted in this film are fictitious. No representation of actual persons and events are intended." Das klingt nach einem typischen Frank-Statement: Das Dokumentarische wird mit der fiktiven, „gespielten" Realität kombiniert. Aber der ganze Filmtext hier ist eine musikalische Nummer. Film-Musik. So ist alles authentisch oder auf dem Weg dorthin. On the road. *Birgit Flos*

Camera? Rolling: Images in Motion   What did the Rolling Stones expect when they hired Frank to make a film about their 1972 tour of Canada and the U.S.? An avant-garde homage? One of Frank's photographs from 1950 was used for the cover of "Exile on Main Street". But afterwards, the band was so dissatisfied with the final product, *Cocksucker Blues*, that they blocked its distribution, though Frank managed to repurchase the rights later. For years, solely bootleg copies of *Cocksucker Blues* have been available, and public showings are supposedly permitted only once a year and in Frank's presence.

All this resulted in certain expectations: Yes, there are scenes in the Stones' private jet in which minor figures have sex with various groupies. There is snorting of cocaine and shooting of heroin. Yes, there is a masturbation scene in which Jagger reveals himself to be the cameraman in a reflected image. Frank put this hot scene near the beginning of the film, possibly to quickly dampen expectations. It could be assumed that Frank's experiences with artists of the Beat Generation such as Kerouac, Ginsberg, and Burroughs were more anarchistic than those with the Stones.

In his 1968 *One plus One*, Godard depicted the Stones as workaholics; they recorded their "Sympathy for the Devil" while neatly separated behind dividing walls. In *Gimme Shelter* by the Maysles brothers they examine footage of the catastrophic concert at Altamont, including the fatal stabbing, earnestly and with shock. *Cocksucker Blues* contains only about fifteen minutes of concert footage. Everything else is set in practice studios, hotel rooms, during preparations and periods of waiting. After a few minutes the viewer might think: I can't stand this trashy handheld camera anymore. It circles the subjects, tolerating all kinds of intrusions. Rather than lying in wait for the stars, it makes them disappear, forgets them completely and then returns them to the picture, seemingly in passing: pure movement for the sake of movement. This movement is initiated almost exclusively by the camera; it infects the picture, and it alone creates the unbelievable filmic energy.

I saw a video copy of *Cocksucker Blues* in which the contrast had been washed out by its being copied so many times. The soundtrack had suffered in similar fashion: What resulted was a collage in which solely snatches of songs are recognizable or parts of sentences can be understood before they go under in the general noise. A magnificent work in progress. No software could produce this kind of wear and tear which gives this film an almost haptic quality: The Stones Rolling (an insert in Godard's *One plus One*).

Before the handwritten title appears, a statement is made: "Except for the musical numbers the events depicted in this film are fictitious. No representation of actual persons and events are intended." This sounds like a typical Frank statement: Documentation has been combined with fictitious, staged reality. But the film's entire text is in this case a song. Film music. As a result everything is authentic or getting there. On the road. *Birgit Flos*

USA 1972, 16 mm, color & black and white, 90 min. this film was made during the U.S.-tour of the Rolling Stones in 1972 ordered by the Rolling Stones. directed by: Robert Frank. cinematography: Robert Frank, Danny Seymour. editing: Robert Frank, Paul Justmann, Susan Steinberg. sound: Danny Seymour, "Flex". music: The Rolling Stones. production: Rolling Stones Presentation, Marshall Chess. cast: Mick Jagger, Keith Richards, Bill Wyman, Mick Taylor, Charlie Watts, Danny Seymour, Andy Warhol, Dick Cavett, Lee Radizwell, Truman Capote, Tina Turner, a.o.

1975

Keep Busy

Verstörungskomödie   "It's important not to neglect the outside in favor of the inside": einer der (meist nicht nur) auf den ersten Blick kryptischen Sätze, die den Großteil des Dialog-Geplappers von *Keep Busy* ausmachen, gibt vielleicht eine Ahnung vom Entstehungsprozess dieses Films. Denn weder Regisseur Robert Frank noch Autor Rudy Wurlitzer haben sich je wirklich erhellend über diese so faszinierende wie ungreifbare knapp dreiviertelstündige Improvisation, ihre erste Zusammenarbeit, geäußert – außer eben, dass sie spontan und fast „wie von selbst" entstanden sei. "I am filming the outside in order to look inside", hat Frank einmal seine Ästhetik formuliert: In *Keep Busy* bildet jedenfalls zum ersten Mal seine kanadische Wahlheimat Nova Scotia jenes „Außen", anhand dessen das „Innen" betrachtet werden soll.

Alles weitere ist Interpretationssache – Frank und Wurlitzer verzichten auf erklärende Maßnahmen und im Gegensatz zu Franks Vorgängerfilm *Cocksucker Blues* kann man sich hier nicht einmal anhand von bisweilen auftauchenden Star-Gesichtern (immerhin ist der Bildhauer Richard Serra im Darsteller-Häuflein auszumachen) oder anhand des Ordnungsprinzips „Tour-Alltag" orientieren, sondern nur den verblüffenden Wortkapriolen und oft unverständlichen Interaktionen der Protagonisten folgen. In der gelegentlichen Neigung zum Nonsens, im synkopierten Rhythmus von Inszenierung und Dialog erinnert das ans spielerische, parodistische Element der Beat-Fantasie *Pull My Daisy*, aber bei *Keep Busy* lässt sich nicht einmal sagen, ob es sich dabei um eine seltsame Idylle oder ein postapokalyptisches Szenario handeln soll.

Lose lässt sich eine Art Handlung ausmachen: Auf einer abgelegenen Insel vor Cape Breton lebt eine kleine Gruppe von Menschen; die einzige Verbindung zur Außenwelt ist das Radio des ansässigen Leuchtturmwärters. Was er von sich gibt, scheint für die anderen von höchster Bedeutung, seien es an Bauernregeln erinnernde Sentenzen ("When the wind is in the west, the weather's always best") oder völlig unbegreifliche Parolen wie das zu Anfang von ihm ausgegebene Mantra "Richard on the fire!", das im Lauf des Films beständig variiert wird. Ähnlich undurchsichtig sind die Aktionen der anderen Figuren (zwei stehen eine Zeitlang unerklärt herum und stützen ein Haus), die Stimmung erinnert ein wenig an Becketts abstrakte Verstörungs-Komödien. Eventuell geht es um die einsame Macht, die der Leuchtturmwärter automatisch über die anderen ausübt (der Turm ragt, in den schönsten der blendenden Schwarzweißbilder hier, symbolhaft am dunstigen Horizont auf), das legt jedenfalls ein Satz nahe, den er gegen Ende äußert: "Once you're up here, you're all alone. You run the show."

Oder es geht doch nur um die Show, die sich hier – im Ineinanderfließen dokumentarischer und fiktiver Elemente – als bienenfleißiges Summen von Aktivität manifestiert: Was man absurderweise so alles tut, um überhaupt etwas zu tun. *Keep Busy* eben. *Christoph Huber*

A comic grotesque   "It's important not to neglect the outside in favor of the inside." This is one of the statements, cryptic at first glance (most of which remain so), which constitute the greater part of the prattling dialogue in *Keep Busy*. At the same time, these dialogues may provide a clue as to how it was produced. Neither director Robert Frank nor screenwriter Rudy Wurlitzer ever really offered any clarification of this equally fascinating and incomprehensible thirty-eight-minute improvisation, their first joint production—except that it was made spontaneously and almost "by itself." "I am filming the outside in order to look inside," Frank once said about his aesthetics. In *Keep Busy* his chosen home of Nova Scotia serves for the first time as the "outside" in an examination of the "inside."

Everything else is a matter of interpretation; Frank and Wurlitzer do not bother with explanations of any sort. In contrast to Frank's previous film, *Cocksucker Blues*, this film does not even orient itself on the basis of stars who appear occasionally or the "daily life on tour" organizing principle (sculptor Richard Serra, however, is recognizable in the jumble of actors). The only thing to do is to follow the protagonists' astounding verbal gymnastics and often incomprehensible interactions. In its occasional tendency to descend into nonsense, and with the syncopated rhythm of its action and dialogue, this film is reminiscent of the playful and parodying elements of the Beat fantasy *Pull My Daisy*, but *Keep Busy* does not even permit a guess as to whether it was intended to represent a strange sort of idyll or a post-apocalyptic scenario.

A plot can be loosely identified: A small group of people live on a remote island near Cape Breton; the sole link to the outside world is the radio owned by the local lighthouse keeper. The other residents put great stock in everything he says, whether it harks back to old sayings ("When the wind is in the west, the weather's always best") or presents a totally incomprehensible mantra such as the one he utters at the beginning, "Richard on the fire!" This statement undergoes constant variation in the course of the film. Similarly enigmatic is the behavior of the other characters (two of them stand around for a while for no apparent reason, apparently holding up a house). The atmosphere is somewhat reminiscent of Beckett's abstract comic grotesques. The focus could be the unchallenged power which the lighthouse keeper automatically exercises over the others (the lighthouse, in the most beautiful of the dazzling black-and-white images, juts symbolically on the hazy horizon). He reinforces this view with a claim made near the film's end: "Once you're up here, you're all alone. You run the show."

Or it's all just about the show, which is manifested here—in the interweaving of documentary and fictitious elements—as a buzz of activity. What absurd things some people do just so they have something to do. Just keeping busy. *Christoph Huber*

CAN 1975, 16 mm, black and white, 38 min. directed by: Robert Frank, Rudy Wurlitzer. script: Rudy Wurlitzer. cinematography: Robert Frank. editing: Robert Frank, sound: Charles Dean. production: Canada Council (support), Robert Frank. world premiere: Berkeley, California. cast: June Leaf, Joan Jonas, Richard Serra, Joanne Akalaitis, Joe Dan MacPherson

1980

Life Dances On...

Ein Film in Möglichkeitsform   Ein kleiner, 1983 in Paris erschienener Band mit Fotografien von Robert Frank schickt einen Text des Künstlers voraus, der *Life Dances On...* als einen im Entstehen begriffenen Film zu beschreiben scheint. Der Text, dessen emblematischer Titel „Ich würde gerne einen Film machen...“[1] lautet, verhandelt nicht weniger als das Verhältnis von Fotografie, Film und Leben. Frank vertritt darin den Anspruch, im Film privates und öffentliches Leben zu verbinden, Zufälligkeiten des Alltags einfließen zu lassen. Fotografien, führt er aus, müssten im Film Atempausen und Fenster sein, die auf eine andere Zeit, andere Orte verweisen. Frank macht nicht viel Aufhebens um ein „perfektes“ Bild. Jean-Paul Fargier[2] hat dies als seine „schwache Stärke“ bezeichnet. Wenn Frank die Kamera führt, agiert und interveniert er meist auf mehreren Ebenen gleichzeitig. Einmal stellt er sich, das Mikrofon in der Hand, einigen New Yorker Amateurfotografen vor, enthüllt sich damit als Subjekt des Films. Ein andermal taucht sein Arm hinter der Kamera hervor, um die Klappe mit einem Fingerschnippen zu ersetzen und aus dem Off weiterzufragen. Zuweilen, wenn er in seinen Unterhandlungen an die Grenzen der Worte gerät, weil seine Gesprächspartner sich verweigern, gibt er gar Regieanweisungen.

Life Dances On... ist Franks verstorbener Tochter Andrea und dem Gedenken an seinen Freund Danny Seymour gewidmet. Wenn der Film Outtakes oder auch Teile früherer Filme in sich aufnimmt, so keineswegs, um die Trauerarbeit erzählerisch wiederzugeben. Franks fragmentarische, metaphorische und assoziative Darstellungsform ist dem Selbstporträt weitaus näher als der Autobiografie. Dies zeigt sich in der scheinbaren Beiläufigkeit der gefilmten Ereignisse. So schwenkt in einer der für *Life Dances On...* aus dem persönlichen Archiv hervorgeholten Schwarzweißaufnahme die Kamera von einem statischen Selbstporträt im kleinen Wandspiegel unvermittelt auf Franks schlafende Frau, zoomt kurz zurück, durchmisst die Wohnung. Ein Wasserkessel auf dem Herd, ein Blick aus dem New Yorker Fenster, morgendliches Sonntagsradio, dann wieder die Frau: „Warum willst du diese Aufnahmen machen?“ Frank entzieht sich einer Antwort; sie ist in der Form zu suchen, mit der der Film Leben in ein zunächst unbewegtes Bild bringt. Fotografien, in Assemblagen präsentiert, aber auch Filmaufnahmen, kaschiert und collagiert, sind für Frank Objekte, deren Materialität mit ihrer Funktion als Erinnerungsträger verbunden sind. Werden sie in ein neues Umfeld gestellt, so tritt ihre zeitliche Spur umso klarer zutage. Frank versteht es aber auch, über Tonbrücken neue Zeitverhältnisse herzustellen. Mit dem Satz „Weißt Du noch, das Filmmaterial, das ich dir in New York zeigte?“ setzt er eine ganze Farbsequenz in die Vorvergangenheit, als etwas innerhalb der Familie bereits Erinnertes. Wir sehen, wie Franks zweite Frau June in einer neuschottischen Küstenlandschaft mit einer Lochkamera einem Blinden zu zeigen versucht, wie man den Wind fotografiert. In *Life Dances On...* geht es letztlich um die Darstellungsgrenzen des Fotografischen. *Christa Blümlinger*

A Film in the Subjunctive Tense   A slim book with photographs by Robert Frank, published in Paris in 1983, begins with a text written by the artist. In it he seems to be describing *Life Dances On...* as a film in production. This text, given the emblematic title "I Would Like to Make a Film...,"[1] deals with nothing less than the relationship between photography, film, and life itself. Frank voices his desire to unite private and public life, including everyday coincidences, in film. Photographs in films, he explained, should function as pauses and windows which show other times and other places.

Frank did not place a great deal of importance on "perfect" images, which Jean-Paul Fargier[2] described as his "weak strength." When Frank operates a camera, he is active and normally intervenes on several different levels simultaneously. He once introduced himself, microphone in hand, to a few amateur photographers in New York, revealing himself to be the film's subject. Another time his arm appeared from behind the camera, replacing the clapboard with a snap of the fingers, and Frank continued asking questions in a voice-over. At times, when his efforts reached the limits of words' capabilities because the interviewee refused to answer, he even provided instructions.

Life Dances On... is dedicated to Frank's deceased daughter Andrea and the memory of his friend Danny Seymour. Though it makes use of outtakes and footage from earlier works, the purpose is not to convey mourning in narrative form. Frank's fragmentary, metaphorical, and associative representational style has more in common with self-portraiture than autobiography. This is demonstrated by the apparently casual nature of the events captured on film. For example, in a black-and-white image taken from the filmmaker's personal archive for *Life Dances On...*, the camera pans suddenly from a static self-portrait in a small mirror on the wall to Frank's sleeping wife, then zooms back briefly and traverses the apartment. A boiling kettle on the stove, a view out a window in New York, a radio program on a Sunday morning, then the woman again: "Why are you filming this?" Frank fails to offer the answer, which can be found only in the way the film brings a motionless image to life.

For Frank, photographs arranged to form assemblages and images taken from film footage, altered and collaged, are objects whose material nature is tied to their function as vehicles of memory. When placed in new surroundings, their timestamp is made clearer. Frank was also skilled at creating new temporal contexts by means of acoustic bridges. The sentence "Do you remember the footage I showed you in New York?" put an entire color sequence into the past perfect tense, as if it were something which had already been remembered within the family. We see Frank's second wife June at Nova Scotia's coast as she attempts to show a blind man how to photograph the wind with a pinhole camera. *Life Dances On...* is in the final analysis of the limits of what photography can depict. *Christa Blümlinger*

USA 1980, 16 mm, color & black and white, 30 min. directed by: Robert Frank. cinematography: Robert Frank, Gary Hill, David Seymour. editing: Gary Hill. sound: Robert Frank, David Seymour, Gary Hill. production: Robert Frank. cast: Pablo Frank, Sandy Strawbridge, Marty Greenbaum, Billy, Finley Fryer, June Leaf

1981

Energy and How to Get It

Mad scientist   Wie man zu Energie kommt: Das künstlerische Credo dieses Films, könnte man meinen, steht schon im Titel. Das kreative Trio hinter *Energy and How to Get It* – neben Robert Frank: Gary Hill und Rudy Wurlitzer – führt jedenfalls vor, wie weit man im narrativen Kino in nicht einmal einer halben Stunde, ohne nennenswerten budgetären Spielraum kommen kann: zu einer vertrackten Reflexion über die „Wahrheit" beispielsweise, zu einem kühn erzählten Minidrama, in dem vieles Platz hat, etwa das Dokumentarische und das Erfundene, Satire, Wissenschaft und Performance-Art. Unter anderem.

Es heißt, Frank sei ursprünglich von der Idee ausgegangen, einen Dokumentarfilm über die ein wenig tragische Existenz des Erfinders Robert Golka zu drehen, der in einem verlassenen Hangar mit Kugelblitzen experimentierte, um aus diesen nutzbare Energie zu gewinnen. Frank, der Golka bereits Ende der siebziger Jahre fotografiert hatte, entwickelte gemeinsam mit Hill und Drehbuchautor Wurlitzer die reale Existenz Golkas dann aber imaginativ weiter, um – im Rahmen einer *fake documentary* – eine von der amerikanischen Regierung, von Behörden und Geschäftemachern in vielfacher Weise behinderte Spielfilmfigur zu entwerfen: eine überraschende Variation über das Motiv des *mad scientist*, der hier Nikola Teslas Erbe zu verwalten scheint.

Das Fragmentarische, Vorläufige der Arbeit Franks bleibt auch in diesem Film erhalten, genau wie der alte Widerspruch zwischen vermeintlicher Kunstlosigkeit (verwackelte Schwarzweißbilder, assoziative Erzählung) und der hohen fotografischen Qualität vieler Einstellungen. Golka selbst erscheint als veritabler Antiheld, als stiller Besessener, der sich noch bei dem Versuch, die Begriffe "fusion" und "fission" zu erklären, argumentativ verheddert.

Viele wunderbare, wunderliche Momente begleiten die (sehr roh belassene) Handlung: William Burroughs etwa legt seinen "energy czar", einen der Gegenspieler Golkas, gewohnt lakonisch an. Und eine fragile alte Dame namens Agnes Moon, im Vorspann als Golkas "companion and witness" angeführt, bereichert die Erzählung mit eigenwilligem Glamour. Mit dem (eher papierenen) Auftritt eines jungen, offen hassenswerten Erfolgsmenschen, der seine absurden Pläne zur globalen Vermarktung von Golkas Arbeit zum Besten gibt, wird die gesellschaftskritische Linie dieses Films für ein paar Augenblicke dann allerdings doch sehr breit.

Improvisierte Musik begleitet den Abstieg Golkas: Ein von Dr. John am Piano intonierter "Lightnin' Boogie" begleitet den glücklosen "Lightnin' Bob", wie man Golka nennt, in den Zynismus, begleitet die trotzige Ankündigung des Wissenschaftlers, unter *diesen* Umständen in Hinkunft eben Bomben bauen (und legen) zu wollen. In Golkas weitläufigem Labor schlägt der Blitz eindrucksvoll noch in ein Auto ein, ehe eine Fahrtaufnahme in die Einsamkeit, nach draußen führt, ins weite, unergründliche Amerika hinaus.
Stefan Grissemann

Mad Scientist   How to obtain energy: This film's artistic creed is, one could say, revealed in its title. The creative trio behind *Energy and How to Get It*—Gary Hill and Rudy Wurlitzer together with Robert Frank—show what can be done in a low-budget narrative film in less than thirty minutes. The result might be, for example, a baffling reflection on "truth," or a boldly related mini-drama offering plenty of room for documentary and fictional elements, satire, science, and performance art (among other things).

It is said that Frank's original idea was to make a documentary about the somewhat tragic existence of inventor Robert Golka, who experimented with ball lighting in an abandoned hangar, intending to use it as a practical source of energy. Frank, who had made photographic portraits of Golka in the late 1970s, Hill, and screenwriter Wurlitzer took off with the real story of Golka's life, creating a *fake documentary* about a man who faced numerous obstacles presented by the American government, various authorities, and wheeler-dealers. This represents a surprising variation on the motif of the *mad scientist*, in this case apparently the administrator of Nikola Tesla's legacy.

The fragmentary, provisional nature of Frank's œuvre is also evident in this film, as is the familiar contradiction between supposed artlessness (jumpy black-and-white images, stream-of-consciousness narration) and the obvious high degree of photographic quality in a number of shots. Golka himself is presented as a true antihero, a quiet and obsessive man who gets tangled in his attempt to explain the terms "fusion" and "fission."

Numerous weird and wonderful moments accompany the (extremely rough) plot, such as William Burroughs playing an energy czar—one of Golka's opponents—in his customarily laconic manner. A fragile old lady by the name of Agnes Moon, identified in the opening credits as Golka's "companion and witness," also adds unusual and individualistic glamour to the story. The (rather wooden) performance of an odious and successful young go-getter, who has masterminded some absurd plans for the global marketing of Golka's work, broadens the film's social criticism to the extreme for a few moments.

Golka's downfall is escorted by improvised music: "Lightnin' Boogie," performed on the piano by Dr. John, accompanies the hapless "Lightnin' Bob," as Golka is familiarly dubbed, into a pool of cynicism and his defiant announcement that he would rather build (and lay) bombs under *these* circumstances. In Golka's huge laboratory, the lightning spectacularly strikes a car before a tracking shot takes us outside, into solitude, into a wide and unfathomable America. *Stefan Grissemann*

USA 1981, 16 mm, black and white, 30 min. directed by: Robert Frank, Rudy Wurlitzer, Gary Hill. script: Rudy Wurlitzer. cinematography: Robert Frank, Gary Hill. editing: Gary Hill. music: Dr. John, Libby Titus. sound: Leanne Ungar, John Knoop. production: Robert Frank, Rudy Wurlitzer, Gary Hill. cast: Robert Golka, Agnes Moon, Rudy Wurlitzer, William S. Burroughs, John Giorno, Robert Downey, Lynne Adams, Alan Moyle

1983

This Song for Jack

Abgesang   Die Traurigkeit in den Filmbildern Robert Franks ist unübersehbar. In *This Song for Jack* findet sich etwa dieses Bild, das Bild einer Lesung im Regen: Jemand trägt öffentlich aus Jack Kerouacs "On the Road" vor, sechs Zuhörer schenken ihm Aufmerksamkeit. Die Kunst – Frank führt das vor – ist Sache eines kleinen Kreises. Und sie ist immer auch, egal wie: Trauerarbeit.

This Song for Jack dreht sich nicht um diese Lesung, aber doch um die Kunst und die Trauer. In Boulder, Colorado, trifft sich 1982 eine Gruppe von Leuten, um eine Konferenz abzuhalten im Naropa Institute, in einem im Grünen gelegenen Haus. Dieses Zusammensein gilt der Erinnerung an einen zeitlebens Einsamen, an ein selbstzerstörerisches Genie: dem Schriftsteller Jack Kerouac. Den eigentlichen Anlass zur Konferenz bietet das 25jährige Jubiläum des Erscheinens von "On the Road". Man sieht Fremde und Bekannte, wartend und plaudernd, auf der Veranda und in den Zimmern: späte Hippies, Freunde und Fans eines Dichters, der seit langem schon, volle dreizehn Jahre, nicht mehr unter ihnen ist. Robert Frank ist gebeten worden, das Treffen zu dokumentieren, wahrscheinlich weil er als einziger von ihnen eine Kamera besitzt.

Er dokumentiert also, und er schießt dabei aus der Hüfte: Franks forschende, suchende Kamera zielt erneut, wie oft im Werk dieses Künstlers, nicht auf „gutes Filmemachen", sondern auf das Festhalten, das Bewahren des Vorläufigen, jener unwiederbringlichen kleinen Momente, die man Leben nennt, aber selten genug im Kino zu sehen kriegt. Als Verteidiger der Wahrheit in der Kunst setzt Frank in *This Song for Jack* nicht nur den schönen Anlass, sondern vor allem auch die Ratlosigkeit seiner Protagonisten und Kollegen (nicht zuletzt: die eigene) ins Bild, zeigt durchaus die Langeweile, die man untereinander, alleingelassen miteinander, fühlt. Aber irgendwann kommt William Burroughs an; er geht am Stock, sehr langsam, aber wenn er über Kerouac zu erzählen beginnt, mit dieser seltsam blechernen, schnarrenden Stimme, kommt doch noch ein wenig Leben in den Film: literarisches Leben, wenn man will.

Ästhetisch bietet *This Song for Jack* nichts Außerordentliches, darum geht es Frank ganz offensichtlich in diesem Fall weniger noch als in anderen Projekten. Die Aufzeichnung selbst ist das Entscheidende, nicht ihr Kunstwert: Als Dokument einer neuen Zusammenkunft der alten Beats hat dieser Film Bedeutung, nicht als dramaturgisch oder visuell genau gestaltete Arbeit. Franks alte Freunde, Weggefährten Kerouacs wie er, sind präsent: Gregory Corso ist da, auch Peter Orlovsky – und Allen Ginsberg predigt vom *angel of death*, der sie alle bislang verschont habe.

Wenn das Lied, das dem Film seinen Titel gibt, der *Song for Jack*, gegen Ende vorgetragen wird, dann klingt das traurig: ein Abgesang, wie der Film selbst, alles andere als eine Feier. *Stefan Grissemann*

Swan Song   The sadness in Robert Frank's film images cannot be overlooked. This also applies to *This Song for Jack*, which depicts a reading held in the rain: Someone reads from Jack Kerouac's "On the Road" for a group of six listeners. Art—which Frank demonstrates—is a matter for a small circle. And it is always, regardless of the specific situation, a form of mourning.

The focus of *This Song for Jack* is not this reading, but art and mourning. In 1982, a number of people gathered in Boulder, Colorado for a conference held at the Naropa Institute, a house in the country. This meeting honored the memory of a man who was lonely his entire life, a self-destructive genius, Jack Kerouac.

The conference's actual occasion was the twenty-fifth anniversary of "On the Road's" publication. Both friends and strangers can be seen there, chatting and waiting, on the porch and in their rooms: old hippies, friends, and fans of a writer who had left them a long time before, thirteen years ago. Robert Frank was asked to document this meeting on film, presumably because he was the only one who owned a camera.

He therefore created a document, and in doing so, he shot from the hip: The goal of Frank's searching, probing camera, as is true for so many of this artist's works, was not "good filmmaking" but capturing something, preserving the past, those irretrievable little moments called life which are rarely seen in film. As a defender of truth in art, Frank created images for *This Song for Jack* showing not only the happy occasion of the conference but most importantly his protagonists' and colleagues' feelings of helplessness (including his own) and the boredom they felt, having been left alone together. But then William Burroughs arrives. Walking with the aid of a cane, he moves at a snail's pace, but when he begins to speak of Kerouac in his oddly tinny, rasping voice, a little life comes into the film: literary life, one could say.

In an aesthetic sense *This Song for Jack* has nothing extraordinary to offer; this was apparently not Frank's goal, even less so than in other projects: The documentation itself is the decisive aspect rather than its value as an artwork. This film is valuable as a record of a gathering of old Beats, not as a film with a precise dramatic or visual structure. Frank's old friends, contemporaries of Kerouac like himself, are there—Gregory Corso, Peter Orlovsky—and Allen Ginsberg speaks of the "angel of death" which has spared the rest of them so far.

When the eponymous song for Jack plays near the film's conclusion, it sounds sad, a swan song like the film itself, anything but a celebration. *Stefan Grissemann*

USA 1983, 16 mm, black and white, 26 min. Shot at the conference "On the Road: The Jack Kerouac Conference" (23.7.–1.8. 1982 Naropa Institute, Boulder/Colorado). directed by: Robert Frank. cinematography: Robert Frank. editing: Sam Edwards. sound: Jay Markel. production: Robert Frank. cast: Allen Ginsberg, Gregory Corso, William S. Burroughs, David Amram, Gary Snyder, Carolyn Cassady, Lawrence Ferlinghetti, a.o. further titles under which the film was screened: *Twenty-five Years Since the Publication of On the Road, Dedicated to Jack Kerouac, This Song for You Jack*

1985

Home Improvements

"Autobiography begins with a sense of being alone. It is an orphan form." (John Berger[3])

Etwas Wahres erzählen   *Home Improvements*, entstanden in den Jahren 1983 und '84, ist eine Art von filmischem Tagebuch. Home-movie-artige Passagen erzählen davon, dass Franks Frau June Leaf erkrankt und sich einer Operation unterziehen muss. Frank bricht mit gemischten Gefühlen zu einem Besuch bei seinem Sohn Pablo in einer psychiatrischen Klinik auf. Seine Gedanken und Handlungen kreisen immer wieder um die Vergangenheit und um seine Versuche, sich von ihren Relikten zu lösen. Diese Ereignisse, die die Tage bestimmen, sind verquickt mit Assoziationen und Fundstücken – wie jenes Bild in einem U-Bahnwaggon, das aus dem Ausschnitt eines Plakats ("SYMPTOMS") und einem Graffiti ("it was dark") ein rätselhaftes Statement formt.

Im Unterschied zu Franks Fotoarbeiten, an die nicht nur diese Aufnahme erinnert, kommen im Film zwei entscheidende Elemente hinzu: die Bewegung und vor allem der Ton, dominiert von Franks Stimme. Sie begleitet die Bilder aus dem Off und hinterfragt dabei nicht selten deren Status, konterkariert deren vermeintliche Aussage – mit einem Zitat etwa oder mit einem akribischen Sequenzprotokoll. Ein Zusammenspiel, das an Patricia Hampls[4] Überlegungen zum Genre der filmischen Lebenserinnerungen erinnert. Die einfachen Mittel, mit denen diese "memory's movies" häufig arbeiten (müssen), schreibt Hampl, erlaubten ihnen eine „Befreiung von der Vorherrschaft des Bildes". Dafür gewinne die Stimme in diesen Arbeiten große (Bedeutungs-)Macht: eine „Stimme, die ihre Bilder versammelt" und einem Erzähler gehöre, der "more eye than I", mehr Auge als Ich geworden sei.

Der Filmemacher nimmt in dieser Konstellation also eine seltsam gespaltene Position ein. Zugleich nah bei den Seinen, bleibt er hinter der Kamera doch allein mit seiner Wahrnehmung. (ALONE: In großen Lettern steht das Wort auf dem Papier. Es fällt ins Auge, während die Kamera über handschriftliche Aufzeichnungen gleitet, ohne diese allerdings als Ganzes lesbar zu machen.) Und nur selten wechselt er hier die Seiten: Einmal filmt June Leaf den Mann, den sie liebt. Frank lächelt verlegen in die Kamera. Das lange Selbstporträt gegen Ende des Films zeigt dagegen den Mann mit der Kamera, wie er sich in einer Scheibe spiegelt. Eine durchsichtige Trennwand und ein Bild, das sich mit Franks Selbstverständnis trifft: „Ich mache immer die selben Bilder. Ich schaue immer nach draußen und versuche dabei, nach Innen zu sehen, etwas Wahres zu erzählen. Aber vielleicht ist nichts wirklich wahr, außer: das, was dort draußen ist, und was dort draußen ist, ist immer anders." *Isabella Reicher*

Telling Something That's True   *Home Improvements*, which was made in 1983 and 1984, is a kind of film diary. Sequences resembling home movies tell the story of how Frank's wife June Leaf becomes ill and has to have surgery. With mixed feelings, Frank sets off to visit his son Pablo in a psychiatric clinic. His thoughts and actions all revolve around the past and his attempts to free himself of its remnants. These events, which define his days, are shot through with associations and *objets trouvés* such as a photograph taken in a subway car. It combines a detail of a poster ("SYMPTOMS") and some graffiti ("it was dark") to form a puzzling statement.

In contrast to Frank's photographic works, of which not only this picture is a reminder, the film contains two further important elements: motion and sound, the latter dominated by Frank's voice. Sound accompanies the images, often questioning their status and presenting a contrast to their presumable statement, for example with a quote or a meticulous log of sequences. This interplay resembles Patricia Hampl's[4] thoughts on the genre of film memoirs. The simple means with which "memory's movies" often (or must) operate, wrote Hampl, "[seem to free] memoir film from the sovereignty of the image." At the same time, the voice in these works takes on great power and significance, "a voice that assembles its pictures" and belongs to a narrator who has become "more eye than I."

The filmmaker therefore assumes a strangely equivocal position in this constellation. Although close to his family, he remains behind the camera, alone with his perception. (ALONE: This word, in large letters, has been written on a piece of paper. It becomes noticeable when the camera glides over some hand-written notes which are never legible in their entirety.) And he changes sides only infrequently: June Leaf films the man she loves. Frank smiles at the camera, somewhat embarrassed. The long self-portrait near the film's conclusion shows the man with the camera reflected in a window pane. A permeable dividing wall and a picture which corresponds to Frank's self-image: "I'm always doing the same images. I'm always looking outside trying to look inside, trying to tell something that's true. But maybe nothing is really true, except: what's out there, and what's out there is always different." *Isabella Reicher*

USA 1985, video, color, 29 min. directed by: Robert Frank. cinematography: Robert Frank, June Leaf. editing: Michael Bianchi, Sam Edwards. sound: Robert Frank. production: Robert Frank. cast: Pablo Frank, June Leaf, Robert Frank, Gunther Moses

1987

Candy Mountain

The Whole Deal   Wanderlust, gleich zu Beginn: Der Blick schweift von New Yorks Skyline ins Innere eines im Umbau befindlichen Lofts. Julius (Kevin J. O'Connor) lässt die Arbeit stehen, geht hinaus. "You don't come back", ruft ihm sein Boss verärgert noch nach. "Right", ist die selbstsichere Antwort. Dann marschiert Julius durch die Straßen der Stadt und hat eine erste rätselhafte Begegnung: Er lacht einem Hotelportier ins Gesicht, der sich mit einer Banane abmüht.

Candy Mountain handelt vom Reisen, physisch wie mythisch – und von Musik: Julius hört vom legendären, verschollenen Gitarrenbauer Elmore Silk, täuscht vor, ihn zu kennen und wird auf die Suche geschickt. Für Julius soll dabei eine Karriere herausspringen, für seine Auftraggeber Silks teure Gitarren. Es ist – Showbiz-Geplauder – viel von Integrität die Rede, vom *walk down rock'n'roll memory lane*, aber eigentlich geht es nur ums Geschäft. "You're telling me he disappeared", sagt ein aufgeblasener Rocker (David Johansen) über Silk, "it`s as if he signed with William Morris or something."

Julius folgt Silks Spuren nach Kanada, seine Reise wird zur Wiederholung der Geschichte als Farce: "He came with very little, he left the same way" sagt Silks ehemalige Geliebte (Bulle Ogier) über den Gitarrenbauer. Wo auch immer Julius hinkommt, geht er mit noch weniger weg: Zu den *running gags* von *Candy Mountain* gehört, dass Julius sein jeweiliges Gefährt – oft auf recht absurde Weise – gegen ein noch schlechteres eintauschen muss, das Spesengeld schwindet ebenfalls rasch.

Dafür gewinnt Julius an Einsicht, vielleicht: Je länger er, mäandernd, tragikomisch, Silks Bewegungen nachvollzieht, desto näher kommt er auch an die Beweggründe für dessen Verschwinden. Aber erst, als er ihn knapp vor Schluss tatsächlich trifft (imposante Erscheinung: Harris Yulin), wird er seine Entscheidung nachvollziehen können. "The whole deal went up in flames", kommentiert Julius das surreale Finale. Dann ist er bereit, weiterzuziehen.

Zu den Vorzügen von *Candy Mountain* zählen neben Robert Franks Sinn für fotografische Komposition ein dankbar unprätentiöser Zugang zum populären Road-movie-Genre, das hier – trotz zahlreicher erinnernswerter Gastauftritte und damit einhergehender guter Musik (u.a. von Dr. John, Tom Waits und Joe Strummer) – vom Independent-Hipstertum der 80er wieder völlig befreit wirkt. Das verdankt sich auch Rudy Wurlitzers knappem, oft giftig-witzigem, stets kritischem Blick auf Mythen (einmal, die Sonnenbrille auf, mit Handschuhen am Lenkrad, erinnert O'Connor an Warren Oates' todtraurigen Träumer GTO in der von Wurlitzer geschriebenen, selbstzerstörerischen Road-movie-Apotheose *Two Lane Blacktop*) und auf ihren falschen Glanz: "Life ain't no candy mountain, you know", sagt ein Autofahrer, der – noch ziemlich zu Anfang – Julius mitnimmt, nachdem dieser an einer herbstlichen Tankstelle sitzen gelassen worden ist. Dann knöpft er ihm 50 Dollar fürs Mitnehmen ab. *Christoph Huber*

The Whole Deal   Wanderlust from the very beginning: The camera sweeps from New York's skyline to the interior of a loft which is under construction. Julius (Kevin J. O'Connor) abandons his work and leaves the room. "You don't come back," shouts his boss angrily. "Right" is the other man's self-assured answer. Julius then marches through the city's streets and has his first puzzling encounter: He laughs in the face of a hotel doorman as the man struggles with a banana.

Candy Mountain is about traveling, both in a physical and mythical sense, and about music. Julius hears about legendary guitar maker Elmore Silk, who disappeared some time before. He pretends to be acquainted with the man and sets off to search for him. Julius's efforts will supposedly be rewarded with a career, and the client will get Silk's precious guitars. There is much discussion of integrity—showbiz talk—and of a "walk down rock-'n'-roll memory lane," but the real issue around which everything revolves is business. "You're telling me he disappeared," says an arrogant rock-'n'-roller (David Johansen) about Silk, "It's as if he signed with William Morris or something."

Julius follows Silk's trail to Canada, and his journey becomes a repetition of history as farce: "He came with very little, he left the same way," says Silk's former lover (Bulle Ogier). Wherever Julius goes, he comes away with even less. One of *Candy Mountain*'s running gags is that Julius repeatedly trades one bad car for an even worse one—often in an absurd situation—and his expense account disappears rapidly. At the same time he gains insight, or at least possibly. The longer he follows Silk's trail, in a meandering and tragicomic way, the closer he comes to discovering the other man's motivation for disappearing. But only after finding Silk (an impressive Harris Yulin) shortly before the film's end is he able to fully understand the decision. "The whole deal went up in flames" is Julius's comment on the surreal finale. He is then prepared to move on.

The outstanding features of *Candy Mountain* include Robert Frank's feeling for photographic composition and a thankfully unpretentious approach to the popular genre of the road movie, which in this case—despite numerous memorable guest appearances and equally good music (Dr. John, Tom Waits, Joe Strummer, etc.)—seems entirely free of 1980s independent hipsterdom. We have Wurlitzer's brief, often bitingly funny and always critical view of myths and their artificial magic to thank for that (once, wearing his sunglasses and his hands on the steering wheel, O'Connor resembles Warren Oates's desperately sad dreamer GTO in the self-destructive road-movie apotheosis *Two Lane Blacktop*, which Wurlitzer co-wrote): "Life ain't no candy mountain, you know," says a driver who, near the film's beginning, gives Julius a ride after he had been abandoned at a gas station. The driver then charges Julius fifty dollars for the ride. *Christoph Huber*

CH / F / CAN 1987, 35 mm, color, 91 min. directed by: Robert Frank, Rudy Wurlitzer. script: Rudy Wurlitzer. cinematography: Pio Corradi. editing: Jennifer Auge. sound: Daniel Joliat. production: Xanadu Films, Ruth Waldburger; Les Films Plain-Chant, Philip Diaz; les Films Vision 4 Inc., Claude Bonim, Suzanne Héncurt. cast: Kevin O'Connor, Harris Yulin, Tom Waits, Bulle Ogier, Roberts Blossom, Leon Redbone, Dr. John, Laurie Metcalf, Rita MacNeil, Joe Strummer, Jane Eastwood, Kazuko Oshima and the musicians: Joey Barron, Greg Cohen, Arto Lindsay, Marc Ribot, Fernando Saunders, John Scofield

1989

Hunter

Stranger Than Paradise   Ein Amerikaner im Ruhrgebiet. Hunter heißt er, und er bereist die Gegend um Duisburg. Ein Reisebericht? Vielleicht. Zwischen Rhein und Ruhr, im industrialisierten Mittelwesten Deutschlands, trifft er auf Einheimische. Ein ethnologisches Projekt? Möglicherweise. Mit den Menschen dort Verbindung aufzunehmen, gelingt kaum. Dennoch das anhaltende Bemühen, zu verstehen, wie man in und mit dem Ruhrgebiet leben kann. Ein Essay? Auch das.

Stephan Balint, Darsteller des Hunter, zugleich Autor des Films, fungiert als Medium dieser Erzählung. Durch ihn erleben wir die Stationen dieses Travelogue. Er spricht nur Amerikanisch – mit ausgeprägtem osteuropäischen Akzent. (Balint war einer der Initiatoren der ungarischen Theater-Gruppe „Squat Theatre" in New York. Seine Schwester, Eszter Balint, spielte die Hauptrolle in Jim Jarmuschs *Stranger Than Paradise*.)

Hunter ist ein Spiel um Fremdheit und den Versuch, diese zu überwinden. Oder: wie Fremdheit Einblicke und Erfahrungen ermöglicht, die sonst verschlossen blieben: kontrolliert scheiternde Kommunikation. Bei vielen Begegnungen, die von einem absurden Überschuss an Sprachbarrieren und Missverständnissen gekennzeichnet sind, lässt sich nicht ausmachen, ob sie verunglückte Passanten-Interviews sind oder tollkühne Spielszenen, ob sie eingefangen oder aufgeführt sind. *Hunter* ist ein komischer Film, dabei allerdings durchzogen von einer wunderbar schwebenden Tristesse – wie der Nachklang bei einem sehr guten Wein.

Hunter entstand im Spätsommer 1989 – also etwa ein Jahr, bevor Godard im geografisch entgegen gesetzten Teil Deutschlands *Allemagne Neuf Zero* drehte – und kann inzwischen als das Festhalten von Merkwürdigkeiten und Schwingungen aus den Monaten kurz vor der Wende gelesen werden. Die Bilder sind als karge Bühnen eingerichtet für naive Selbstdarstellungen von Menschen aus Deutschland. Ein junger Ausländer erzählt seine Version vom Zusammenhang zwischen Ausländerhass heute und Judenhass früher. Die Ausländer heute und die Juden früher haben einfach immer die besseren Mädchen gekriegt, das hat die Deutschen wütend gemacht. Zum Abschluss sagt er: „Ich sprech' zwar die Sprache perfekt von denen hier. Aber ich bin kein Deutscher. Ich bin in Spanien geboren. Ich bin Marokkaner und will Marokkaner bleiben. Ich nehm' keine andere Nationalität an." (Ein Zwischentitel: "History / His Story" – eine Reverenz an Godard, die man nicht wirklich braucht.) Dann die ältere Dame in einem Souvenirshop, die ohne eigene Vorlieben mit filigranen Hitler-, Elvis- und anderen Statuetten handelt. Oder die Bäckerei-Fachverkäuferin an ihrer Auslage in der Fußgängerzone. Enthusiastisch referiert sie über die Vorlieben ihrer Kundschaft: „Was heute in Deutschland verlangt wird, sind meistens diese Vollkornbrote."

P. S.   In einer Hinsicht kommen *Hunter* und *Allemagne Neuf Zero* übrigens zu einem identischen Fazit über Deutschland. Sie orten eine Grundstimmung, die von der Romantik her über die Distanz von fast zwei Jahrhunderten in die Gegenwart ragt: Einsamkeit. Mehrfach operiert Godard in seinem Deutschland-Film mit dem Wort "Solitude", stellt es geradezu aus. *Hunter* endet mit dem wackeligen Abschwenken eines Graffiti an einer Brandmauer: „Wir sind immer alleine ... bis zum Tode!!" *Ralph Eue*

Stranger Than Paradise   An American visits Germany's Ruhrgebiet. His name is Hunter, and he's touring the area around Duisburg. A travelogue? Maybe. Somewhere between the Rhine and Ruhr rivers, in the country's industrialized midwest, he meets some locals. An ethnological project? Possibly. His attempts to

establish contact with the people there are unsuccessful. But he keeps trying to understand how someone can live in this area and cope with it. An essay? That too.

Stephan Balint, who also wrote the film's screenplay, plays the role of Hunter, the story's mediator. We experience the locations in this travelogue through him. He speaks American English, but with a strong Eastern European accent. (Balint was one of the founders of Squat Theatre, a Hungarian theater troupe in New York. His sister, Eszter Balint, was the female lead in Jim Jarmusch's *Stranger Than Paradise*.)

Hunter is a play on foreignness and the attempt to overcome it; or how this state enables insights and certain experiences which would have been otherwise inaccessible. In other words: controlled communication breakdowns. It is not certain whether the many encounters, which are characterized by an absurd excess of language barriers and misunderstandings, are unsuccessful attempts at interviewing passers-by or boldly staged scenes; whether they were captured or planned. *Hunter* is an amusing film, though at the same time it is imbued with wonderful shades of sadness, like the lingering taste of an excellent wine.

Hunter was made late in the summer of 1989—one year before Godard shot *Allemagne Neuf Zero* on the opposite side of the country. It can now be read as a record of curiosities and the general vibrations in the months shortly before the fall of the Berlin Wall. Its scenes serve as bare stages for a naïve presentation of the German experience. A young foreigner tells us his idea of the relationship between modern xenophobia and past anti-Semitism: Like foreigners in today's Germany, Jews always got a higher class of women, which made other Germans angry. At the conclusion he says, "I speak their language perfectly. But I'm not German. I was born in Spain. I'm Moroccan and want to stay Moroccan. I'm not going to change my citizenship." (An insert appears: "History / His Story"—a demonstration of reverence for Godard which is not really necessary.) Then there is an elderly woman in a souvenir shop who, indifferently, sells delicate statuettes of Hitler, Elvis, and other personalities. And a bakery clerk at the window in a pedestrian zone enthusiastically reporting on her customers' buying habits: "What most people want in Germany today is this whole-grain bread."

P. s. In one sense *Hunter* and *Allemagne Neuf Zero* come to the same conclusion with regard to Germany. They identify an underlying theme extending from Romanticism through two centuries to the present day: solitude. In his film Godard operates on multiple levels with the word solitude, virtually putting it on display. *Hunter* ends with a shaky pan of some graffiti on a firewall: "We're always alone ... until we die!!" *Ralph Eue*

D 1989, 16 mm, color & black and white, 37 min. directed by: Robert Frank. script: Stephan Balint. cinematography: Clemens Steiger, Bernhard Lehner, Robert Frank (Video). editing: Jolie Gorchov. sound: Gerhard Metz. production: Kulturstiftung Ruhr (Kinemathek im Ruhrgebiet), Essen; Westdeutscher Rundfunk. world premiere: Kinemathek Duisburg. cast: Stephan Balint, Gunter Burchart, Sabine Ahlborn - Gockel, Laurenz Berges, Fosco Dubini, Familie Topuz, a.o.

1989

Run

What the hell is happening?   Wo es ästhetische Gesetze gibt, schlägt Robert Frank sie in den Wind. Den Auftrag, 1989 ein Musikvideo für die renommierte britische Band New Order zu drehen, erfüllt er, indem er seine Grundlagen verweigert. Zwar stellt Frank die verlangten drei Minuten dreißig Sekunden Film her, die dem New-Order-Song "Run" eine visuelle Basis geben sollen. Aber er inszeniert Bilder, die in heftigem Gegensatz zu den Ansprüchen und Anmaßungen der Branche stehen, für die er dabei arbeitet; er produziert, was die Industrie am wenigsten brauchen kann: einen Anti-Clip.

Die Bilder, die Frank dem melancholischen Pop der Briten beistellt, sind unansehnlich, billig, „arm" – Arte povera. Sie verklären und erzählen nichts, bleiben bloßes Splitterwerk, Impressionen einer heruntergekommenen Rockindustrie. New Order selbst sind nur zwischendurch zu sehen, auf einer vernebelten Bühne, im Trockeneis verschwindend; die Band spielt keine Hauptrolle in dieser Arbeit. Frank stellt eine fragmentarische Spielhandlung ins Zentrum seines Clips, ein Stück Fiktion, geprägt von Resignation und Einsamkeit: Ein älterer Mann geht, scheinbar unschlüssig, in einer unbefahrenen Straße auf und ab, setzt sich schließlich an einen präparierten Tisch. Er sinniert, dann lacht er plötzlich auf, ganz für sich, wie einer, der auf die Absurdität der Welt nur noch mit Lachen, höhnisch fast, reagieren kann.

Franks grundlegender Pessimismus scheint sich im Text des Songs zu spiegeln, in den Worten, die die seltsam bedeutungsentleerten Bilder des Clips mit einem Rest von Sinn konfrontieren: "Answer me / Why won't you answer me / I can't recall the day that I last heard from you", heißt es in dem Lied – und wenig später: "What the hell is happening / I can't think of everything / I don't know what day it is / Or who I'm talking to".

Ein Kind, ein Mädchen, beginnt in *Run* ohne Grund vor dem Mann, der da an seinem Tisch sitzt, zu tanzen, auf der Straße, einfach so; wie aufgezogen, mechanisch, absolviert das Mädchen seinen Tanz – eine Miniatur-Madonna, die ihr Rätsel auch nicht preisgibt. Anderswo sehen eine Handvoll Zuschauer auf irgendeiner Brüstung in die Ferne, vielleicht auf eine Konzertbühne. Eine Serie von Gesichtern, gefilmte und fotografierte, letztere in Schwarzweiß, rücken kurz ins Bild. Die Idee der Formlosigkeit, des assoziativen Stückwerks, durchdringt Franks erstes Promo-Video. Es sieht anders aus als jenes, das er ein paar Jahre später für Patti Smith inszenieren wird: wie ein Amateurfilm nämlich, wie ein verzweifelter Versuch, alternative *images* zu finden für eine Industrie, die in ihrer laufenden Selbstüberbietung längst schon das Entscheidende – die Musik, das Bild – nicht mehr berücksichtigen kann. Franks *Run* ist ein Plädoyer für die Verlangsamung, für das Ungelenke, das Alltägliche. Robert Frank tritt einen Schritt hinter alles zurück, das sein Arbeitsgebiet definiert: das bescheidenste Musikvideo der Welt. *Stefan Grissemann*

What the hell is happening?   Whenever there are aesthetic rules in force, Robert Frank ignores them. While making a music video for the famous British band New Order in 1989 he simply refused to follow the usual guidelines. Although Frank did produce a three-minute thirty-second film as called for in his contract, thereby providing a visual basis for New Order's song "Run," he created images which contrasted starkly with the industry's assumptions and presumptions. The type of film he made was what the industry has the least possible use for, an anti-clip.

The images Frank produced to accompany the British band's melancholy pop are unattractive, cheap, and "poor"—Arte Povera. Rather than telling a story, they confuse matters, remaining little more than fragments, impressions of a rock industry which has seen better days. The band New Order itself is visible only occasionally, on a misty stage, disappearing in the dry-ice fog. In fact, the musicians play a secondary role in this work. Frank's clip features a fragmentary plot, a piece of fiction characterized by resignation and solitude. An elderly man paces an empty street, apparently with some indecision, then sits at a table in front of a drink. He ponders something, then begins laughing to himself as if somewhat derisive hilarity were the only possible reaction to the absurdity of the world.

Frank's underlying pessimism seems to be reflected in the song's lyrics, in the words which confront the strangely meaningless images with some remnant of sense: "Answer me / Why won't you answer me / I can't recall the day that I last heard from you," and somewhat later, "What the hell is happening / I can't think of everything / I don't know what day it is / Or who I'm talking to."

Without any obvious reason a child, a girl, begins to dance in the street in front of the man as he sits at the table. Mechanically, as if she were a wind-up toy, she completes her dance—a miniature Madonna who does not provide an answer to her puzzle. Somewhere else a few people look at a low wall or embankment in the distance, possibly a stage. A series of faces, both in film footage and photographs, the latter black and white, move briefly into the picture. The idea of formlessness, the associative patchwork, shows through Frank's first promotional video. In all it looks quite different than the one he would make for Patti Smith a few years later; this video resembles the work of an amateur, a desperate attempt to create alternative "images" for an industry no longer able to take the decisive factors—the music, the picture—into account in its constant attempts to outdo itself. Frank's *Run* is a plea for deceleration, for the awkward, the everyday. Robert Frank took a step behind everything defining the industry in which he was working, and the result was the most modest music video ever made. *Stefan Grissemann*

USA 1989, video, color & black and white, 3 min. 35 sec. music film for New Order's song "Run". directed by: Robert Frank. cinematography: Robert Frank. editing: Laura Israel. music: New Order. cast: New Order, a.o.

1990

C'est vrai! (One Hour)

Metaphysisch   „Ich habe *La chouette aveugle* sieben Mal gesehen", schrieb Luc Moullet einmal über Raul Ruiz' störrisches Meisterwerk, „und nach jedem Ansehen weiß ich etwas weniger über den Film." Ich kann nicht sagen, dass *One Hour* irgendetwas mit Ruiz' Film gemeinsam hat, doch dasselbe Paradox macht auch ihn zu einem Meisterwerk und störrisch: je mehr ich mich einem Verständnis annähere, desto mysteriöser wird er.

Mein erster Blick auf diesen Bericht in einer einzigen Einstellung von Frank und dem Schauspieler Kevin O'Connor, die entweder zu Fuß oder auf dem Rücksitz eines Minivan einige Straßenzüge der Lower East Side von Manhattan durchqueren – gedreht zwischen 15:45 und 16:45 am 26. Juli 1990 – führte mich dazu, ihn als ein räumliches Ereignis zu interpretieren, das die ein wenig unheimliche Gemütlichkeit des New Yorker Straßenlebens einfängt, die seltsame Erfahrung, unbeabsichtigt Fremde zu belauschen, die ein essentieller Teil davon ist, sich in Manhattan zu befinden, einer Insel, auf der so viele Menschen zusammengepfercht sind, dass die existentielle Herausforderung ihrer alltäglichen Koexistenz zentral für die Energie und die Aufregung der Stadt scheint.

Aber das war nur ein erster Eindruck. Ein zweiter Blick hob hervor, in welchem Ausmaß Franks planlose Reiseroute scheinbar eine Tradition des nordamerikanischen experimentellen Kinos rekapituliert, das auf der fortwährenden Bewegung des Protagonisten und/oder der Kamera herumreitet und so verschiedene Arbeiten wie *At Land, Dog Star Man* und Michael Snows Trilogie der Kamerabewegung umfasst, in denen die Erzählung sowohl zu einer Art von Bewusstseinsstrom wie auch zu einer Art von Reise wird, auch wenn die Reise (wie bei Snow) mechanisch und in aufeinander folgenden ruckartigen Zooms oder in pendelnden Bogen oder Kreisen fortschreitet und dieselben Muster und/oder Räume zurückverfolgt. Dann stieß ich auf etwas, das einem Nachschlüssel für *One Hour* am Nächsten kommt – ein kleines Buch, 1992 von Hanuman Books herausgegeben, das vor allem eine Transkription des gehörten Dialoges (über 74 Seiten), aber auch zwei Seiten mit Credits beinhaltet: ein halbes Dutzend Mitarbeiter der Produktion oder des Aufnahmeteams und 27 Schauspieler. Und eine Bestätigung, dass der Film ein Skript (von Frank und seinem Assistenten Michal Rovner) hat, dass die in einem Diner zu hörende Unterhaltung von Mika Moses geschrieben wurde und dass der Text von Peter Orlovsky (Frank fängt ihn nach ungefähr einer halben Stunde vor dem Angelika Kino auf der Houston Street ab) – der O'Connor den Mittelpunkt des Films nach und nach entwindet – „völlig improvisiert" ist. Hier beginnen die Rätsel erst wirklich. Wie viel von Franks anscheinend zufälligem Dahintreiben ist präzise geplant, wie viele der scheinbar zufälligen Begegnungen sind inszeniert und aufs Genaueste koordiniert, wie viel von dem, was wir sehen und hören, geschieht aus dem Stegreif? Über die unbeständigen, labilen Mischungen von Zufall und Kontrolle kann man sich nie völlige Klarheit verschaffen. Kurz und gut, in welchem Maß dies ein hingeworfenes Home Movie über Franks Viertel ist und in welchem Maß es ein erfundenes Brettspiel ist, das sich über mehrere Blocks erstreckt, wird letztendlich zur metaphysischen Frage. Also ist Frank vielleicht doch nicht so weit von Ruiz entfernt. *Jonathan Rosenbaum*

Metaphysical   "I've seen *La chouette aveugle* seven times," Luc Moullet once wrote of Raúl Ruiz's intractable masterpiece, "and I know a little less about the film with each viewing." I can't say *One Hour* has anything in common with the Ruiz film, yet what also makes it a masterpiece and intractable is the same paradox:

the closer I come to understanding it, the more mysterious it gets. My first look at this single-take account of Frank and actor Kevin O'Connor either walking or riding in the back of a mini-van through a few blocks of Manhattan's Lower East Side—shot between 3:45 and 4:45 pm on 26 July 1990—led me to interpret it as a spatial event capturing the somewhat uncanny coziness and intimacy of New York street life, the curious experience of eavesdropping involuntarily on strangers that seems an essential part of being in Manhattan, an island where so many people are crammed together that the existential challenge of everyday coexistence between them seems central to the city's energy and excitement.

But this was just a first impression. A second look highlighted the degree to which Frank's rambling itinerary seems to recapitulate a tradition of North American experimental cinema harping on the perpetual motion of protagonist and/or camera, encompassing such varied works as *At Land, Dog Star Man*, and Michael Snow's camera movement trilogy, in which narrative becomes a kind of stream of consciousness as well as a sort of journey, even if the journey (as in Snow's) proceeds mechanically and in successive jerky zooms or pendulum-like arcs or circles, retracing the same patterns and/or spaces. Then I encountered the closest thing *One Hour* has to a skeleton key—a tiny book issued by Hanuman Books in 1992, comprising mainly a transcription of the dialogue heard
(over 74 pages), but also two pages of credits: half a dozen production or crew workers and 27 actors. Plus an acknowledgement that the film has a script (by Frank and his assistant, Michal Rovner), that a conversation heard in a diner is written by Mika Moses, and that the lines of Peter Orlovsky (intercepted by Frank roughly halfway through the hour, in front of the Angelika Cinema on Houston Street)—who gradually wrests the film's apparent center away from O'Connor— are "total improvisation".

Here's where the mysteries truly begin. How much of Frank's apparently random drift is precisely plotted, how many seeming chance encounters are staged and intricately coordinated, how much of what we see and hear is extemporaneous? The volatile, unstable mixtures of chance and control can never be entirely sorted out. In short, how much this is a tossed-off home movie about Frank's neighborhood and how much it's a contrived board game spread out over several city blocks ultimately becomes a metaphysical question. So perhaps Frank isn't so far away from Ruiz after all. *Jonathan Rosenbaum*

F 1990, video, color, 60 min. directed by: Robert Frank. script: Robert Frank, Michal Rovner. cinematography: Robert Frank. production: La Sept, Prony Production, Paris; Philippe Grandrieux. world premiere: TV (F), La Sept. cast: Kevin O'Connor, Peter Orlovsky, Taylor Mead, Willoughby Sharp, Bill Rice, Tom Jarmusch, Zsigmond Kirschen, Sid Kaplan, Odessa Taft, Sarah Penn, Margo Grip, a.o.

1992

Last Supper

Würgeengel   *Last Supper* erscheint streckenweise wie ein Lehrfilm mit Gebrauchsanweisung. Es geht um die Unmöglichkeit der Abbildung. Geht es um die Unmöglichkeit der Abbildung? Was ist real? Was ist inszeniert? Was ist vom Zufall inszeniert? Und: Welche Realität zeichnet die Videokamera auf?

Auf einem verwahrlosten Grundstück zwischen heruntergekommenen Häuserblocks in New York treffen Gäste ein. Der Einladende ist ein Autor, der mit seinen Freunden und Bekannten die Publikation seines neuen Buches feiern will. Ein Buffet ist aufgebaut. Warten auf den Autor. Warten auf Godot. Er kommt nicht. Diese Filmebene ist als Theater konstruiert. Die Dialoge wirken holografisch: In fast jeder zitierbaren Teilaussage spiegelt sich die Bedeutung des Ganzen.

Aber der Film beginnt mit einer menschenleeren Videoeinstellung auf dieses Gelände – mit eingeblendeter Datumsangabe: 9-18-91. Die unregelmäßige Serie solcher Einstellungen strukturiert das inszenierte Geschehen; die Daten variieren, die Abläufe erweisen sich als nicht chronologisch. Die Videoaufnahme zeigt: Das ist so gewesen, Ort und Zeit werden festgestellt. Da ist also die Gruppe der Schauspielenden: weiß, middleclass. Über das Gelände kommen auch die realen BewohnerInnen dieses Wohnbezirks in das Bild, in den Film. Sie sind AfroamerikanerInnen. Manche gehen an dem Schauspiel einfach vorbei. Andere zögern oder drehen wieder um.

Das Aufregende an diesem komplexen Filmtext spielt sich an den Übergängen ab. Was macht eine reale Umgebung mit ihren zufälligen Details, die von der Kamera wahllos registriert werden, aus einer kontrollierten Inszenierung? Ist nicht im Grunde *jede* Kameraaufzeichnung dokumentarisch? Wie sieht es mit den unterschiedlichen Darstellungsmodi aus? Der „Kellner", der das Buffet beaufsichtigt, wird von Bill Rice, einem bekannten Darsteller in Independent-Produktionen, verkörpert. Wie ist sein Zusammenspiel mit den Gästen einzustufen, die schauspielerisch mehr oder weniger professionell agieren? Und die LaiendarstellerInnen? Wann wird die quasi versteckte Kamera für sie spürbar, wann wird ihre „Natürlichkeit" zur forcierten Performance?

Viel Autobiografisches aus Robert Franks Leben ist in diese Arbeit eingeflossen: der Sohn, der nicht für die Kunst des Vaters ausgenutzt werden will; der Vater / Ehemann, der verschwinden möchte und das Bedürfnis hat, dem „Kunstdiskurs" zu entgehen. Die Textur deutet auf Bunuel; der Flügelschlag des *Würgeengels* ist zu spüren: Die bürgerlichen Gäste sind in ihrer *smalltalk- / art-talk*-Arena eingeschlossen. Warum verlassen sie die Party nicht? Auch das Abendmahl produziert Filmverweise, etwa auf das Essen der Bettler in Bunuels *Viridiana*. Auch dort sitzen Menschen an einem gedeckten Tisch, der eigentlich nicht für sie bestimmt ist, und genießen auf andere Weise als die ‚Berechtigten'. Auch sie spielen das biblische „Abendmahl" nach. Aber: Werden diese Menschen ausgestellt? Werden sie für den Film ausgenutzt?

Die radikalen Bildbefragungen des Robert Frank riskieren auch das Verstummen: den schwarzen Kader. *Birgit Flos*

Exterminating Angel   Parts of *Last Supper* resemble an educational film with directions for its use. It deals with the impossibility of depicting something. Or is it really about the impossibility of depicting something? What is real? What is staged? What can be staged by coincidence? And which reality does a video camera record?

Guests arrive at a vacant lot in New York, which is surrounded by rundown apartment buildings. The host is a writer, and he intends to celebrate the publication of his latest book with his friends and acquaintances. A buffet has been laid out. Waiting for the writer. Waiting for Godot. He fails to show up. This level of the film is constructed in the same way as a theatrical work. The dialogues seem holographic: Almost every quotable phrase reflects the meaning of the entire statement.

But the film begins with a video image of this empty lot, and with an indication of the date: 9-18-91. The irregular series of similar shots gives structure to the staged events. The dates vary; it turns out that the story is not being told in chronological order. The video picture shows what happened and indicates time and place. There is the group of actors: white, middle-class. The actual residents of this neighborhood walk across the lot and enter the picture, and the film. They are African-Americans. Some of them simply walk past the scene; others hesitate or turn around to leave.

The exciting aspect of this complex film text plays out in the transitions. What kinds of effects can a real environment and its incidental details, randomly captured by a camera, have on a controlled, staged scene? Strictly speaking, is not *every* camera shot documentary in nature? And what about the various modes of portrayal by actors? The Waiter watching over the buffet is played by Bill Rice, who has appeared in a number of independent productions. How could one categorize his interaction with the guests, whose acting is more or less professional? And the amateurs? When do they first sense the presence of the virtually hidden camera, when does their natural behavior turn into a forced performance?

A great deal of autobiographical elements from Robert Frank's life were used in this work, such as the son who does not want to be exploited for his father's art, and the father/husband who wants to disappear and feels a need to escape "art discourse." This film's texture is reminiscent of Buñuel; the beating wings of the *Exterminating Angel* are apparent: The bourgeois guests are trapped in their arena of small talk and art talk. Why do they not leave the party? Even the evening meal supplies film references, such as to the beggar's banquet in Buñuel's *Viridiana*. In the latter film, people also sit at a table which has been set, one that was not set for them, enjoying the meal in a manner differing from that of the "authorized" group. They too are acting out the Biblical Last Supper. But are these people on display? Are they being exploited for the film?

Robert Frank's radical questions directed at images also run the risk of losing their voice: in the black frame. *Birgit Flos*

CH/GB 1992, 16 mm, color, 50 min. directed by: Robert Frank. script: Robert Frank, Sam North, Michal Rovner. cinematography: Kevin Kerslake, Mustapha Barat (video), Robert Frank (video). editing: Jay Rabinowitz. art director: Tom Jarmusch. production: Vega Film, Zurich; World Wide International Television, BBC; Ruth Waldburger, Martin Rosenbaum. cast: Zohra Lampert, Bill Youmans, Bill Rice, Taylor Mead, John Larkin, Odessa Taft, a.o.

1994

Moving Pictures

Weiße Seiten   "I have a faible for fragments which reveal and hide truth", verkündet die Schrift im Bild, in Großbuchstaben. Am Anfang von *Moving Pictures* aber steht das Wort "memory", mehrmals untereinander auf ein in die Schreibmaschine eingespanntes Blatt geschrieben: Das Fragmentarische der Erinnerung setzt sich parallel zum Fragmentarischen des fotografischen Bildes in einer assoziativen Aneinander-reihung neu zusammen.

Ohne Ton gedreht, verhandelt diese Arbeit einmal mehr die Übergänge Robert Franks von der Fotografie zum Film und seine Suche nach einer „tragfähigen Ausdrucksform".[5] Frank montiert seine eigenen Fotografien in räumlichen und zeitlichen Sequenzen: so werden sie eine nach der anderen übereinandergelegt, Fotobücher werden durchgeblättert, Streifen von Fotoabzügen mit langsamem, tastendem Blick abgefilmt.

Seit den fünfziger Jahren betrachtet Robert Frank das einzelne, ikonische Bild kritisch und ent-wickelt Strategien gegen dessen Absolutheitsanspruch. In *Moving Pictures* verschwimmen die Grenzen zwischen Fotografie, Found Footage, Filmprojektion und gefilmter Realität durch lange Zooms bis in die Details von Fotos, in Schleier von Staubschichten oder Fensterglas und die verwaschene, von wenigen Akzenten belebte Farbgebung. Dazu verwendet Frank vorwiegend bereits vorhandenes Material seiner eigenen künstlerischen Produktion. Die Art des Vorüberziehens dieser Bilder entspricht der Doppeldeutigkeit des Titels. *Moving Pictures* verweist einerseits auf ein Handlungsmoment des Betrachters, in diesem Fall des Filmemachers selbst – nämlich das Bewegen von Bildern (als Objekte), andererseits auf den Charakter von Film im Gegensatz zu Fotografie oder Malerei.

Moving Pictures handelt auch vom Tod. Der Grabstein von Franks Eltern als erstes Bild, die Fotos von Raoul Hague oder Jack Kerouac am Totenbett, eine Blumenwiese mit der Aufschrift „Pour la Fille" (in Anspielung auf seine im Alter von 20 Jahren verstorbene Tochter Andrea) sind überaus traurige Bilder, die von einer ehrlichen Aggression gegen Tod und Alter konterkariert werden – wenn etwa Franks alter Freund Harry Smith auf die Frage nach dem Gefühl, heute Geburtstag zu haben, mit einer wegwerfenden Geste bellt: "It sucks!".

Wie eine Ergänzung zur Stille des Films wirken die Fotos von menschenleeren Räumen, die hier als Klammern eingesetzt werden – ein verlassener Strand, sterile Hochhauslandschaften, ein weiter Park-platz, eine leere Asphaltfläche, die ausgestorbene Straße einer Industriegegend: Orte, an denen jemand war und nun nicht mehr ist. Ein temporärer Zustand der Leere, der Stille. Im letzten Bild, auf einem Feld, bewegen Frauen einen Sack, mit dem Übertitel "Keep busy". Die Leerstellen und die Stille stellen im permanenten Fluss von Bildern, Gedanken und Erinnerungen ein notwendiges Innehalten dar, wie die weißen Seiten in Franks Fotobüchern. Oder, wie der Titel einer Fotografie Robert Franks sagt: "HOLD STILL keep going".
Nina Schedlmayer

Blank Pages   "I have a faible for fragments which reveal and hide truth," announces the text in capital letters. But the word "memory," written several times on a sheet of paper in a typewriter, appears at the beginning of *Moving Pictures.* The fragmentary nature of memory is reordered in an associative sequence parallel to the fragmentary nature of the photographic image.

This silent work deals once again with Robert Frank's transition from photography to film and his search for a "solid form of expression."[5] Frank assembled his own photographs in temporal and spatial sequences: One is laid atop another, photo albums are flipped through; strips of prints are filmed with a slow and probing gaze.

Ever since the 1950s, Frank has regarded the solitary iconic image with a critical eye, developing strategies to counteract its claims to absolutism. In *Moving Pictures* the borders between photography, found footage, projected film footage, and filmed reality blur in long zooms to details of photographs, in veils of dust or windowpanes, and washed-out colors with a few brighter contrasts. To this end, Frank mostly employed material he had already shot for his artworks. The way in which these images pass by, parallels the title's dual meaning. *Moving Pictures* refers firstly to a moment in the viewer's action, in this case that of the filmmaker himself, namely the movement of images (as objects), and secondly to the nature of film as opposed to photography and painting.

Moving Pictures also deals with death. The headstone of Frank's parents is the first image we see, then the photos of Raoul Hague and Jack Kerouac on their deathbeds, a meadow covered with flowers captioned "Pour la Fille" (a reference to his daughter Andrea, who died at the age of 20): These quite sad images are counteracted by honest feelings of aggression directed at death and aging, such as the reaction of Frank's old friend Harry Smith when asked how he felt about having a birthday: He made a dismissive gesture and bellowed, "It sucks!"

Photos of empty spaces seem to complement the stillness of this film, and they are employed as punctuation—a deserted beach, sterile landscapes of apartment buildings, a large parking lot, an empty asphalt surface, an abandoned street in an industrial district. All these places were once inhabited but are no longer: A temporary state of emptiness, of silence. The last scene shows a group of women dragging a sack across a field with the caption "Keep busy." The emptiness and the silence represent a needed pause in a constant flow of images, thoughts, and memories, like the blank pages in Frank's photo albums. Or, as the title of one of Frank's photographs says: "HOLD STILL keep going." *Nina Schedlmayer*

USA 1994, video, color & black and white, silent, 16 min. 30 sec. directed by: Robert Frank. cinematography: Robert Frank. editing: Laura Israel. production: Vega Film, Zurich. world premiere: Washington D.C. , NGA. cast: Allen Ginsberg, Raoul Hague, Harry Smith, June Leaf, Jean Luc Godard, a.o.

1996

The Present

Handwerk des Lebens Eines Montags … Der Gestus des Tagebuchs: zerstreut schweifender Video-Blick. Die Umgebung jedes Tages im Haus des Autors. Und dessen Off-Stimme: "I'm glad I have found my camera. Now I can film. But I don't know what. I don't know what story I would like to tell. But looking around this room, I should be able to find something. Don't you think so? Don't we know? Isn't it all there?" Worte eines assoziativen Selbstgesprächs im Moment der Aufnahme. Außerdem: die Erschaffung eines kommunikativen Raums zwischen Ich und Du, Ihr und Wir. Dann erst, nach etwa zwei Minuten, eine deutliche Fokussierung: das Bild einer Pappe auf dem Fußboden. Was verbirgt sich dahinter? Einerseits die Geschichte: "I'm gonna begin this film with this picture. What's behind this board?" Andererseits gibt es auch die Fliegen an den Fenstern, den Freund Fernando, das Zusammenleben mit June Leaf, die Erinnerungen an Tochter Andrea, den verstorbenen Sohn Pablo, das Apartment in New York, den Bruder in der Schweiz und die Krähen im Winter …

Der Versuch, Verbindung aufzunehmen zu den Dingen, Menschen, Tieren und Ereignissen vor der Kamera. Auch zu potentiellen Betrachtern des Films.

Ein Tagebuch, das Frank an irgendeinem Montag zwischen 1994 und 1996 begonnen haben mag. Worum es darin geht? Um das Handwerk des Lebens in diesen Jahren. Das Ineinander, Miteinander und Durcheinander von Schüben der Erinnerung, fortwährenden Versuchen, die eigenen Angelegenheiten zu ordnen, der Gegenwart von Tieren vor den Fenstern des Hauses, von Reisen oder unerledigt gebliebenen Vorhaben – so liest Frank einmal den melancholischen Satz aus einem Brief an ihn vor: "We should go on making this film about life…" Es wird nicht weiter verhandelt, was das sein könnte, ein Film über's Leben. Im gleichen Atemzug aber, da *The Present* nicht über etwas erzählt, sondern Teil hat am Vorantasten im Leben von Tag zu Tag, findet sich Franks Arbeit (und Kunst) bereits eingeschrieben in die Realisierung jenes vielleicht (wahrscheinlich) unmöglichen Films.

Immer wieder auch Momente des Abschieds, des Aufbruchs, der Trennung. Etwas (jemand) bleibt zurück, jemand anderer tritt eine Reise an: In der Schweiz stirbt ein Freund. "I am almost sure I will not see him again." Das nächste Bild zeigt eine Tafel am Zürcher Hauptbahnhof: „Noch 1347 Tage bis zum Jahr 2000." Zurück im Haus des Filmemachers an der Küste von Nova Scotia. An einer Wand steht das Wort "Memory" geschrieben. Im Off räsonniert der Autor/Filmemacher: "Today I'm going to ask Luigi to erase the word 'Memory'." Frank schaut zu, wie der junge Mann sich plagt, vom Ende des Wortes her die Buchstaben wegzukratzen, bis nur noch die Silbe "Me" (Ich) stehen bleibt. Sich verankern und sich herauslösen – zwischen beidem besteht ein Zusammenhang. Daran zu arbeiten ist schmerzhaft. Irgendwann betrachtet Luigi die Wand und sagt in die Kamera: "It's kind of sad."

Ganz am Ende spielt ein Freund gegen sich selbst. Dafür hat er zwei Würfel aus einem großen Glas mit vielen anderen geholt. Als erstes Ich würfelt er insgesamt zehn Punkte, als zweites Ich sieben. "I've lost", sagt das eine Ich. "But so what?", erwidert das andere. "That's the question." *Ralph Eue*

Life as a Craft One Monday… The semblance of a diary: the sweeping gaze of a video camera. Everyday surroundings in the screenwriter's house. And his off-camera voice: "I'm glad I have found my camera. Now I can film. But I don't know what. I don't know what story I would like to tell. But looking

around this room, I should be able to find something. Don't you think so? Don't we know? Isn't it all there?" The filmmaker talks to himself in an associative monolog at the moment of filming. In doing so, he creates a communicative space between I and you, you all and we. Then, roughly two minutes later, the picture focuses clearly on a piece of cardboard on the floor. What is hiding behind it? On the one hand, the plot: "I'm gonna begin this film with this picture. What's behind this board?" On the other, there are the flies on the windows, his friend Fernando, his life together with June Leaf, his memories of his daughter Andrea, his deceased son Pablo, the apartment in New York, his brother in Switzerland, and the crows in the winter.

His attempt to connect with the things, people, animals, and events in front of the camera, and also with the film's potential viewers.

A diary which Frank presumably started some Monday between 1994 and 1996: What might it be about? The craft of his life during those years; the combined, parallel and chaotic onslaughts of memory, constant attempts to order his private affairs, the presence of animals in front of the house's windows, of trips, and unfinished projects. At one point Frank reads a melancholy sentence from a letter he received: "We should go on making this film about life...." What that could be, a film about life, is not dealt with. But in the same breath, because *The Present* does not say anything about a subject, it represents a part of feeling one's way in daily life, as Frank's work (and art) has marked the realization of this possibly (probably) impossible film.

There are repeated moments of saying farewell, departure, separation. Something (someone) is left behind, and someone else begins a journey. A friend in Switzerland dies: "I am almost sure I will not see him again." The next scene shows a sign at Zurich's main train station: "Another 1,347 days until the year 2000." Back in the filmmaker's house on the Nova Scotia coast, the word "memory" has been written on a wall. Off-camera, the screenwriter/filmmaker grumbles: "Today I'm going to ask Luigi to erase the word 'Memory.'" Frank watches as the young man scrapes the letters away with difficulty, beginning at the end of the word and working back until only "me" is left. Putting down roots and ripping them up—the two acts are connected. Working on that is painful. At one point, Luigi takes a look at the wall, and then says into the camera, "It's kind of sad."

At the very end of the film, a friend plays against himself. He has taken a pair of dice from a large jar that is filled with them. First he rolls a ten as his first self, then a seven as his second self. "I've lost," says one self. "But so what?" answers the other. "That's the question." *Ralph Eue*

CH 1996, video/35 mm, color, 27 min. directed by: Robert Frank. cinematography: Robert Frank, Paulo Nozzolino. editing: Laura Israel. sound: Robert Frank. production: Vega Film, Zurich, Ruth Waldburger. world premiere: New York

1996

Summer Cannibals / Patti Smith

Horrorfilm   "I went down to Georgia / Nothing was as real / As the street beneath my feet / Descending into air." Das knurrende Timbre von Patti Smith, der Frau, die sich nur in Schwarzweiß fotografieren lässt, begleitet die Einleitung eines rätselhaften Textes, der möglicherweise von einem Hexensabbat erzählt, von Vampirismus und einer mystischen Kommunion in einer Welt, deren Regeln auf den Kopf gestellt sind. "Summer Cannibals" heißt der Song, wie ein Kapitel aus James G. Ballards experimentellem Roman "The Atrocity Exhibition", was höchstwahrscheinlich kein Zufall ist. Dort gibt es keinen Unterschied mehr zwischen Außen- und Innenwelt – die Trennlinie zwischen der überreizten, fragmentierten Psyche des/der Protagonisten und den allgegenwärtigen Stimuli der Mediengesellschaft ist ausgelöscht. Und in Smiths treibender Musik überwältigt das Lyrische Ich ab der zweiten Zeile eine archaische Vision, „von der dunklen Seite dessen, was es heißt, ein Rockstar zu sein", wie Smith angemerkt hat.

Es wäre der ideale Stoff für einen Horrorclip, aber Robert Franks lichter, energetischer Kurzfilm zu *Summer Cannibals* versagt sich naheliegende illustrative Bilder, so sie nicht zu Patti Smiths Selbstinszenierung vor der Kamera gehören: Zur Zeile "The viscous air / Pressed against my face" etwa drückt sie sich theatralisch die Hände ans Gesicht, am Höhepunkt ihres Lieds; nachdem sie mit einem rollenden, gutturalen "Eat!"-Schrei zum peitschenden Refrain überleitet, beißt sie sich in die Armbeuge. *Summer Cannibals* bedient sich einer typischen, eigentlich banalen Musikvideo-Situation – Smith und Band tun in einem spärlich dekorierten Zimmer so, als gäben sie ein Konzert –, seltsamerweise besitzt Franks Film aber eine Aura des Unerklärlichen.

In hohem Tempo – Franks Bilder folgen intuitiv dem Rhythmus des Songs – entsteht ein verspieltes Assoziationsgeflecht: Zu Beginn gleitet die Kamera soghaft an der Decke entlang, es folgt ein Kreisschwenk, der in seinem Versuch, die gesamte Örtlichkeit zu erfassen, eher desorientierend wirkt (eben wie das widersprüchliche "descending into air"), wenig später wird man Zeuge eines heiter-makabren Mysterienspiels, das Smith und Band aufführen (einmal flüstert sie einem Musiker eine Botschaft ins Ohr). Manchmal beteiligt sich Frank daran, indem er irritierende Großaufnahmen einfügt, deren Effekt zunächst eher sinnlich als sinnstiftend ist. Manchmal – ein Stich des „Letzten Abendmahls" – scheinen christliche Symbole die heidnischen Metaphern des Textes umzudeuten, aber letztlich führt auch diese Spur ins Leere: Als Smith Gegenstände aus ihren Taschen kramt, holt sie zunächst einen Rosenkranz heraus – und dann noch Kleingeld. Was weniger ein Kommentar zum Themenkreis Religion/Pop/Geschäft zu sein scheint als reiner Zufall. Oder auch nicht: In *Summer Cannibals* sind die Dinge und Handlungen gleichzeitig unergründlich und aufreizend konkret. Vielleicht doch ein Horrorfilm: eine Arbeit über die beunruhigenden Geheimnisse, die jenseits des Offensichtlichen lauern. *Christoph Huber*

Horror Movie   "I went down to Georgia / Nothing was as real / As the street beneath my feet / Descending into air." The growling timbre of Patti Smith, the woman who only allows herself to be photographed with black-and-white film, accompanies the introduction of a cryptic text, apparently about a witch's Sabbath, vampirism, and a mystic communion ceremony in a world where all the rules have been turned upside down. The song is entitled "Summer Cannibals," the same as a chapter in James G. Ballard's experimental novel "The Atrocity Exhibition", which is most probably not a coincidence. In it there is no difference between the

outer and inner worlds—the line dividing the overwrought, fragmented psyche of the protagonist(s) and the omnipresent stimuli from a media-obsessed society have been obliterated. And in Smith's music and its driving rhythm, the lyric self overcomes an archaic vision beginning in the second line, which addresses "the darker side of being a rock musician," as Smith later remarked.

This would be ideal material for a horror movie, but Frank's lighthearted, energetic short film made to accompany *Summer Cannibals* dispenses with logical illustrative images to the extent they fail to serve Patti Smith's performance for the camera: For example, at the lines "The viscous air / Pressed against my face" at the song's climax she theatrically presses her hands to her face; after a thundering, guttural cry of "Eat!" leads to the lashing refrain, she bites herself in the crook of her arm. *Summer Cannibals* makes use of a typical, in fact banal music-video situation: Smith and her band put on a make-believe concert in a sparsely furnished room. Oddly enough though, Frank's film has an aura of the inexplicable.

Frank's images intuitively follow the song's rhythm, and a high speed playful web of associations is created. At the beginning, the camera glides along the ceiling as if it were being pulled by an invisible current. This is followed by a 360-degree pan which has a rather disorienting effect in its attempt to capture the entire scene (just like the contradictory phrase "descending into air"). A little later the viewer is witness to an amusingly macabre mystery play acted out by Smith and band (at one point she whispers something into a musician's ear). Frank participated occasionally by inserting irritating closeups which tended to add sensuousness rather than meaning. At times, Christian symbols such as an engraving of the Last Supper seem to demand reinterpretation of the lyrics' heathen metaphors, but this is misleading: When Smith takes some objects out of her pocket the first thing to appear is a rosary—and then some coins. This seems to happen more out of coincidence rather than as commentary on the related topics of religion, pop, and economics. Or maybe not: Things and actions in *Summer Cannibals* are simultaneously inexplicable and provocatively concrete. Maybe it is a horror movie after all, specifically, a story of the unpleasant secrets hidden from the public eye.
Christoph Huber

USA 1996, 35 mm, black and white, 5 min. music film for Patti Smith´s song "Summer Cannibals". directed by: Robert Frank. cinematography: Kevin Kerslake. editing: Laura Israel. music: Patti Smith. production: Cascando Studios. producer: Michael Shamberg. cast: Patti Smith & Band

1996

Flamingo

Strukturen der Behausung   Ein Haus, hoch über dem Meer; ein Lichtstrahl, der auf alte Fotografien fällt; eine Stimme, die das Sichtbare benennt: *Flamingo* ist eng verwandt mit *What I Remember from My Visit (with Stieglitz)* und verläuft doch gänzlich anders, denn Frank selbst ist nur flüchtig anwesend in dieser schwarzweiß gehaltenen Notiz über die elementaren Strukturen der Behausung. Der Kommentar von Miranda Dali klingt objektiv, die Stimme ist disloziert von den Bildern, wie in einer Ausstellungsinstallation, in der es darum geht, einen Raum zu füllen (das Thema von *Flamingo*). Dali benennt, was zu sehen ist: die Silhouette eines riesigen Baggers (auf einem Foto). Souvenirs: eine Buddhastatue, eine Postkarte mit dem Empire State Building. Arbeiter kommen, um an dem Haus in Nova Scotia zu bauen, das Frank mit seiner Frau June be- wohnt. Es soll ein zusätzliches Geschoß errichtet werden, der Ausblick auf den Ozean wird dann noch besser sein. Die routinierten Handgriffe, die Präzision und Geschwindigkeit der Arbeit werden in Franks Bildern zu Formen und Abläufen der Natur, qualitativ nicht unterschieden von der Bewegung, die der Wind in einem Stapel Blätter verursacht. Der Schnee, die Schlange, die das Weite sucht, die Himmelsrichtungen, die Holz- wände, das Meer – alles zusammen ergibt einen Assoziationsraum, der von Miranda Dali bestimmt wird, auch dann, wenn sie auffällig verstummt und die schattenhaften Aufnahmen allein die Verrichtungen der Arbeiter zeigen. Das "all patient house" hat in *Flamingo* eine doppelte Struktur: eine materielle und eine biografische. Es besteht aus Wänden und aus den Fragmenten eines Lebens (die häufig an die Wand geheftet oder projiziert werden). "This is the time to say a few words: about building a house, about projecting slides": Der biblische Tonfall, mit dem diese Aussage beginnt, wird in eine medienarchäologische Überlegung aufgenommen – das Haus erst wirft die Bilder zurück, verwandelt sie in Erinnerungen, lässt sie zueinander in Bezug treten. Die Wände bilden nach innen eine Zuflucht, in die sich Frank mit seiner Frau zurückziehen kann, um wie Philemon und Baucis („Wog' auf Woge, schäumend wild / Seht als Garten ihr behandelt", heißt es in Goethes „Faust" über das Refugium am Meer, in dem das alte Ehepaar sein Ausgedinge hat) den Gang der Zivilisation durch den der Natur zu verstehen. Das Bild von Buddha hat in *Flamingo* keinen herausragenden Stellenwert, es erscheint flüchtig und in einer Reihe gleichwertiger Eindrücke. Aber es könnte ein Schlüssel für die Organisation des Films sein, wie der Beginn einer Zen-Meditation: Eindrücke wirken aus allen Richtungen auf das Bewusstsein, das sich davon nur allmählich zu befreien vermag. Wenn die Baufahrzeuge schließlich das Feld räumen, bleibt ein Gebäude zurück, das noch zusätzlich abgedichtet wird. "Paint it black".

Flamingo ist datiert wie ein Gemälde, aber die Unterschrift ist kein Zertifikat, sondern – als Spur im Schnee – wiederum nur der Hinweis auf eine Gegenwart, die es im Film nicht gibt. *Bert Rebhandl*

Structures of Residential Buildings   A house high above the sea. A ray of light falls on some old photographs. A voice names the things we see. *Flamingo* closely resembles *What I Remember from My Visit (with Stieglitz)*, yet it develops in a completely different way, because Frank himself is visible only briefly in this black-and-white report on the elementary structures of residential buildings. Miranda Dali's commentary sounds objective, her voice dislocated from the images like in an art installation intended to fill a space (*Flamingo*'s theme). Dali names what is visible in the picture: the silhouette of a huge excavator (in a photograph); and souvenirs, specifically a statue of Buddha and a postcard with the Empire State Building. Laborers arrive to work

on the house in Nova Scotia where Frank lives with his wife June. An addition to the house is planned to provide an even better view of the ocean. In Frank's film, routine movements, the precision and speed with which they work, become organic shapes and processes, similar to a stack of paper fluttering in the wind. The snow, the retreating snake, various landscapes, the wooden walls, and the sea— everything together provides latitude for associations, as defined by Miranda Dali, even when she conspicuously stops talking and the indistinct images show the workers going about their business. The "all-patient house" has a dual structure in *Flamingo*, both material and biographical. It consists of four walls and the fragments of someone's life (which are repeatedly projected onto or attached to the walls). "This is the time to say a few words: about building a house, about projecting slides." The Biblical tone at the beginning of this statement is employed in a reflection on media archeology—at first the house reflects the images, transforming them into memories, allowing them to enter a joint context. The walls form an inner refuge where Frank can retire with his wife to contemplate the progress of civilization through nature; like Philemon and Baucis, the lines "You, on shores of breaking foam, / See, a garden lies completed" in Goethe's "Faust" refer to the couple's seaside retreat where they are spending their golden years. The picture of Buddha has no particular significance in *Flamingo*; it appears only briefly in a series of equally important images. But this could also provide a key to the film's organization, like the beginning of a Zen meditation: consciousness is bombarded by sensory stimuli from all directions and liberates itself only gradually from them. When construction vehicles finally clear the field, a house is left behind for final insulating. "Paint it black."

     Flamingo is dated like a painting, but the signature, rather than certification, is written in the snow—another reference to a present which does not exist in this film. *Bert Rebhandl*

CAN 1996, video, black and white, 5 min. made for the lending out of the Hasselblad Award. directed by: Robert Frank. cinematography: Robert Frank. editing: Laura Israel. narrator: Miranda Dali. production: Robert Frank. world premiere: Sweden

1998

What I Remember from My Visit (with Stieglitz)

Das Ende der Bilder   Eine Stimme mit französischem Akzent wiederholt den Titel des Videos und suggeriert damit den Beginn einer persönlichen Erzählung. Das Home-movie-Setting unterstreicht diesen Eindruck. Eine nackte Glühbirne hängt an der Decke, eine Hand schaltet die Lampe ein: die Attraktion der filmischen Beobachtung kann beginnen, wenn auch mit einfachsten Mitteln. "What I remember from my visit with Stieglitz: the hospitality, the wood-stove in the kitchen, chicken for lunch, Stieglitz, waiting for the sun to appear through the clouds...."

Der Mann hinter der Kamera ist auch der Erzähler: Jerome Sother, ein junger Filmemacher, der von Robert Frank eingeladen wurde, während seines Besuchs in Mabou einen Kurzfilm zu drehen. Wie schon in seinen Filmen *Me and My Brother*, *About Me: A Musical*, *Candy Mountain* und *Last Supper*, schafft sich Frank mit diesem Projekt wieder die Möglichkeit, über das Alter ego einer fiktiven oder wirklichen Künstlerpersönlichkeit seine eigene Rolle als Fotograf und Filmemacher zu hinterfragen. Kein Geringerer als der große frühe amerikanische Fotograf Alfred Stieglitz, der unter anderem durch die Portraits seiner Frau, der Malerin Georgia O'Keefe berühmt wurde, steht hier als Stellvertreter eines *grand old man*. Die Ähnlichkeit zu Franks eigener Lebensgeschichte – er war zweimal mit Künstlerinnen verheiratet – ist wieder eines der vielen Details, die mit der Biografie Franks zu tun haben, mit seinem Privatleben und seiner Arbeit als Fotograf. Er selbst spielt die Rolle des Stieglitz, seine Frau June Leaf spielt Georgia, "who comes from her studio in the rain." Aber einige Elemente früherer Frank-Selbstspiegelungen fehlen hier: Die Kinder können keinen Widerstand mehr leisten, ihr Tod liegt lange zurück; der Rückzug ins rauhe Neuschottland vor der Fangemeinde und den Kunstvermittlern ist gelungen; die Geister der Erinnerung suchen ihn nicht mehr heim, die Familienalben sind leer, die Fotos der Vergangenheit fehlen. Traurig mutet sie an, diese Absenz von Bildern, aber vielleicht betrifft sie nur Franks Abneigung gegen den Ausverkauf seiner Icons, seine Abneigung gegen die Selbstwiederholung. "And I'm thinking of Kerouac when he said: ,Being famous is like old newspapers, blowing down Bleecker Street.'", sagt Robert Frank in *Home Improvements*. Eine solch abwertende Bemerkung scheint in *What I Remember* nicht mehr notwendig, vielmehr kann die Rolle des Kreativen, der Leben und Kunst, äußere Wirklichkeit und Autobiografisches verbindet, spielerisch dargestellt werden. Frank verkörpert den alten Mann mit der Kamera auf Motivsuche, einen, der Holz hackt, seine "steel-toes" zum Einkaufen umschnallt und mit seiner rauhen Hand die faltige Wange seiner Lebensgefährtin streichelt.

Es ist, als hätte sich Frank mit der Rolle des alten Meisters angefreundet, der das Häusliche und die Kunst als wiederholtes Zusammenspiel von Ritualen darstellen kann. Die Spontaneität sitzt ihm noch in den Gliedern, er ist jederzeit bereit für "more photographs." ... Trotzdem ist eines klar: Es ist alles nur Spiel. Die Verletzungen des Lebens haben in einem Portrait, das der Bewunderung entspringt, keinen Platz.
Brigitta Burger-Utzer

The End of Images   The video's title is repeated by a voice with a French accent, suggesting the beginning of a personal narration. The home-movie touch underlines this impression. A naked light bulb hangs from the ceiling; the hand of an unseen person switches the lamp on. The main attraction—the cinematic observation—can begin, though with the most basic means available. "What I remember from my visit with

Stieglitz: the hospitality, the wood-stove in the kitchen, chicken for lunch, Stieglitz, waiting for the sun to appear through the clouds...."

The man behind the camera is also the narrator: Jerome Sother, a young filmmaker invited by Robert Frank to make a short film during his visit in Mabou. As was the case in his films *Me and My Brother*, *About Me: A Musical, Candy Mountain,* and *Last Supper,* this project provided Frank once again with an opportunity to question his role as a photographer and filmmaker through the alter ego of a real or fictitious artist. No less a personality than the great American photographer Alfred Stieglitz, whose fame was based in part on the portraits of his wife, painter Georgia O'Keefe, represents a "grand old man" in this film work. The similarity to Frank's life story—he had been married twice, to two different artists—is another one of the details that evoke his own biography, private life, and work as a photographer. Frank plays the role of Stieglitz, his wife June Leaf plays Georgia, "who comes from her studio in the rain." But some of the elements employed in earlier self-referential works are missing: The children, having passed away long before, are no longer able to offer resistance. The retreat from his fans and other members of the art industry into the rough landscape of Nova Scotia was successful. The ghosts of memory no longer plague him; the family albums are empty; there are no pictures from the past. It seems somehow sad, this absence of images, though this might be no more than the product of Frank's distaste for the sellout of his icons, his loathing to repeat himself. "And I'm thinking of Kerouac when he said, 'Being famous is like old newspapers, blowing down Bleecker Street,'" says Robert Frank in *Home Improvements*. Such a dismissive statement seems unnecessary in *What I Remember*; the role of a creative personality who combines life and art, external reality and autobiography is easy to play. Frank becomes the old man with a camera who is on the lookout for motifs, someone who chops wood, puts on his steel-toed shoes to go shopping, and caresses his wife's wrinkled cheek with a rough hand.

It is almost as if Frank had come to enjoy this role of an old master, able to present art and domestic life as a repetitive interplay of rituals. Spontaneity still comes naturally to him; he is always ready for "more photographs."

At the same time one thing is certain: It is nothing more than a game. Life's scars have no place in a portrait motivated by admiration. *Brigitta Burger-Utzer*

CAN 1998, video, color, 7 min. directed by: Robert Frank. cinematography: Jerome Sother. editing: Laura Israel.
production: Robert Frank. cast: Robert Frank, June Leaf, Jerome Sother

2000

San Yu

Ein Requiem? In Taiwan und Paris begibt sich Robert Frank auf eine Spurensuche nach dem 1966 erst 65jährig verstorbenen, mit ihm befreundeten Maler San Yu. Eine Suche, die sich selbst dokumentiert: eine Landkarte von China, auf der San Yus Geburtsort lokalisiert werden soll; Pfeile auf der Straße und auf Verkehrsschildern weisen auf das Prozesshafte und die Selbstreflexivität dieses Films hin. "No clear direction or substance of what I will be trying to say and to show" gesteht Frank und fragt sich: "Is this a requiem?" Frank hatte San Yu in den sechziger Jahren kennengelernt und mit ihm für kurze Zeit sein New Yorker Studio gegen dessen Pariser Atelier getauscht. Dreißig Jahre nach dem Tod des Malers wird er von seiner Witwe Rita Wong kontaktiert, die ihn nach bei ihm verbliebenen Skulpturen fragt.

Ohne spektakulären dramaturgischen Aufbau, strukturiert nur durch Zwischentitel, dokumentiert Robert Franks Film die eigene Entstehungsgeschichte: Korrespondenz mit San Yus Witwe, mit Auktionshäusern und Journalisten wird eingeblendet. Frank erzählt nicht nur über seinen Freund San Yu, sondern auch über sich selbst, zeigt sich in behutsamer, fast zärtlicher Interaktion mit dessen Werken. Im Gegensatz zu anderen Dokumentationen über Künstler filmt er nicht Zeichnungen, Gemälde und Skulpturen ab, sondern zeigt sie ausschließlich in ihren Kontexten: als Objekte einer Auktion oder als Exponate einer Ausstellung, die gerade aufgebaut wird.

Ähnlich wie in *Last Supper* berichtet Frank von San Yu, dessen (ganz dem Klischee entsprechender) Verarmung und seinem posthum entdeckten Œuvre, durch andere Personen, die sich über diesen äußern. Nur selten kommt der Künstler selbst ins Bild – bezeichnenderweise einmal auf einem Foto mit dem Filmemacher selbst. "I wanted to show something between him and me, and not just his pictures", sagt Frank in einem Interview.[6] Signifikant für diesen Zugang ist die Frage eines Journalisten: "What do you want to tell San Yu?". So spricht Frank den Maler, im Pariser Studio mit der Kamera am Boden liegend, selbst an: "The sun is shining on your tree. No more paintings. So this would be your story about the few moments I remember."[7]

In Schwarzweiß-Aufnahmen, die sich vom Rest des Films abheben, verbindet Frank Reales, Fiktives und Autobiografisches[8]: In der Pariser Umgebung, in der San Yu gelebt hat, spricht ein Schauspieler in der Rolle des Künstlers über künstlerische Arbeit, die Geschichte, das Träumen und die Liebe. Die Frage nach dem Realitätsanspruch dieser Figur bleibt offen. Damit ist *San Yu* nicht nur eine Untersuchung über das Sprechen von Kunst und Künstlern, sondern auch über die Authentizität dokumentarischer Darstellungen.
Nina Schedlmayer

A Requiem? In Paris and Taiwan, Robert Frank sets off on a search for traces of a friend, the painter San Yu, who died in 1966 at the age of sixty-five. At the same time, this search documents itself: San Yu's birthplace has supposedly been marked on a map of China, arrows on the street and street signs indicate the film's procedural and self-reflexive nature. There is "no clear direction or substance of what I will be trying to say and to show," admits Frank, and then asks himself, "Is this a requiem?" Frank met San Yu in the 1960s and briefly traded his studio in New York for the latter's in Paris. Thirty years after the painter's death, Frank was contacted by his widow Rita Wong, who asked him about her husband's sculptures.

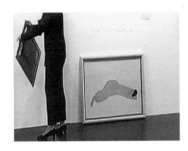

Dispensing with a spectacular dramatic structure, organized solely by means of inserts, Frank's film documents the story of its own production. Correspondence with San Yu's widow, auction houses and journalists appear occasionally. Frank tells us not only about his friend San Yu, but about himself also, showing his careful and almost tender interaction with the other man's works. In contrast to other documentaries about artists, he did not simply shoot footage of drawings, paintings, and sculptures; they appear within their contexts exclusively, as lots at an auction or as exhibits at a show as it is being set up.

In a way similar to *Last Supper*, Frank has made a report on San Yu, his descent into poverty (thoroughly clichéd), the painter's œuvre and its posthumous discovery on the basis of third-party statements. The artist himself is shown infrequently—once quite significantly in a photograph with the filmmaker. "I wanted to show something between him and me, and not just his pictures," said Frank in an interview.[6] Significant for this approach is a question posed by a journalist: "What do you want to tell San Yu?" In response, Frank addresses the painter himself, who is lying on the Paris studio's floor with the camera: "The sun is shining on your tree. No more paintings. So this would be your story about the few moments I remember."[7]

In black-and-white footage set apart from the rest of the film Frank combines real, fictitious, and autobiographical elements.[8] In Paris, the city where San Yu lived, an actor playing the role of the artist talks about creative work, history, dreaming, and love. The issue of this character's authenticity remains open. *San Yu* is therefore not only an examination of the discussion of art and artists, but also about the authenticity of documentary depictions. *Nina Schedlmayer*

CH / F 2000, video/35 mm, color & black and white, 27 min. directed by: Robert Frank. cinematography: Robert Frank, Paolo Nozzolino. editing: Laura Israel. production: Vega Film, Zurich, Paris: Yves Riou, Didier Fouquier. world premiere: Locarno. cast: Nikolaï Boldaïen

2002

Paper Route

Nichts als Kreise   *Paper Route*, eine Auftragsarbeit der Schweizer Expo 2002, ist ein kleiner, lakonischer Videofilm über Aufbruch und Heimkehr, über die zyklische Bewegung der Natur und die nicht weniger zirkelhafte Bewegung einer Reise. Anfangs- und Endpunkt fallen gleich im ersten Bild zusammen. Franks Videokamera streicht über eine Collage von Fotografien und Notizen; von Hand und mit Maschine beschriebene Zettel, der Briefkopf eines Hotels. "Leaving Home" steht da, und: "Coming Home"; eine Frauenstimme aus dem Off – "Story A", "Story B" treibt diese Zweiteilung voran. "The voyage of an ordinary man with important memories".

Aufblende, Krähenschreie, ein Gartenzaun im Schnee. Neuschottland, Kanada. Robert Frank filmt sich selbst im Spiegel, wartet darauf, dass es hell wird. "I wonder about the paper route… getting the news…". Wie so oft in den Arbeiten Franks steht eine flüchtige Frage, die beiläufige Beobachtung der Welt vor der eigenen Haustür am Anfang einer fotografischen Medïtation. Wie kommt die Zeitung jeden Tag vor die Türen entlegener, eingeschneiter Häuser? Der Filmemacher begibt sich also erneut auf die Reise, diesmal auf die „Zeitungstour"; er begleitet Bobby McMillan, einen drahtigen, aufgekratzten Zeitungsausträger auf seiner nächtlichen Route rund um Mabou, Neuschottland. 158 Abonnenten, jeder hat einen Namen und eine Geschichte, und Bobby kennt sie alle.

Anfangs ist es noch stockfinster, Schneegestöber, im Autoradio laufen Middle-of-the-Road-Hits für Frühaufsteher, von "The Time of my Life" bis zu Rod Stewart. Franks Kamera wechselt zwischen Bobbys Profil und dem Blick durch die Windschutzscheibe. *Paper Route* widmet sich auf gänzlich unprätentiöse und humorvolle Weise der Vermessung der zeitlichen und räumlichen Parameter des Lebens eines Mannes, der „seine Arbeit in der Nacht verrichtet" (Frank). „Nichts dabei" sagt Bobby, "a good job". Beide lachen, als sie draufkommen, dass die Zeitungsroute im Kreis verläuft: "Circles – that's all we do" grummelt Frank; "that's all we do, when it comes to the end!".

Am Ende ist es hell geworden, auch die Musik hat sich verändert. Pink statt Jennifer Garner, und der vorletzte Kunde wartet schon am Treppenaufgang. Zuletzt sitzt Bobby wieder in seinem eigenen Wohnzimmer, den Staubsauger neben sich. "What was it like being filmed?" fragt Frank diesmal nach der Qualität *seiner* Arbeit. "Good" sagt Bobby. Story A, Story B.

Paper Route wurde bezeichnenderweise, im Rahmen einer Video- und Fotoinstallation Franks, im August 2002 auf einem Schiff, der Barke des "Arteplage mobile de Jura" präsentiert. Ein schöner Schauplatz, um über ein „Leben unterwegs" zu erzählen – ohne festen Ort, im Aufbruch von A nach B, endlos seine Kreise ziehend. *Michael Loebenstein*

Nothing but Circles   *Paper Route*, which was commissioned for the 2002 Expo in Switzerland, is a short, laconic video film about departures and returns, about cyclical movement in nature and the equally circular movement of a journey. Both the starting point and destination are shown in the first scene. Frank's video camera skims over a collage of photographs and notes, typed and handwritten, hotel stationery. "Leaving Home" is visible, and "Coming Home"; a woman's voice from off-camera —"Story A," "Story B" continues this bisection. "The voyage of an ordinary man with important memories."

Fade-in, crows cawing, a garden fence in the snow: Nova Scotia, Canada. Robert Frank films himself in a mirror, waiting for the sun to come up. "I wonder about the paper route… getting the news…" As is so often the case in Frank's works, a casual question, a passing remark about the world before one's own doorstep, is the starting point for a photographic meditation. How is the daily newspaper delivered to remote, snowed-in houses? The filmmaker once again sets off on a journey, this time a paper route: He accompanies Bobby McMillan, a wiry, high-spirited paperboy on his evening route around Mabou, Nova Scotia. One hundred fifty-eight subscribers, each with a name and a story, and Bobby knows every one of them.

At the beginning it is still pitch black; snowflakes swirl and easy listening hits for early risers, from "The Time of My Life" to Rod Stewart, play on the radio. Frank's camera alternates between Bobby's profile and the view through the windshield. *Paper Route* is a humorous and wholly unpretentious survey of the spatial and temporal parameters in the life of a man who "does his work at night" (Frank). "No big deal," says Bobby, "a good job." Both men laugh when they realize that the paper route takes them in a circle: "Circles—that's all we do," grumbles Frank; "that's all we do, when it comes to the end!"

At the conclusion, the sun is up and the music has changed; Pink rather than Jennifer Garner. One of the last customers is already waiting at his stairway. Then Bobby is back in his own living room, sitting next to his vacuum cleaner. "What was it like being filmed?" asks Frank, this time about the quality of *his* work. "Good," answers Bobby. Story A, Story B.

Significantly, *Paper Route* was presented on a ship, the "Arteplage mobile de Jura," in August 2002 as part of an installation of Frank's video and photographic works. A beautiful venue for a tale about a "life on the move," without a fixed location, on the way from A to B, endlessly moving in circles.
Michael Loebenstein

CAN / CH 2002, video, color, 23 Min. made by order of the Expo project „Le Cafard". directed by: Robert Frank. editing: Laura Israel. production: Vega Film, Zurich; Robert Frank. cast: Bobby McMillan

Life Dances On...

[1] Robert Frank, „J'aimerais faire un film...", in: "Robert Frank," coll. Photo Poche, Paris: Centre National de la Photographie, 1983 (o.S).

[2] Jean-Paul Fargier, „La Force faible", in: *Cahiers du Cinéma* N° 380/Februar 1986, S. 35-39.

[1] Robert Frank, "J'aimerais faire un film...," "Robert Frank," coll. Photo Poche, Paris: Centre National de la Photographie, 1983.

[2] Jean-Paul Fargier, "La Force faible," *Cahiers du Cinéma*, N° 380, February 1986, pp. 35-39.

Home Improvements

[3] John Berger, "Mother", in: ders., Keeping a Rendezvous. New York: Vintage 1992, S. 43-52.

[4] Patricia Hampl, "Memory's Movies", in: Charles Warren (Ed.), Beyond Document. Essays on Nonfiction Film. Hanover: Wesleyan University Press 1996, S. 51-79.

[3] John Berger, "Mother," Berger, "Keeping a Rendezvous". New York: Vintage, 1992, pp. 43-52.

[4] Patricia Hampl, "Memory's Movies," Charles Warren (ed.), "Beyond Document. Essays on Nonfiction Film". Hanover: Wesleyan University Press, 1996, pp. 51-79.

Moving Pictures

[5] Sarah Greenough: „Fragmente, die ein Ganzes ergeben. Zur Bedeutung in fotografischen Sequenzen", in: dies., Philip Brookman (Hg.): "Moving Out – Robert Frank", Ausst. Kat. National Gallery of Art, Washington, Scalo Verlag, Zürich 1995, S. 97f.

[5] Sarah Greenough, "Fragments That Make a Whole: Meaning in Photographic Sequences," Greenough, Philip Brookman (eds.), "Robert Frank: Moving Out," exhib. cat., National Gallery of Art, Washington, Scalo publisher, Zurich, 1995, pp. 97.

San Yu

[6] Interview mit Ute Eskildsen, in: „HOLD STILL_keep going", Ausst. Kat. Museum Folkwang, Essen, hg. von Ute Eskildsen, Scalo Verlag, Zürich – Berlin – N. Y., S. 111

[7] „Indem er die Wahrheit des fotografischen Bildes hinterfragt und vorschlägt, die Kamera, die zwischen Erlebnis und Dokumentation steht, zu eliminieren, erklärt Frank, dass Erinnerungen an ein Erlebnis realer seien als Fotos davon.", Philip Brookman: „Fenster auf eine andere Zeit. Autobiographische Fragen", in: "Robert Frank: Moving Out", Ausst. Kat. National Gallery of Art, Washington, Scalo Verlag, Zürich 1995, S. 153.

[8] Siehe dazu auch: Philip Brookman über *Last Supper*, in: ders., „Fenster auf eine andere Zeit. Autobiographische Fragen", in: Ausst. Kat. National Gallery of Art, Washington 1995, S. 143.

[6] Interview with Ute Eskildsen, Eskildsen (ed.), "HOLD STILL_keep going," exhib. cat., Museum Folkwang, Essen, Scalo, Zurich, Berlin, New York, p. 111.

[7] "By questioning the veracity of photographic images and by proposing to eliminate the camera that stands between experience and documentation, Frank declares that memories of an experience are more real than photographs of it." Philip Brookman, "Windows on Another Time: Issues of Autobiography," Sarah Greenough, Brookman (eds.), "Robert Frank: Moving Out," exhib. cat., National Gallery of Art, Washington, Scalo, Zurich, 1995, p. 153.

[8] See also Philip Brookman on *Last Supper*, Brookman, op. cit., p. 143.

1924	geboren am 9. 11. in Zürich.
1941-44	kurze Lehre und Assistenzen als Fotograf in der Schweiz (u.a. bei Hermann Segesser und Michael Wolgensinger).
1946	macht sein erstes Buch *40 Fotos* mit Originalfotografien.
1947	Emigration nach New York.
	Alexey Brodovitch engagiert Frank für *Harper's Bazaar* als Modefotograf.
1948	Reisen nach Peru und Bolivien. Die dabei entstandenen Fotografien werden erstmals 1952 in Robert Delpire's Revue *Neuf* und 1956 als Buch mit dem Titel *Indiens pas morts* veröffentlicht.
1949	Reise nach Europa (Frankreich, Italien, Schweiz und Spanien). Produziert ein Buch mit 74 Originalfotografien von Paris für die Künstlerin Mary Lockspeiser.
1950	heiratet Mary Lockspeiser.
	Edward Steichen zeigt Franks Arbeiten im Museum of Modern Art in der Gruppenausstellung "51 American Photographers".
1951	Sohn Pablo wird in New York geboren.
1952-53	lebt und arbeitet in Europa, hauptsächlich in Paris; Reisen nach Spanien, London, Wales und die Schweiz. Er gibt die Modefotografie auf und arbeitet als freier Fotojournalist.
1954	Tochter Andrea wird geboren.
1955-56	Robert Frank erhält als erster europäischer Fotograf ein Guggenheim-Stipendium für ein Jahr.
	Reisen durch die Vereinigten Staaten, erreicht eine Verlängerung des Stipendiums um ein weiteres Jahr.
1958	Robert Delpire publiziert *Les Américains* in Paris, das erst 1959 in den USA bei Grove Press herauskommt. Robert Frank reist mit Jack Kerouac nach Florida. Er arbeitet für die Werbeabteilung der *New York Times* und fährt mit dem Bus durch New York, unter anderem die 42. Straße ab, die Fotoserie *Bus Series* entsteht.
1959	*Pull My Daisy* entsteht in Co-Regie mit Alfred Leslie.
1961	Reisen nach Europa, fotografiert beim Filmfestival Venedig.
	Hugh Edwards kuratiert Franks erste Einzelausstellung "Robert Frank: Photographer" für das Art Institute of Chicago.
1962	Ausstellung im Museum of Modern Art, New York: "Photographs by Harry Callahan and Robert Frank", kuratiert von Edward Steichen. Daraufhin widmet die Schweizer Zeitschrift *Du* eine Ausgabe den Fotografien von Frank.
1963	Regie bei *OK End Here.*
1964	George Eastman House kauft 25 der Fotografien von *The Americans* für eine Wanderausstellung.
1964-66	dreht und reist mit dem Regisseur und Produzenten Conrad Rooks für den Film *Chappaqua*

	nach Frankreich, Mexico, Indien, Ceylon, England, Jamaica und Amerika. Sie gewinnen damit 1967 in Venedig den silbernen Löwen.
1965	beginnt mit seinem ersten Langfilm *Me and My Brother,* der 1968 fertiggestellt wird.
1969	trennt sich von Mary, später dann Scheidung. Lebt mit der Künstlerin June Leaf in der Bowery.
	Er publiziert fünf monatliche Kolumnen für das Magazin *Creative Camera* in London.
	Regie und Produktion seines ersten autobiografischen Films *Conversations of Vermont* und des Dokumentarfilms *Liferaft Earth.*
1970-71	Frank kauft ein Stück Land und ein Haus in Nova Scotia mit June Leaf.
	Lehrt an mehreren Colleges und Universitiäten in den USA.
	Er bekommt eine Unterstützung vom American Film Institute, um den Film *About Me: A Musical* zu produzieren.
1971	Kazuhiko Motomura publiziert *The Lines of My Hand* in Tokyo, in den USA wird das Buch danach von Lustrum Press herausgegeben.
1972	beginnt eine Polaroid-Kamera zu verwenden.
1974	Franks Fotos werden in einer retrospektiven Ausstellung im Kunsthaus Zürich, kuratiert von Rosselina Bischof, gezeigt.
	Im Dezember stirbt seine Tochter Andrea bei einem Flugzeugabsturz in Guatemala.
1975	heiratet er June Leaf in Reno am Weg nach Californien, wo er zwei Monate Film unterrichtet.
	Fotografiert mit einer Wegwerfkamera.
	Robert Frank als Teil der Reihe *Aperture History of Photography Monographs* mit einem Vorwort von Rudy Wurlitzer veröffentlicht.
1976	beginnt mit einer professionellen Polaroid-Kamera mit einem Positiv/Negativfilm der Type 665 zu arbeiten. Er macht Collagen mit Text von diesen Negativen.
1978	Retrospektive in Ottawa, kuratiert von Lorraine Monk vom National Film Board of Canada, sie reist auch zum Fogg Museum an die Harvard University nach Cambridge, Massachusetts.
1979	Einzelausstellung "Robert Frank: Photographer / Filmmaker, Works from 1945–1979", kuratiert von Philip Brookman am Long Beach Museum of Art in California.
1980	Retrospektive "The New American Filmmakers Series: Robert Frank", kuratiert von John Hanhardt am Whitney Museum of American Art in New York.
	Seinen Film *Life Dances On...* widmet er seiner Tochter Andrea und seinem Freund Danny Seymour.
1981	Franks Filme werden beim Rotterdam Filmfestival gezeigt.
	Er reist nach Israel und lehrt dort drei Wochen an der Camera Obscura School.

1982	Robert Delpire veröffentlicht *Robert Frank* bei Photo Poche mit einer Einleitung von Rudy Wurlitzer. Es erscheint die Sondernummer über Robert Frank von *Les Cahiers de la Photographie*, von Gilles Mora herausgegeben.

Beginnt mit der Arbeit an dem Video *Home Improvements* (1985).

1985 „Robert Frank: Fotografias/Films 1948–1984": Ausstellung und Katalog für den Salla Parpallo in Valencia, kuratiert von Vicente Todoli.

Er erhält den Erich Salomon Preis der Deutschen Gesellschaft für Fotografie in Berlin.

1986 arbeitet mit Rudy Wurlitzer an dem Drehbuch zu *Candy Mountain*.

The Americans wird neu herausgegeben.

Ausstellung und Katalog *Robert Frank: New York to Nova Scotia* im Museum of Fine Arts in Houston, kuratiert von Anne Wilkes Tucker und Philip Brookman. Die Ausstellung wird 1987 auch im Folkwang Museum in Essen gezeigt.

1987 The Friends of Photography in San Francisco verleihen Frank den Peer Award for Distinguished Career in Photography.

Filmreihe: "In the Margins of Fiction: The Films of Robert Frank", American Film Institute, John F. Kennedy Center for the Performing Arts, Washington.

Ausstellung "The Lines of My Hand", Museum für Gestaltung, Zürich.

1988 Regie beim Musikvideo *Run* für New Order. Reist mit Stephan Balint vom Squat Theater in New York ins Ruhrgebiet, um den Film *Hunter* zu drehen.

1990 The National Gallery of Art, Washington gründet die Robert Frank-Collection. Frank stiftet Negative, Kontaktbögen, Arbeits- und Ausstellungsprints.

Das Video *C'est vrai! (One Hour)* wird für den französischen Fernsehsender La Sept produziert.

1991 Frank dreht einen Kurzfilm für den Modeschöpfer Romeo Gigli in Florenz.

Er fotografiert in Beirut und im Libanon für ein Projekt für Dominique Eddé.

1992 Frank reist nach Ägypten. Beginn eines Filmes mit Dominique Eddé und Dina Haidar, der nicht fertiggestellt wird.

Reise mit June an den Baikalsee.

1993 Reise mit Kazume Kurigami nach Hokkaido in den Norden Japans.

Buch *Black White and Things*, das zum ersten Mal 1952 in drei handgemachten Kopien hergestellt wurde, wird in Paperback von The National Gallery of Art und Scalo veröffentlicht.

1994 Retrospektive „Robert Frank: Moving Out", National Gallery of Art, Washington, kuratiert von Sarah Greenough und Philip Brookman.

Im November stirbt sein Sohn Pablo in Allentown, Pennsylvania.

1995 „Robert Frank: Moving Out" wird im Kunsthaus Zürich, im Stedelijk Museum in Amsterdam, dem Whitney Museum of American Art in New York und im Yokohama Museum of Art gezeigt.

Frank gründet die Andrea Frank Foundation in New York.

Ausstellung: „Robert Frank: Flower is...", Mole Gallery, Tokyo.

1996 erhält den International Photography Award der Hasselblad Stiftung, Göteborg.

Beendet den Film *The Present* mit der Cutterin Laura Israel.

Ausstellung „Robert Frank: Photographies de 1941 à 1994", Centre Culturel Suisse, Paris.

1997 besucht Allen Ginsberg am Abend vor seinem Tod.

Reise nach Taiwan und Kopenhagen.

Ausstellung „Flamingo" im Hasselblad Center in Göteborg.

Ausstellung: „Robert Frank: Flower is...Paris" in der Pace/MacGill Gallery, New York.

Restaurierung und Verkauf der Gemälde des Malers San Yu.

1998 reist nach Madrid und besucht Vicente Todoli. Autounfall in Spanien.

Beginnt mit der Arbeit an dem Film *San Yu*.

1999 Ausstellung „From the Canadian Side" in der Pace/MacGill Gallery, New York.

Verleihung der Ehrendoktorwürde der Universität Göteborg.

Fotografiert für die Zeitung *Libération*.

2000 Frank erhält den ersten Cornell Capa Award des International Center of Photography, New York.

2000-01 Ausstellung und Katalogbuch „Robert Frank. HOLD STILL_keep going" im Museum Folkwang, Essen. Die Ausstellung reist weiter zum Museo Nacional Centro de Arte Reina Sofia, Madrid und zum Centro Cultural de Belém, Lisboa.

2002 Robert Frank präsentiert persönlich sein neuestes Video *Paper Route*, das von der „Expo. 02" in der Schweiz in Auftrag gegeben wurde.

2003 Ausstellung „Robert Frank: London / Wales" in der Corcoran Gallery of Art, Washington, kuratiert von Philip Brookman und begleitet von dem Buch gleichen Titels.

Die Biografie stützt sich auf Angaben der Chronologie in „Robert Frank: Moving Out", hg. von Sarah Greenough und Philip Brookman und auf die Chronologie in „New York to Nova Scotia", hg. von Anne W. Tucker and Philip Brookman. Zusätzliche Informationen und eine Überarbeitung stellten Stuart Alexander und die Pace/MacGill Gallery zur Verfügung.

1924	Born in Zurich on November 9th.
1941-44	Brief apprenticeship and employment as a photographer's assistant in Switzerland (including with Hermann Segesser and Michael Wolgensinger).
1946	Makes first book, *40 Fotos* with original photographs.
1947	Emigrates to New York.
	Alexey Brodovitch hires Frank to work for *Harper's Bazaar* as a fashion photographer.
1948	Trips to Peru and Bolivia. The resulting photographs are first published in Robert Delpire's revue *Neuf* in 1952 and later in a book entitled *Indiens pas morts* in 1956.
1949	Trip to Europe (France, Italy, Switzerland and Spain). Produces a book with 74 original photographs of Paris for artist Mary Lockspeiser.
1950	Marries Mary Lockspeiser.
	Edward Steichen includes Frank's photographs in a group show entitled "51 American Photographers" at New York's Museum of Modern Art.
1951	Son Pablo is born in New York.
1952-53	Lives and works in Europe, primarily Paris; trips to Spain, London, Wales, and Switzerland. Gives up fashion photography and begins working as a freelance photojournalist.
1954	Daughter Andrea is born in New York.
1955-56	Frank is the first European photographer to receive a one-year Guggenheim Fellowship.
	Travels across United States; fellowship is extended for a second year.
1958	Robert Delpire publishes *Les Américains* in Paris; Grove Press later publishes it in the United States in 1959.
	Frank travels to Florida with Jack Kerouac.
	Works for advertising department of *New York Times*. Rides buses throughout New York including 42nd Street to create *Bus Series*.
1959	Co-directs *Pull My Daisy* with Alfred Leslie.
1961	Travels to Europe, takes photographs at Venice film festival.
	Hugh Edwards curates Frank's first one-man show, "Robert Frank: Photographer," in the Spring at The Art Institute of Chicago.
1962	Exhibition at New York's Museum of Modern Art: "Photographs by Harry Callahan and Robert Frank," curated by Edward Steichen.
	The Swiss magazine, *Du*, dedicates an issue to Frank's photographs.
1963	Directs the film *OK End Here.*
1964	George Eastman House purchases twenty-five of the photographs which appeared in *The Americans* for a traveling show.
1964-66	Frank travels throughout France, Mexico, India, Sri Lanka, England, Jamaica, and America with director and producer Conrad Rooks and shoots

	the film *Chappaqua*. They win the Silver Lion at Venice in 1967.
1965	Begins his first feature, *Me and My Brother,* which is finished in 1968.
1969	Seperates from Mary and later divorces.
	Lives with artist June Leaf in New York's Bowery.
	Frank writes five monthly columns for London's *Creative Camera* magazine. Produces and directs his first autobiographical film, *Conversations in Vermont* and the documentary, *Liferaft Earth.*
1970-71	Frank buys land and a house in Nova Scotia with June Leaf.
	Teaches at several American colleges and universities.
	Receives funding from the American Film Institute to produce *About Me: A Musical.*
1971	Kazuhiko Motomura publishes *The Lines of My Hand* in Tokyo; this book is later published in the USA by Lustrum Press.
1972	Begins to use a Polaroid Land pack film camera.
1974	Frank's photographs are shown in a retrospective at Zurich's Kunsthaus, curated by Rosselina Bischof.
	In December, his daughter Andrea dies in a plane crash in Guatemala.
1975	Marries June Leaf in Reno on the way to California, where he teaches filmmaking for two months.
	Takes photographs with a disposable camera. *Robert Frank* is published as part of the *Aperture History of Photography Monographs* series with an introduction by Rudy Wurlitzer.
1976	Begins to use a professional Mode 195 Polaroid pack film camera with Type 665 Positive/Negative film. Makes collages with text from these negatives.
1978	Retrospective in Ottawa, curated by Lorraine Monk of the National Film Board of Canada; also shown at Harvard University's Fogg Museum in Cambridge, Massachusetts.
1979	Exhibition "Robert Frank: Photographer / Filmmaker, Works from 1945–1979," curated by Philip Brookman, at the Long Beach Museum of Art in California.
1980	Retrospective "The New American Filmmakers Series: Robert Frank" in New York, curated by John Hanhardt, at the Whitney Museum of American Art.
	Dedicates his film *Life Dances On...* to his daughter Andrea and his friend Danny Seymour.
1981	Frank's films are screened at the Rotterdam film festival.
	Frank travels to Israel to teach at the Camera Obscura School for three weeks.
1982	Robert Delpire publishes *Robert Frank* as part of the "Photo Poche" collection with an introduction by Rudy Wurlitzer.

A special edition of *Les Cahiers de la Photographie*, edited by Gilles Mora, is dedicated to Frank.

Starts working on the video *Home Improvements* (1985).

1985   "Robert Frank: Fotografias/Films 1948–1984": exhibition and catalog for the Salla Parpallo in Valencia, Spain, curated by Vicente Todoli.

Frank receives the German Photography Society's Erich Salomon Prize in Berlin.

1986   Works on the screenplay *Candy Mountain* with Rudy Wurlitzer.

A new edition of *The Americans* appears.

Exhibition and catalog entitled *Robert Frank: New York to Nova Scotia* at the Museum of Fine Arts in Houston, curated by Anne Wilkes Tucker and Philip Brookman. This exhibition later travels to Museum Folkwang, Essen, Germany in 1987.

1987   The Friends of Photography, San Francisco gives Frank the Peer Award for Distinguished Career in Photography.

Retrospective entitled "In the Margins of Fiction: The Films of Robert Frank" at the American Film Institute, John F. Kennedy Center for the Performing Arts, Washington, D.C.

Exhibition entitled "The Lines of My Hand" at the Museum für Gestaltung, Zurich.

1988   Directs music video *Run* for New Order.

Goes to the Ruhrgebiet to shoot *Hunter* together with Stephan Balint from the Squat Theater, New York.

1990   The National Gallery of Art, Washington D.C. establishes the Robert Frank Collection. Frank donates negatives, contact sheets, work and exhibition prints.

Video entitled *C'est vrai! (One Hour)* is produced for the French television broadcaster La Sept.

1991   Frank produces a short film for fashion designer Romeo Gigli in Florence.

Takes photographs in Beirut and around Lebanon for a project organized by Dominique Eddé.

1992   Frank travels to Egypt. Begins making a film with Dominique Eddé and Dina Haidar which is never completed.

Travels to Lake Baikal with June.

1993   Travels to Hokkaido in the north of Japan with Kazume Kurigami.

A book entitled *Black White and Things*, first created in 1952 in three handmade copies, is published in paperback by The National Gallery of Art and Scalo.

1994   Retrospective entitled "Robert Frank: Moving Out," National Gallery of Art, Washington, D.C., curated by Sarah Greenough and Philip Brookman.

Frank's son Pablo dies in November in Allentown, Pennsylvania.

1995   "Robert Frank: Moving Out" travels to Zurich's Kunsthaus, Stedelijk Museum in Amsterdam, the Whitney Museum of American Art in New York, and Yokohama Museum of Art, Japan.

Frank establishes Andrea Frank Foundation in New York.

Exhibition entitled, "Robert Frank: Flower is...," Mole Gallery, Tokyo.

1996   Receives the International Photography Award from the Hasselblad Foundation, Göteborg.

Completion of the film *The Present* with editor Laura Israel.

Exhibition entitled "Robert Frank: Photographies de 1941 à 1994" at the Centre Culturel Suisse, Paris.

1997   Visits Allen Ginsberg the evening before the poet's death.

Travels to Taiwan and Copenhagen.

Exhibition entitled "Flamingo" at the Hasselblad Center in Göteborg.

Exhibition entitled "Robert Frank: Flower is...Paris" at the Pace/MacGill Gallery, New York.

Restoration and sale of paintings by San Yu.

1998   Travels to Madrid and visits Vicente Todoli. Car accident in Spain.

Begins working on the film *San Yu*.

1999   Exhibition entitled "From the Canadian Side" at the Pace/MacGill Gallery, New York.

Frank receives an honorary Ph.D. from the University of Göteborg.

Takes photographs for the newspaper *Libération*.

2000   Frank receives the first Cornell Capa Award from the International Center of Photography, New York.

2000-01   Exhibition and catalog entitled "Robert Frank. HOLD STILL_keep going" at Museum Folkwang, Essen, Germany. The exhibition travels to Museo Nacional Centro de Arte Reina Sofia, Madrid and Centro Cultural de Belém, Lisbon.

2002   Robert Frank personally presents his new video *Paper Route*, which was commissioned for the "Expo.02" in Switzerland.

2003   Exhibition „Robert Frank: London / Wales," at the Corcoran Gallery of Art, Washington, curated by Philip Brookman and accompanied by the book of the same title.

The biography is based on the chronology by Paul Roth in "Robert Frank: Moving Out," ed. by Sarah Greenough and Philip Brookman and the chronology in "New York to Nova Scotia," ed. by Anne W. Tucker and Philip Brookman. Additional information and revision was provided by Stuart Alexander and Pace/MacGill Gallery.

Publications by Robert Frank (selection)

Frank, Robert: **Les Américains**, Photographies de
Robert Frank. Selection of texts and edited by Alain
Bosquet, Encylopédie Essentielle, no 5, Série Histoire,
no 3. Robert Delpire, Paris, 1958.

Frank, Robert: **The Americans**, Photographs by Robert
Frank. Introduction by Jack Kerouac. Grove Press, New
York, 1959.
German edition: **Die Amerikaner**. Introduction by Jack
Kerouac. Scalo Verlag Zurich – Berlin – New York, 1993.

Frank, Robert: **Black White and Things**, National Gallery of
Art Washington/Scalo, Washington, Zurich 1993 (concept
from 1952).

Frank, Robert: "Films: Entertainment Shaked Up With Art,"
in: **Artsmagazine** 41, 5th of March 1967, p. 23.

Frank, Robert: "It's all true," in: **LimeLight – Cinéma** 57,
February 1997, p. 32-36.

Frank, Robert: **The Lines of My Hand**. Parkett / Der Alltag,
Zurich, 1989. First published in Japan by Kazuhiko
Motomura, Tokyo, 1971.

Frank, Robert: **London / Wales**. Edited by Philip Brookman.
Scalo, Zurich – Berlin – New York, 2003.

Frank, Robert: **New York Is**. Photographs by Robert Frank.
Introduction by Gillbert Millstein. In: **The New York Times**,
New York 1959

Frank, Robert: **Pull My Daisy**. Text ad-libbed by Jack
Kerouac for the film of Robert Frank and Alfred Leslie.
Introduction by Jerry Tallmer. Grove Press, New York, 1961.
(Based on the film *Pull My Daisy*).

Frank, Robert: **Robert Frank. The Aperture History of
Photography Series. no. 2**. Introduction by Rudolph
Wurlitzer. Millerton, New York: Aperture, 1976. Published
simultaneously in London by Gordon Fraser Gallery, Ltd.
and in Paris by Nouvel Observateur / Delpire.

Frank, Robert: **Texts by Robert Frank**. Thames and
Hudson Ltd, London, 1991. Originally published in France
by Centre National de la Photographie, Paris, 1983.

Frank, Robert; Grazda, Ed: **Thank You**. For the 10th
anniversary of Pace MacGill Gallery. Scalo, Zurich – Berlin
– New York, 1996.

Frank, Robert: "Transcript from the lecture of his
presentation on 7. Symposium for photography at
Steirischer Herbst," on 5.10.1985, Forum Stadtpark Graz,
in: **Camera Austria** 22, 1987, pp. 17-23.

Interviews with Robert Frank (selection)

Bertrand, Anne: "Robert Frank de passage / Passing
Through" in: **Art Press** 207, November 1995, pp. 39-43.

Garel, Alain: "Robert Frank: Entretien: Images en
mouvement," in: **La Revue du Cinéma** 435, February 1988,
pp. 49-52.

Glicksman, Marlaine: "Highway 61 Revisited," in: **Film
Comment** 23, 4, July / August 1987, pp. 32-39.

Johnson, William: "The Pictures are a Necessity: Robert
Frank in Rochester, NY 1988," in **Rochester Film and
Photo Consortium Occasional Papers** Nr. 2, Jan. 1989.

Schaub, Martin: "FotoFilmFotoFilm: Eine Spirale: Robert
Franks Suche nach den Augenblicken der wahren
Empfindung," in: **Cinema: unabhängige Schweizer
Filmzeitschrift** 30, November 1984, pp. 75-94.

Sargeant, Jack: "An Interview with Robert Frank," in: **The
Naked Lens. An Illustrated History of Beat Cinema**.
Creation Cinema Collection # 7. Creation Books 1997,
reprinted 2001. pp. 38-53.

Wallis, Brian:"Robert Frank: American Visions," in: **Art in
America** 84, 3, 1996, pp. 74-79.

Publications about Robert Frank (selection)

lAlexander, Stuart: **Robert Frank: A Bibliography, Filmography and Exhibition Chronology 1946–1985**. Center for Creative Photography, University of Arizona, Tucson, in association with Museum of Fine Arts Houston, Tucson 1986.

Bertrand, Anne: "Le Présent de Robert Frank," in: **Trafic. Revue de Cinema** 21, spring 1997, pp. 50-57.

Eskildsen, Ute: **Robert Frank: HOLD STILL _ keep going**. Exhibition catalog Museum Folkwang, Essen 2000.

Gasser, Martin: " ... really more like Russia in feeling and look ...: Robert Frank in Amerika," in: Beat Schläpfer: **Swiss Made**, Zürich 1998, pp. 79-92.

Gosgrove, Gillian: "On the Road with the Rolling Stones – The Film That Can't Be Shown," in: **The Montreal Star**, 12 September 1977, Sek. C-2.

Greenough, Sarah; Brookman, Philip: **Robert Frank: Moving Out**. Exhibition catalog National Gallery of Art, Washington 1994.
German edition: National Gallery of Art, Washington, Scalo, Zurich 1995.

Hagen, Charles: "Robert Frank: Seeing Through the Pain," in **Afterimage** 1, 5, february 1973, pp. 1, 4-5.

Hall, Lars; Knape, Gunilla: **Robert Frank. Flamingo**. The Hasselblad Award 1996, exhibition catalog Hasselblad Center, Göteborg 1997.

Hanhardt, John: "A Movement Toward the Real. *Pull My Daisy* and the American Independent Film, 1950-65," in: Lisa Philipps: **Beat Culture and the New America: 1950–1965**. Exhibition catalogue Whitney Museum of American Art, New York in association with Flammarion, Paris, New York 1995.

Hanhardt, John: "Kenner des Chaos. Die Filme und Videos," in: **Robert Frank: Moving Out**. Exhibition catalogue National Gallery of Art, Washington 1994, German edition: National Gallery of Art, Washington, Scalo, Zurich 1995.

Horak, Jan-Christopher: "Robert Frank: Daddy Searching for the Truth," in: **Making Images Move. Photographers and Avant-Garde Cinema**. Washington, London 1997, pp. 161-190.

Lifson, Ben: "Robert Frank and the Realm of Method," in **Village Voice** 24, 8, febr. 1979, pp. 75.

MacDonald, Scott: "An Interview with Amos Vogel," in: **Cinema 16–Document Toward a History of the Film Society**. Temple University 2002, pp. 55, 364.

Martiradonna, Sabino: **Robert Frank.** Catalog on the occasion of Mostra Internationale Riminicinema, Rimini 1990.

Meier, Marco: "Robert Frank. Part Two." **Du. Die Zeitschrift der Kultur**, No. 731, Zurich, November 2002.

Mekas, Jonas: "Cinema of the New Generation," in: **Film Culture** 21, Sommer 1960, pp. 1-20.

Perret, Jean; Biamonte, Francesco: "Robert Frank: atelier," in: **Catalog of Visions du Réel No. 5**, Nyon 1999, pp. 158-177.

Noll Brinckmann, Christine: "Vom filmischen Alltag der Beats. *Pull My Daisy*" (Robert Frank und Alfred Leslie, USA 1959), in: **Cinema 30**: Bild für Bild – Photographie und Film, Chronos, 1997.

Rotzler, Willy: "Robert Frank." **Du. Kulturelle Monatsschrift**, volume 22, Zurich January 1962.

Sargeant, Jack: **The Naked Lens. An Illustrated History of Beat Cinema**. Creation Cinema Collection # 7. Creation Books 1997, reprinted 2001.

Schaub, Martin: "Postkarten von überall und innere Narben. Porträt des sechzigjährigen Fotografen und Filmemachers Robert Frank...," in: **Tagesanzeiger Magazin** 44, 3. November 1984, pp. 8-13, 15-16.

Searle, Leroy: "Symposium: Poems, Pictures and Conceptions of >Language<," in: **Afterimage** 3, 1/2 (May / June) 1975, pp. 33-39.

Tucker, Ann Wilkes; Philip Brookman: **Robert Frank: New York to Novia Scotia**. Exhibition catalog Museum of Fine Arts Houston, Boston, 1986.

Tyler, Parker: "For *Shadows,* Against *Pull My Daisy,*" in **Film Culture** #24, spring 1962, pp. 29.

Watson, Steven: **Die Beat Generation. Visionäre, Rebellen und Hipsters, 1944–1960**. Hannibal, St. Andrä-Wördern, 1997.
English edition: **The birth of the beat generation – visionaries, rebels, and hipsters 1944–1960**. Pantheon Books, a division of Random House, Inc., New York 1995.

Ziegler, Ulf Erdmann: "Der desperate Blick," in: **Die Zeit**, 16 June 1995, pp. 50.

Michael Barchet Dr. phil. Hochschulassistent am Lehrstuhl „Geschichte und Ästhetik der Medien" der Friedrich-Schiller-Universität Jena. Studium der Amerikanistik, Filmwissenschaft und Germanistik an der University of California at Berkeley und an der Johann-Wolfgang-Goethe-Universität Frankfurt am Main, dort 1998 Promotion mit dem Titel „Figures of Unlikely Plots: American Documentary Film, Spectatorship and the Work of Errol Morris". Publikationen über Dokumentarfilm, frühes Kino, Videokunst, amerikanisches Fernsehen.

Christa Blümlinger Dr. phil, lehrt als Maître de conférences im Fach Filmwissenschaft an der Universität Sorbonne Nouvelle (Paris 3). Davor Universitätsassistentin an der Freien Universität Berlin. Lehr-, und Forschungstätigkeiten in Wien und Paris, zahlreiche kuratorische und journalistische Tätigkeiten. Jüngste Publikationen: Harun Farocki: „Reconnaître et poursuivre", Paris: THTY 2002 (Hg.); „Das Gesicht im Zeitalter des bewegten Bildes", Wien: Sonderzahl 2002 (hg. gem. mit Karl Sierek).

Philip Brookman ist Chefkurator für Fotografie und Medienkunst der Corcoran Gallery of Art, Washington, DC. Zuvor war er als Kurator beim Washington Project for the Arts, El Centro Cultural de la Raza, San Diego und der University of California, Santa Cruz tätig. Er organisierte auch wichtige Ausstellungen für andere Museen, u.a. die National Gallery of Art, Washington und das Museum of Fine Arts, Houston. Er ist auch Autor, Herausgeber, Filmemacher und Fotograf. Kürzlich stellte er die Ausstellung und das Buch „Robert Frank: London/Wales" fertig.

Brigitta Burger-Utzer Geboren 1960 in Wien; Studien der Theaterwissenschaft und Fotografie; Diplom der Kepler-Universität Linz für Kulturelles Management; 1990 Gründung von Sixpack Film (gemeinsam mit Martin Arnold, Alexander Horwath, Lisl Ponger und Peter Tscherkassky); seit 1992 Geschäftsführerin von Sixpack Film (Organisation für Verleih und Vertrieb österreichischer künstlerischer Filme und Videos); Konzept und/oder Organisation von zahlreichen Filmreihen in Wien; seit 1994 Betreuung der Reihe "IN PERSON: Internationale KünstlerInnen der Avantgarde stellen ihr Werk zur Diskussion".

Ralph Eue Geboren 1953 in Blankenburg/Ex-DDR. Republikflucht der Eltern. Studium in Marburg, Paris und Frankfurt. Autorentätigkeit und Szenenbild bei Film und TV. Head of Public Relations bei Tobis-Filmkunst. Herausgeber mehrerer Bücher, u.a. "Donald Albrecht", "Architektur im Film" und "Marcel Ophüls, Widerreden und andere Liebeserklärungen" (gemeinsam mit Constantin Wulff). Publizist und Realisator von Beiträgen und Dokumentationen für verschiedene TV-Redaktionen. Lebt und arbeitet in Berlin.

Birgit Flos Geboren 1944. Literaturstudium an der City University of New York. Mitarbeit an Dokumentar-/ Filmprojekten. Gastprofessur an der HdK und arbeitslos in Berlin (1980er Jahre). Seit 1988 LA für Filmgeschichte an der Wiener Filmakademie. Ausstellungskonzepte. (u.a. 1995/96 medien, apparate kunst im MAK, Wien); Redaktionsmitglied der Filmzeitschrift „Meteor". Moderatorin der Grazer Diagonale bis 2003. Texte zu Kunst + Film für Radio und Printmedien.

Michael Barchet Dr. phil., university assistant, Professorship for History and Media Aesthetics at the Friedrich-Schiller-Universität, Jena. American Studies, Film Studies, and German at the University of California, Berkeley and at the Johann-Wolfgang-Goethe-Universität, Frankfurt am Main. Graduated with the thesis: "Figures of Unlikely Plots: American Documentary Film, Spectatorship and the Work of Errol Morris." Publications on documentary film, early cinema, video art, and American television.

Christa Blümlinger Dr. phil, teaches as Maître de conférences in film studies at the Universität Sorbonne Nouvelle (Paris 3). Previously university assistant at the Freie Universität Berlin. Teaching and research activities in Vienna and Paris, numerous curatorial and journalistic activities. Most recent publications: "Harun Farocki: Reconnaître et poursuivre," Paris: THTY 2002 (ed.); "Das Gesicht im Zeitalter des bewegten Bildes," Vienna: Special edition 2002 (co-edited with Karl Sierek).

Philip Brookman is Senior Curator of Photography and Media Arts at the Corcoran Gallery of Art, Washington DC. He has previously held curatorial positions at Washington Project for the Arts, El Centro Cultural de la Raza, San Diego, and the University of California, Santa Cruz. He has also organized major exhibitions for other museums including the National Gallery of Art, Washington, and the Museum of Fine Arts, Houston. He is also a writer, editor, filmmaker, and photographer. He recently completed the exhibition and book "Robert Frank: London/Wales."

Brigitta Burger-Utzer Born in 1960 in Vienna; studied theater and photography; degree in Cultural Management from the Kepler University, Linz. Founded Sixpack Film in 1990 (together with Martin Arnold, Alexander Horwath, Lisl Ponger, and Peter Tscherkassky); since 1992 managing director of Sixpack Film (association for lending and distribution of Austrian art films and videos); concept and/or organisation of numerous film series in Vienna; since 1994 in charge of the series "IN PERSON: International avant-garde artists bring their work up for discussion."

Ralph Eue Born in 1953 in Blankenburg in former East Germany. Defected with parents from GDR. Studied in Marburg, Paris, and Frankfurt. Worked as an author and stage builder for film and television. Head of Public Relations at Tobis-Filmkunst. Has published several books, including: "Donald Albrecht," "Architektur im Film," and "Marcel Ophüls, Widerreden und andere Liebeserklärungen" (together with Constantin Wulff). Journalist and director for contributions and documentaries for various television programs. Lives and works in Berlin.

Birgit Flos Born in 1944. Studied literature at the City University of New York. Has worked together with various documentary and film projects. Guest professor at the HdK and unemployed in Berlin (1980s). Since 1988, lecturer in film history at the Wiener Filmakademie. Exhibition concepts: (1995/96 medien, apparate kunst at the MAK, Vienna, among others); Member of the editorial board of the film journal "Meteor." Moderator for the Graz Diagonale through 2003. Texts on art and film for radio and print media.

Stefan Grissemann Geboren 1964. Leiter des Kultur-
ressorts des Wochenmagazins „profil". 1989 bis 2002
Filmkritiker der Tageszeitung „Die Presse". Kuratorentätig-
keit für Kino-Retrospektiven in Wien, Graz und Basel.
Veröffentlichungen u.a. in „Berliner Zeitung", „Tip", „Film
Comment" und „Süddeutsche Zeitung". Buchbeiträge
zu Maya Deren, Fritz Lehner und Alfred Hitchcock, zur
österreichischen Avantgarde und zur amerikanischen
Filmgeschichte. Publikationen: „Haneke / Jelinek: Die
Klavierspielerin" (2001), "Mann im Schatten: Der Filmemacher Edgar G. Ulmer" (2003). Lebt und arbeitet in Wien.

Isabella Heugl Geboren 1966. Studium der Romanistik
und Publizistik in Wien. Diplomarbeit über Michelangelo
Antonioni. Gründerin von H2-arts&acts. Mitarbeit und
Produktionsleitung bei diversen Theaterprojekten.

Christoph Huber DI, geboren 1973 in Vöcklabruck, aufge-
wachsen in Attnang-Puchheim. Studium der Technischen
Physik in Wien. Ab 1999 Filmkritiker und redaktionelle
Tätigkeit für diverse Webseiten. Seit 2000 Film- und Musik-
kritiker der Tageszeitung „Die Presse". Publikationen in
„Senses of Cinema", „Schnitt", „RAY" u. a. Schreibt die
Programmtexte des Österreichischen Filmmuseums. Lebt
und arbeitet in Wien.

Kent Jones ist Filmkritiker und Filmkurator. Er ist Chefredakteur von "Film Comment", für das er, neben vielen
anderen Zeitschriften, auch regelmäßig schreibt. Autor des
Buches "L'Argent", das in der Reihe BFI Modern Classics
erschien, und Co-Autor der Dokumentation *Il mio Viaggio
in Italia* von Martin Scorsese. Er lebt in Brooklyn, New York.

Michael Loebenstein Geboren 1974. Studiert Theater-,
Film-, und Medienwissenschaft, ist als freiberuflicher Autor
und Filmkritiker (Mitarbeiter der Stadtzeitung „Falter"),
Kurator (u.a. der Dokumentarfilminitiative „Kinoreal") und
Mediengestalter (CD-Roms, DVD und Installationsprojekte)
tätig und lebt in Wien.

Thomas Mießgang Geboren 1955 in Bregenz. Studium
der Germanistik und Romanistik in Wien. Journalistische
Tätigkeit bei u.a. „Falter", „profil", „Die Zeit", ORF-Hörfunk
(„Musicbox", „Diagonal") Von 1994 – 1996 Berater der
Wiener Kulturstadträtin Ursula Pasterk. Seit 2000 Kurator
der Kunsthalle Wien. Buchveröffentlichungen: „Semantics"
(Wolke, 1991) und „Semantics II" (Triton, 2002), „Der
Gesang der Sehnsucht - Die Geschichte des Buena Vista
Social Club" (Kiepenheuer + Witsch, 2000).

Pia Neumann Dr. phil. Amerikanistin und Fotografie-
theoretikerin. Dissertation über amerikanische Fotografie
der 60er Jahre. Langjährige wissenschaftliche Mitarbeit am
Museum für Moderne Kunst Frankfurt. Lehrtätigkeit am
Institut für England- und Amerikastudien Frankfurt und am
Lehrstuhl für Geschichte und Ästhetik der Medien Friedrich
Schiller Universität Jena. Arbeit als freiberufliche Fotografin,
Übersetzerin und Redakteurin. Veröffentlichungen u.a.:
„Metaphern des Mißlingens: Amerikanische sozialdoku-
mentarische Fotografie der sechziger Jahre zwischen
Konzeptkunst und Gesellschaftskritik", Frankfurt, 1995.

Stefan Grissemann Born in 1964. Head of the cultural
section of the weekly magazine "profil." From 1989 to
2002 film critic for the daily paper "Die Presse." Curatorial
activities for cinema retrospectives in Vienna, Graz, and
Basel. Publications in "Berliner Zeitung," "Tip," "Film
Comment" and "Süddeutsche Zeitung," among others.
Book contributions on Maya Deren, Fritz Lehner, and Alfred
Hitchcock; Austrian avant-garde film and American film
history. Publications: "Haneke / Jelinek: Die Klavierspielerin"
(2001), "Mann im Schatten: Der Filmemacher Edgar G.
Ulmer" (2003). Lives and works in Vienna.

Isabella Heugl Born 1966. Studied Romance languages
and literature and journalism in Vienna. Master's thesis
on Michelangelo Antonioni. Founded H2-arts&acts.
Collaboration and head of production for diverse theater
projects.

Christoph Huber Born in 1973 in Vöcklabruck, childhood
in Attnang-Puchheim. Studied technical physics in Vienna.
Engineering degree. Since 1999 film critic and journalist for
diverse websites. Since 2000, film and music critic for the
daily paper "Die Presse." Publications in "Senses of
Cinema," "Schnitt," and "RAY," among others. Writes film
program texts for the Austrian Film Museum. Lives and
works in Vienna.

Kent Jones is a film critic and programmer. He is the
editor-at-large of "Film Comment" and a regular contributor
to that magazine, as well as many others. He is the author
of the BFI Modern Classics book on *L'Argent*, and the
co-writer of the documentary *Il mio Viaggo in Italia* by
Martin Scorsese. He lives in Brooklyn, New York.

Michael Loebenstein Born in 1974. Studied theater, film,
and media studies. Works as a freelance writer and film
critic on the staff of the Viennese weekly, "Falter." Curator for
the documentary film project *Kinoreal*, among others, and
media designer (CD-Rom, DVD, and installation projects).
Lives in Vienna.

Thomas Mießgang Born in 1955 in Bregenz. Studied
German and Romance languages and literature in Vienna.
Works as a journalist for "Falter," "profil," "Die Zeit," ORF
radio ("Musicbox," "Diagonal"). From 1994–1996 advisor for
Vienna's city cultural councillor Ursula Pasterk. Since 2000
curator of the Kunsthalle Wien. Book publications include:
"Semantics" (Wolke, 1991) and "Semantics II" (Triton,
2002), "Der Gesang der Sehnsucht – Die Geschichte des
Buena Vista Social Club" (Kiepenheuer + Witsch, 2000).

Pia Neumann Dr. phil., American Studies and
Photography, dissertation on American photography of
the 1960s. Long-term academic work at the Museum für
Moderne Kunst, Frankfurt. Teaching duties at the Institute
for English and American Studies, Frankfurt, Professorship
for History and Media Aesthetics at the Friedrich Schiller
Universität, Jena. Works as a freelance photographer,
translator, and editor. Publications include: "Metaphern
des Mißlingens: Amerikanische sozialdokumentarische
Fotografie der sechziger Jahre zwischen Konzeptkunst
und Gesellschaftskritik," Frankfurt, 1995.

Klaus Nüchtern   Geboren 1961 in Linz. Studium der Germanistik und Anglistik. Kulturredakteur der Wiener Stadtzeitung „Falter" (seit 1990) sowie stellvertretender Chefredakteur (seit 1998). Als Literaturkritiker arbeitet er auch regelmäßig für den ORF und veröffentlichte u.a. in „Die Zeit", „Weltwoche", „Tagesredakteur", „Taz" et al. Ausgewählte seiner wöchentlich im „Falter" erscheinenden Kolumnen „nüchtern betrachtet" erschienen in den Büchern „rain on my crazy bärenfellmütze" (2001) und „kleines gulasch in st. pölten" (2003) – beide: Falter Verlag.

Bert Rebhandl   Geboren 1964. Studium der Germanistik, Philosophie und Kath. Theologie in Wien. Lebt als freier Journalist und Autor in Berlin. Lehraufträge an der FU Berlin und Universität Jena.

Isabella Reicher   Geboren 1967. Studierte Theater-, Film- und Fernsehwissenschaften in Wien, Berlin und Amsterdam; arbeitet seit 1994 vor allem als Filmkritikerin („Falter", „Der Standard") und Filmpublizistin; gemeinsam mit Andrea Pollach und Tanja Widmann Kuratorin und Herausgeberin von „Singen und Tanzen im Film" (Wien, Zsolnay 2003 bzw. Österreichisches Filmmuseum, Mai 2003).

Jonathan Rosenbaum   ist Filmkritiker beim Chicago Reader. Zu seinen Büchern zählen u.a. "Moving Places", "Midnight Movies" (mit J. Hoberman), "Placing Movies", "Movies as Politics", "Greed", "Dead Man", "Movie Wars", Abbas Kiarostami (mit Mehrnaz Saeed-Vafa), und "Movie Mutations" (herausgegeben mit Adrian Martin).

Nina Schedlmayer   Geboren 1976 in St. Pölten. Studierte Kunstgeschichte in Wien und Hamburg. Diplomarbeit über "Technik, Maschinen und Mechanik im Werk von Hannah Höch in den Zwanziger Jahren". Ausstellungskuratorin und Kritikerin. Beiträge und Reviews für u. a. „profil", „art-magazine", „Wiener Zeitung Extra" und „Camera Austria International" und für Publikationen des Filmarchivs Austria. Lebt und arbeitet in Wien und Krems.

Amy Taubin   ist Redakteurin der Zeitschriften "Film Comment" und "Sight and Sound", für die sie auch schreibt. Ihr Buch "Taxi Driver" erschien in der Film Classics-Serie des British Film Institute. Sie war 14 Jahre lang Kritikerin für die "Village Voice". Sie drehte Avantgarde-Filme, unter anderem In the Bag (1982), und tritt in Filmen von Jonas Mekas, Michael Snow und Andy Warhol auf. Sie unterrichtet an der School of Visual Arts, wo sie 2003 eine Auszeichnung als lehrende Kunsthistorikerin erhielt.

Gerald Weber   Geboren 1965. Studium der Geschichte, Geographie und Philosophie in Wien. Film- und Medienwissenschafter. Gründungsmitglied von „Projektor – Diskussionsforum Film & neue Medien". Mitarbeiter bei Sixpack Film. Diverse Vorträge und publizistische Beiträge.

Klaus Nüchtern   Born in 1961 in Linz. Studied German and English. Cultural journalist since 1990 for the Viennese weekly "Falter" and deputy chief editor since 1998. Literary critic for Austrian radio with publications in "Die Zeit," "Weltwoche," "Tagesanzeiger," "TAZ," etc. Author of: "rain on my crazy bärenfellmütze" (2001) and "kleines gulasch in st. pölten" (2003) – both published by Falter Verlag.

Bert Rebhandl   Born in 1964. Studied German, philosophy, and Catholic theology in Vienna. Lives in Berlin as a freelance journalist and author. Lectures at the FU Berlin and the Universität Jena.

Isabella Reicher   Born in 1967. Studied theater, film, and television in Vienna, Berlin, and Amsterdam. Since 1994 she has mainly worked as a film critic ("Falter," "Der Standard") and film journalist. Co-curator and publisher (together with Andrea Pollach and Tanja Widmann) of "Singen und Tanzen im Film" (Vienna, Zsolnay 2003 and Austrian Film Museum, May 2003).

Jonathan Rosenbaum   is film critic for the "Chicago Reader." His books include, among others, "Moving Places," "Midnight Movies" (with J. Hoberman), "Placing Movies," "Movies as Politics," "Greed," "Dead Man," "Movie Wars," "Abbas Kiarostami" (with Mehrnaz Saeed-Vafa) and "Movie Mutations" (coedited with Adrian Martin).

Nina Schedlmayer   Born 1976 in St. Pölten. Studied art history in Vienna and Hamburg. Master's thesis on "Technik, Maschinen und Mechanik im Werk von Hannah Höch in den Zwanziger Jahren" (Technology, machines, and mechanics in the work of Hannah Höch in the 1920s). Exhibition curator and critic. Contributions and reviews for the magazins "profil", "artmagazine", "Wiener Zeitung Extra", "Camera Austria International" and for publications of the Filmarchive Austria. She lives and works in Vienna and Krems.

Amy Taubin   is a contributing editor to "Film Comment" and "Sight and Sound" magazines. Her book, "Taxi Driver," is published in the British Film Institute's Film Classics series. She was a critic for fourteen years for the "Village Voice." She has made avant-garde films, among them In the Bag (1982) and appears in films by Jonas Mekas, Michael Snow and Andy Warhol. She teaches at the School of Visual Arts where she received the 2003 Art Historian/Teaching Award.

Gerald Weber   Born in 1965. Studied history, geography, and philosophy in Vienna. Film and media scientist. Founding member of "Projektor – Diskussionsforum Film & neue Medien." Staff member at Sixpack Film. Diverse lectures and journalistic contributions.